Neuroeconomics and the Firm

Neuroeconomics and the Firm

Edited by

Angela A. Stanton

Center for Neuroeconomics Studies, Claremont Graduate University, USA

Mellani Day

Colorado Christian University, USA

Isabell M. Welpe

Professor of Strategy and Organization, Munich University of Technology, Germany

Edward Elgar
Cheltenham, UK • Northampton, MA, USA

Published by
Edward Elgar Publishing Limited
The Lypiatts
15 Lansdown Road
Cheltenham
Glos GL50 2JA
UK

Edward Elgar Publishing, Inc.
William Pratt House
9 Dewey Court
Northampton
Massachusetts 01060
USA

A catalogue record for this book
is available from the British Library

Library of Congress Control Number: 2009938415

Mixed Sources
Product group from well-managed
forests and other controlled sources
www.fsc.org Cert no. SA-COC-1565
© 1996 Forest Stewardship Council

ISBN 978 1 84844 440 9

Printed and bound by MPG Books Group, UK

Contents

Figures

Tables

Contributors

David B. Audretsch, PhD, is Director of the Max Planck Institute of Economics in Jena, Germany; Honorary Professor at the Friedrich Schiller University of Jena; Research Professor at Durham University; Distinguished Professor and the Ameritech Chair of Economic Development; Director of the Institute for Development Strategies at Indiana University; External Director of Research at the Kiel Institute for the World Economics; and Research Fellow of the Centre for Economic Policy Research (London). Audretsch's research has focused on the links between entrepreneurship, government policy, innovation, economic development and global competitiveness. His research has been published in over 100 scholarly articles in the leading academic journals. His books include *Entrepreneurship and Economic Growth* (2006) and *The Entrepreneurial Society* (2007). He is co-founder and co-editor of *Small Business Economics: An Entrepreneurship Journal*. He was awarded the 2001 Global Award for Entrepreneurship Research by the Swedish Foundation for Small Business Research. He received an honorary doctorate degree from the University of Augsburg. He is a member of the Advisory Board to a number of international research and policy institutes, including the Zentrum fuer Europaeisch Wirtschaftsforschung (ZEW, Centre for Economic Research), Mannheim, the Deutsches Institut fuer Wirtschaftsforschung (German Institute for Economic Analysis), the Basque Institute for Competitiveness, the Deutsche Telekom Foundation, and the Swedish Foundation for Research on Entrepreneurship and Small Business.

Norman A. Baglini, PhD, CPCU, CLU, AU, ARe, is Professor of Risk Management, Insurance and Business Ethics at Temple University in Philadelphia. He is also President Emeritus and Life Trustee of the American Institute for Chartered Property Casualty Underwriters, the Insurance Institute of America and the Insurance Institute for Applied Ethics, where he served as chief executive officer. He currently chairs the Ethics Policy Committee of the Board. Upon his retirement, the Board of Trustees established an ethics endowment in his name to support the projects of the Insurance Institute for Applied Ethics. He is the author of *Risk Management in International Corporations and Global Risk*

Management (1976) and co-author of two books: *Principles of Property and Liability Underwriting and Insurance Company Operations* (1976) as well as numerous articles and professional papers in risk management, professional education and business ethics. He is a member of the Scientific Committee of the Geneva Association and an associate editor of the *Geneva Papers on Risk and Insurance Issues and Practice*, the *John Liner Review* and *Insurance Research and Practice*, the journal of the Chartered Insurance Institute of Great Britain. He also taught at the Wharton School, University of Pennsylvania. Norm earned BS and MBA degrees from the University of Rhode Island and MA and PhD degrees in economics from Temple University.

Frédéric Basso has received his MSc in economics and management. Currently a doctoral candidate in consumer research at the University of Rennes 1, he is the Laureate of the 2006 National 'Agrégation d'économie' award. He is teaching graduate courses in law, economics and management at the Rennes 1 Graduate School in Business Administration and at the Ecole Normale Supérieure de Cachan. Basso's research focuses on emotions in organizational theory, aesthetics and risk perception in consumer behavior and metaphors in social neuroscience.

Constant D. Beugré, PhD, received his doctorate at Rensselaer Polytechnic Institute and is Professor of Management at Delaware State University, College of Business. He teaches courses in organizational behavior and strategic management at the undergraduate level and organizational leadership at the graduate level. Dr Beugré also served as the Chair of the Department of Business Administration. Prior to joining Delaware State University, Dr Beugré was an assistant professor of management and information systems at Kent State University, Tuscarawas Campus, and visiting fellow at Harvard University. His research interests include organizational justice, offshoring and neuroeconomics. Dr Beugré has published three books and more than 30 refereed academic journal articles, such as *Decision Sciences*, the *International Journal of Human Resource Management*, *International Journal of Manpower*, *Journal of Applied Behavioral Science*, *Journal of Applied Social Psychology* and *Research in the Sociology of Organizations*.

Eden S. Blair, PhD, is Assistant Professor of Entrepreneurship at Bradley University in Peoria, Illinois. She received her doctorate from the University of Wisconsin, Madison, in organizational behavior with a concentration in entrepreneurship. Her work examines entrepreneurial cognition, particularly unconscious behaviors and unconscious priming.

She has published in the *Journal of Applied Psychology* and *Frontiers of Entrepreneurship Research*. Her teaching interests include social entrepreneurship and creativity and innovation.

Mellani Day, PhD, is Dean of the Business and Technology Division College of the College of Adult and Graduate Studies at Colorado Christian University. Over the course of her career she has worked in both higher education and in business in the USA and for over 13 years in Germany. On the business side she has been a founder of and worked primarily in entrepreneurial ventures, including over five years as CFO of a small high-tech entrepreneurial company in Colorado, and an import business in Germany. Day earned her doctorate in business administration from Nova Southeastern University and a Master's degree in systems management from the University of Southern California. Day's research interests include entrepreneurship (social/sustainable, neuroentrepreneurship, environments that foster it), spirituality and religion in management and adult education (transformational learning and entrepreneurship).

Kristina M. Durante, PhD, received her MA in social sciences from the University of Chicago and her PhD in evolutionary social psychology from the University of Texas at Austin. Her research investigates strategic shifts in female social behavior. Durante's work on ovulatory shifts in women's choice of dress and the influence of women's fertility on mate choice has been published in *Personality and Social Psychology Bulletin* and the Royal Society journal, *Biology Letters*. Her research on the hormonal correlates of female mating behavior has received worldwide media attention. She is currently a post-doctoral research associated investigating the role of intrasexual competition on consumer behavior and risky decision making.

Donald E. Gibson, PhD, is Professor of Management and Chair of the Management Department at the Charles F. Dolan School of Business, Fairfield University in Fairfield, Connecticut. Professor Gibson's research examines the attributes and impact of organizational role models, the management of individual emotional experience and expression in organizations, anger in the workplace and conflict management. He has published in *Organization Science*, *Journal of Management*, *Journal of Vocational Behavior*, *Academy of Management Perspectives*, *Journal of Business Ethics*, *International Journal of Conflict Management* and *Journal of Applied Social Psychology*, as well as a book for practicing managers, *Managing Anger in the Workplace*. He received his MBA and PhD from the University of California at Los Angeles, and was a professor for six years at the Yale University School of Management. He also has served as Executive Director and Program Chair of the International Association for Conflict Management, a professional organization whose mission is to understand and improve conflict management in family, organizational, societal and international settings.

Laurent Guillou has received his MSc in economics. He is currently a doctoral candidate in economics at the University of Paris X where he is also a research assistant for the 'Law and Economics' program. Guillou is teaching economics and sociology at the University of Paris I and at the Champagne School of Management in Troyes. His research interests focus on the links between law, economics and entrepreneurship.

Michael P. Haselhuhn, PhD, received his doctorate from the University of California, Berkeley, and is currently a post-doctoral fellow at the Wharton School at the University of Pennsylvania. Haselhuhn's research focuses on the motivational and emotional facets of human interaction, particularly as they relate to bargaining and negotiation. His work has been published in *Cognitive Brain Research* and *Journal of Personality and Social Psychology*.

Jane E. Joseph, PhD, received her doctorate in cognitive psychology from the University of Virginia and completed post-doctoral work at Georgetown University. She is presently an Associate Professor in the Department of Anatomy and Neurobiology at the University of Kentucky Chandler Medical Center. Her laboratory focuses on the neural basis of cognition and motivation and how these brain systems undergo developmental change. Ongoing projects include understanding the neural basis of cognitive, emotional and motivated behavior in individuals at risk for drug abuse (funded by the National Institute on Drug Abuse), the neural basis and developmental trajectory of object and face recognition in typical and atypical development (funded by Autism Speaks and the National Institute on Child Health and Human Development), and neurobiological and functional neuroanatomical sex differences in cognition (funded by the National Center for Research Resources). Dr Joseph serves on the editorial board for the *Journal of Neuroscience Methods*.

Laura J. Kray, PhD, is the Harold Furst Associate Professor of Management Philosophy and Values and the Chair of the Organizational Behavior and Industrial Relations Group at the Walter A. Haas School of Business, University of California at Berkeley. Professor Kray earned her doctorate in social psychology and she applies this lens to her work on

negotiations, women's unique leadership challenges, counterfactual thinking, and individual and team-level performance.

Xun Liu, PhD, is Assistant Professor in the Department of Psychiatry at
Mount Sinai School of Medicine. He received his Bachelor and Master's
degrees from Peking University, China and his PhD from the University of
California, Los Angeles. His primary research interests are in behavioral
and neural mechanisms of cognitive and affective controls and their interaction in human decision making. His publications have focused on atten-
tional control and reward-related processes, and appeared in *NeuroImage*,
Cerebral Cortex, *Journal of Cognitive Neuroscience*, *Cognitive*, *Affective*,
and *Behavioral Neuroscience* and the *Journal of Neuroscience*.

Connson C. Locke, PhD, is a lecturer (Assistant Professor) in the
Department of Management at the London School of Economics. She
participated in the research for this volume while obtaining her PhD
in organizational behavior from the Haas School of Business at the
University of California, Berkeley. Before entering academia, she worked
for 16 years as an educator, manager and consultant in the USA and Asia.
Her current research explores power, voice and leadership.

John F. McCarthy, PhD, is Associate Professor of Psychology and Chair
of the Psychology Department in the College of Arts and Sciences at
Fairfield University in Fairfield, Connecticut. Trained as a clinical psychologist, Professor McCarthy's research in the last ten years has focused
on the relationship between syntax and cognition. Studies of behavioral
and neurophysiological differences between native German and native
English speaking people have been the research area. In this period he
has been a regular presenter at the International Academy of Linguistic
Behavioral and Social Sciences, the Association for Psychological Science
and the International Association for Conflict Management. He received
his BS at Boston College and his MA and PhD from the Catholic
University of America.

Theresa Michl is a doctoral student of economics at the Munich School
of Management of the Ludwig-Maximilians-University, Munich,
Germany. At present Michl is Assistant Professor for telecommunica-
tions and innovation management at the Department for Information,
Organization and Management of the Ludwig-Maximilians-University
and for statistics, methodology and organization theory at the University
of Applied Management, Erding, Germany. She is working on theoretical and empirical research projects in economics and psychology, such as

entrepreneurship, innovation management, cognitive emotion theories, management training and coaching.

Amos Nadler is an economics doctoral student specializing in neuroeconomics at Claremont Graduate University. His undergraduate degree is in economics from the University of Oregon. His interests include neuroeconomics research and strategic institutional design. Nadler has extensive professional experience in consulting, branding, strategy and positioning in the healthcare industry. He is the principal of Advanced Marketing – Organizational Strategies, LLC, a company specializing in business-to-business marketing for the healthcare profession.

Katherine A. Nelson is on the faculty of the Fox School of Business and Management, Temple University, teaching business ethics and introduction to management. She also teaches ethics to executive MBAs at the University of Delaware and to executives at Wharton Executive Education at the University of Pennsylvania. She was a senior fellow in ethics at the Wharton School for several years. She was vice president and head of worldwide HR communication at Citicorp in New York and has held similar positions at Merrill Lynch and at Honeywell. The Work Ethic and similar games that she developed have been used in numerous business schools including Harvard, Wharton, Columbia, Oxford and INSEAD; and by numerous organizations including NASA, General Electric and J.P. Morgan. Nelson received her BA from the College of Mount St Vincent in New York City and will receive her MS in human resources management from Temple University.

Olivier Oullier, PhD, received his doctorate from the University of the Mediterranean. He has worked at the Center for Complex Systems and Brain Sciences. He is currently Associate Professor of Neuroscience at Aix-Marseille University, and serves as a research associate at the Center for Complex Systems and Brain Sciences and the Groupement de Recherche en Economie Quantitative d'Aix-Marseille. Oullier teaches neuroeconomics, neuroethics, neurophysiology, endocrinology and coordination dynamics. In 2005 he founded the first graduate courses in neuroeconomics and neuroethics in France and is now teaching these topics in various business schools and universities, including the Ecole Normale Supérieure. His main research areas are social neuroscience, the role of bodily information on decision making and neuroeconomics. Dr Oullier is frequently consulted as an advisor on neuroeconomics and neuroethics by various national and international institutions including the French and European Parliaments and various ethics committees. In 2009 he was appointed to be a scientific advisor at the French Prime Minister's Center for Strategic Analysis where he heads the 'Neuroscience and public policy' program.

Helen Pushkarskaya, PhD, is Assistant Professor in the Department of Agricultural Economics at the University of Kentucky. She received her PhD at the Ohio State University, where she also did post-doctoral work at the Department of Psychology. In her research she utilizes multidisciplinary approaches, and works on the intersection of economics, psychology, sociology and neuroscience. Her primary research interests are in judgment and decision making under uncertainty, individual differences in perceptions of and attitudes toward different types of uncertainty, strategic interaction under different types of uncertainty and intertemporal choice. She publishes in various economics and agricultural economics journals.

Gad Saad, PhD, is Associate Professor of Marketing at the John Molson School of Business. He holds the Concordia University Research Chair in Evolutionary Behavioral Sciences and Darwinian Consumption. He is the author of *The Evolutionary Bases of Consumption* (2007), the first academic book to demonstrate the Darwinian roots of a wide range of consumption phenomena. He has published over 45 scientific articles in a broad range of disciplines, including marketing, psychology, medicine, economics and bibliometrics. He is currently editing a book on the applications of evolutionary psychology in the business sciences (2010). He is serving as a guest editor of a special issue on the futures of evolutionary psychology to be published in *Futures*. Dr Saad obtained his BSc in mathematics and computer Science and MBA, both from McGill University, and an MS in Management and PhD degrees in marketing (dissertation area psychology of decision making; minors in statistics and cognitive studies), both from Cornell University.

Carl A. Scheraga, PhD, is Professor of Business Strategy and Technology Management. His fields of research and teaching include transportation and international logistics, global strategic management, cross-cultural management, and the management of technology and innovation. Scheraga has published numerous articles in *Transportation Research Series A*, *Journal of Transportation Management*, *Transportation Journal*, *Journal of the Transportation Research Forum*, *Journal of Public Policy and Marketing*, *Technology in Society: An International Journal*, *Journal of Banking and Finance*, *Global Business and Finance Review*, *Journal of Investing*, *Management International Review*, *International Journal of Advertising* and *International Review of Economics and Finance*. He has also published chapters in such volumes as *Research in International Business and International Relations, Japanese Direct Investment in the United States: Trends, Developments and Issues* (1993) and *International Financial Market Integration* (1993). As a co-author, he received the Transportation Research Forum Outstanding Research Paper Award in 1998 and the Aviation Research Paper Award in 1999. Scheraga received his PhD in economics from the University of Connecticut, an MA in economics, and a BSc in mathematics and engineering from Brown University.

Robert Smith, PhD, earned his MA from Aberdeen University and his PhD in relation to the social construction of entrepreneurship from the Robert Gordon University, Aberdeen. He is currently employed as a lecturer in police leadership and management at Aberdeen Business School. Smith, who was born and raised in Aberdeenshire, was formerly a police officer before entering into academia. His research interests are eclectic and include social constructionism, semiotics, criminology, policing studies, criminal entrepreneurship, illegal rural enterprise and rural entrepreneurship as well as family business. His numerous and varied publications are testament to this eclectic streak. He is particularly interested in the effect of learning difficulties on entrepreneurial and criminal proclivity and his interest in neurological aspects stems from this facet of his work.

Michael Smithson, PhD, is Professor in the Department of Psychology at the Australian National University in Canberra, and received his doctorate from the University of Oregon. He is the author of *Confidence Intervals* (2003), *Statistics With Confidence* (2000), *Ignorance and Uncertainty* (1989) and *Fuzzy Set Analysis for the Behavioral and Social Sciences* (1987); co-author of *Fuzzy Set Theory: Applications in the Social Sciences* (2006); co-editor of *Uncertainty and Risk: Multidisciplinary Perspectives* (2008) and *Resolving Social Dilemmas; Dynamic, Structural, and Intergroup Aspects* (1999). His other publications include more than 100 refereed journal articles and book chapters. His primary research interests are in judgment and decision making under uncertainty, social dilemmas, applications of fuzzy set theory to the social sciences and statistical methods for the social sciences.

Angela A. Stanton, PhD, is a neuroeconomist, who is currently a visiting scholar at the Center for Neuroeconomics Studies in Claremont, California, and external research fellow at the Max Planck Institute of Economics in Jena, Germany. She received her BSc in mathematics from UCLA, MBA from UC Riverside, MS in management science of engineering from Stanford University, and PhD in economics from Claremont

Graduate University. Dr Stanton focuses on the interplay between hormones, environmental stimuli and economic decision making. In particular, her dissertation research showed that elevated oxytocin levels make people more generous ('Oxytocin increases generosity in humans' with Paul J. Zak and Sheila Ahmadi (2007), *PLoS ONE*, **2** (11), e1128). Currently she experiments in search of understanding the different brain mechanisms used for solving risky and ambiguous choices using both fMRI and hormonal analysis. Prior to receiving her PhD, Dr Stanton spent many years in the corporate world, with various working experience, including managerial and executive roles. She has taught at the Argyros School of Business and Economics at Chapman University and at the International Finance Diploma Program at UC Berkeley Extension.

Stefan Taing is a doctoral candidate of business administration at the Munich School of Management of the Ludwig-Maximilians-University in Munich, Germany. He earned a Bachelor's degree in management information systems, a Bachelor's degree in Chinese studies from University of Vienna and a Master's degree in industrial engineering from Vienna University of Technology. Taing has worked as a strategy consultant in Berlin, Paris and Zurich for a leading international consultancy. His current research focuses on technology innovation and organizational management of virtual teams.

Donald T. Wargo, PhD, has been Assistant Professor of Economics at Temple University in Philadelphia for the past five years. He teaches economics and business ethics to undergraduate and graduate students. For 30 years prior to that he held executive positions in a number of large real estate companies in the Philadelphia area, including vice president of finance and president. Thus, he brings an entire career of experience and expertise to his academic work. Dr Wargo holds a BA in philosophy from St Charles Seminary in Philadelphia, an MA in philosophy from Villanova University, and an MA and PhD in economics from Temple University. His current research and published work is in the areas of business ethics and neuroeconomics. In addition to his academic work, Dr Wargo is active in many charitable organizations, including personal advisor to the Conference Bishops and to the President of the United Church of Christ.

Isabell M. Welpe, PhD, received her MSc in management science and her doctorate in high technology entrepreneurship at the Ludwig-Maximilians-University in Munich, Germany. She also studied at the Massachusetts Institute of Technology, Boston and at the European Institute of the London School of Economics. She has worked as advisor to the European

Union EU delegation on Economic and Social Development – Trade and Development at the United Nations in New York and as consultant with biotechnology start-ups. She was visiting professor at the Keck Graduate Institute, post-doctoral fellow at the Carlson School of Business at the University of Minnesota and senior research fellow at the Max Planck Institute for Economics. Currently she is Chair for Strategy and Organization at the Technical University of Munich, Germany.

Paul J. Zak, PhD, is the founding Director of the Center for Neuroeconomics Studies and Professor of Economics, Psychology and Business at Claremont Graduate University. Zak also serves as Professor of Neurology at Loma Linda University Medical Center, and is a senior researcher at UCLA. He has degrees in mathematics and economics from San Diego State University, a PhD in economics from the University of Pennsylvania and post-doctoral training in neuroimaging from Harvard. Professor Zak is credited with the first published use of the term 'neuroeconomics' and has been a vanguard in this new discipline. He organized and administers the first doctoral program in neuroeconomics in the world at Claremont Graduate University. He is a recognized expert in oxytocin. His laboratory discovered in 2004 that oxytocin allows us to determine who to trust. This knowledge is being used to understand the basis for modern civilizations and modern economies, improve negotiations, and treat patients with neurologic and psychiatric disorders.

Foreword by David B. Audretsch

For many decades, the firm has primarily been looked at as an organizational unit with the sole objective of providing profits to shareholders. To assist management in accomplishing this goal, management researchers have focused on resource acquisition, operational efficiencies and taking advantage of strategic opportunities. Although some academic fields do consider human resources as core resources, they do so under the auspices of skills as resources. The branch of research that deals with human behavior within the firm mostly focuses on employee well-being and motivation factors that are evaluated somewhat distinctly from the firm. To date, little effort has been placed on understanding the connection of what happens to the firm as a consequence of the human within. Refreshingly, the editors of this volume selected contributors who wrote carefully crafted chapters that focus attention to new ways of looking at the interaction of the firm and its human actors.

The environment of the firm has frequently been discussed in the past but never in terms of its variability and the affect this variability has on the employees. There is a two-way communication between the decision-making abilities of the employees and the environment in which they have to make those decisions. The decisions they make affect the environment of the firm and the environment of the firm in turn affects the decision-making abilities of its employees. Thus the question is not just how the firm may manage the people within, but what is the influence of the people on the organization of the firm. The question is not just about who to hire or promote to advance the success of the firm, but how does the environment of the firm affect its own success by influencing the decision-making abilities of those it hires or promotes.

Looking at the firm, human decision-making processes have been paid scant attention. The models of economic theories, based on rational choice and their logical means by which decisions are supposed to be made, preclude behavioral processes from being incorporated as important parts of decision making. Human behavioral processes are understood to be important in psychology, and business education and research have certainly benefitted from them. Still, the tendency has been to treat the human brain as a black box by scientists studying the firm and its employees. It has been almost axiomatic that institutions set rules and humans adjust according to their personalities. It has also been assumed that there is little difference between the human at work and the human away from work. Personality tests, typically employed as part of the hiring/promoting process, have been designed to measure a desired bundle of skills and knowledge and some basic psychological traits. These tests assume that the personality traits of humans are stable. It is assumed that no factors may induce a different personality type on a person in the business practices of the firm. The concept of the resource-based view that considers humans as a resource of skills and knowledge posits exactly that.

Management education includes economics, accounting, strategy, law, ethics and even psychology as its core requirements, yet the connecting element in the application of all these remains elusive and is not taught. The connecting element is the human mind that must apply everything that was learned whether in a split-second decision or in a long and deliberate plan. Would a human mind end up with the same decision in a split second as it would when it has the time to think for several days about the same issue? What are those elements that influence the variability of decision-making?

Corporate managers, leaders and entrepreneurs come with all types of education and from various backgrounds. What makes some of them successful and others unsuccessful at leading or managing the firm? Are there biologically measurable abilities that help some people feel more comfortable and thus be more successful in certain business environments? For example, how would a firm know who exactly makes a great leader versus a great manager? What is the affect of risk and ambiguity on decision-making? We already know that some people are crippled with discomfort when it comes to risky decisions while others thrive. Who are the people who excel in a challenging environment of little information and who are those who excel in an environment of stability? We now understand that many decisions we make are on a subconscious level, yet we believe that within the firm all decisions are made consciously and deliberately. How do decisions made at the subconscious level affect the firm? Can the firm create an environment in which more of the decisions are based on conscious deliberate evaluations rather than on heuristics? Can a firm change how much people trust each other inside the firm?

Human decision-making is strongly influenced by hormones. Many hormones are essential to everyday life but we rarely focus on them in terms of the firm. For example, dopamine, ocytocin, testosterone and cortisol are some of the hormones that are naturally released in the brain in levels that change continuously in response to changes in the environment. Some of these hormones make people impulsive and restless while others make them relaxed, trusting and more generous. Some of these hormones allow for better decision-making in some people and worse decision-making in others. Do people with high testosterone levels make decisions the same way as people with lower testosterone? Do men change their behavior when a pretty woman enters the office? Do women change their behavior when a handsome man enters the office? Do men and women affect each other within the firm to the detriment or the benefit of the firm?

In some way, the questions this book addresses are questions that we are all familiar with and have asked for many years. It suggests looking for answers in places that that we have never thought of before. Some of the chapters will surprise you with their ingenious, simple answers and propositions; some will perhaps make you feel uncomfortable with their straightforward way of presenting what we all suspected but felt uncomfortable to talk about. Many ideas will need further research. Nonetheless, this is a book where every chapter provides leading edge information to today's business and economics students and should be of great interest to corporate leaders and managers. The book also points the way toward new research methods and opportunities in management and entrepreneurial research. More than anything else, this book captures the excitement and spirit that accompanies the discovery and working out of a new and promising area for research. We are fortunate that, by compiling these chapters which, taken together, constitute a pioneering approach to understanding the firm, the editors share their exciting intellectual journey with us.

Introduction

Angela A. Stanton, Mellani Day and
Isabell M. Welpe

The ideal firm has been studied and analyzed by numerous researchers over several centuries. Yet today little is known about what makes one firm successful and another fail. From the perspective of economics, the firm is an entity whose sole purpose is to maximize shareholders' wealth. The firm does so by applying strategic steps using its internal resources and external opportunities to navigate the turbulent seas of the market. While there is nothing specifically wrong with this view, it treats all resources as commodities, each with a particular supply and demand curve that can be manipulated by the firm to its benefit. Although some economic theories ask what the purpose and the processes of the firms are, these theories do not ask much about the purpose and the processes of the people who make up the firm.

Economic theories analyze the employees of the firm in the context of contracts between principals and agents. The principal–agent theory assumes predictable automatons bargaining along the lines of their own supply and demand curves in game-theoretic steps, following mathematical laws of optimization based on axioms that are frozen in *ceteris paribus* moments of time.

Principals and agents maximize their benefits and minimize their efforts for the purpose of maximizing utility to self. They have no emotions or personal lives that may interfere with the goal of the firm any more than what the principal already knows, which is the agent's tendency to shirk at every opportunity. But is this really what a firm is all about? If it were this simple, there would be very little need to model and simulate firm strategy, market ups and downs, and financial crises. Economic theories suggest that complex models are necessary because the markets are uncertain and decision options must be simulated in uncertain environments. And so decision theory has advanced. But decision theory still looks upon the humans within the firm as automatons whose actions can be calculated by simply finding a mathematical optimum of all possible outcomes. It has been believed that humans only care about the outcomes of their choices and that their preferences are thus revealed by the outcomes they choose.

In the late 1970s and early 1980s clever and simple economic games were used to test if humans really do behave in accordance with the maximization concept. One after the other, these games showed that humans appear not to maximize benefits to self but to consider the welfare of others. At first these findings were dismissed. It was suggested that people did not understand the games or that they did not decide the same way in classrooms and computer laboratories as they do in real life; but after 20 years of robust stable results in various cultures and levels of civilization, humans consistently defy the rules of self-maximization in order to consider the benefit of others. When modern technology allowed researchers to peer inside the physiology of the human brain while playing these games, it became clear that the mistake is on the part of those economic theories that considered only the outcome as important. When technologies became available to stimulate the chemical components (hormones and neuropeptides) of some of the decision-making processes, it also became clear that often there is more value found in maximizing the decision-making process than maximizing the outcome itself. Humans are rewarded by giving as well as by receiving, and taking may feel more punishing than rewarding. If giving is as rewarding as receiving, the outcome need not be the one that is maximized; the process itself may be better maximized for a self-regarding rational agent! Emotional states are influenced by hormones and hormone level variations are influenced by the environment. Both hormones and emotions influence the decisions that humans make.

The latest warning about the lack of applicability of mainstream economic theories is the global financial crisis that started in 2007. This event gave pause to economic purists of academia, business and government. Now is a good time to evaluate what really is happening within the firm and why and where does the human fit into the process of forming the firm. This book opens the black box of decision-making by evaluating factors other than outcome that influence what happens to the firm.

THE REASON FOR THIS BOOK

In August 2007 two of the three editors of this volume, Angela A. Stanton and Mellani Day, met by accident at the Philadelphia airport after attending a very hot and humid conference of the Academy of Management (AOM). They did not actually know each other prior to this airport meeting. They ended up sitting next to each other in a cafeteria awaiting their flight and Stanton accidentally bumped into Day's table, nearly spilling her drink. A conversation started and they discovered that they had both left the AOM a day earlier than planned. Stanton complained about her experience since she found all presentations that she had attended were based on 'old-fashioned' research. Everything she saw and heard completely ignored new findings in brain research – the heart of her field of specialty: neuroeconomics. Coincidentally, during the last meeting Day attended, the following comment was made: 'if only we could peer into the mind of the entrepreneur'. Not surprisingly, their conversation accelerated with hot ideas and great excitement. The chance meeting turned into an online 'Google document' collaboration, digging deeper into how neuroeconomics may enhance entrepreneurial research. In this book the terms 'firm' and 'entrepreneur' are often used as synonyms. Although the prevailing view is that the firm is a legal entity while the entrepreneur is an individual and one might argue that the two are distinct, it is the core aim of this book to realign the widespread concept about the firm as a 'thing' to what it really is: the decisions of the individuals within. The firm henceforth gains the personality of the people who make up the firm.

Soon Isabell M. Welpe joined the discussion online. It took little time to decide to present along the concept of neuroeconomics and the firm at the 2008 AOM meeting in Anaheim, California. The editors of this book organized three very successful and well-attended sessions at the conference: a symposium, a workshop and a caucus, each identifying how neuroeconomics may be used for the purpose of identifying the personality, the role and the decision methods of the entrepreneur. Importantly, the word 'neuroentrepreneurship' was coined by the three editors of this volume on the last day of the conference. Neuroentrepreneurship is the application of neuroeconomic tools and methods to entrepreneurial research. This book represents the foundation, gives meaning to and defines some of the possible variables used by neuroentrepreneurship to aid the development of this new field of study.

OVERVIEW

The book is made up of five interconnected sections that revolve around the examination of what is inside the 'black box' of the human brain and how it works as an economic decision-making and processing center. The 'black box' concept is used in many fields and is typically associated with a mysterious object or process. In this volume we evaluate the firm by considering the human decision-making process in the brain as the 'black box' and the connection of what is in the 'black box' to the success of the firm. Chapters of this volume examine the external forces that act upon this 'black box' and how forces inside this mysterious processing machine respond to external stimuli.

In Part 1, we examine the black box from the outside by looking at factors of uncertainty as they affect decision-making. There are three chapters in this part; two discuss how humans feel and relate to uncertainty and the third chapter questions whether all entrepreneurial activities are conducted at a conscious level.

An important factor in the success of the firm is how the firm responds to market uncertainties. The problem with this sentence is that the firm does not respond to anything; people who work for the firm act on their beliefs and they represent the firm in its actions. Thus it is people who respond to market uncertainties and it is they who navigate the market under the auspices of the firm. How do people relate to having to make decisions in an uncertain environment? Do all people relate to uncertainty in the same way? Entrepreneurial researchers have shown the complexity of people's behavior when dealing with uncertainty. Indeed, the definition of uncertainty itself is variable. Two chapters open this volume by introducing the variety of definitions of uncertainties as well as some of the issues the many definitions have caused.

In Chapter 1, Helen Pushkarskaya, Michael Smithson, Xun Liu and Jane E. Joseph describe an extended definition of uncertainty that includes some subjective factors, such as intent and ignorance. They define uncertainty differently from mainstream economic theories. Economic theories view risk as an objective phenomenon that, when it exists, can mathematically be resolved. Pushkarskaya and colleagues show that various perceptions of risk modify how risk is experienced in various ways. For example, they argue based on experimental results that being unaware of something as a result of deliberately withheld information by others is treated differently in the brain of the unaware subject from the situation when information simply does not exist.

By contrast, in Chapter 2 Angela A. Stanton and Isabell M. Welpe define choice under uncertainty in a more classical way. They argue that using a variety of definitions without standardization, research in entrepreneurship results in conflicting findings. In the management literature the talent of the entrepreneur is synonymous with risk handling ability. However, management researchers use the models of economic theories of uncertainty, in which risk is defined as a simple gamble of full information akin to casino roulette or the purchase of lottery tickets. Entrepreneurs seldom have full information and thus seldom play gambles. Rather an entrepreneur is surrounded with ambiguity, a type of risk that arises from having partial information. Entrepreneurial research, in line with the management literature, uses tools that measure risk and conclude solution to ambiguity. Stanton and Welpe question whether this approach is mathematically, logically and epistemologically acceptable and if research on brain processes can justify the use of risk as proxy for measuring ambiguity. Since neuroeconomics research found that separate brain regions respond to risk and ambiguity and that frequent natural hormonal variations influence perception bias in risk assessment, it is not possible to suggest that ambiguity may be resolved by computing it as risk, as some economic theories suggest and which management research so often applies.

In Chapter 3 Eden S. Blair reviews research on how unconscious processes impact business behaviors and decisions. Unconsciousness is defined as a mental process that is not consciously realized, planned or done. Blair looks at how memory and heuristics allow individuals to make decisions unconsciously. Unconscious processes cannot be measured using conventional social science methods that can be successfully used to analyze the processes of the conscious mind. Blair discusses the pros and cons of the different ways of measuring unconscious processes.

Chapter 4 opens the second part in the book. In Part 2 the authors 'open the black box' of the information processing and decision-making brain. The discussion is moving toward human emotions and their influence on decision-making. In Chapter 4 Paul J. Zak and Amos Nadler discuss the importance of trust. Trust in businesses has recently hit an all-time low. Yet trust is essential to effective management. Zak and Nadler present new findings from brain science, much of it from work done at Zak's laboratory, identifying how managers can build trust. They introduce a simple tool, the O-Factor (O-Factor), and provide suggestions for its use. They suggest the following ingredients of the trust recipe: praise, anticipation, delegation, transparency, empathy, autonomy and authenticity. Zak and Nadler's studies show how these techniques activate regions of the brain that produce trust. As trust increases, management becomes more effective; higher morale, productivity and profits follow.

In Chapter 5 Donald T. Wargo, Norman A. Baglini and Katherine A. Nelson look at some of the causes of the global financial crisis. Financial markets around the world experienced profound losses in 2008 and 2009 as a result of the worldwide credit crisis. The crisis was caused by the collapse of the market for collateralized debt obligations (CDOs). These CDOs were bonds backed by mortgages on houses in the USA but were bought not only by US banks but also by many municipalities and by European banks. 'Greed and fear' appear to be the overwhelming cause of this financial crisis. Wargo and colleagues show a biological cause; the reward and loss system of the brain. They argue that reward is normally counterbalanced by risk perception and greed is counterbalanced by fear of loss. They conclude that as a result of the sophisticated financial engineering tools that purportedly spread the risk, the perception of risks was removed by making risk invisible or difficult to perceive. The human reward and loss system, the danger-alerting system, was bypassed.

Chapter 6 opens Part 3, in which we start our exploration of what happens inside the black box of the brain and why. In this part we introduce a commonly misunderstood topic: stereotyping. Stereotyping is a 'negative' word, meaning that it implies a particular look, a particular behavior, or a particular ability or lack of ability that is generalized. Although this topic is usually shunned, here we face stereotyping head on. In addition to showing that it exists, we also take it a step further and evaluate the evolutionary roots for the reasons and meaning of stereotyping and how that may impact the firm.

Laura J. Kray, Connson C. Locke and Michael P. Haselhuhn present two experiments in Chapter 6 that explore what stereotypes mean in terms of beliefs about innate ability differences between men and women. As negotiations are important in corporate success, stereotyping might have a significant influence over who is negotiating with whom and with what success. With their first experiment, Kray and colleagues demonstrate that gender stereotype endorsement impairs performance for positively stereotyped negotiators relative to negatively stereotyped negotiators. Stereotyping decreases joint performance by causing both negotiators to overlook commonalities. In their second experiment they explore whether reactions to stereotype endorsement are moderated by negotiators' implicit beliefs about the malleability of performance. Kray and colleagues demonstrate that stereotype reactance (a performance boost by the negatively stereotyped negotiator) is promoted by a belief that negotiating ability is malleable. Fixed beliefs about negotiating ability render negotiators immune to the endorsement of gender stereotypes.

In Chapter 7 Kristina M. Durante and Gad Saad explore factors that are associated with stereotyping women. Women have made significant progress in today's workforce, with an increasing number of women holding senior corporate positions. Research shows that evolutionary and biological factors influence strategic shifts in women's behaviors, cognitions and emotions: the monthly ovulatory cycle. This chapter is not discussing changes in women's behaviors, cognitions and emotions as a result of premenstrual syndrome (PMS). Rather Durante and Saad look at the evolutionary role of those changes, which then manifest themselves in the stereotyped term PMS. As the probability of conception increases by an ovulating egg each month, women experience shifts in their social motives and behaviors. But these shifts are strategic from the perspective of evolution. For instance, research has found that near ovulation women become more attracted to masculine and socially dominant men, and are more competitive with other women. As these behavioral changes have serious evolutionary strategic roles in terms of ensuring the best possible chance for the mother's and the child's survival, they impact women's decision-making across multiple social arenas – including the business setting. Durante and Saad examine how a woman's fertility status might affect her behavior and performance within the workplace and discuss the implications that these shifts in behavior may have on intra-office relations.

In Chapter 8 Angela A. Stanton provides an unusual look at how men's hormonal variations affect the workplace. While women's hormonal variations and the corresponding physiological mechanisms that influence their mood, motivation and behavior have received significant scientific attention, male hormonal variations are typically only discussed in terms of aggression and dominance without context. Similarly to females, males experience hormonal variations that are shaped by selection forces in response to environmental stimuli. Stanton synthesizes extant literature on male hormonal variation in response to environmental stimuli that manifests itself as competitiveness, aggression, dominance, status-seeking, risk-taking, wealth creation and mate selection and shows how female hormonal cyclicality affects male hormonal variability. Men and women respond to each other's hormone concentrations by subconsciously reading each other's facial cues. As such, hormonal communication between the sexes is constant and is a key element of doing business inside the firm.

In Chapter 9 Donald T. Wargo, Norman A. Baglini and Katherine A. Nelson discuss the importance of understanding the mechanisms underlying the economic model of decision making and the dopamine-mediated reward system, which is the neurological correlate of decision-making. The dopamine-mediated reward system has profound implications for decision-making in the firm. They suggest that there are three interconnected decision-making systems in the human brain and dopamine is the principal neurotransmitter that is involved in these three systems. They present current neuroeconomic research on how the dopamine reward system is used to make economic decisions.

Chapter 10 opens Part 4 of the book. In this part we move from what is in the black box and how it reacts to the environment to how the black box influences the entrepreneur and entrepreneurial proclivity. Since risk is considered to be synonymous with the entrepreneur in most management literature, the brain's functions that identify and respond to risk and the associated strategic decision-making processes are important to understand. In Chapter 10 Theresa Michl and Stefan Taing introduce us to the differences between economic and neuroscientific understandings of entrepreneurial strategic decision making. There are no agreed upon strategic decision-making models in economics that can provide a realistic estimation of risk and ambiguity in light of the brain processes associated with monetary and social rewards. Although aspects of uncertainty and reward are assumed to be integrated in strategic decision-making processes, the sub-processes are not fully understood. Michl and Taing draw a theoretical comparison of cognitive and affective aspects of uncertainty and reward in strategic decision-making processes through neuroscientific and economic findings. They find the conclusions in these research fields only partly congruent. They apply the similarities and the differences by extending strategic decision-making models in economics and provide propositions for how to evaluate uncertainty and reward in strategic decision-making.

In Chapter 11 Robert Smith provides an overview of emerging research in entrepreneurship and neuroeconomics from a theoretical and practical perspective. He maps and unites research in a narrative that is understandable to economists, entrepreneurship scholars and the social scientific communities. Smith links disparate theories and discusses them at a layman's level. He develops a conceptual model that illustrates linkages with other human drives, such as spiritual fulfillment and libido. He questions whether some people are genetically and psychologically hard-wired to become successful entrepreneurs. Finally, he considers the theoretical contributions, which point to the emergence of a new genre of entrepreneurship research that is both scientifically and empirically rigorous.

In Chapter 12 Frédéric Basso, Laurent Guillou and Olivier Oullier introduce the sensory theory of value (STV) in the context of entrepreneurship. Their theory originates in Friedrich Hayek's seminal work that brought together neurophysiology and political economics. Main elements are discussed in light of recent developments in economic, cognitive and brain sciences. They argue that STV is a theory of mind. They show that determining market prices, as a cognitive mechanism, provides information on the behavior of the entrepreneur. Finally, they discuss the relevance of prices as sensory data, through recent advances in the fields of motor cognition, social coordination dynamics and neuroeconomics.

The final part in this volume, Part 5, is about corporate ethics and the influence of culture. This part opens with Chapter 13 by Donald T. Wargo, Norman A. Baglini and Katherine A. Nelson, who discuss ethics from a neuroeconomic perspective. Recent research in the areas of moral psychology, biological anthropology, neuroscience, game theory, behavioral economics, neuroeconomics and institutional theory present overwhelming evidence that ethical decisions are not made rationally. They are emotional and are typically made under stress.

Chapter 14 by John F. McCarthy, Carl A. Scheraga and Donald E. Gibson discusses cultural differences in negotiation and conflict management from the perspective of neuroeconomics. In negotiation and conflict management situations, understanding cultural patterns and tendencies is critical to whether a negotiation will accomplish the goals of the parties involved. McCarthy and colleagues suggest that a fine-grained approach is needed that examines cultural differences below the level of behavioral norms. Drawing on recent social neuroscience approaches, they propose that differing negotiating styles may not only be related to differing cultural norms, but to differences in underlying language processing strategies in the brain. They suggest that cultural differences may influence neuropsychological processes, and they anticipate that individuals from different cultures would exhibit different neuropsychological tendencies. Consistent with their hypothesis, they show in an experiment, using EEG measured responses, that native German-speaking participants took significantly more time to indicate when they understood a sentence than did native English-speaking participants of the same sentence (each time the native language of the participant was used). In a second experiment the same phenomenon was observed when participants were presented with positively and negatively framed situations which required decisions to be made. These results are consistent with the theory that individuals from different cultures develop unique language processing strategies that affect behavior. A deliberative cognitive style used by Germans, meaning logical assessment of sentences based on their structures, could account for these differences in comprehension reaction time relative to Americans, who looked more toward the meaning of the sentences rather than their structures. Their findings demonstrate that social neuroscience may provide a new way of understanding micro-processes in cross-cultural negotiations and conflict resolution.

In Chapter 15 the final chapter in this volume, Constant D. Beugré introduces a new discipline that he calls 'neuro-organizational behavior'. Beugré defines this new discipline as one that studies the impact of brain structures on human behavior in organizations and as a sub-field of organizational behavior. It integrates three levels of analysis: neural, mental and behavioral and considers neural circuitry as a key point in explaining human behavior in organizations. Beugré construes this new discipline as multidisciplinary that draws its knowledge and tools from various established disciplines, such as cognitive psychology, neuroeconomics, neuroscience, organizational behavior and social cognitive neuroscience.

We hope that you enjoy reading every chapter of this book. As the numerous chapters associated with the firm suggest, the firm needs new theories, definitions and models that are more person-centric in order to successfully explain how the firm achieves its goals and how it may optimize its performance using its resources. Both emotional and cognitive factors belong to the resources of the firm. These resources are rich with potential, but only to those firms who understand the neuroeconomics of the firm: neuroentrepreneurship. Since neuroentrepreneurship is a new field, we hope to have made the readers curious enough to follow new research that will most certainly reshape our understanding of the firm.

PART 1

The black box

Uncertainty about the future and risks in the present make decision-making under uncertainty a frequent area of research. In the recent past researchers typically probed human decision-making by looking at the outcomes of those decisions. They took these findings and inferred the intentions and decision-making processes from these outcomes. Studying decision-making this way is equal to treating the brain as a black box whose functions are of little importance. Although significant advances have been made in understanding what is inside the black box and how it works, there is room for further development. Part 1 looks at the black box from the outside and shows how it is influenced by the uncertainty of the environment.

1. Neuroeconomics of environmental uncertainty and the theory of the firm

Helen Pushkarskaya, Michael Smithson, Xun Liu and Jane E. Joseph

There is a need to be much more precise in defining, using, and measuring the construct of environmental uncertainty.

Frances J. Milliken (1987, p. 135)

Since Knight's (1921) suggestion that the acts of entrepreneurship are closely associated with environmental uncertainties, interest in research on environmental uncertainty has experienced ebbs and flows. This area of research reached a peak of popularity in the 1970s (for review, see Downey et al., 1975) when various researchers proposed different frameworks for describing it, including unpredictability (Cyert and March, 1963), lack of knowledge (Duncan, 1972) and complexity (Galbraith, 1973). Then the interest in the topic fell off dramatically, to reach another peak during the 1990s, when it was found that perceptions and beliefs about the environment affect top management decision-making more strongly than do actual environmental realities (Isabella and Waddock, 1994). Particular attention was paid to organizational response to perceived environmental uncertainties (for example, Kumar and Seth, 1998). In addition, by the 1990s, tools of experimental economics allowed researchers to collect sufficient empirical evidence that supported differentiation between two types of uncertain environments: risk and ambiguity, which provided an empirical ground for further theoretical advances (see Camerer and Weber, 1992 for a review of empirical and theoretical work). Milliken (1987) suggested that a reason for such an unsteady dynamic of development of this research area might be that 'the results of the research were not easily interpretable' (p. 135). She also argued that 'there is a need to be much more precise in defining, using, and measuring the construct of environmental uncertainty' (ibid.) and suggested that a clear classification of environmental uncertainty can help with interpretation of the empirical results.

The 1990s also ushered in new brain imaging technology, functional magnetic resonance imaging (fMRI), which measures neurobiological responses, and allows researchers to analyze them together with behavioral measures. The introduction of fMRI facilitated a renewed increase of interest in the topic of environmental uncertainty (Platt and Huettel, 2008). However, many researchers remain skeptical about the usefulness of fMRI findings in providing practical advice to decision-makers. These researchers claim that fMRI research is limited to localization of function, which alone would not help to advance psychological theory (for example, Coltheart, 2006a, b). This chapter discusses how Milliken's (1987) suggestion to use a 'clear classification' of the types of environmental uncertainty helps to interpret the results of the recent fMRI studies and to apply them to modeling decision-making.

Milliken (1987) classified environmental uncertainty into three types: uncertainty related to the environmental state (state uncertainty), uncertainty as to the effect of the environment or environmental changes on the individual (effect uncertainty), and uncertainty as to the number and type of individual responses to a given environment or environmental change (response uncertainty).

State uncertainty was classified further based on information available about outcomes and/or probabilities of these outcomes. Environments with known outcomes were classified as risk known probabilities (von Neumann and Morgenstern, 1944); and ambiguity (probabilities are unknown either due to the lack of reliable information or due to the presence of conflicting information about probabilities; Ellsberg, 1961). Budescu and Wallsten (1995) pointed out that the studies of decision-making under ambiguity had focused only on environments with imprecise probabilities rather than on unknown probabilities, and did not utilize Ellsberg's definition of ambiguity as an environment 'when there are questions of reliability and relevance of information, and particularly where there is conflicting opinions and evidence' (Ellsberg, 1961, p. 659). Later Smithson (1999) suggested considering a conflict environment (equally reliable sources provide conflicting information about probabilities associated with known outcomes) separately from ambiguity (vague probabilities are associated with known outcomes).

Environments where information about possible outcomes is not fully available were classified into unawareness (that is, decision-makers are unaware that some unknown outcomes are possible; Modica and Rustichini, 1994), and sample space ignorance (SSI; decision-makers are aware that some unknown outcomes are possible; Smithson et al., 2000). The main difference between these two environments is that during a decision stage under unawareness a decision-maker is likely to perceive the

Table 1.1   Classification of uncertainty environments

	Risk	Ambiguity	Conflict	SSI	Unawareness
Probabilities	Known	Imprecise	Conflictive estimates	Unknown	Not known to be unknown
Outcomes (state uncertainty), or					
Impacts (effect uncertainty), or	Known	Known	Known	Unknown	Not known to be unknown
Actions (response uncertainty)					

environment as risk, ambiguity or conflict (Modica and Rustichini, 1999), whereas under SSI a decision-maker acknowledges that some unknown outcomes are possible and has to adjust decision-making strategies accordingly (for example, Smithson et al., 2000). Table 1.1 summarizes these classifications.

A similar classification can be applied to both effect and response uncertainties. Effect uncertainty, when all potential impacts are known, can be classified as risk (that is, known probabilities), ambiguity (that is, vague probabilities) and conflict (that is, equally reliable sources provide conflicting information about probabilities); and when some impacts are not known to decision-makers, can be classified as unawareness (that is, decision-makers are unaware that the event can have some unknown impacts on them) and SSI (that is, decision-makers are aware that the event can have some unknown impacts on them). Response uncertainty, when all actions available to all agents are known, can be classified as risk (known probabilities), ambiguity (vague probabilities) and conflict (equally reliable sources provide conflicting information about probabilities); and, when all actions available to all agents are not known, can be classified as unawareness (that is, decision makers are unaware that some unknown actions are available) and SSI (that is, decision-makers are aware that some unknown actions are available).

Distinguishing between risk, ambiguity, SSI and conflict is important for two reasons. First, a coherent nomenclature for different kinds of unknowns is essential for theoretical development in organizational research. All too often, researchers use terms such as 'uncertainty,' 'ambiguity' and 'risk' imprecisely or even interchangeably. Aside from the traditional distinction between risk, ambiguity and uncertainty in the economists' sense, there has been little attention paid to distinctions among different kinds of uncertainty. The second set of reasons pertains to the psychological and social realities of organizational life, which are: (1) Psychological responses to them are distinct in important ways. People think and act as if these are different kinds of uncertainty. (2) People have distinct strategic uses for them. They play specific roles in interpersonal communication and interaction. (3) They underpin specific kinds of institutional arrangements, group norms and social capital that operate in a wide variety of organizational contexts. (4) They invoke different control strategies and orientations towards the future.

Beginning with psychological factors, behavioral studies have demonstrated that people show aversion or attraction to ambiguity (Ellsberg, 1961), conflict (Smithson, 1999) and SSI (Smithson et al., 2000) separately from risk. At the very least, these operate like additional components above and beyond risk to the overall impact of uncertainty. For example, insurers ask for higher premiums and insured persons are willing to pay more under ambiguity than under risk (Hogarth and Kunreuther, 1989).

Furthermore, risk, ambiguity, conflict and SSI appear to have a partial ordering whereby under some conditions conflict and SSI are regarded as more severe than ambiguity or risk. Smithson (1999) found that two ambiguous but agreeing messages from two sources are preferred over informatively equivalent precise but conflicting messages from two equally believable sources, and conflicting sources are perceived as less credible or knowledgeable than ambiguous sources. People are conflict-averse in the sense that they behave as if conflict is a more consequential kind of uncertainty than ambiguity. Likewise, Baron and Frisch (1994) find that people regard alternatives with missing information as inferior, and Smithson et al. (2000) extended this idea by experimentally demonstrating ignorance aversion. One possible consequence of ignorance and conflict aversion is that people may be more reluctant to actually make decisions under SSI or conflict because those decisions are perceived as more difficult (Anderson, 2003).

Another important psychological factor introduced by ambiguity, conflict and SSI is miscalibration. People can and do misestimate probabilities, but these three additional uncertainties bring in new and systematic biases to perceptions of uncertainty. First, people typically underestimate ambiguity in the sense that, when asked to construct confidence intervals, they make them too narrow (Alpert and Raiffa, 1982). More generally, people underestimate variability. Second, they underestimate the probability of a novel (previously unobserved) event occurring (Russo and

Kozlow, 1994), or even of an event that has been observed but is 'lumped together' with other events (Tversky and Koehler, 1994). Finally, both conflict and SSI render people especially vulnerable to confirmation bias (Nickerson, 1998), a tendency to seek out and overweigh information that confirms current beliefs.

Ambiguity and SSI often are implicated in motivations to seek, create or maintain uncertainty, rather than always trying to avoid, banish or reduce it. Everyday examples include pleasant surprises (such as unexpected gifts), and indeed there is evidence that people feel better about such events if their outcomes are not prematurely revealed or explained (Wilson et al., 2005). Likewise, undertakings such as discovery, creative work and entrepreneurship and positive future-oriented emotions, such as hope and aspiration, all require a supply of at least short-term uncertainties about what the future will bring (for example, Smithson, 1993, 2008).

Now let us move to the strategic interpersonal level (that is, the response uncertainty). Tetlock (2002) points out that there is more to uncertainty management than being an intuitive statistician/scientist. His templates are the 'intuitive politician', 'intuitive prosecutor' and 'intuitive theologian'. The adaptive challenges implicit in these metaphors are thrown at people by the social inter-firm environment: dealing with accountability and social exchange, negotiating the ground rules for accountability and exchange, and defending fundamental values.

Ambiguity in communication in the sense of unspecified probabilities occurs when an utterance has two or more possible meanings with no indication of which is the more likely. The word 'hot' in the sentence 'This food is hot', with no additional contextual information, could refer to heat or spiciness but we have no grounds for believing that one meaning has greater probability than the other. In manager–subordinate relationships both state and response ambiguity might be created intentionally either by manager or by subordinate. In an early reformulation of Durkheimian ideas, Eisenberg (1984) listed several reasons for strategic use of ambiguous environments. One is to achieve 'unified diversity', whereby a diversity of interpretations of such things as mission statements or organizational goals are permitted to exist and dysfunctional conflicts are avoided. Another is to enable deniability, for example, the ability to claim that a face-threatening interpretation was not the intended meaning of what was said. A third is increasing capacity for organizational change and adaptability by permitting diverse possible interpretations of organizational goals and rules while still appearing consistent. SSI, on the other hand, is more likely to be of strategic use for entrepreneurs and workers in creative professions. When viewed as knowledge 'gaps' to be filled, SSI is a resource for researchers, artists, entrepreneurs and even risk managers.

For instance, Carl Macrae's (2009, in press) study of risk assessment practices by airline flight safety investigators begins with the finding from studies of major organizational accidents that risks may remain unnoticed or misunderstood for long periods despite warning signals. His study reveals interpretative processes by which investigators 'enlarge small moments of doubt', a sense that current knowledge is suspect or inadequate. It also highlights an ambivalent tendency for the investigators to regard their own risk assessments and knowledge-base as fallible and incomplete, but also an intolerance of ignorance and a view of it as signaling novel risks. In short, ignorance is used by the investigators as a proxy indicator of risk.

In a somewhat more sinister vein, people may use the deliberate production of ignorance and uncertainty as a way to dominate or manipulate others. Proctor's (1995) work on the tobacco industry's efforts to manufacture doubt about the hazards of tobacco is an excellent case study of the use of pseudo-science by an industrial giant to protect and expand its investments. The industry generated doubt in three ways: by feigning its own ignorance of the hazards of smoking, repeatedly claiming the absence of proof from scientific research and publicizing in-house research that appeared to be addressing relevant health issues while actually sidestepping them. Likewise, Michaels and Monforton (2005) have elaborated the thesis that opponents of health and environmental regulation are able to prosecute their ends 'without being branded as anti-environmental, by focusing on scientific uncertainty and by manufacturing uncertainty if it does not exist' (ibid., p. S43).

Specific kinds of group norms, institutional arrangements and even social capital are underpinned by particular kinds of uncertainty. Examples of group norms involving risk are fairness in games and sports via randomizing devices and handicapping, and standards of proof imposed on juries in civil versus criminal trials. The sports norms regulate the risks of winning or losing, while the standards of proof regulate the risk of returning erroneous verdicts. Organized specialization is an example of an institutional ignorance arrangement that spreads risks associated with SSI in two ways. First, the risk that ignorance about specific matters might be consequential is spread by diversifying ignorance. Second, the risks associated with knowledge also are diversified. Any one of the myriad of institutional arrangements and forums for regulated debate stands as an example of a longstanding Western tradition for dealing with the uncertainties arising from conflict.

Trust is an example of social capital that trades on uncertainty. A primary source of that risk is a virtual requirement that the truster remain partially ignorant about the trustee, because trust relationships place limitations on overt monitoring or demands for accountability. Yamagishi and colleagues (for example, Yamagishi et al., 1998) argue that trust and 'commitment formation' are alternative solutions to what they call 'social uncertainty', chiefly the risk of being exploited in social interactions. Commitment formation involves the development of mutual monitoring and powers to sanction and reward each other's behavior. However, the reduction of transaction costs in commitment formation via uncertainty reduction comes at a price, namely the difficulty and costliness in exiting from the relationship and foregoing opportunities to form other relationships. Trust, on the other hand, entails running the risk of being exploited but increases opportunities by rendering the truster more mobile and able to establish cooperative relations more quickly. Trust, therefore, trades undesired uncertainty (the risk of being exploited) against desired uncertainty (freedom to seize opportunities for new relations).

These issues are exemplified and extended in 'Mattera's Dilemma' (Smithson, 1989), a conundrum in regulation with tradeoff and dilemmatic components. The tradeoff arises from the fact that a climate favoring creativity and entrepreneurship requires the toleration of SSI and possibly conflict in the service of freedom. Insistence on full knowledge and control eliminates the latitude needed for creativity. The dilemmatic component arises from the fact that the greater the attempts to regulate behavior, the more people attempt to generate ignorance in the would-be controllers by withholding or giving false information. If both parties pursue their self-interest then the end result is a system of constraints and controls built on disinformation.

Finally, we briefly turn to orientations towards control and the future. Smithson and Bammer (2008) observe that environments with known outcomes and probabilities (that is, merely risky) invoke forecasting and an 'anticipatory' stance towards the future. With ambiguity, conflict and (most of all) SSI comes an inability to forecast outcomes and quantify uncertainty. Dovers et al. (2008) claim that recognition among environmental risk assessors and managers that 'precise predictions of the scale or probability of impacts is not possible', and that meaningful probability distributions (or even second-order distributions) cannot be constructed has led to the realization that 'not even the broad directions of change are known' and 'thresholds [of dramatic change] and surprise are understood as likely'. These conditions have motivated a shift in control orientation from a solely anticipatory to a more resilience-oriented managerial style. That style emphasizes methods such as 'robust decision-making' (Lempert et al., 2002), crisis management and recovery, and resilient system design (for example, Boin and McConnell, 2007).

NEUROIMAGING

Neuroimaging studies make three important contributions to the understanding of decision-making under uncertainty. First, they provide new empirical support to the hypothesis that decision-making and other psychological processes are different in different uncertain environments by revealing differential patterns of brain activation across these environments (see, for example, Hsu, et al., 2005). Second, they contribute to a better understanding of what cognitive processes are involved during decision-making in various environments by revealing what psychological measures correlate with the brain activation in the areas that are involved in decision-making in these environments (see, for example, Huettel et al., 2006). And third, they contribute to a better understanding of individual differences in decision-making under uncertainty by informing what brain regions are correlated with individual economic preferences toward different types of uncertainties (ibid.).

Neuroimaging studies mainly focus on state uncertainty. It is worth noting that the majority of these studies use 'simple-gambles' setups. In these studies subjects are presented with the list of available options (for example, certain payoff, gamble 1 or gamble 2) and associated with each option a list of possible outcomes (for example, receive monetary rewards, lose money or receive nothing). Each outcome is associated with either precise (risk) or vague (ambiguity) probability. We model the SSI environment by informing decision-makers that the list of possible outcomes associated with some of the options are not complete. A simple gamble setup allows manipulating the types of uncertainty clearly, since a researcher can control how much information about outcome and/or probabilities is available to the subjects. In other settings the classification is less obvious. For instance, in the Balloon Analog Risk Task, subjects inflate a virtual balloon that can either grow larger or explode (Lejuez et al. 2002). This task is likely to model an ambiguous environment, since probabilities associated with each event (balloon grows larger or balloon explodes) are not known precisely. It is important to keep in mind while interpreting the results of these studies what type of uncertain environment is used in the experiment.

Earlier studies compared neurobiological responses to two uncertain environments – risk and ambiguity (for example, Hsu et al., 2005; Huettel et al., 2006). These studies revealed that individuals recruited different brain regions when dealing with each type of uncertainty. In particular, Hsu et al. (2005) found that ambiguity relative to risk trials facilitated stronger activation in the lateral orbitofrontal cortex and the amygdala, while risk relative to ambiguity trials activated more strongly the striatum and precuneus. Behavioral performance on this task in orbitofrontal lesion patients corroborated these claims.

In a previous study we employed a simple gamble setup to compare neurobiological responses to ambiguity and SSI (Pushkarskaya et al., 2007). We found that while ambiguity and SSI (uncertainties with missing information) shared activation in six regions, located primarily in the frontal lobe and also in the left fusiform gyrus, they also activated some regions differently. The ambiguity condition activated the left insula, associated with the parasympathetic system ('rest and repose' response) more extensively than the other conditions, whereas the SSI condition activated the left mid-orbitofrontal cortex (implicated in anticipation anxiety), the left anterior cingulate cortex (implicated in flexible adaptation response) and bilateral inferior parietal cortices (implicated in numerical representation) more than the other conditions. These results not only provide empirical support for the theoretical distinction between risk, ambiguity and SSI conditions, but also contradict the reductive viewpoint of the Subjective Expected Utility (SEU) framework and related theories, such as Prospect Theory (PT; Tversky and Kahneman, 1992) and Rank-Dependent Expected Utility Theory (RDEU; Quiggin, 1993). All these theories assume that individuals reduce any type of uncertainty to a risk environment by forming subjective beliefs about both the partition of a sample space and the corresponding probabilities. Consequently, a 'null' hypothesis, informed by these theories, implies that activation under ambiguity should be subsumed by the activation under SSI. The reason is that, according to existing theories, under SSI a decision-maker needs to partition the sample space in addition to estimating probabilities and deriving a subjective expected value of each prospect.

These results imply that a theory of the firm needs to model risky, ambiguous and SSI environments differently. In particular, while models of decision-making in risky and ambiguous environments might follow the reductive approach of SEU, PT and RDEU, a different approach needs to be used to model decision-making in the SSI environment. As we noted earlier, the SSI environment is more likely to be of strategic use for entrepreneurs, while ambiguity or risk is more likely to describe a decision-making environment of managers of established firms. Consequently, better models of decision-making in the SSI environment might help to answer the important but challenging question: 'how is the firm created?'

Entrepreneurial literature documents a few attempts to employ an approach different from the reductive approach of SEU. For instance, the Creation Theory (for example, Alvarez and Barney, 2007) assumes that entrepreneurs have to deal with a higher level of uncertainty than risk, and that possible outcomes of a stream of decisions over time can generally not be anticipated. Therefore, opportunities do not exist objectively and do not exist currently as market imperfections, but rather are created by individuals – individuals searching for ways to gain real economic wealth. Importantly, this search process is not governed by traditional profit maximizing and cost minimizing logic (Kohn and Shavell, 1974). The results of fMRI studies support further development of these models.

The results of neurobiological studies also help us to understand what psychological and other cognitive processes are likely to be involved during decision-making in various environments, by revealing what cognitive processes are associated with the brain areas that are involved in decision-making in these environments. For instance, in the risky environments relative to ambiguous environment subjects more strongly activated the striatum and precuneus, whereas the ambiguity condition relative to risky condition more strongly activated the orbitofrontal cortex and the amygdala (Hsu et al., 2005). Furthermore, SSI activated the orbitofrontal cortex more strongly than other uncertain environments (Pushkarskaya et al., 2007, 2008). The lateral orbitofrontal cortex was consistently implicated in the processes associated with punishment (Kringelbach and Rolls, 2004) and anticipation anxiety (Chua et al., 1999). Therefore, fMRI data are consistent with the results of Baron and Frisch (1994) who found that people regard alternatives with missing information as inferior, that is, they treat the pure absence of information as a punisher and are likely to experience higher levels of anxiety.

The increased selective activation in the left insula under the ambiguity condition suggests that the ambiguity condition provokes a 'rest and repose' response in individuals; on the other hand, the increased selective activation in the anterior cingulate cortex (ACC) under the SSI condition suggests that SSI invokes a flexible adaptation response (Pushkarskaya et al., 2007). Under ambiguity, when all possible outcomes are known, Bayesian updating suggests that waiting can be beneficial, since more information about relative frequencies of the outcomes helps to estimate unknown probabilities of these outcomes with a greater precision; that is, when all possible outcomes are known, people think the environment is stable enough that waiting for more information is going to be worthwhile. If not all outcomes are known (that is, SSI environment), and the subjects are aware of this fact, then they are more likely to think that the environment is not stable. In unstable (or non-stationary) environments accumulating information over time is not worthwhile. These findings might explain why, once a business is established and the economic environment is stable, it can be beneficial to transfer a decision-making power from an entrepreneur to a manager (for example, De Fraja, 1996). Perhaps, entrepreneurs are accustomed to making decisions in the SSI environment, and develop a tendency not to wait too long for more information about the likelihoods of potential outcomes, which becomes inefficient in an ambiguous environment.

Finally, neuroimaging studies that investigate individual preferences toward uncertainty can help answer another important question for the theory of the firm: do attitudes toward different types of uncertainty constitute distinct personality traits? If so, then do entrepreneurs and managers differ in their attitudes toward different types of uncertainty? The literature on entrepreneurship has examined a wide variety of possible differences between entrepreneurs and non-entrepreneurs (Begley and Boyd, 1986). While this research has continued for over two decades, the only two systematic differences between entrepreneurs and non-entrepreneurs identified so far concern first, the extent to which these two groups manifest particular cognitive biases and heuristics (Busenitz and Barney, 1997), and second, the level of self-efficacy in the domains of dealing with environmental uncertainties/coping with unexpected and developing new opportunities/innovation (Chen et al., 1998; DeNoble et al., 1999).

A number of fMRI studies investigated individual preferences toward different types of state uncertainty. Studies that compared risk, ambiguity and SSI directly found that preferences toward different types of uncertainty correlate with activation in different brain regions. For instance, activation of the posterior parietal cortex was predicted by risk preference; whereas activation in the lateral prefrontal cortex was predicted by ambiguity preferences (Huettel et al., 2006). Activation in the brain regions in the frontal and mid-frontal cortex that were implicated in intuitive reasoning, cognitive control strategy, goal maintenance and the selection of a task context positively correlated with ignorance aversion (Pushkarskaya et al., 2007, 2008). This result might suggest that individuals who dislike an unstable SSI environment make a stronger effort to resolve the multiplicity of its interpretations. Consequently, the inability or refusal to accept instability of the SSI environment is likely to contribute to ignorance aversion.

We also found that individual preferences toward ambiguity predict the ambiguity effect relative to SSI in all regions differentially activated by ambiguity and SSI. These results suggest that when ambiguity tolerant individuals receive full information about the potential outcomes (but not about probabilities), in addition to the 'flexible adaptation' system they activate the parasympathetic nervous system ('rest and repose response'), whereas ambiguity averse individuals use a 'flexible adaptation' network less intensively. This result also suggests that the ability to wait might be a key component for ambiguity tolerance. If, for external or internal reasons, individuals cannot wait (that is, they cannot employ the 'rest and repose' response) they avoid making decisions under ambiguity. If they can wait then, consistent with Bayesian updating, they 'rest and repose' in anticipation that more information about unknown probabilities will become available.

These results imply that studies interested in systematic differences between entrepreneurs and non-entrepreneurs need to investigate their preferences toward different types of uncertainties. We suggest that, even though managers and entrepreneurs do not differ significantly in their risk-attitudes (Brockhaus, 1980), they might differ in how much ambiguity or ignorance they are willing to tolerate. The development of the scales that measure individual ambiguity and ignorance aversion may take into account findings of fMRI studies that the inability or refusal to accept the instability of a SSI environment is likely to contribute to ignorance aversion, while the inability or refusal to wait might be a key component for ambiguity aversion. Furthermore, theories of decision-making under uncertainty, instead of modeling individual attitudes toward uncertainty by a single parameter (usually risk-aversion), can consider incorporating several parameters that reflect individual attitudes toward different types of uncertain environments.

Studies that focus on effect uncertainty are virtually non-existent; however, there are some fMRI studies that have started moving in this direction. For instance, Plassmann et al. (2008) demonstrated that marketing actions can modulate neural correlates of experienced pleasantness and suggested the mechanisms through which the effect operates.

Few fMRI studies applied tools of game theory to investigate the neural mechanisms recruited by the response uncertainties (for a review, see Sanfey, 2007). These studies have found that the key brain areas involved reinforcement learning, such as the striatum and orbitofrontal cortex, also support decision-making in social settings. Importantly, it was found that activity in some cortical areas is often enhanced during interactions with human partners compared with activity during similar interactions with computer partners, suggesting that decisions made during social interactions might be influenced by factors not directly related to payoffs (Lee, 2006). This reinforces the idea that state uncertainty (generated by computer) is distinct from response uncertainty (generated by humans). However, these studies mostly modeled ambiguous environments (vague probabilities are associated with known actions).

We suggest that neuroeconomists need to pay more attention to other types of response uncertainties. For instance, a classical trust game (Berg et al., 1995) models ambiguity in the response uncertainty setting, since all possible actions of the Trustee are known to the Investor *ex ante*. In reality, however, managers often have to trust their subordinates to choose from the set of actions that is not completely known to them a priori (SSI in the response uncertainty setting), or when they have conflicting information about the set of available actions (conflict in the response uncertainty setting). Since individuals behave differently in ambiguity, SSI and conflict environments in the state uncertainty setting, they might also differentiate between ambiguity, SSI and conflict environments in the response uncertainty setting. Neurobiological data, if they support the differentiation between different types of response uncertainty, might motivate social scientists to investigate manager–subordinate relationships in these settings further, which in turn might contribute to the further development of the theory of the firm. Overall, neuroimaging is an important new tool in the toolbox of empirical researchers, as it provides new behavioral hypotheses and data that can evaluate current theories. However, these new data might not be easily interpreted, and, consequently, not helpful to the theoretician, unless they can be clearly classified. We recommend that both experimenters and theoreticians follow the suggestions here regarding classification of environmental uncertainty when creating new models, interpreting the data and applying the results of the literature on environmental uncertainty to the theory of firms.

REFERENCES

Alpert, W. and Raiffa H. (1982), 'A progress report on the training of probability assessors', in D. Kahneman, P. Slovic and A. Tverksy (eds), *Judgment Under Uncertainty: Heuristics and Biases*, New York: Cambridge University Press, pp. 294–305.

Alvarez, S.A. and J. Barney (2007), 'A creation theory of entrepreneurial opportunity formation', Working paper available at http://www.uky.edu/Ag/AgEcon/seminars/alvarez-may07-txt.pdf.

Anderson, C.J. (2003), 'The psychology of doing nothing: forms of decision avoidance result from reason and emotion', *Psychological Bulletin*, **129**, 139–67.

Baron, J. and D. Frisch (1994), 'Ambiguous probabilities and the paradoxes of expected utility', in P. Ayton and G. Wright (eds), *Subjective Probability*, Chichester, Sussex: Wiley, pp. 293–94.

Begley, T. and D. Boyd (1986), 'Psychological characteristics associated with entrepreneurial performance', *Frontiers of Entrepreneurship Research*, 146–65.

Berg, J., J. Dickhaut and K. McCabe (1995), 'Trust, reciprocity, and social history', *Games and Economic Behavior*, **10**, 122–42.

Boin, R.A. and A. McConnell (2007), 'Preparing for critical infrastructure breakdowns: the limits of crisis management and the need for resilience', *Journal of Contingencies and Crisis Management*, **15**, 50–59.

Brockhaus, R.H. Sr (1980), 'Risk taking propensity of entrepreneurs', *The Academy of Management Journal*, **23** (3), 509–20.

Budescu, D. and T. Wallsten (1995), 'Processing linguistic probabilities: general principles and empirical evidence', in J. Busemeyer, R. Hastie and D.L. Medin (eds), *Decision making from a Cognitive Perspective*, San Diego, CA: Academic Press, pp. 275–318.

Busenitz, L.W. and J.B. Barney (1997), 'Differences between entrepreneurs and managers in large organizations: biases and heuristics', *Journal of Business Venturing*, **12** (1), 9–30.

Camerer, C. and M. Weber (1992), 'Recent developments in modeling preferences: uncertainty and ambiguity', *Journal of Risk and Uncertainty*, **5** (4), 325–70.

Chen, C.C., P.G. Greene and A. Crick (1998), 'Does entrepreneurial self-efficacy distinguish entrepreneurs from managers?', *Journal of Business Venturing*, **13**, 295–316.

Chua, P., M. Krams, I. Toni, R. Passingham and R. Dolan (1999), 'A functional anatomy of anticipatory anxiety', *NeuroImage*, **9** (6), 563–71.

Coltheart, M. (2006a), 'What has functional neuroimaging told us about the mind (so far)?', *Cortex*, **42**, 323–31.

Coltheart, M. (2006b) 'Perhaps functional neuroimaging has not told us anything about the mind (so far)', *Cortex*, **42**, 422–7.

Cyert, R. and J. March (1963), *Behavioral Theory of Firm*, Englewood Cliffs, NJ: Prentice Hall.

De Fraja, G. (1996), 'Entrepreneur or manager: who runs the firm?,' *Journal of Industrial Economics*, **44** (1), 89–98.

DeNoble, A.F., D. Jung and S.B. Ehrlich (1999), 'Entrepreneurial self-efficacy: the development of a measure and its relation to entrepreneurial action', in P.D. Reynolds, W.D. Bygrave, S. Manigart, C.M. Mason, G.D. Meyer, H.J. Sapienza and K.G. Shaver (eds), *Frontiers of Entrepreneurship Research*, Wellesley, MA: Babson College, pp. 73–87.

Dovers, S., M. Hutchinson, D. Lindenmayer et al. (2008), 'Uncertainty, complexity and the environment', in G. Bammer and M. Smithson (ed.), *Uncertainty and Risk: Multidisciplinary Perspectives*, London: Earthscan, pp. 245–60.

Downey, H.K., D. Hellriegel and J.W. Slocum, Jr (1975), 'Environmental uncertainty: the construct and its application', *Administrative Science Quarterly*, **20**, 613–29.

Duncan, R. (1972), 'Characteristics of organizational environments and perceived environmental uncertainty', *Administrative Science Quarterly*, **17**, 313–27

Eisenberg, E.M. (1984), 'Ambiguity as strategy in organizational communication', *Communication Monographs*, **51**, 227–41.

Ellsberg, D. (1961), 'Risk, ambiguity, and the savage axioms', *Quarterly Journal of Economics*, **75**, 643–69.

Galbraith, J.R. (1973), *Designing Complex Organizations*, 1st edn, Boston, MA: Addison-Wesley Longman Publishing Co.

Hogarth, R. and H. Kunreuther (1989), 'Risk, ambiguity and insurance', *Journal of Risk and Uncertainty*, **2**, 5–35.

Hsu, M., M. Bhatt, R. Adolphs, D. Tranel and C.F. Camerer (2005), 'Neural systems responding to degrees of uncertainty in human decision-making', *Science*, **310** (5754), 1680–83.

Huettel, S., C. Stowe, E. Gordon, B. Warner and M. Platt (2006), 'Neural signatures of economic preferences for risk and ambiguity', *Neuron*, **49** (5), 765–75.

Isabella, L.A. and S.A. Waddock (1994), 'Top management team certainty: environmental assessments, teamwork, and performance implications', *Journal of Management*, **20** (4), 835–58.

Knight, F.H. (1921), *Risk, Uncertainty and Profit*, Boston, MA: Hart, Schaffner and Marx.

Kohn, M. and S. Shavell (1974), 'The theory of search', *Journal of Economic Theory*, **9**, 93–123.

Kringelbach, M.L. and E.T. Rolls (2004), 'The functional neuroanatomy of the human orbitofrontal cortex: evidence from neuroimaging and neuropsychology', *Progress in Neurobiology*, **72** (5), 341–72.

Kumar, S. and A. Seth (1998). 'The design of coordination and control mechanisms for managing joint venture–parent relationships', *Strategic Management Journal*, **19** (6), 579–99.

Lee, D. (2006), 'Neural basis of quasi-rational decision-making', *Current Opinion in Neurobiology*, **16** (2), 191–8.

Lejuez, C.W., J.P. Read, C.W. Kahler et al. (2002), 'Evaluation of a behavioral measure of risk taking: the Balloon Analogue Risk Task BART', *Journal of Experimental Psychology and Applications*, **8**, 75–84.

Lempert, R.J., S.W. Popper and S.C. Bankes (2002), 'Confronting surprise', *Social Science Computing Review*, **20**, 420–40.

Macrae, C. (2009, in press), 'Making risks visible: identifying and interpreting threats to airline flight safety', *Journal of Occupational and Organizational Psychology*.

Michaels, D. and C. Monforton (2005), 'Manufacturing uncertainty: contested science and the protection of the public's health and environment', *American Journal of Public Health Supplement*, **95**, S39–S48.

Milliken, F. (1987), 'Three types of perceived uncertainty about the environment: state, effect, and response uncertainty', *Academy of Management Review*, **12**, 133–43.

Modica, S. and A. Rustichini (1994), 'Awareness and partitional information structures', *Theory and Decision*, **37**, 107–24.

Modica, S. and A. Rustichini (1999), 'Awareness and partitional information structures', *Games and Economic Behavior*, **27**, 265–98.

Nickerson, R.S. (1998), 'Confirmation bias: a ubiquitous phenomenon in many guises', *Review of General Psychology*, **2**, 175–220.

Plassmann, H., J. O'Doherty, B. Shiv and A. Rangel (2008), 'Marketing actions can modulate neural representations of experienced pleasantness', *Proceedings of the National Academy of Sciences of the United States of America*, **105**, 1050–54.

Platt, M.L. and S.A. Huettel (2008), 'Risky business: the neuroeconomics of uncertainty', *Nature of Neuroscience*, **11** (4), 398–403.

Proctor, R.N. (1995), *Cancer Wars: How Politics Shapes What We Know and Don't Know about Cancer*, New York: Basic Books.

Pushkarskaya, H., X. Liu, M. Smithson and J.E. Joseph (2007), 'Neurobiological responses in individuals making choices in uncertain environments: ambiguity and sample space ignorance', SABE annual meeting, New York, 15–18 May.

Pushkarskaya, H., X. Liu, M. Smithson and J.E. Joseph (2008), 'Neurobiological responses in individuals making choices in uncertain environments: ambiguity and sample space ignorance versus conflict', Society for Neuroeconomics annual meeting, Park City, Utah, 25–28 September

Quiggin, J. (1993), *Generalized Expected Utility Theory: The Rank Dependent Model*, Boston, MA: Kluwer Academic Publishers.

Russo, J.E. and K. Kozlow (1994), 'Where is the fault in fault trees?', *Journal of Experimental Psychology: Human Perception and Performance*, **20**, 17–32.

Sanfey, A.G. (2007), 'Social decision-making: insights from game theory and neuroscience', *Science*, **318**, 598–602.

Smithson, M. (1989), *Ignorance and Uncertainty: Emerging Paradigms*, New York: Springer.

Smithson, M. (1993), 'Ignorance and science: dilemmas, perspectives, and prospects', *Knowledge: Creation, Diffusion, Utilization*, **15**, 133–56.

Smithson, M. (1999), 'Conflict aversion: preference for ambiguity vs. conflict in sources and evidence', *Organizational Behavior and Human Decision Processes*, **79**, 179–98.

Smithson, M. (2008), 'The many faces and masks of uncertainty', in G. Bammer and M. Smithson (eds), *Uncertainty and Risk: Multidisciplinary Perspectives*, London: Earthscan, pp. 12–25.

Smithson, M. and G. Bammer (2008), 'Coping and managing under uncertainty', in G. Bammer and M. Smithson (eds), *Uncertainty and Risk: Multidisciplinary Perspectives*, London: Earthscan, pp. 321–33.

Smithson, M., T. Bartos and K. Takemura (2000), 'Human judgement under sample space ignorance', *Risk, Decision and Policy*, **5**, 135–50.

Tetlock, P.E. (2002), 'Social functionalist frameworks for judgment and choice: intuitive politicians, theologians, and prosecutors', *Psychological Review*, **109**, 451–71.

Tversky, A. and D. Kahneman (1992), 'Advances in prospect theory: cumulative representation of uncertainty', *Journal of Risk and Uncertainty*, **5** (4), 297–323.

Tversky, A. and D.J. Koehler (1994), 'Support theory: a nonextensional representation of subjective probability', *Psychological Review*, **101**, 547–67.

von Neumann, J. and O. Morgenstern (1944), *Theory of Games and Economic Behavior*, Princeton, NJ: Princeton University Press.

Wilson, T.D., D.B. Centerbar, D.T. Gilbert and D.A. Kermer (2005), 'The pleasures of uncertainty: prolonging positive moods in ways people do not anticipate', *Journal of Personality and Social Psychology*, **88**, 5–21.

Yamagishi, T., K.S. Cook and M. Watanabe (1998) 'Uncertainty, trust and commitment formation in the United States and Japan', *American Journal of Sociology*, **104**, 165–94.

2. Risk and ambiguity: entrepreneurial research from the perspective of economics

Angela A. Stanton and Isabell M. Welpe

We took risks. We knew we took them. Things have come out against us. We have no cause for complaint.

Robert Falcon Scott, 1868–1912

INTRODUCTION

As we are entering a new season of heated debates over the financial meltdown and try to point fingers to 'who done it', a key comment made in the *Atlantic Magazine* is apt to be shown here as one of the reasons why this chapter is of importance. Simon Johnson, professor at MIT Sloan School of Management and Chief Economist at the International Monetary Fund in 2007 and 2008, in his superb essay quotes Ben Bernanke saying in 2006 that 'The management of market risk and credit risk has become increasingly sophisticated . . .. Banking organizations of all sizes have made substantial strides over the past two decades in their ability to measure and manage risks'. Johnson continues: 'To date, the U.S. government, in an effort to rescue the company, has committed about $180 billion in investments and loans to cover losses that AIG's sophisticated risk modeling had said were virtually impossible' (Johnson, 2009, p. 50). Why are these sentences the introduction to this chapter? Both Bernanke and Johnson discuss 'risks' to be managed, controlled and modeled. But what they are really talking about are not risks but ambiguities. The differences are not semantics; they are referring to economic models that are not capable of modeling both risk and ambiguity. And this is one of the reasons for the failure of market analysts, bankers and specialists in not discovering early enough that the models they use do not fit the problem.

Modeling some phenomenon implies that some information is missing and the model represents possible outcomes with various probability assessments. Risk need not be modeled accordingly, because, by standard economic definition, in risky situations one has full information about the outcomes and of the probability distribution of those outcomes. Indeed, pure risk is defined in economics as gamble. However, in the case of ambiguity, we lack some information about the probability. It is in the case of ambiguity where modeling is necessary. But one may not use the mathematics created for solving risk to solve problems of ambiguity.

A problem with the word 'risk' is that it is a general term that means risk, ambiguity and uncertainty at the same time as it also means just pure risk (as in known probabilities, which is the definition of a gamble). The word 'uncertainty' is also used to mean either risk, ambiguity or uncertainty. In everyday discussions of uncertainties the distinctions between these three words is not enforced. The English language is often noted to have words with multiple meanings and they are normally of no concern. Since in academia clarity and sharp definition is of essence, in most cases proper definitions pre-empt any possibility of confusion. Not so in the case of 'risk' and 'uncertainty'. Although economics has strong definitions for each of these risk types, even it uses these terms confusingly. For example, the field of study in economics that concerns itself with decision-making under risk, ambiguity and uncertainty is called 'choice under uncertainty'. In this chapter, for lack of better options, we use 'risk types' to refer to the family of risks that include risk, ambiguity and uncertainty among a few other types, which are introduced in later sections.

The purpose of this chapter is to detail the differences between the various risk types. We provide the standard economic definition of risk, ambiguity and uncertainty and compare them to the definitions used by other research fields, such as business management and psychology. We then show why each risk type is distinct and why the model created for one cannot be used for the other. We introduce findings of recent research that show what parts of the brain are solving risky versus ambiguous problems. As we shall see, the two types of risks are treated very differently from each other in the human brain. Therefore, one needs to use caution when applying models originally developed for risk calculations to problems of ambiguous nature because the human mind does not work according to economic theories developed to solve these problems. The faulty assumption that standard economic models are good enough to model real-life decision-making is quite common. In this chapter we focus our analysis on the field of entrepreneurial research because the conflicts arising from the misuse of these models have surfaced a long time ago but have remained to date unresolved. Here we summarize, extend and synthesize these findings.

CLEARING THE CLUTTER OF DEFINITIONS

Distinguishing between risk and ambiguity in entrepreneurial theories is important in order to build sound theories about decision-making. Building strong theories requires consistent definitions within and across fields. Within the field of entrepreneurship risk is the only type of uncertainty discussed but various versions of its definitions coexist, while economics uses different definitions for several categories of uncertainties, of which risk is only one type. The many definitions can become a serious hindrance to science and are cause for concern. Issues associated with inconsistent definitions, for example, surface even in the academic peer review system as some submissions receive conflicting requests from anonymous reviewers on the use and/or definition of risk or uncertainty (this is a comment based on experience of one of the authors of this chapter and also of several colleagues who shared their experiences). Confused definitions in entrepreneurial research have led to conflicting results (Newman, 2007; Stewart and Roth, 2001). A prime question that entrepreneurial researchers try to find an answer for is whether successful entrepreneurs differ in their propensity to deal with risks from non-entrepreneurs. However, research results have been inconclusive and contradictory in finding both yes and no answers with about equal frequency.

In the following sections we introduce the main concepts associated with the terms risk, ambiguity and uncertainty, and provide a definition of each.

RISK

The meaning of the term 'risk' is defined in economics in the following way: risk is a gamble of possible loss with full information. Information is given about all possible outcomes and the probability distribution associated with those outcomes is also fully disclosed. For example, flipping a fair coin provides such a risk if one wishes to bet on the outcome of the next flip. Mainstream economic theories posit that people evaluate risk based on the expected value of the outcomes. To calculate the expected value, economics uses the model in which the probabilities are multiplied with their respective outcomes and then these are summed. To choose between two gamble sets, the gambles with the higher expected value would consistently be chosen. For instance, in the case of the coin flip, if one is offered a gamble to place a free bet on the next flip yielding a head, and if it is heads the winning is $30 but if it is tails the loss is $10, one can calculate the expected value of that gamble: $(0.5)*(\$30) + (0.5)*(-\$10) =$

$15 − $5 = $10. Economic theory posits that this gamble with its positive expected value would be accepted by all types of people, regardless of their risk aversion levels. But if the gamble provided a slightly negative expected value, only people who prefer risk would choose that gamble.

It has been shown in a variety of experiments that humans behave differently from economic expectations. People consider losses more important than gains by about 2:1, implying that the gains need to be about twice as large as the losses before they choose to engage in the gamble (Kahneman and Tversky, 1972, 1979, 2000). Economic theories have also failed to predict that people are sensitive to more than just the expected value of the outcomes. Keeping the expected value of several gambles constant but varying the magnitude of potential gains and losses may prompt an inconsistent choice by a decision maker. For example, given gambles (1) 50 percent chance of winning $10 and 50 percent chance of losing $10 versus (2) 50 percent chance of winning $100 and 50 percent of losing $100, those who fear risk more will likely prefer (1) whereas those who prefer risk might choose (2), even if the expected value of (1) and (2) are equal. Economic theory assumed that given identical expected values, the decision makers would be indifferent between these choices but research shows that they are not indifferent. It has been suggested that people suffer from cognitive bias (Kahneman and Tversky, 1972, 1979, 2000; Tversky and Kahneman, 1992) but, as discussed later in more detail, hormonal expectations of the brain, error calculations and brain adaptations may override financial expectations.

While mainstream economics considers risk only in terms of mathematical definition (potential outcomes and probability distribution), other sciences, such as management and psychology, consider risk in terms of how people relate to a risky situation. And herein lies the first cause for the confused results: economics looks at risk 'objectively', whereas other fields look at the 'subjective' effect of risk on decision-making. The two types of views of risk are very different. The mathematics associated with calculating risk in its objective sense is very different from the mathematics that might be useful to calculate risk in its subjective sense.

When management researchers discuss the risk propensity of an agent, the propensity they describe has little similarity to what economics defines as risk propensity. In economics risk propensity is merely a measure of divergence from risk neutrality, whereas in entrepreneurship risk propensity comes in degrees and types. Researchers in entrepreneurship look for differences in how people relate to risks and not the differences in the types of risks themselves. The types of bundles they use in their search for finding entrepreneurial propensity often lead to Prospect Theory type analysis (Einhorn and Hogarth, 1986). Prospect Theory, in brief, suggests that people do not consider losses and gains perfectly symmetrical (Kahneman and Tversky, 1979). In standard economic theories a dollar gained with 50 percent chance and a dollar lost with 50 percent chance lead to the expected value of $0 (losses and gains of equal magnitude and probability are symmetrical) but in Prospect Theory the dollar lost is about twice as important as a dollar gained (given the same probability). In Prospect Theory the options of gain and loss are not symmetrical. For this reason, Prospect Theory is distant from the risk models used to define risk propensity. Since risk propensity is a property of an economic model reflecting on a desired form of decision-making under risk, the mathematics associated with risk propensity can only be used when full information is provided. Risk propensity models of economics are not appropriate for analyzing choice outcomes in ambiguous settings, when some information is not provided to the decision-maker.

The second problem arising from the various definitions of risk is that in economics risk is applicable only if (1) a loss is a possible outcome. In management research, surveys of risk questions often contain bundles in which subjects have to decide between options with larger versus smaller gain or some gain versus status quo. As there is no loss, this is not risk under the strict economic definition of risk. (2) All information must be known – as summarized above – in order to use economic models of risk. Not much in entrepreneurship fits this concept because the probability distribution and the factors associated with success or failure are not known. Thus research in entrepreneurship is not really about 'risk' but about some other form of uncertainty in which the rules do not call for full information. It follows that the use of the term 'risk' and the use of risk models is inappropriate for business problems. Rather than having full information, an entrepreneur needs to make an educated guess or use past results to calculate a probability scenario associated with success. Economics calls these types of problems ambiguous.

AMBIGUITY

When management researchers discuss 'risk', they almost always mean 'ambiguity', as it is rare in management that one has full information about probabilities and their associated outcomes. As discussed above, one cannot use the mathematical models created for resolving risky problems to resolve ambiguous problems. In economics ambiguity is defined as a decision problem of partial information, in which the outcomes are known but some information is lacking about the probability distribution. Since ambiguity is not a gamble in the same way as risk is, it need not have a loss component. However, as not all information is provided, using the mathematics of expected value is not possible.

Ellsberg introduced a classic example of ambiguity, which is referred to as the Ellsberg Paradox (Brown and Bracha, 2008; Ellsberg, 1961; Hsu et al., 2005). For example, a decision-maker is facing two urns of blue and red colored balls. She is told that Urn A has 20 percent red and 80 percent blue balls and is not told about the color distribution of Urn B. Thus Urn A represents a risky urn and Urn B an ambiguous urn. It is entirely possible that the two urns are identical in every respect but since the decision-maker does not know the probability distribution of colors in Urn B, she is more likely to try her luck from Urn A when given the choice to pull a blue ball.

Economics defines ambiguity as something that can be resolved mathematically by forming beliefs about the probability distribution. For example, in the urn example above, the decision-maker may eyeball Urn B and decide (believe) that Urn B has 40 percent red and 60 percent blue balls. Thus given her belief about the probability distribution of Urn B and full information about Urn A, she may decide to bet on Urn B if the gamble calls for larger winning in case a red ball is drawn. Once those beliefs are formed, the ambiguous problem of economics reduces to risk. However, one of the facts about such beliefs is that there may be an infinite number of beliefs all leading to the same choice outcome. One may use the flip of a coin to form some guess about the odds of red to blue ball ratio in Urn B, or one may use data from past draws from that urn, or even fancy models, like financial analysts do. The method of forming those beliefs is not important in terms of the economic definition of ambiguity but since there are an infinite number of such possible beliefs, there is a mathematical problem in equating a particular belief with a particular probability distribution and using that as though it has become a risk problem.

To elaborate, imagine that the decision-maker believed that 40 percent of the balls were red in Urn B and 60 percent were blue. As a result, when the choice to pull from an urn is given such that if red is pulled, she wins $20 but if blue is pulled, she loses $10, she will pull from Urn B because she believes that Urn B has more red balls than Urn A. She might believe that 39 percent of the balls are red in Urn B, or 41 percent, or anything in between. There are an infinite number of probabilities between 39 percent and 40 percent (39.1 percent, 39.2 percent and so on) and they would all lead to her drawing from Urn B. Thus a researcher may say little about the subject's beliefs, as an infinite number of them will lead to the same decision: she pulled from Urn B. It follows that one may not assume that ambiguity, once a belief is made, is the same as risk, since in the case of risk, there is only one set of probability distribution given whereas in ambiguity it is infinite in numbers.

Economics resolves ambiguity as risk after a particular belief was made but requires consistency of choices, *ceteris paribus*. The human brain uses special compartments to form beliefs that are emotional and call on memory as well as on a variety of other social functions (Hamann, 2009; Kapogiannis et al., 2009; Kensinger, 2009; Larson and Steuer, 2009; Mather and Sutherland, 2009; Moll et al., 2006; Young et al., 2007). No level of consistency may be assumed from an emotion-based decision. Since economic decision-making of rational agents requires consistency, inconsistent experimental results have often been dismissed as human weakness or anomalous findings. Although economic researchers have come far in understanding the importance of decision-making processes in decision outcomes, they do not usually accept that it may be the models that do not apply to human decision-making. Here we show that such anomalies are the results of measurement error stemming from models that are not applicable to human decision-making.

Since the human brain calls on emotions and memory when forming beliefs but not when faced with evaluating risks of full information, it is not possible to say that in the brain ambiguity is resolvable as risk once beliefs are formed. In all likeliness, ambiguity cannot be reduced to risk because the areas used to solve them in the brain reside in distinct physiological locations, use different hormonal chemical processes and often work at a different time as well. Furthermore, the brain appears very plastic in that it is able to change its decision-making process instantaneously in adaptation to new information – see Chapter 8 in this volume on how fast men change their decisions when testosterone-increasing stimuli (pictures of young women or lingerie) are presented (Van den Bergh and Dewitte, 2006); see also a multitude of research on dopamine adaptation in error response (Schultz, 1998, 2001; Schultz and Dickinson, 2000; Schultz et al., 1997); the influence of reward as a process rather than an outcome that produces adaptations in the brain (Kobayashi and Schultz, 2008); and later in this chapter about how such quick changes in testosterone and cortisol may influence financial success (Coates and Herbert, 2008). When ambiguity is present, its existence appears to affect the perception of risk as well – in fact, when risky choices are made after ambiguous ones, the human brain may distort the true probability, leading to the possibility that decision-makers might end up treating risks as though they were ambiguity (Tobler et al., 2008). For example, research shows that a 'near miss' is enough to make the gambler 'believe' that the next gamble has a better chance (Clark et al., 2009). Thus this makes us question if risk is even a component of business decision-making.

UNCERTAINTY

And finally, let us mention uncertainty. Although in management (and in common everyday thinking) uncertainty implies risk or ambiguity inter-changeably, in economics it does not. In economics 'uncertainty' refers to something that (1) does not exist – has neither outcome nor probability, and (2) is mathematically non-resolvable (see Knight, 1921; discussed in detail later). For example, if you think back to the tragic terrorist attack of 9/11: on 9/10 what was the probability associated with terrorists flying commercial jets into the Twin Towers? Did people ask (or even think of) this specific question? In other words, was it something that someone con-ceived of (in the USA populace)? Both the outcome and the probability associated with that outcome were complete unknowns to people in the USA. This we call uncertainty in a 'milder' sense. It is 'milder' because some people knew that it was going to happen: the terrorists had a plan; they knew. Thus, in reality, this was not true fundamental uncertainty – it was simply uncertainty in that some people held back information from others.

Some researchers argue that uncertainty is context specific in that strong uncertainty that is truly fundamental is different from mild uncertainty in which only the subjects under observation lack information. To them, the milder form of uncertainty is an example of 'ignorance' or 'unawareness' and is treated by the brain differently from fundamental uncertainty (see Chapter 1 of this volume). It may be successfully argued that this is seman-tics. It is not possible to test fundamental uncertainty experimentally because if the researchers know about it, this is no longer fundamental uncertainty but milder uncertainty, which has been labeled ignorance or unawareness. In this chapter we mention uncertainty only in terms of its definition.

THEORIES OF RISKS

Many researchers refer to the theory of risk and uncertainty developed by Knight when they introduce a risky problem in their research (Knight, 1921). It is generally assumed that risk is inseparable from entrepreneurship (Barbosa et al., 2007; Brockhaus Sr, 1980; Cramer et al., 2002; Folta, 2005; Forlani, 2000; Grichnik, 2008; Janney and Dess, 2006; Kamalanabhan et al., 2006; Keh et al., 2002; Legoherel et al., 2004; Miner and Raju, 2004; Naldi et al., 2007; Newman, 2007; Stewart and Roth, 2001; Wu and Knott, 2006; Xu and Ruef, 2004). Typically, risk in management theories is defined as something that is affected by emotions, goals and other drive states (for a review, see Maner and Gerend, 2007). Indeed, the confused definition of risk and how researchers are probing to find risk-management in entrepreneurs has been questioned for quite some time (Alvarez, 2005; Grichnik, 2008; Slovic, 1964; Stewart and Roth, 2001).

A good discussion of the various interpretations of risk is presented by Gilboa and colleagues in their review of probability and uncertainty modeling in economics (Gilboa et al., 2008). Their paper adds to our discussion in two significant ways: first, they show how people might have the tendency to consider simple risks with full information as if some information were missing. This they refer to as 'subjective probability', which implies that one may form a subjective belief about the probability in spite of the fact that an objective probability is given. In effect, Gilboa and colleagues show that subjective probability is equal to ambiguity. Second, they state that subjective probability is ignorance about the true probability. Thus this suggests that ambiguity and ignorance are two words for the same phenomenon. By contrast, in Chapter 1 of this volume, Pushkarskaya and colleagues refer to ignorance as being unaware of some potential outcome or potential action opportunity. Rather than subjectivity in probability, they see it as subjective outcome (see also Smithson et al., 2000). Furthermore, Pushkarskaya and colleagues in Chapter 1 suggest that ambiguity is different from ignorance in that often ambiguity is used as proxy for risk but ignorance is not. Thus, for them, ambiguity and ignorance are different from each other. With the many definitions about risk and what is understood to be unknown, no wonder that research in entrepreneurship has yielded conflicting results.

The main divide between risk in economic versus entrepreneurial research is that one is looking at an outcome and the other a process within a particular context. That is why entrepreneurial literature refers to risk using terms that involve behavioral components, such as risk perceptions 'given the desirability of the benefits', the 'utility of negative outcomes', how 'severe the costs are judged to be', the likelihood associated with 'both the potential gain and the severity of losses'. It is not surprising then to find mixed risk and ambiguity statements such as that when people 'judge positive outcomes as strong and likely to occur, they tend to make action-oriented choices; when people judge negative outcomes as strong and likely to occur, they tend to make risk-avoidant choices' (Maner and Gerend, 2007, p. 257).

Entrepreneurial researchers neither use risk in the way that it is defined in economics, nor as it is defined by Prospect Theory, but in a behavioral term that reflects on brain processes that are influenced by environmental factors and which are distinct from the problems of risks themselves (Baron, 1998, 2004, 2008; Brockhaus Sr, 1980). Part of the confused results stem from using the economic term of risk but formulating the research about it as a behavioral process. As mentioned earlier, a key factor of the confused results is the use of risk models to derive choices to ambiguous situations. Entrepreneurial researchers have suggested that risky options might evoke fear and thus influence risk-avoidance (Maner and Gerend, 2007) but it is our opinion that it is ambiguity that they elicited, which recruits emotions to form beliefs. They suggest that risk is handled by the part of the brain where fear is resolved. However, research in neuroscience shows that the center for fear is the amygdala (Hsu et al., 2005; Rustichini et al., 2005; Smith et al., 2002) and the primary hormones associated with fear are dopamine and serotonin (Garpenstrand et al., 2001). The primary hormone associated with taking risks is testosterone (Mazur and Booth, 1999) and the location of solving risky problems is in the prefrontal cortex (Hsu et al., 2005, 2009; Rustichini et al., 2005; Smith et al., 2002). This shows that there is a strong mismatch between what entrepreneurial researchers test for as risk and what the human brain considers as risk. This may explain some of the conflicting findings. This also indicates that risk might not be all that important in entrepreneurial decision-making.

Most entrepreneurial researchers open their discussions about risk leaning on the theories of Knight, but then they seem to ignore most of the key points (Knight, 1921). Knight defined risk as 'a measurable uncertainty, or "risk" proper, as we shall use the term, is so far different from an *unmeasurable* one that it is not in effect an uncertainty at all' (Chapter I, p. I.I.26, italics in original). Since all information is provided, this constitutes a mathematically resolvable problems that is 'measurable', as per Knight's definition.

It is seldom if ever noted that Knight also defined a kind of risk that is akin to what we today call ambiguity. This he said is 'neither entire ignorance nor complete and perfect information, but partial knowledge' (Chapter VII, p. III.VII.5). This is ambiguity. Thus ambiguity is resolvable mathematically by guessing the probability of each possible outcome.

Uncertainty, on the other hand, he defined as immeasurable. He suggested to 'restrict the term "uncertainty" to cases of the non-quantitive type. It is this "true" uncertainty, and not risk, as has been argued, which forms the basis of a valid theory of profit and accounts for the divergence between actual and theoretical competition' (Chapter I, p. I.I.26). The difference between risk and uncertainty is so grand (risk is mathematically resolvable and uncertainty is not) that one may not use risk and use its mathematics to derive a solution for uncertainty. Knight further suggested that '[m]ost of the real decisions of life are based on "reasoning" (if such it may be called) of this still more tenuous and uncertain character, and not even that which has already been described', meaning that the reason why we cannot solve uncertainty mathematically is because we do not actually know all possible outcomes, let alone the probability associated with each (Chapter VII, p. III.VII.25). In this chapter we consider uncertainty as Knight did; uncertainty refers to outcomes that do not exist and cannot be accounted for and hence their probability distributions are also unknown. Thus uncertainty, viewed this way, cannot be used for calculations as it does not exist – it has to be ignored.

Various other definitions exist for uncertainties. New institutional economics defined different types and different degrees of uncertainty, such as substantial and procedural uncertainty and strong and weak uncertainty while others added fundamental uncertainty (for a full review of the various definition, see and (Camerer and Weber, 1992; Dequech, 1997, 2006; Dosi and Egidi, 1991). In this chapter we treat uncertainty as Knight did: some information is lacking both in the probability distribution of the possible outcomes and also not all possible outcomes are known at the time of the decision-making.

RESEARCH PROBLEMS

In entrepreneurial research, risk propensity surveys and problem sets are often used to find entrepreneurial skills that are unique distinguishing marks from non-entrepreneurs. We found that most research using these surveys assume unsupported stable human biases and risk preferences (Wang, 2008; Xu and Ruef, 2004). Risk-bias instability is well understood (Kahneman and Tversky, 1972, 2000) and can clearly be seen from contradictory findings, which define the entrepreneur to be any of the following: risk-averse, risk-seeking and no different from non-entrepreneurs and managers (Acedo González and Florin, 2007; Stewart and Roth, 2001; Xu and Ruef, 2004). Some researchers suggest that entrepreneurs might not even discover risk (Krueger and Brazeal, 1994). Stewart and Roth and White and colleagues go as far as suggesting that research in entrepreneurship has come to a dead end as a result of the variety of methods and scales used with confused parameters and without definitions (Stewart and Roth, 2001; White et al., 2006).

Entrepreneurial research is also facing a framing problem in that the way something is presented affects the thing being presented (Kahneman and Tversky, 2000). The representation of the term 'risk' may become a positive, a negative or a neutral term in the mind of the research participant, affecting her perceptions as well as her propensity to risks for the moment. Janney and Dess report that there are significant differences between risks represented as variance (neutral), as opportunity (positive challenge) and as potential loss (negative downer) (Janney and Dess, 2006). We would like to add that research in the field of neuroeconomics has provided very useful results particularly in this area, offering neurological proof of how framing affects risk propensity and perception – as discussed later.

Even in a state of neutrality (if such exists), the mind of a person is directed to decisions by perceptions that questionnaires may find impossible to decipher. To highlight the complexity, we provide an example of how perceived risks of an individual may change the risks provided by the experimenter into ambiguity by the participant, making measurement of risk propensity by surveys and scales impossible. Lottery tickets represent pure gambles in which the odds of winning or losing are known to all participants. A person's valuation of a lottery ticket is variable and she may consider that purchasing a lottery ticket provides a good investment (in spite of the known odds) (Fong and McCabe, 1999). For example, in a state lottery when no winning ticket was purchased, the amount of money in the bucket is applied toward the next draw. The lines of ticket-purchasers lengthens as the amount of money in the pot increases and each person purchases more tickets. It is assumed that as the pot increases in its value, it makes more sense to invest. The prize money increases but at the same time the odds of winning actually decrease. Furthermore, the more tickets one purchases, the more the odds decrease for each ticket purchased. Thus the intuition is that it makes more sense to purchase more tickets when the bucket has more money in it, but this bias is based on the size of the pot that disregards the decreased probability.

Recent research found that the human brain separates the utility of the reward amount (possible gain) from the odds of winning (Tobler et al., 2009). Tobler and colleagues show that as the reward amount increases, activation in the striatum increases with the increase in amount and that this increase is independent from the decrease in probability of actually achieving this winning (the aggregate function activated the lateral regions of the prefrontal cortex, which the authors suggest is equivalent to the mean-variance approach to utility) (ibid.). Therefore, a person may purchase more tickets because she increases her utility in the amount to be won, disregarding and forming false beliefs about the associated probability. Although the separation of risk from reward amount in the brain (as in economics models) implies that the human brain does utility calculations similar to the way economics models suggest, the fact that subjects disregard (or consider less) the decrease in probability than the increasing outcome opposes the consistency of utility calculation. Rather we suggest that these cases are examples of when subjects turn risk into belief-driven ambiguity in which the expected outcome is based on a believed probability rather than on the actual one. Here then we deal with someone who is facing perceived ambiguity and not risk, even though she has been provided complete information.

It is often assumed that the bias in assessing risk as ambiguity is systematic, for example, it remains the same both in size and in direction over time (Grichnik, 2008). This understanding has provided the base for a variety of risk scales and personality scales that researchers use to assess the risk propensity of an individual. Studies show, and as the lottery example shows above, that risks may be overestimated or underestimated in gambles, showing that there is motion in the direction and size of bias (Acedo González and Florin, 2007; Cramer et al., 2002; Krueger and Brazeal, 1994; Miner and Raju, 2004; Weber and Milliman, 1997; White et al., 2006). Part of the reason for such variations has to do with hormones that are released in the brain in varying amounts in response to environmental stimuli, such as fighting in traffic on the way to the experiment, having had sex the night before, or even the type of commercials or advertisements one saw on the way to the office (Garcia and Saad, 2008).

HORMONES OF RISKY AND AMBIGUOUS DECISION-MAKING

Hormones are an integral part of decision-making. Technically we should be talking about neurotransmitters but many of the neurotransmitters that assist in decision-making are also hormones. The distinction between hormones and neurotransmitters is a technical detail at the chemical level and is of no importance here. Neurotransmitters are released into the synapses (spaces) between neurons and are used for communication between neurons. Neurons are brain cells, whose communication is facilitated by electrical signals. As electrical signals pulse through a neuron, it releases its neurotransmitter into the synapse, which other neurons in the neighborhood may or may not absorb. If absorption occurs, the signal is transmitted from one neuron to the next. These transmissions are the messages passed down the line from neuron to neuron until an arm is moved in the decision to place a risky bet, for example. Many key neurotransmitters are hormones that have major evolutionary roles in guiding decision-making. Most of these have been researched to a various extent, such as testosterone (see Chapter 8 in this volume), estrogen (see Chapter 7 in this volume), dopamine (Chapter 9 in this volume), oxytocin (Kosfeld et al., 2005; Stanton, 2007; Zak et al., 2004, 2005, 2007), vasopressin (Stanton, 2007) and serotonin (Birger et al., 2003; Crockett et al., 2008; Garpenstrand et al., 2001; Hariri et al., 2002; Jorgensen, 2007; Jorgensen et al., 2003; Kavoussi et al., 1997; King et al., 2003). However, these hormones work together in various ways and their interactions are not well understood.

Recent research shows a bidirectional influence between hormonal fluctuations and bias-inducing mood, such that hormonal changes influence bias and the bias of the moment may influence the level of hormones the subject has at her disposal (Booth et al., 2006; Coates and Herbert, 2008; Knutson et al., 2008; Mazur and Booth, 1999; Mazur and Lamb, 1980; Petrovic et al., 2008; White et al., 2006). It is now understood that a person's risk preferences are not stable even over a short period of time (Berg et al., 2005). Therefore, if an agent is participating in research and we are to evaluate his entrepreneurial decision-making methods and skills, by asking pure gamble questions we may only evaluate his risk propensity – assuming we could ensure that he views gambles as risks and has not converted them in his mind into ambiguities and that his hormones remain stable for the duration of the experiment. Given that one cannot control hormonal stability and that the researchers cannot control the subject's frame of mind, it is not possible to state with certainty that research with questionnaires yields the desired risk propensity of the agent.

Examples of conflicting findings abound. Miner and Raju, for example, produced results that conflicted with the results of previous studies, and so they indicated their concern over the researchers' true understanding of the underlying parameters (Miner and Raju, 2004).

Studies have shown that risk and ambiguity are resolved by different parts of the brain (Bach et al., 2009; Daw et al., 2006; Hsu et al., 2008; Post et al., 2008; Sanfey et al., 2006; Seymour, 2008; Seymour et al., 2007) and thus risks and ambiguities are treated differently from each other (Coates and Herbert, 2008; Holland and Gallagher, 1993; Hsu et al., 2005; Post et al., 2008; Rangel et al., 2008; Sanfey et al., 2006; Seymour, 2008). Risky decisions appear to be solved by the insular cortex (Hsu et al., 2008), whereas ambiguous ones in the amygdala (Cohen and Ranganath, 2005). The cortex is considered to solve problems of a more calculative and abstract nature whereas the amygdala is part of the emotional center of the brain, the limbic system. Parameters of risk and ambiguity, as solved by the different parts of the human brain, are not combinable. Although economics currently proposes that ambiguity is compound risk and thus it can be resolved by breaking it into bits of risk packets, based on fMRI and hormonal experimental findings, this does not appear to be the case. As the brain uses different processing methods for the two types of risks, it is questionable if the resultant data can be combined as one.

As far as we know, to date, only a single hormonal experiment exists that has been able to pinpoint the hormonal variant of ambiguity (Coates and Herbert, 2008). Hormonal experiments so far have shown that risk is inherently associated with changes in testosterone levels (Booth and Mazur, 1998; Booth et al., 2006; Coates and Herbert, 2008; Mazur and Booth, 1998; Mazur and Lamb, 1980) while cortisol fluctuates with the level of uncertainty (Coates and Herbert, 2008). An important finding is that testosterone does not fluctuate with risk in the female brain, although it does in the male brain (Booth et al., 2006), yet there are female entrepreneurs. The study by Coates and Herbert showed that market traders on the London trading floor make their investment decisions driven by their particular hormone levels for the day and also of the time of day (Coates and Herbert, 2008). If traders started the day with high testosterone levels, their profits were higher than if they started with lower levels. This thus shows both that risk preferences are not stable and that decision-making is in the hormone of the beholder.

CONCLUSION

In this chapter we introduced the reader to the many definitions of risks and uncertainties used in various research fields that are connected to entrepreneurial and management research. It is not surprising that researchers have found conflicting results in their experiments, given the confused interpretations of what risk is, how that differs from ambiguity and uncertainty in terms of entrepreneurial decision-making, and which mathematical models may be used to analyze the outcomes.

In summary of the previous sections, we may provide the following five reasons for the errors that lead to the contradictory findings in entrepreneurial literature: (1) researchers use risk questions that do not relate to entrepreneurial decision-making tasks, which do not contain full information and are more like ambiguity than risk; (2) decision-makers have the propensity to turn risk problems into ambiguity by formulating beliefs even when full information is provided; (3) researchers often analyze answers to risk questions as though they were answers equally fit for risk, ambiguity or uncertainty; (4) researchers combine parameters of risk, ambiguity and uncertainty into a single parameter for statistical analysis, which ignores the fact that these variables are not of the same type and are not combinable; (5) risk is defined as the probability of losses; yet many questions on risk scale questionnaires contain only various levels of gain versus the return to status quo but often no loss. Such scales could not possibly provide information about the risk propensity of an individual.

As it is unclear to us if pure risk experiments allow researchers to resolve anything about the entrepreneur, we are hesitant to suggest that testosterone, the hormone associated with assessing risks, should be the key hormone of study for entrepreneurial researchers, as some suggest (White et al., 2006). As we have shown, a multitude of hormones interact, influencing decision-making in particular ways, some of which are already predictable by neuroeconomic techniques.

We recommend that researchers first establish if a given level of risk stimulus activates particular hormone levels differently for entrepreneurs and non-entrepreneurs under varying environmental conditions. Perhaps some of the hormones, such as testosterone, cortisol, vasopressin, dopamine and others that are potentially associated with risk and ambiguity can be tested by exogenously administering them, as in a few experiments already conducted with oxytocin and vasopressin (Kosfeld et al., 2005; Stanton, 2007; Zak et al., 2007). As different receptor concentrations of particular hormones likely predispose certain individuals to handle risk problems differently from others, exogenous hormonal stimulus could show some of the required trait differences and could help researchers identify what might be unique in the brains of entrepreneurs.

It is time to settle on one particular definition of risk, one for ambiguity and one for uncertainty and to use these definitions consistently within the field of management and entrepreneurial research. We suggest choosing the ones that economics uses because they are simple and clearly only apply to objective facts that are mathematically defined. This would also ensure that the appropriate mathematical models are used for the particular risk type. This would allow researchers to clearly identify and separate emotional behavioral responses that have no mathematical solutions at the moment from those that are of simple mathematics. This would advance research in the field of entrepreneurship and management in general. Researchers could focus on what is really important to them: finding what differentiates the decision-making ability of entrepreneurs from non-entrepreneurs.

REFERENCES

Acedo González, F. and J. Florin (2007), 'Understanding the risk perception of strategic opportunities: a tripartite model', *Strategic Change*, **16** (3), 97–116.
Alvarez, S.A. (2005), *Theories of Entrepreneurship: Alternative Assumptions and the Study of Entrepreneurial Action*, Boston, MA: Now Publishers.
Bach, D.R., B. Seymour and R.J. Dolan (2009), 'Neural activity associated with the passive prediction of ambiguity and risk for aversive events', *Journal of Neuroscience*, **29** (6), 1648–56.
Barbosa, S.D., M.W. Gerhardt and J.R. Kickul (2007), 'The role of cognitive style and risk preference on entrepreneurial self-efficacy and entrepreneurial intentions', *Journal of Leadership and Organizational Studies*, **13** (4), 86–104.

Baron, R. (1998), 'Cognitive mechanisms in entrepreneurship: why and when entrepreneurs think differently from other people', *Journal of Business Venturing*, **13** (4), 275–94.

Baron, R.A. (2004), 'The cognitive perspective: a valuable tool for answering entrepreneurship's basic "why" questions', *Journal of Business Venturing*, **19**, 221–39.

Baron, R.A. (2008), 'The role of affect in the entrepreneurial process', *Academy of Management Review*, **33** (2), 328–340.

Berg, J., J. Dickhaut and K. McCabe (2005), 'Risk preference instability across institutions: a dilemma', *Proceedings of the National Academy of Sciences of the United States of America*, **102** (11), 4209–14.

Birger, M., M. Swartz, D. Cohen, Y. Alesh, C. Grishpan and M. Kotelr (2003), 'Aggression: the testosterone–serotonin link', *Israel Medical Association Journal*, **5** (9), 653–8.

Booth, A. and A. Mazur (1998), 'Old issues and new perspectives on testosterone research – response', *Behavioral and Brain Sciences*, **21**, 386–97.

Booth, A., D.A. Granger, A. Mazur and K.T. Kivlingham (2006), 'Testosterone and social behavior', *Social Forces*, **85**, 168–91.

Brockhaus Sr, R.H. (1980), 'Risk taking propensity of entrepreneurs', *Academy of Management Journal*, **23** (3), 509–20.

Brown, D.J. and A. Bracha (2008), 'Affective decision making and the Ellsberg Paradox', Discussion paper no. 1667R, Tel Aviv Universtiy, *SSRN eLibrary*.

Camerer, C. and M. Weber (1992), 'Recent development in modeling preferences: uncertainty and ambiguity', *Journal of Risk Uncertainty*, **5**, 325–70.

Clark, L., A.J. Lawrence, F. Astley-Jones and N. Gray (2009), 'Gambling near-misses enhance motivation to gamble and recruit win-related brain circuitry', *Neuron*, **61**, 481–90.

Coates, J.M. and J. Herbert (2008), 'Endogenous steroids and financial risk taking on a London trading floor', *Proceedings of the National Academy of Sciences of the United States of America*, **105** (16), 6167–72.

Cohen, M.X. and C. Ranganath (2005), 'Behavioral and neural predictors of upcoming decisions', *Cognitive Affective, and Behavioral Neuroscience*, **5** (2), 117–26.

Cramer, J.S., J. Hartog, N. Jonker and C.M. van Praag (2002), 'Low risk aversion encourages the choice for entrepreneurship: an empirical test of truism', *Journal of Economic Behavior and Organization*, **48**, 29–36.

Crockett, M.J., L. Clark, G. Tabibnia, M.D. Lieberman and T.W. Robbins (2008), 'Serotonin modulates behavioral reactions to unfairness', *Science*, **320**, 1739–39.

Daw, N.D., J.P. O'Doherty, P. Dayan, B. Seymour and R.J. Dolan (2006), 'Cortical substrates for exploratory decisions in humans', *Nature*, **441**, 876–9.

Dosi, G. and M. Egidi (1991), 'Substantive and procedural uncertainty: an exploration of economic behavior in changing environments', *Journal of Evolutionary Economics*, **1**, 145–68.

Duquech, D. (1997), 'Uncertainty in a strong sense: meaning and sources', *Economic Issues*, **2**, 21–43.

Duquech, D. (2006), 'The new institutional economics and the theory of behavior under uncertainty', *Journal of Economic Behavior and Organization*, **59**, 109–31.

Einhorn, H.J. and R.M. Hogarth (1986), 'Decision making under ambiguity', *The Journal of Business*, **59** (4), S225–S250.

Ellsberg, D. (1961), 'Risk, ambiguity, and the Savage axioms', *Quarterly Journal of Economics*, **75**, 643–69.

Folta, T.B. (2005), *Entrepreneurial Risk*, Malden, MA: Blackwell.

Fong, C. and K. McCabe (1999), 'Are decisions under risk malleable?', *Proceedings of the National Academy of Sciences of the United States of America*, **96** (19), 10927–32.

Forlani, D.M.J.W. (2000), 'Perceived risks and choices in entrepreneur's new venture decision', *Journal of Business Venturning*, **15** (4), 305–22.

Garcia, J.R. and G. Saad (2008), 'Evolutionary neuromarketing: Darwinizing the neuroimaging paradigm for consumer behavior', *Journal of Consumer Behavior*, **7**, 397–414.

Garpenstrand, H., P. Annas, J. Ekblom, L. Oreland and M. Fredrikson (2001), 'Human fear conditioning is related to dopaminergic and serotonergic biological markers', *Behavioral Neuroscience*, **115** (2), 358–64.

Gilboa, I., A.W. Postlewaite and D. Schmeidler (2008), 'Probability and uncertainty in economic modeling', *Journal of Economic Perspectives*, **22** (3), 173–88.

Grichnik, D. (2008), 'Risky choices in new venture decisions – experimental evidence from Germany and the United States', *Journal of International Entrepreneurship*, **6**, 22–47.

Hamann, S. (2009), 'Towards understanding emotion's effects on memory', *Emotion Review*, **1** (2), 114–15.

Hariri, A.R., V.S. Mattay, A. Tessitore et al. (2002), 'Serotonin transporter genetic variation and the response of the human amygdala', *Science*, **297** (5580), 400–403.

Holland, P.C. and M. Gallagher (1993), 'Amygdala central nucleus lesions disrupt increments, but not decrements, in conditioned stimulus processing', *Behavioral Neuroscience*, **107**, 246–53.

Hsu, M., M. Bhatt, R. Adolphs, D. Tranel and C.F. Camerer (2005), 'Neural systems responding to degrees of uncertainty in human decision-making', *Science*, **310**, 1680–83.

Hsu, M., C. Anen and S.R. Quartz (2008), 'The right and the good: distributive justice and neural encoding of equity and efficiency', *Science*, **320**, 1092–5.

Hsu, M., I. Krajbich, C. Zhao and C.F. Camerer (2009), 'Neural response to reward anticipation under risk is nonlinear in probabilities', *Journal of Neuroscience*, **29** (7), 2231–7.

Janney, J.J. and G.G. Dess (2006), 'The risk concept for entrepreneurs reconsidered: new challenges to the conventional wisdom', *Journal of Business Venturning*, **21**, 385–400.

Johnson, S. (2009), 'The Quiet Coup', *The Atlantic*, **303**.

Jorgensen, H., M. Riis, U. Knigge, A. Kjaer and J. Warberg (2003), 'Serotonin receptors involved in vasopressin and oxytocin secretion', *Journal of Neuroendocrinology*, **15** (3), 242–9.

Jorgensen, H.S. (2007), 'Studies on the neuroendocrine role of serotonin', *Danish Medical Bulletin*, **54** (4), 266–88.

Kahneman, D. and A. Tversky (1972), 'Subjective probability: a judgment of representativeness', *Cognitive Psychology*, **3**, 430–54.

Kahneman, D. and A. Tversky (1979), 'Prospect theory: an analysis of decision under risk', *Econometrica*, **47**, 263–91.

Kahneman, D. and A. Tversky (2000), *Choices, Values, and Frames*, New York: Russell Sage Foundation.

Kamalanabhan, T.J., D.L. Sunder and A.T. Manshor (2006), 'Evaluation of entrepreneurial risk-taking using magnitude of loss scale', *Journal of Entrepreneurship*, **15** (1), 37–46.

Kapogiannis, D., A.K. Barbey, M. Su, G. Zamboni, F. Krueger and J. Grafman (2009), 'Cognitive and neural foundations of religious belief', *Proceedings of the National Academy of Sciences*, **106**, 4876–81.

Kavoussi, R., P. Armstead and E. Coccaro (1997), 'The neurobiology of impulsive aggression', *Psychiatric Clinics of North America*, **20** (2), 395–403.

Keh, H.T., M.D. Foo and B.C. Lim (2002), 'Opportunity evaluation under risky conditions: the cognitive processes of entrepreneurs', *Entrepreneurial Theory and Practice*, **28**, Winter, 419–29.

Kensinger, E.A. (2009), 'Remembering the details: effects of emotion', *Emotion Review*, **1** (2), 99–113.

King, J.A., J. Tenney, V. Rossi, L. Colamussi and S. Burdick (2003), 'Neural substrates underlying impulsivity', *Annals of the New York Academy of Sciences*, **1008**, 160–69.

Knight, F.H. (1921), *Risk, Uncertainty, and Profit*, Boston, MA: Hart, Schaffner and Marx, Houghton Mifflin Company, The Riverside Press.

Knutson, B., G.E. Wimmer, C.M. Kuhnen and P. Winkielman (2008), 'Nucleus accumbens activation mediates the influence of reward cues on financial risk taking', *Neuroreport*, **19**, 509–13.

Kobayashi, S. and W. Schultz (2008), 'Influence of reward delays on responses of dopamine neurons', *Journal of Neuroscience*, **28** (31), 7837–46.

Kosfeld, M., M. Heinrichs, P.J. Zak, U. Fischbacher and E. Fehr (2005), 'Oxytocin increases trust in humans', *Nature*, **435** (7042), 673–6.

Krueger, N. and D. Brazeal (1994), 'Entrepreneurial potential and potential entrepreneurs', *Entrepreneurship Theory and Practice*, **18**, 91–104.

Larson, C.L. and E.L. Steuer (2009), 'Motivational relevance as a potential modulator of memory for affective stimuli: can we compare snakes and cakes?', *Emotion Review*, **1** (2), 116–17.

Legoherel, P., P. Callot, K. Gallopel and M. Peters (2004), 'Personality characteristics, attitude toward risk, and decisional orientation of the small business entrepreneur: a study of hospitality managers', *Journal of Hospitality and Tourism Research*, **28** (1), 109–20.

Maner, J.K. and M.A. Gerend (2007), 'Motivationally selective risk judgments: do fear and curiosity boost the boons or the banes?', *Organizational Behavior and Human Decision Processes*, **103**, 256–67.

Mather, M. and M. Sutherland (2009), 'Disentangling the effects of arousal and valence on memory for intrinsic details', *Emotion Review*, **1** (2), 118–19.

Mazur, A. and A. Booth (1998), 'Testosterone and dominance in men', *Behavioral and Brain Sciences*, **21** (3), 353–63; discussion 363–97.

Mazur, A. and A. Booth (1999), 'The biosociology of testosterone in men', *Social Perspectives on Emotion*, **5**, 311–38.

Mazur, A. and T.A. Lamb (1980), 'Testosterone, status, and mood in human males', *Hormones and Behavior*, **14**, 236–46.

Miner, J.B. and N.S. Raju (2004), 'Risk propensity differences between managers and entrepreneurs and between low- and high-growth entrepreneurs: a reply in a more conservative vein', *Journal of Applied Psychology*, **89**, 3–13.

Moll, J., F. Krueger, R. Zahn, M. Pardini, R.d. Oliveira-Souza and J. Grafman (2006), 'Human fronto-mesolimbic networks guide decisions about charitable donation', *Proceedings of the National Academy of Sciences of the United States of America*, **103** (42), 15623–8.

Naldi, L., M. Nordqvist, K. Sjoberg and J. Wiklund (2007), 'Entrepreneurial orientation, risk taking, and performance in family firms', *Family Business Review*, **XX** (1), 33–47.

Newman, A. (2007), 'Risk-bearing and entrepreneurship', *Journal of Economic Theory*, **137**, 11–26.

Petrovic, P., R. Kalisch, T. Singer and R.J. Dolan (2008), 'Oxytocin attenuates affective evaluations of conditioned faces and amygdala activity', *Journal of Neuroscience*, **28** (26), 6607–15.

Post, T., M. van den Assem, G. Baltussen and R.H. Thaler (2008), 'Deal or no deal? Decision making under risk in a large-payoff game show', *American Economic Review*, **98**, 38–71.

Rangel, A., C. Camerer and P.R. Montague (2008), 'A framework for studying the neurobiology of value-based decision making', *Nature Reviews Neuroscience*, **9** (7), 545–56.

Rustichini, A., J. Dickhaut, P. Ghirardato, K. Smith and J.V. Pardo (2005), 'A brain imaging study of the choice procedure', *Games and Economic Behavior*, **52**, 257–82.

Sanfey, A.G., G. Loewenstein, S.M. McClure and J.D. Cohen (2006), 'Neuroeconomics: cross-currents in research on decision-making', *Trends in Cognitive Sciences*, **10**, 108–16.

Schultz, W. (1998), 'Predictive reward signal of dopamine neurons', *Journal of Neurophysiology*, **80**, 1–27.

Schultz, W. (2001), 'Reward signaling by dopamine neurons', *Neuroscientist*, **7** (4), 293–302.

Schultz, W. and A. Dickinson (2000), 'Neuronal coding of prediction errors', *Annual Review of Neuroscience*, **23**, 473–500.

Schultz, W., P. Dayan and P.R. Montague (1997), 'A neural substrate of prediction and reward', *Science*, **275**, 1593–9.

Seymour, B., N. Daw, P. Dayan, T. Singer and R. Dolan (2007), 'Differential encoding of losses and gains in the human striatum', *Journal of Neuroscience*, **27**, 4826–31.

Seymour, B.D.R. (2008), 'Emotion, decision making, and the amygdala', *Neuron*, **58**, 662–71.

Slovic, P. (1964), 'Assessment of risk taking behavior', *Psychological Bulletin*, **61**, 220–33.

Smith, K., J. Dickhaut, K. McCabe and J.V. Pardo (2002), 'Neuronal substrates for choice under ambiguity, risk, gains, and losses', *Management Science*, **48**, 711–18.

Smithson, M., T. Bartos and K. Takemura (2000), 'Human judgment under sample space ignorance', *Risk, Decision and Policy*, **5**, 135–50.

Stanton, A.A. (2007), 'Neural substrates of decision-making in economic games', *Journal of Dissertation*, **1** (1), 1–63.

Stewart, W.H. and P.L. Roth (2001), 'Risk propensity differences between entrepreneurs and managers: a meta-analytic review', *Journal of Applied Psychology*, **86** (1), 145–53.

Tobler, P.N., G.I. Christopoulos, J.P. O'Doherty, R.J. Dolan and W. Schultz (2008), 'Neuronal distortions of reward probability without choice', *Journal of Neuroscience*, **28** (45), 11703–11.

Tobler, P.N., G.I. Christopoulos, J.P. O'Doherty, R.J. Dolan and W. Schultz (2009), 'Risk-dependent reward value signal in human prefrontal cortex', *Proceedings of the National Academy of Sciences*, **106**, 7185–90; published online before print 15 April 2009, doi: 10.1073/pnas.0809599106.

Tversky, A. and D. Kahneman (1992), 'Advances in prospect theory: cumulative representation of uncertainty', *Journal of Risk Uncertainty*, **5**, 297–323.

Van den Bergh, B. and S. Dewitte (2006), 'Digit ratio (2D:4D) moderates the impact of sexual cues on men's decisions in ultimatum games', *Proceedings of the Royal Society B: Biological Sciences*, **273** (1597), 2091–5.

Wang, X.T. (2008), 'Risk communication and risky choice in context: ambiguity and ambivalence hypothesis', *Annals of the New York Academy of Sciences*, **1128** (1), 78–89.

Weber, E.U. and R.A. Milliman (1997), 'Perceived risk attitudes: relating risk perception to risky choice', *Management Science*, **43**, 123–44.

White, R.E., S. Thornhill and E. Hampton (2006), 'Entrepreneurs and evolutionary biology: the relationship between testosterone and new venture creation', *Organizational Behavior and Human Decision Processes*, **100**, 21–34.

Wu, B. and A.M. Knott (2006), 'Entrepreneurial risk and market entry', *Management Science*, **52**, 1315–30.

Xu, H. and M. Ruef (2004), 'The myth of the risk-tolerant entrepreneur', *Strategic Organization*, **2** (4), 331–55.

Young, L., F. Cushman, M. Hauser and R. Saxe (2007), 'The neural basis of the interaction between theory of mind and moral judgment', *Proceedings of the National Academy of Sciences of the United States of America*, **104** (20), 8235–40.

Zak, P.J., R. Kurzban and W.T. Matzner (2004), 'The neurobiology of trust', *Annals of the New York Academy of Science*, **1032**, 224–7.

Zak, P.J., R. Kurzban and W.T. Matzner (2005), 'Oxytocin is associated with human trustworthiness', *Hormones Behavior*, **48** (5), 522–7.

Zak, P.J., A.A. Stanton and S. Ahmadi (2007), 'Oxytocin increases generosity in humans', *PLoS ONE*, **2** (11), e1128.

3. What you think is not what you think: unconsciousness and entrepreneurial behavior

Eden S. Blair

INTRODUCTION

An entrepreneur who develops fitness equipment comes home from a long day at work. She has spent the past week thinking about new ideas, drawing figures on white boards and in journals and talking to others about their fitness needs with frustratingly few results. She sits down and relaxes in front of the television. Twenty minutes later, she sits up straight, excited about a new idea to improve the way people strengthen their back, arm and leg muscles. Her new device allows people to lie on their stomachs and use a pulley system to move their legs and arms as if they were swimming. The entrepreneur believes that she can make this relatively inexpensively and that it will sell well. The entrepreneur tells others, and believes herself, that her idea was developed after long hours of deep thought and introspection. In fact, the idea was unconsciously and almost instantaneously triggered from seeing a hawk gliding through a car commercial.

There is often an assumption that most work in organizations is based on slow, deliberate and conscious thought processes (Locke and Latham, 2002). In fact, much of people's behavior seems to be based on unconscious[1] control (Bargh, 2005). Unconsciousness can be defined as a mental process outside of an individual's awareness. These unconscious processes are much faster than conscious deliberations and occur with little or no awareness (Bargh, 1997). This chapter is designed to look at what scholars understand about unconsciousness and specifically about unconscious behaviors in entrepreneurship. Different methods for studying unconsciousness, such as priming and methods from neuroscience, will be described briefly. Examples from the field of entrepreneurship will be used to help explain these concepts and several propositions relating to entrepreneurial and venture capitalist research will be developed.

Entrepreneurship is an encouraging field in which to study unconscious processing. First, entrepreneurs are required to be involved in dozens of intellectual tasks simultaneously. For example, a typical entrepreneur might be developing an idea, building a prototype, writing a business plan, talking to investors, developing relationships with clients, leading employees and branding the venture's image. These mental processes require a great deal of both technical and conceptual skill in a significantly short period of time, and it would be difficult, if not impossible, to do them with conscious deliberation. Second, they are in situations with a great deal of novelty, emotion and uncertainty (Baron, 1998), suggesting that multiple mental processes, both cognitive and affective, might be occurring simultaneously. Third, research suggests that entrepreneurs do not have great insight into what they do and how it might lead them to success (Forbes, 2005). Finally, most entrepreneurs are involved in the creation of new ideas, products and/or services and are successful at recognizing opportunities that others do not. Scholars argue that the differences between entrepreneurs and non-entrepreneurs is not an individual characteristic like personality, but in how they think (Baron, 1998). All of these aspects of entrepreneurship likely can be informed by research on unconscious processing. I include some propositions involving research on unconscious processes and entrepreneurs and venture capitalists. Venture capitalists are investors who invest specifically in high-risk, relatively young ventures for equity in the firm. Research in entrepreneurship and venture capitalists are inherently linked, as both make decisions under risk, uncertainty and ambiguity (Shepherd et al., 2003).

WHY USE UNCONSCIOUS PROCESSES?

Based on research in areas such as cognitive psychology, social psychology and neuroscience, conscious, controlled processes – those that are intentional and achieved with effort (Wegner, 2005) – have severe limitations (Bargh, 2005; Camerer et al., 2005). Human senses are constantly bombarded with information. Research suggests that our senses (touch, sight, hearing, smell, taste) can handle about 11 million bits of information per second, with the visual system itself handling 10 million bits (see Nørretranders, 1998 for a review). Bits are the smallest unit of information that can be distinguished from another unit. Our conscious capacity to process information is much less than our unconscious capacity. When individuals read silently, they can process at most 45 bits per second on average, when reading aloud 30 bits, and when calculating two numbers together they can process 12 bits, making our total capacity on average at least 200 000 times as strong as our conscious capacity (Nørretranders, 1998). Thus, using unconscious, automatic processes becomes not only useful in making decisions and determining our actions, but vital. Without the ability to use this type of processing, individuals would be bogged down trying to make even the simplest decision. Quick, seemingly instantaneous decisions often occur after a great deal of unconscious processing of information (Dijksterhuis et al., 2005). This unconscious processing can be effective for screening information quickly and making judgments (Shiffrin and Dumais, 1981). Unconscious behavior allows individuals, such as entrepreneurs and venture capitalists, to make a myriad of decisions in very little time. By automating routing tasks, which have been learned through experience, individuals can free up the conscious mind for more complex processing (Bargh, 1994).

HOW DO WE STUDY UNCONSCIOUSNESS?

If these unconscious processes are so important, then how do researchers study them? This has often been difficult. Asking an individual what he or she is thinking unconsciously is impossible, as by definition the individual is unaware of what is happening and cannot consciously retrieve the information. If they can retrieve it, these individuals will alter the situation by consciously processing it. One of the ways to study these processes is called 'priming'. In priming researchers argue that much of behavior is triggered by external cues. The unconscious controls the conscious self, which is controlled, effortful and intentional (Wegner, 2005; Wegner and Bargh, 1998). Several researchers in social psychology (see Bargh, 1997; Prinz, 2003; Wegner, 2005) argue against a purposeful, conscious self at all (they believe in a lack of free will, for instance), but rather suggest that most behaviors are due to environmental triggers, leading to automatic behaviors (Bargh, 1997). Many researchers still argue for conscious processes being an important part of everyday life (Baumeister and Sommer, 1997). They do agree that environmental cues trigger the unconscious, which then guides the individual to act. However, the conscious is important for overriding automatic, habitual responses when needed, even if infrequent (Camerer et al., 2005). For example, habitual automatic behavior while driving is generally useful, which is why drivers can suddenly realize they do not recall driving the last few miles they safely drove, but it is important for the conscious processes to kick in and override automatic processes when there is a sudden emergency, such as needing to avoid unexpected debris or other vehicles on the road.

Mental Constructs

These environmental cues are triggering mental constructs. Over time, individuals, through their experience, create mental constructs that are representations of patterns of experiences, which in turn provide guidance about certain ways to feel, think or act in situations similar to those they have experienced in the past (Chartrand and Bargh, 2002; Kelly, 1963). George A. Kelly (1963) defines these mental constructs as templates that an individual 'creates and then attempts to fit over the realities of which the world is composed' (p. 9). In these constructs some things are considered to be alike but different from others. These templates may give an accurate or inaccurate construction of the reality around the individual. Individuals can have many personal, at least slightly unique constructs about many things in their everyday lives, such as a construct of family, integrity, patriotism and achievement. Entrepreneurial constructs could be, for example, representations of opportunity, uncertainty or relationship building with investors.

Heuristics

One type of mental construct is a heuristic. This is a simplified set of decision rules that allows individuals to reduce complex judgments to relatively quick and simple cognitive decisions (Busenitz and Barney, 1997; Kahneman and Tversky, 1982). Heuristics can be an especially important cognitive device for entrepreneurs, who often face novel situations of uncertainty with ambiguous information (Holcomb et al., 2009). Three common heuristics apply to entrepreneurs: the availability heuristic, the representativeness heuristic, and the anchoring and adjustment heuristic (ibid.; Kahneman and Tversky, 1973).

The availability heuristic states that people base decisions about a class of events on how easily information about that class comes to mind (Kahneman and Tversky, 1973). Repetition and greater exposure increase this information to be readily accessible in memory and increase the perceived probability that this will occur in the future (Holcomb et al., 2009). This can lead decision-makers to inaccurately discount objective information that could be relevant. For example, a successful entrepreneur who sells discount jewelry may ignore an upcoming economic crisis because his past success makes him believe in the high probability that he can continue to sell his product. With this heuristic, people stop seeking additional information for making decisions once they gather enough information to make a decision with what they believe is sufficient certainty (Cassar and Gibson, 2007). However, an entrepreneur who has found success launching start-ups in one domain may find the heuristic useful when seeking opportunities in that domain (Holcomb et al., 2009).

The representativeness heuristic suggests that people generalize about a phenomenon based only on a few observations of that phenomenon (Busenitz and Barney, 1997; Kahneman and Tversky, 1973). For example, this heuristic leads entrepreneurs to develop theories of success based on a single successful experience without any real understanding of what made them successful. When a venture capitalist is examining which entrepreneurial ventures to fund, they examine features that have commonly led past ventures to succeed (Zacharakis and Shepherd, 2001). Entrepreneurs, especially ones without prior entrepreneurial experience, tend to underestimate the complexity of new venture situations and fail to understand the true causal relationships that lead to success or failure (Baron and Ensley, 2006).

An anchoring and adjustment heuristic is one where people start with an initial value or anchor and then adjust it upwards or downwards to account for additional information. This anchor can be based on prior experience, partial calculations, or unintentional or arbitrary factors (Holcomb et al., 2009). For example, entrepreneurs will often arbitrarily set the amount of ownership they are willing to give to outsiders in return for equity investment at 49 percent, even when the amount of capital needed to be successful would require them to give up much more ownership. This heuristic also means that entrepreneurs tend to overestimate the likelihood of conjunctive events (for example, a great idea will lead to success) and underestimate the likelihood of chain-like, disjunctive events (for example, success is due to a series of independent acts – a great idea, a great venture team, knowledge of how to market it, understanding of current economic conditions and so on) (ibid.).

Schemas

A schema is a generalized cognitive framework that an individual uses to impose a structure and give meaning to data (for example, social information, situations, stimuli) in order to gain a better understand of the world around him or her (Gioia and Poole, 1984). A great deal of work has been done in organizational behavior on scripts, defined as a schema held in memory that describes a behavior for a particular context (ibid.). These scripts allow people to act in predictable ways in frequently encountered occasions. Information that is organized into schemas is more useful and easier to access than information that is not (Ozgen and Baron, 2007). A common entrepreneurial schema is entrepreneurial alertness. Those with entrepreneurial alertness schemas are more likely to notice changing environmental stimuli, match them with information they have already stored in memory about entrepreneurial opportunities, and discover new ones (Gaglio and Katz, 2001).

These mental constructs lie in our implicit memory, memory that works without the use of our consciousness (Nørretranders, 1998). Performance of a task can be influenced by memories even if they are not consciously present during the performance. Nørretranders describes it thus: 'What is remembered was conscious when it was remembered but is not so when it was used' (p. 302). This can commonly be seen in several ways, such as when people know that they recognize a face but do not know immediately who the person is, or the example mentioned earlier: when someone drives down a highway and has no memory of driving the past few miles. This is in contrast to explicit memory, which refers to the conscious recollection of information (Schacter, 1987). Implicit and explicit memory seem to be mostly independent but do appear to interact with each other. Thus, information can be retrieved from implicit memory without it shifting into explicit memory so a subject becomes consciously aware of it (ibid.).

Importantly, the mental representations discussed in this section are anticipatory. Individuals will use mental constructs to forecast their future behavior in anticipated environments rather than reacting to environments as they arrive. A person will unconsciously behave in a new situation on the basis of prior entrepreneurial triggers that occur even before that person enters the new situation. For example, entrepreneurs will react to a new opportunity in the same way they reacted to a prior one even before they have enough information to understand if the new opportunity is similar to or very different from the previous opportunities. Work in the field of social psychology (Chartrand and Bargh, 2002; Dijksterhuis et al., 2005) and, more recently, the field of organizational behavior (Stajkovic et al., 2006) has tried to activate these constructs by 'priming' them unconsciously with environmental cues. In this methodology the experimenter attempts to activate one of these mental constructs without an individual's awareness of doing so. This can affect an individual's behavioral decisions, impressions or evaluations because the experimenter has changed the interpretations of the 'reality' that the individual is anticipating (Bargh, 1990). Priming helps provide evidence that these unconscious processes are occurring and that these constructs exist (Kihlstrom, 1987). In priming, these unconscious processes become evident and observable, at least indirectly. Experimenters can measure the behaviors or evaluations that are elicited in those that are primed and compare them to those in a control group to measure the difference.

PRIMING

Constructs can be primed either subliminally or supraliminally. In subliminal priming a word or image is flashed in front of the individual too quickly for them to consciously see, generally using a device such as a computer and monitor. For example, in the Bargh et al. (1996) study the authors used a subliminal methodology, where the participants were given ten adjectives on a computer screen. Each participant pronounced the adjective and was then asked to label them good or bad by pushing a button on the computer keyboard. The participants then were told to just pronounce the words as quickly as they could when they flashed on the screen. For those words that the participants had the strongest attitudes about in the earlier task, they had a faster response time in the pronunciation task, suggesting no conscious goal is necessary to get them to act faster. Supraliminal priming occurs when the subject can see the words or images but is not aware of any patterns or significance. In the Stajkovic et al. (2006) study participants were given 20 sets of scrambled words. Each set contained five words which could be unscrambled to make a four-word sentence with one word left over. In the treatment group 12 of these sets contained a word related to the construct of achievement. Those in the treatment group were able to develop more uses for a common object (like a wire hanger) than those in the control group.

There are limitations to priming studies. Priming measures are relatively complicated, require a significant amount of technological expertise and time to administer and require very tightly controlled experimental situations (Wittenbrink, 2007). This can make it very difficult not only to develop and administer these experiments, but makes replication of prior work difficult. Research in priming, especially subliminal priming, can be controversial. Some researchers still do not believe that effects exists while others worry about the ethical implications if one can subliminally persuade someone to evaluate or behave in a way they cannot consciously control (Dijksterhuis et al., 2005). Additionally, effect sizes are small, reliability is low and there is a lack of standards for how to implement priming experiments (Wittenbrink, 2007).

NEUROSCIENCE AND THE UNCONSCIOUS

Although priming literature has been able to explain some of what is happening unconsciously in implicit memory, work in cognitive neuroscience has been able to answer some questions that priming has not. Neuroscience uses such techniques as brain imaging, animal studies, hormone tests and other methods to attempt to infer details about how the brain works (Camerer et al., 2005). Research in neuroscience has helped explain how unconscious, automatic processes work and when they are in use. Neuroentrepreneurship, a new field, has borrowed from work in neuroscience, neuropsychology and neuroeconomics to better understand and test how entrepreneurs think, behave and make decisions.

Research in neuroscience has helped researchers better understand the types and speed of mental processes used in a particular situation. The unconscious brain works efficiently because it uses a network of interconnected systems in parallel. Thus, multiple computations in different parts of the brain can occur simultaneously and sometimes even interact with each other (ibid.). Research in neural networks suggests that neurons can actively invoke other neurons, allowing cognitive processing such as analogies to happen (Choe, 2003). In analogy two or more mental structures/constructs somehow correspond with each other (Wharton et al., 2000). Analogies allow entrepreneurs to take very different concepts and develop a novel idea that others did not see (Ward, 2004). Since analogy is often important for recognizing opportunities, a neuroscientific explanation of analogy may be useful in entrepreneurship research. Wharton and colleagues found activation in four areas of the brain when their participations engaged in analogical reasoning, the medial frontal cortex, the left prefrontal cortex, the anterior insula and the left inferior parietal cortex. A possible neuroentrepreneurship study could involve asking entrepreneurs to consider new potential opportunities and see if similar parts of the brain are activated.

Proposition 1: An entrepreneur uses analogical reasoning during opportunity recognition.

AFFECTIVE AND COGNITIVE PROCESSES

Unconscious and conscious processes can both be divided further into affective and cognitive processes (Camerer et al., 2005). Research suggests that the emotional aspects of a stimulus might be processed more automatically than the stimulus of a non-emotional aspect and have greater impact on decisions than originally thought. Cognitive processes are those that answer true/false questions, either at the conscious or unconscious level (ibid.). Affective states are more than just what humans feel. Most affects fall below conscious awareness. Our emotions often motivate us to behave in certain ways at an unconscious level (Zajonc, 1998) and appear to actually have an impact on individuals physically, such as with changes in heart rates (Cacioppo et al., 2000). For example, if a person is angry, she might show aggressive behavior. A person who is fearful might try to escape a dangerous situation (Camerer et al., 2005). Affective processes leading to go/no-go decisions, such as approaching or avoiding a particular situation, may be due to how the individual feels about that situation (Zajonc, 1998).

One possible unconscious affective state is trust. Research on trust has suggested a biological component (Zak, 2005a, 2005b; Zak et al., 2007). Trust occurs not just among people who have known each other for a long time, but also among strangers or brief acquaintances (Zak, 2005b). Travelers trust the airline pilot to get them safely to their destination despite not knowing anything about the pilot or the pilot's experience. This trust is important in many ways. It aids in economic growth by reducing transaction costs and in investment decisions. More homogeneous groups – ones similar in ethnicity, income, education, language and so on – are also more likely to trust one another than groups that are more heterogeneous (Zak, 2005a). Oxytocin, a naturally occurring hormone in the body, increases when a transaction involving trust in another occurs (Zak, 2005b) and promotes generosity towards strangers (Zak et al., 2007).

Research on trust suggests that venture capitalists, when reading entrepreneurial business plans, might be making investment decisions based on more than just the financial factors of the business, such as expected internal rates of return. I have often heard venture capitalists argue that they 'would rather invest in an A team with a B idea than a B team with an A idea'. Whether venture capitalists actually use this as the primary decision factor in investing is far from certain. While some research suggests that the qualities of the venture team matter (for example, Muzyka et al., 1996), venture capitalists do not appear to have much insight into how they make investment decisions (Hall and Hofer, 1993; Tyebjee and Bruno, 1984; Zacharakis and Meyer, 1998) and often make mistakes about the people that they back (Smart, 1999). This lack of insight and the speed in which they make judgments about a business after reading a business plan (an average of around six minutes; see Hall and Hofer, 1993) suggests that an automatic process is occurring. Neuroscientific research would support this idea as well. The brain, in trying to increase processing efficiency, appears to automate complex processes as often as possible. This occurs with experience (Camerer et al., 2005). Thus, an experienced venture capitalist is more likely to have automated most investment decisions, while a novice investor would probably require more conscious activity in the brain. If this process is automated, venture capitalists would not be aware of the heuristics they use.

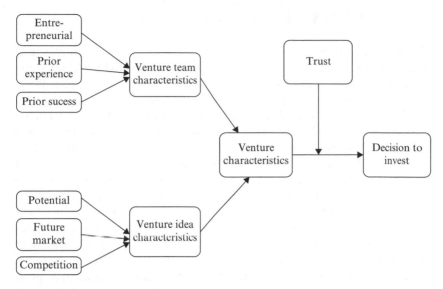

Figure 3.1   Proposition 2b – moderating relationship of trust with venture characteristics and investment decisions

Proposition 2a: Venture capitalists have more automated judgment processes than novice investors when evaluating business plans.

Other researchers have argued that trust matters in investment decisions (Harrison et al., 1997). A relatively simple study of oxytocin levels on venture capitalists while making business plan decisions might shed some light on whether trust is a factor in which ideas the venture capitalists fund. I would suggest that other factors of the venture team, such as level of entrepreneurship experience, prior experience in the new venture field, prior entrepreneurial success, viability of the idea demonstrated by the potential market for the idea, future market growth and amount of competition all matter but are likely moderated by the level of trust the venture capitalist has in the venture team. Thus, at least some of these characteristics are necessary, but they will have a greater impact on the decision with higher levels of trust (Figure 3.1).

Proposition 2b: As the level of trust a venture capitalist has with the venture team increases, the characteristics of the venture team and the venture opportunity are a more attractive investment to the venture capitalist.

OPPORTUNITY RECOGNITION

The idea that individuals demonstrate less brain activity in a complex task after repeated experiences with that task might also help explain some processes involved in opportunity recognition. Opportunity recognition is the process in which a particular person identifies new and potentially profitable ideas (Baron, 1998). The phenomenon of entrepreneurial alertness may be a useful place for neuroentrepreneurship researchers to test this. Some researchers argue that successful entrepreneurs have higher levels of entrepreneurial alertness (Baron and Ensley, 2006; Gaglio and Katz, 2001). Individuals with high entrepreneurial alertness appear to use a schema that enables them to detect informational cues, such as an economic disequilibrium, from the environment. These cues inform them that the current way of doing business will no longer work and that something new (for example, producing a new product or a change in how to market the product or service) must be done (Gaglio and Katz, 2001). At least some aspects of entrepreneurial alertness schema appear to happen at an unconscious level. Research suggests that experienced entrepreneurs seem to be able to better detect meaningful patterns than novices (Baron and Ensley, 2006). Again, brain imaging studies may be useful in detecting these schemas. Examining the differences between an experienced entrepreneur and a novice when attempting to scan the environment to recognize opportunities may help us to better understand the importance of experience in opportunity recognition.

Proposition 3: Brain activity in experienced entrepreneurs will differ from those of novices.

CONCLUSION

This chapter was designed to help readers better understand unconsciousness and our knowledge of how unconscious processes work. Research in unconscious behavior over the past few decades, which is studied using such practices as priming, brain imaging and other neuroscience techniques, has increased researchers' understanding of how individuals process information unconsciously and how it compels them to act in ways outside of their conscious control and without their awareness. We know that individuals have very little insight into much of their behavior, largely because they are unaware of what causes them to act. People develop mental constructs, representations of past experiences that assist them at an unconscious level to interpret and understand new experiences and act accordingly. These constructs are developed over time through past experience. They may or may not be accurate representations.

Free Will?

Some scholars of unconsciousness argue that humans are so controlled by unconscious processes that they have little or no free will or the volition to change their behavior (Bargh, 2005). These researchers argue that we are in essence prisoners to our mental constructs, developed through past experiences, and their activation through environmental stimuli. Experiments by Libet (1994) demonstrate, not without controversy, that conscious acts were preceded by a readiness potential that occurred an average of 350 milliseconds prior to conscious thought. This has been interpreted by some to suggest an unconscious initiation but conscious behavior can veto unconscious acts (Libet et al., 2000). The existence of free will is still highly debatable. Unconscious processes are the default mode of the brain (Camerer et al., 2005). Since unconscious processes are by nature outside the realm of awareness, individuals tend to exaggerate the importance of conscious processes.

If these unconscious processes play such an important part, when are conscious processes activated? Usually significant disconfirming evidence in the environment is needed for individuals to consciously change behavior that generally responds unconsciously. A possible lack of free will might suggest that formal analytical models of proper decision-making behavior may not be as useful as encouraging entrepreneurs and venture capitalists to gain experience, which might inform their heuristics and schemas. Another option is to teach entrepreneurs or venture capitalists to search for more disconfirming evidence. This search, for most, is difficult because we unconsciously tend to seek confirming and ignore disconfirming evidence. One of the interesting aspects of the entrepreneurial alertness schema is its ability to seek and recognize disconfirming evidence from the environment that is ignored by other individuals. Entrepreneurs that have this schema may also be more likely to ignore the initiation behavior described by Libet.

Emotion

Another important aspect about unconscious processes discussed in this chapter is that a large part of these are affective rather than cognitive. People make decisions based more often on what we unconsciously feel than what we unconsciously think and both occur more often than what we consciously feel and think. Baron (2008) has developed a framework that suggests that affect has an impact on entrepreneurial behaviors such as opportunity recognition, developing networks, acquiring resources and dealing with dynamic environments. Others argue that entrepreneurs seem uniquely passionate compared to others in the workplace. Cardon et al. (2005) have developed a framework based on a parenting model to suggest that entrepreneurs nurture their ventures like parents do children, and like parent–child relationships, can be healthy, nurturing the venture until it can stand on its own, or unhealthy. Further research in neuro-entrepreneurship is needed to empirically explore this implicit emotional link to decisions and behavior.

Implications

From a practitioner standpoint, research in unconscious behavior and neuroentrepreneurship can help entrepreneurs and venture capitalists gain a better understanding of what makes the other behave and how to evaluate the way they do. While I am not suggesting that entrepreneurs should spray oxytocin in a venture capitalist's face, I do think finding ways to gain each other's trust is beneficial for a long-term business relationship. Understanding the opportunity recognition process more clearly will help entrepreneurs seek better opportunities to exploit. Finding ways to help a novice gain entrepreneurial experience that helps them develop relatively accurate heuristics and schemas can make them more successful entrepreneurs.

Finally, I believe that entrepreneurship research and neuroscience research can learn a great deal from each other. Entrepreneurs do seem to be different from non-entrepreneurs, at least in how they think (Baron, 1998). Entrepreneurs see things that others do not, and work, if not thrive, in situations surrounded by risk, uncertainty and ambiguity. Entrepreneurs and venture capitalists do not seem to have great insight into how they make decisions. Researchers might be able to gain insight using the techniques briefly described in this chapter. Entrepreneurship can use theories and techniques developed in the neurosciences to help better understand these phenomena, while neuroscientific research can exploit scientifically interesting phenomena in the field of entrepreneurship.

NOTE

1. In this chapter I use the term unconscious to describe thought processes outside of an individual's awareness. Other terms, such as non-conscious, subconscious, automatic behavior and automaticity are also used. Automaticity and automatic behavior is

behavior that occurs reflexively and without conscious guidance when a trigger condition is in place (Bargh, 1997). Non-conscious and subconscious are often used interchangeably with unconscious, although subconscious is sometimes used to describe what is below or beneath conscious thought, while the other two can be described as the behavior that is not conscious or without awareness (Chartrand and Bargh, 2002).

REFERENCES

Bargh, J.A. (1990), 'Auto-motives: preconscious determinants of thought and behavior', in E.T. Higgins and R.M. Sorrentino (eds), *Handbook of Motivation and Cognition*, 2nd edn, Hillsdale, NJ: Erlbaum, pp. 1–40.

Bargh, J.A. (1994), 'The four horsemen of automaticity: awareness, intention, efficiency, and control in social cognition', in R.S. Wyer and T.K. Scrull (eds), *Handbook of Social Cognition*, Vol. 1, Hillsdale, NJ: Erlbaum, pp. 1–40.

Bargh, J.A. (1997), 'The automaticity of everyday life', in R.S. Wyer (ed.), *Advances in Social Cognition*, Vol. 10, Mahwah, NJ: Lawrence Erlbaum Associates, pp. 1–49.

Bargh, J.A. (2005), 'Bypassing the will: toward demystifying the nonconscious control of social behavior', in R.R. Hassin, J.S. Uleman and J.A. Bargh (eds), *The New Unconscious*, Oxford: Oxford University Press.

Bargh, J.A., S. Chaiken, P. Raymond and C. Hymes (1996), 'The automatic evaluation effect: unconditional automatic attitude activation with a pronunciation task', *Journal of Experimental Social Psychology*, **32** (1), 104.

Baron, R.A. (1998), 'Cognitive mechanisms in entrepreneurship: why and when entrepreneurs think differently than other people', *Journal of Business Venturing*, **13** (4), 275–94.

Baron, R.A. (2008), 'The role of affect on the entrepreneurial process', *Academy of Management. The Academy of Management Review*, **33** (2), 328.

Baron, R.A. and M.D. Ensley (2006), 'Opportunity recognition as the detection of meaningful patterns: evidence from comparisons of novice and experienced entrepreneurs', *Management Science*, **52** (9), 1331–44.

Baumeister, R.F. and K.L. Sommer (1997), 'Consciousness, free choice, and automaticity', in R.S. Wyer (ed.), *Advances in Social Cognition*, Vol. X, Mahwah, NJ: Erlbaum, pp. 75–81.

Busenitz, L.W. and J.B. Barney (1997), 'Differences between entrepreneurs and managers in large organizations: biases and heuristics in strategic decision-making', *Journal of Business Venturing*, **12** (1), 9–30.

Cacioppo, J.T., G.G. Berntson, J.T. Larsen, K.M. Poehlmann, and T.A. Ito (2000), 'The psychophysiology of emotions', in M. Lewis and J.M. Haviland Jones (eds), *Handbook of Emotions*, 2nd edn, New York: Guilford Press, pp. 173–91.

Camerer, C.F., G. Loewnstein and D. Prelec (2005), 'Neuroeconomics: how neuroscience can inform economics', *Journal of Economic Literature*, **XLIII** (1), 9–64.

Cardon, M.S., C. Zietsma, P. Saparito, B.P. Matherne and C. Davis (2005), 'A tale of passion: new insights into entrepreneurship from a parenthood metaphor', *Journal of Business Venturing*, **20** (1), 23–45.

Cassar, G. and B. Gibson (2007), 'Forecast rationality in small firms', *Journal of Small Business Management*, **45** (3), 283–302.

Chartrand, T.L. and J.A. Bargh (2002), 'Nonconscious motivations: their activation, operation, and consequences', in A. Tesser, D.A. Stapel and J.V. Wood (eds), *Self and Motivation*, Washington, DC: American Psychological Association, pp. 13–41.

Choe, Y. (2003), 'Processing of analogy in the thalamocortical circuit', Paper presented at the Proceedings of the International Joint Conference on Neural Networks.

Dijksterhuis, A., H. Aarts and P.K. Smith (eds) (2005), *The Power of the Subliminal: On Subliminal Persuasion and Other Potential Applications*, Oxford: Oxford University Press.

Forbes, D.P. (2005), 'Are some entrepreneurs more overconfident than others?', *Journal of Business Venturing*, **20** (5), 623–40.

Gaglio, C.M. and J.A. Katz (2001), 'The psychological basis of opportunity identification: entrepreneurial alertness', *Small Business Economics*, **16** (2), 95.

Gioia, D.A. and P.P. Poole (1984), 'Scripts in organizational behavior', *Academy of Management Review*, **9** (3), 449–59.

Hall, J. and C.W. Hofer (1993), 'Venture capitalists' decision criteria in new venture evaluation', *Journal of Business Venturing*, **8**, 25–42.

Harrison, R.T., M.R. Dibben and C.M. Mason (1997), 'The role of trust in the informal investor's investment decision: an exploratory analysis', *Entrepreneurship: Theory and Practice*, **21** (4), 63–81.

Holcomb, T.R., R.D. Ireland, R.M.J. Holmes and M.A. Hitt (2009), 'Architecture of entrepreneurial learning: exploring the link among heuristics, knowledge, and action', *Entrepreneurship Theory and Practice*, **33** (1), 167.

Kahneman, D. and A. Tversky (1973), 'On the psychology of prediction', *Psychological Review*, **80** (4), 237–51.

Kahneman, D. and A. Tversky (1982), 'Intuitive prediction: biases and corrective procedures', in D. Kahneman, P. Slovic and A. Tversky (eds), *Judgment under Uncertainty: Heuristics and Biases*, Cambridge, MA: Cambridge University Press.

Kelly, G.A. (1963), *The Psychology of Personal Constructs*, New York: Norton.

Kihlstrom, J.F. (1987), 'The cognitive unconscious', *Science*, **237**, 41–7.

Libet, B. (1994), 'A testable field theory of mind–brain interaction', *Journal of Consciousness Studies*, **1** (1), 119–26.

Libet, B., A. Freeman and K. Sutherland (eds) (2000), *The Volitional Brain: Towards a Neuroscience of Free Will*, Exeter: Imprint Academic.

Locke, E.A. and G. Latham (2002), 'Building a practically useful theory of goal setting and task motivation', *American Psychologist*, **57**, 705–17.

Muzyka, D., S. Birley and B. Leleux (1996), 'Trade-offs in the investment decisions of European venture capitalists', *Journal of Business Venturing*, **11** (4), 273–87.

Nørretranders, T. (1998), *The User Illusion: Cutting Consciousness Down to Size*, New York: Viking.

Ozgen, E. and R.A. Baron (2007), 'Social sources of information in opportunity recognition: effects of mentors, industry networks, and professional forums', *Journal of Business Venturing*, **22** (2), 174.

Prinz, W. (2003), 'How do you know about our own actions?', in S. Maasen, W. Prinz and G. Roth (eds), *Voluntary Action: Brains, Minds, and Sociality*, New York: Oxford University Press, pp. 21–33.

Schacter, D.L. (1987), 'Implicit memory: history and current status', *Journal of Experimental Psychology: Learning, Memory, and Cognition*, **13** (3), 501–18.

Shepherd, D.A., A. Zacharakis and R.A. Baron (2003), 'VCs' decision processes: evidence suggesting more experience may not always be better', *Journal of Business Venturing*, **18** (3), 381.

Shiffrin, R.M. and S.T. Dumais (1981), 'The development of automatism', in J.R. Anderson (ed.), *Cognitive Skills and their Acquisition*, Hillsdale, NJ: Erlbaum, pp. 111–40.

Smart, G.H. (1999), 'Management assessment methods in venture capital: an empirical analysis of human capital valuation', *Venture Capital*, **1** (1), 59–82.

Stajkovic, A.D., E.A. Locke and E.S. Blair (2006), 'A first examination of the relationships between primed subconscious goals, assigned conscious goals, and task performance', *Journal of Applied Psychology*, **91** (5), 1172–80.

Tyebjee, T.T. and A.V. Bruno (1984), 'A model of venture capitalist investment activity', *Management Science*, **30**, 1051–66.

Ward, T.B. (2004), 'Cognition, creativity, and entrepreneurship', *Journal of Business Venturing*, **19** (2), 173–88.

Wegner, D.M. (2005), 'Who is the controller of controlled processes?' in R.R. Hassin, J.S. Uleman and J.A. Bargh (eds), *The New Unconscious*, New York: Oxford University Press, pp. 19–36.

Wegner, D.M. and J.A. Bargh (1998), 'Control and automaticity in social life', in D.T. Gilbert, S. Fiske and G. Lindzey (eds), *Handbook of Social Psychology*, Boston, MA: McGraw-Hill.

Wharton, C.M., J. Grafman, S.S. Flitman, et al. (2000), 'Toward neuroanatomical models of analogy: a positron emission tomography study of analogical mapping', *Cognitive Psychology*, **40** (3), 173–97.

Wittenbrink, B. (2007), 'Measuring attitude through priming', in B. Wittenbrink and N. Schwarz (eds), *Implicit Measures of Attitudes*, New York: Guilford Press.

Zacharakis, A.L. and G.D. Meyer (1998), 'A lack of insight: do venture capitalists really understand their own decision process?', *Journal of Business Venturing*, **13** (1), 57–76.

Zacharakis, A.L. and D.A. Shepherd (2001), 'The nature of information and overconfidence on venture capitalist's decision making', *Journal of Business Venturing*, **16** (4), 311.

Zajonc, R.B. (1998), 'Emotions', in D.T. Gilbert, S.T. Fiske and G. Lindzey (eds), *Handbook of Social Psychology*, New York: Oxford University Press, pp. 70–74.

Zak, P.J. (2005a), 'The neuroeconomics of trust', in R. Frantz (ed.), *Two Minds: Intuition and Analysis in the History of Economic Thought*, London: Springer.

Zak, P.J. (2005b), 'Trust: a temporary human attachment facilitated by oxytocin', *Behavioral and Brain Sciences*, **28** (3), 368–9.

Zak, P.J., A.A. Stanton and S. Ahmadi (2007), 'Oxytocin increases generoisty in humans', *PLoS ONE*, **2** (11), e1128.

PART 2

Trust, greed and the black box

During the credit crises and global financial meltdown, the most commonly used terms in the news have been 'greed' and 'trust'. It is said that greed is responsible for the crisis and the lack of trust that followed does not allow the healing of the economy. But what exactly is greed and where does it come from? And what is trust and where does it come from? And, more importantly, why did trust leave us and how can it return? Part 2 starts the process of opening the black box to understand how these two key components of economic exchange – greed and trust – work, what causes them, what affects them and how we can control them.

4.   Using brains to create trust: a manager's toolbox
Paul J. Zak and Amos Nadler

WHY TRUST IS ESSENTIAL

In 2009 people's trust in US businesses fell to 38 percent from 58 percent a year earlier, the lowest level since records have been kept (Edelman Trust Barometer, 2009). And the bigger the business, the lower the trust. Perhaps this is unsurprising as monthly layoffs are comparable to Super Bowl attendance and consumers are hoarding their money like thirsty wanderers in the dry economic desert. Egregious institutional and individual indiscretions have marred the business landscape, prompting the frequent use of the word 'crisis'. While politicians design the next multi-billion dollar 'bailout' plan, managers of belt-tightening organizations have a more immediate problem: how to maintain employee motivation when pink slips are flying, and at the same time how to sustain customer loyalty.

Distrust undercuts effective management because when trust is low, employees are less likely to understand and react to a manager's goals. In 2009 60 percent of employees reported that they needed to hear information three to five times before believing it. Equally worrisome, only 17 percent of employees in 2009 trusted statements made by a CEO (ibid.). Without trust, organizational goals will literally fall on deaf ears. At the same time, economic downturns are precisely when managers have more latitude to make organizational changes in order to staunch hemorrhaging profits. An additional concern is that reductions in trust often occur outside a manager's awareness, pulling down productivity. This hidden effect can diminish a manger's effectiveness over time. For this reason, it is essential that managers take a trust inventory at regular intervals, just as merchandise on the shelf must be inventoried regularly to maintain sufficient stock. One way to assess your organization's trust is to use the O-Factor Survey we have developed (find it at http://www.ofactor.pro).

There is a way to actively build interpersonal trust in your organization and protect it against reductions in morale and profitability. This chapter uses recent discoveries in brain science, much of it from our laboratory, to describe a seven-step process that managers can use to effectively build (and rebuild) trust.

This is where the science comes in. Our laboratory has shown recently that how much we trust others is determined by the release of a brain chemical called oxytocin (Kosfeld et al., 2005; Zak et al., 2004, 2005a). Oxytocin release is not consciously controlled but responds to the social and organizational environment in which we find ourselves. Indeed, our neuroeconomics experiments have produced a solid understanding of the situations in which oxytocin is released by the brain and its effect on peoples' behaviors. Oxytocin reduces anxiety and motivates us to engage with others to achieve win–win solutions. Our research indicates that a high-trust, high-oxytocin environment is the foundation for an effective and well-functioning organization. If one thinks of for- and non-profit organizations as simply individuals working together to achieve common goals, the crucial role of trust becomes apparent. Managers can increase the likelihood of meeting organizational goals by actively managing an organization's trust, the platform on which employees interact with each other and with clients.

When trust is low, people focus their energy on their own protection and survival, with fear their primary motivator. Instead of focusing on innovation and excellence, scarce mental resources are spent on vigilance, safety and survival. The human brain is resource constrained and quickly adapts to the environment we find ourselves in, creating behavioral biases that can be hard to break (Zak, 2008a). For example, the 'rank and yank' survive-at-all-costs culture at Enron was a crucial part of its implosion (Zak, 2008b). When survival requires making up the numbers, eventually people start making up the numbers; lying is rampant and interpersonal trust hits a nadir. In high-trust environments people can productively and respectfully discuss and resolve issues, whereas in low-trust environments conflict is arbitrated institutionally in a slow and costly manner. In high-trust environments people can speak their minds directly, respectfully and effectively, sharing leadership. In low-trust organizations, management is top-down and can seem coercive. For example, managers who amass critiques to unload during annual reviews create an environment of surveillance for employees who sense that their errors are being tabulated. On the other hand, managers who provide constructive on-the-spot feedback let people know where they stand and permit on-the-spot corrections. All managers know that time and energy are chronically scarce and corrections mid-flight are preferable to allowing failing programs to continue to waste resources.

To be clear, a no- or low-stress workplace should not be the objective

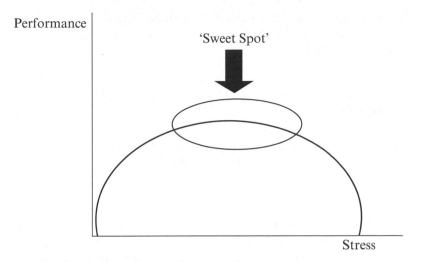

Figure 4.1   Drive, cognition and performance are maximized at the 'sweet spot'

for your organization. Figure 4.1 illustrates the relationship between stress and performance. There is an optimal point on the stress continuum where performance peaks; if stress is too low or too high, performance on nearly any type of task suffers. Organization leaders should push those they manage into the 'sweet spot' on the stress curve, where drive, cognition and performance are maximized.

The art, of course, is finding the appropriate level of, and kind of, stress that drives productivity. There are two general types of stress that affect employee performance; we call these Type I and Type II stress. Type I stress is characterized by chronic fear. This occurs when managers demand perfection, leading to loss avoidance behaviors. This is the kind of stress that is associated with heart disease, diabetes and depression because it chronically raises our vigilance systems, reducing our ability to think clearly. Behaviorally, chronic Type I stress produces 'learned helplessness' where people give up trying to do better or to do more, and instead simply seek to survive.

Conversely, Type II stress is associated with excitement and motivation, high energy and enjoyment. This type of stress is episodic, and the brain responds by releasing energy stores. When we have a deadline, when we are in 'flow' and are creative and open, Type II stress is high. The physiologic effects of Type II stress are short term and motivate collaborative bonding. It quickly gets people into the stress sweet spot. The nuanced goal of managers is to activate people with Type II stress and to avoid, when possible, its sinister cousin, Type I stress. The O-Factor inventory provides a measure of Type I stress as a guide to managers to identify when levels are high.

HOW TO RAISE YOUR ORGANIZATION'S O-FACTOR

The remainder of this chapter provides seven techniques that managers can use to raise their organization's O-Factor.

Technique 1: Praise

When someone in your organization reaches a goal or engages in a positive behavior, such as helping a colleague, recognize them privately and especially publicly. Indeed, recognition has the most powerful effect on brain and behavior when it is public and unexpected. Having systems in place to regularly recognize exemplary employees certainly facilitates this process. But, after five years of awarding it, the 'employee of the month parking spot' loses its punch. Change it up and release a surge of the rewarding neurotransmitter dopamine (see Chapter 9 in this volume) by surprising an exemplary employee with a gift of a spa massage or a $50 coffee card. Do not dismiss the value of massage by the way: we recently showed that massage primes the brain to release the social-bonding molecule oxytocin and this radically ramps up cooperative behaviors (Morhenn et al., 2008). Oxytocin induces dopamine flow and makes cooperation feel good, promoting trust.

A program that empowers employees to recognize each other in meaningful ways is an effective way to energize people in an organization to acknowledge excellence. Relying on recognition solely from managers is both time-intensive and may generate envy. You have eyes and ears all over your organization constantly observing magnificence from others, and when these behaviors are transmitted to colleagues and managers, a culture of excellence can be built.

On the other hand, when mistakes occur the best approach is usually to identify the mistake and the ways to fix it in private. While public lashings do send a message to others, it a fear-based risk-avoidance message. You should embrace mistakes as learning experiences to foster creativity and innovation. Managers, too, must be open to critiques by others. If they are not, such a two-tiered system undermines organization-wide trust. The manager's job is not to be a disciplinarian, but to coach employees in order to stimulate productivity, morale and magnificence.

Technique 2: Anticipation

The brain's dopamine reward system is associated with motivation and drive to obtain goals. Use this system to promote excellence by setting obtainable goals and then offering immediate rewards when goals are reached. These rewards need to be fun and tangible, such as a lunch out or happy hour for the project team. Rewards should be public and immediate (Technique 1), but need not be large. Think how much you enjoy anticipating an upcoming dinner with friends; you can use this same anticipatory response to reward to put employees into Type II stress. This will optimize their drive and creativity.

The dopamine system is driven by novelty, so change rewards often (Schultz, 2002). Although it is important to maintain consistency with traditions, such as holiday parties and bonuses, even these are better if they vary from year to year. Trust is built by groups of people going through difficult experiences together and anticipating the rewards at the end. This could be a grueling audit, but it could also be a day riding roller coasters at an amusement park, or a whitewater rafting trip.

Technique 3: Delegation

The essence of trust is the empowerment of others. You can do this by distributing tasks to others that are within their realm of interest and expertise. Managers should do this personally whenever possible to maximize the impact of oxytocin release on motivation to achieve a goal. A leader cannot 'cut and run' when delegating, but must provide the resources and tools needed to hit the mark. President Woodrow Wilson used not only his brains, 'but all he could borrow'. But the key is motivating these other brains to engage with the task. Delegating tasks to others creates Type II stress and gives those receiving an assignment ownership in a project's outcome. Delegation also provides an opportunity to recognize and reward colleagues. And, if the outcome does not hit its mark, this is a chance to teach someone in a constructive manner how improvements can be made (Technique 1).

Delegation is empowering in a trusting, collaborative environment. Delegating tasks to others is part of shared leadership and is essential in knowledge-based industries (really, all industries are knowledge-based). It permits those being delegated to meet their own needs for self-direction and recognition, and also allows them to draw on the organization's collaborative resources. Delegation can therefore foster trust between organization members as they seek to work together towards a common goal. Clear delegation of tasks also draws on people's anticipation of how it will feel to complete the task and earn the reward for it (Technique 2). Recognition of a completed delegated task is also essential (Technique 1).

Technique 4: Transparency

Sunlight nurtures trust, darkness destroys it. Leaders in a trusting environment have nothing to hide, and work 'in the trenches' with everyone else. When Jerre Stead took over as CEO at NCR Corp in 1993, he instituted an 'open door' policy. And he really meant open doors – he actually had the doors removed from his and other senior executives' offices. While this can be dismissed as a publicity ploy, it certainly sets the expectations employees have for leadership. Transparency facilitates trust by reducing uncertainty and suspicion. Our laboratory has shown that distrust causes the release of testosterone and is associated with aggressive responses (especially in men) that inhibit cooperation and destroy morale (Zak et al., 2005b).

Communication is the key. Directives that obfuscate true intentions or generate confusion undermine trust. Transparency is also facilitated by identifying trust as a core organization value, and acting on it. This means that building trust is explicitly discussed in company meetings and trust inventories such as the O-Factor are taken regularly. Trust must be made a priority, and breaches of trust must be quickly addressed to sustain organizational confidence. The corporate response by Johnson and Johnson to tainted Tylenol that killed seven people in Chicago in 1982 is a model of transparency. Every organization will face crises, though seldom this severe, and transparency maintains company cohesion when they arise.

Technique 5: Empathy

Leaders should see themselves as information aggregation devices. One can effectively manage people only if one is responsive to them behaviorally and emotionally. Yes, leaders need empathy. It allows you to 'read' people and appropriately anticipate what they will do and what they need rather than waiting until all this is laid out (which might never occur). Empathy promotes trust and efficiency because employees' needs are met and uncertainty is reduced. Employees rate empathy as one of the most important attributes in an effective leader (Macaluso, 2003).

The necessity of empathy also runs in the other direction, from employees to managers. When leaders transparently communicate the needs of the organization (Technique 4), then empathy and a desire to cooperate to reach the organization's goals is produced. For example, we have shown recently that watching a 100-second emotional video causes oxytocin to spike and this strongly correlated with the subjective experience of empathy. In this same experiment those who were empathically engaged were substantially more generous when promoted to help a stranger with their own money (Barraza and Zak, 2009). Empathy connects us to others and motivates us to satisfy their needs and goals – especially when the other is one's manager.

Empathy can be built in leaders and in followers. One must be unafraid to embrace it, and continually practice being emotionally open. This is difficult in the workplace because constant demands and working at lightning speed inhibit oxytocin release. Empathy requires that we, at least at some times, slow down and listen.

Technique 6: Autonomy

Giving those you manage autonomy is perhaps the ultimate demonstration of trust. It is delegation on steroids. Yes, this is risky. Autonomy with accountability is a mantra for an effective leader. Delegating tasks to employees (Technique 1) will backfire if you are constantly looking over their shoulders to get updates on their work. High degrees of autonomy are associated with greater productivity and employee morale. In a landmark study of British civil servants those with less autonomy had a threefold increase in mortality and substantially higher rates of cardiovascular disease. A lack of autonomy has been shown to raise Type I stress. The primary human stress hormone, cortisol, initiates the cascade of factors that damage the heart and other organs. Cortisol suppresses oxytocin and, you guessed it, reduces interpersonal trust.

Autonomy works because rather than being the innately selfish homo economicus you have heard so much about, our research shows that human beings are more accurately described as homo reciprocans, or reciprocal creatures. You cannot get someone to trust you unless you first give them your trust. That is just the way the human brain works. People trust those who trust them, and distrust those who distrust them. Leaders must choose which side of the trust/distrust dichotomy they want to be on.

Technique 7: Authenticity

All of the techniques described here must be practiced authentically to improve the work lives of those around you or they will backfire. Human beings are hypersocial creatures, and our brains are exceptionally good at identifying liars and cheats. This includes inauthentic managers. If you try to fake your way to creating a trusting workplace without really investing thought and emotion into it, your artifice will eventually back-fire. Cons and cardsharps always get caught because they all have 'tells'. In the *Nicomachean Ethics*, Aristotle identified the virtues that, when prac-ticed, lead to a fulfilled and satisfied life. One of these is magnificence. A high-trust workplace permits those in it to be magnificent. In a high-trust organization employees are productive and collaborate easily, customers are delighted, and a manager is therefore effective. Authenticity is telling it the way it is. Magnificence is authenticity put to work. Both of these can only arise when trust is high.

SUMMARY

In a study of architectural firms, companies whose principals displayed empowering, trusting behaviors were also the most innovative (Burpitt and Bigoness, 1997). Your organization can replicate this by applying the seven techniques that raise trust we have described: praise, anticipation, delegation, transparency, empathy, autonomy and authenticity. A mne-monic for these is PADTEAA ('pad-tea'). These factors combine to create organizations with high levels of trust. High-trust companies have high productivity and greater stock market returns than low-trust companies. Trust initiates a positive feedback loop that reinforces and sustains trust.

So why not implement these techniques today? Changing your organi-zation's culture requires that managers change entrenched behavioral patterns. Because our brains are designed to save energy, behaviors are dif-ficult to change once we have got used to them (Zak, 2008a). Implementing change requires energy and perseverance, but this can renew the energy in your organization. As discussed in Techniques 1 and 2, novelty and anticipation draw on the brain's reinforcement system, driving us to achieve new goals. These goals can be implemented by clearly stating them (Technique 4) and delegating the steps needed to create a trusting organi-zation to groups of employees (Technique 3).

There will be complaints, of course, because to a greater or lesser extent we all fear the uncertainty of change. Listen to the fears of those around you with empathy (Technique 5), and provide support during the tran-sition period. Provide autonomy to those around you (Technique 6) by putting your fate into their hands and ask them to reciprocate. Our studies have shown that the brains of 98 percent of people who are shown trust release oxytocin and this causes them to reciprocate by being trustworthy (Zak, 2007). The other 2 percent will remain in self-serving 'survival' mode and will be unlikely to change. These people have difficulty connecting to others and as a result do not consistently reciprocate with others. Perhaps most importantly, change begins with you. If you authentically adopt the approach we have outlined (Technique 7), those around you will follow. After all, as herd species humans crave leadership. If you wholeheartedly adopt the PADTEAA techniques, trust in your organization will increase and everyone (including you) will benefit. That is magnificence.

REFERENCES

Barraza, J.A. and P.J. Zak (2009), 'Empathy towards strangers triggers oxytocin release and subsequent generosity', *Annals of the New York Academy of Sciences*, **1167**, 182–9.

Burpitt, W.J. and W.J. Bigoness (1997), 'Leadership and innovation among teams: the role of empowerment', *Small Group Research*, **28**, 414.

Edelman Trust Barometer (2009), Available at http://www.edelman.com/TRUST/2009/.

Kosfeld, M., M. Heinrichs, P.J. Zak, U. Fischbacher and E. Fehr (2005), 'Oxytocin increases trust in humans', *Nature*, **435** (2), 673–76.

Macaluso, J. (2003), 'Harnessing the power of emotional intelligent leadership. The CEO refresher', available at http://www.refresher.com/.

Morhenn, V.B., J.W. Park, E. Piper and P.J. Zak (2008), 'Monetary sacrifice among strangers is mediated by endogenous oxytocin release after physical contact', *Evolution and Human Behavior*, **29**, 375–83.

Schultz, W. (2002), 'Getting formal with dopamine and reward', *Neuron*, **36** (2), 241–63.

Zak, P.J. (2005), 'Trust: a temporary human attachment facilitated by oxytocin', *Behavioral and Brain Sciences*, **28** (3), 368–9.

Zak, P.J. (2007), 'The neuroeconomics of trust', in R. Frantz (ed.), *Renaissance in Behavioral Economics*, Routledge, pp. 17–33.

Zak, P.J. (2008a), 'Rational rationality', Psychology Today Blog: The Moral Molecule, available at http://blogs.psychologytoday.com/blog/the-moral-molecule/200810/rational-rationality.

Zak, P.J. (2008b), 'Value and values: moral economics', in Paul J. Zak (ed.), *Moral Markets*, Princeton, NJ: Princeton University Press, pp. 259–79.

Zak, P.J., R. Kurzban and W.T. Matzner (2004), 'The neurobiology of trust', *Annals of the New York Academy of Sciences*, **1032**, 224–7.

Zak, P.J., R. Kurzban and W.T. Matzner (2005a), 'Oxytocin is associated with human trustworthiness', *Hormones and Behavior*, **48**, 522–7.

Zak, P.J., K. Borja, W.M. Matzner and R. Kurzban (2005b), 'The neuroeconomics of distrust: sex differences in behavior and physiology', *American Economic Review Papers and Proceedings*, **95**, 360–64.

5. The new millennium's first global financial crisis: the neuroeconomics of greed, self-interest, deception, false trust, overconfidence and risk perception

Donald T. Wargo, Norman A. Baglini and Katherine A. Nelson

INTRODUCTION

Politicians, professors and pundits will analyze and memorialize the causes of the new millennium's first global financial crisis for years to come. One of the most discussed topics will be the alleged 'irrational' behavior of 'sophisticated investors' (Zweig, 2007). To what extent did behavior that is inconsistent with the basic assumptions of investor rationality contribute to the crisis? This chapter hypothesizes that the originators of the collateralized debt obligations – investment banks, commercial banks and mortgage companies – acted with complete disregard to risks attached to these investment vehicles. Similarly, the purchasers of the collateralized debt obligations – banks, investment funds, municipalities and individuals – acted with disregard to risks attached to these bonds. The answer to why this happened cannot be found in economic or business textbooks. It was the result of overconfidence and the willingness to ignore risks. However, the authors contend that a neuroeconomic analysis of the reward and loss systems of human investors gives us deep insight into the decision failings of the human investors in this crisis.

THE MILLENNIUM'S FIRST GLOBAL FINANCIAL CRISIS

Financial markets around the world experienced profound losses in 2008 and early 2009 as a result of the worldwide credit crisis. The crisis was caused by the collapse of the markets for what were termed collateralized debt obligations (CDOs). These CDOs were bonds backed by mortgages on houses in the USA but the bonds were bought not only by US banks but also by many municipalities and by European banks. The attractiveness of these bonds was higher interest rates than US Treasury or corporate bonds. When the CDO markets collapsed (due to massive defaults on the underlying mortgages) the CDOs became worthless and the banks holding large numbers of them became insolvent. In order to avoid the collapse of the entire US financial system, the US government has already given $350 billion in federal bailout money to over 200 banks and financial institutions and governments similarly rescued many other banks in Europe.

In the USA, however, since the majority of the bailed-out banks did not increase lending and used the money to bolster their liquidity or for employee bonuses or acquisitions, a hue and cry was arising for nationalization of the financial system, if only temporarily (Paletta et al., 2009). The USA has already (effectively) nationalized AIG, the largest insurance company in the world and the two largest mortgage lenders in the world, Fannie Mae and Freddie Mac. Nationalization was the solution for the United Kingdom, Sweden and Iceland in the current crisis. Meanwhile, in 2009, the Obama administration began dispensing an additional $350 billion authorized by Congress under the Troubled Asset Relief Program (TARP).

World stock markets reflected the crisis. Beginning in the summer of 2007 and continuing all through 2008, the US S&P 500 Index sank 37.1 percent. It was the index's second-worst loss since its founding in 1923 and its worst since a decline of 43.1 percent during the Great Depression. The Dow Jones Industrial Average also had its third-worst loss in its 113-year history. The global pain was even sharper – the MSCI All Country World Index excluding USA dropped 47.0 percent. About $7 trillion of shareholders' wealth on the US stock markets – the gains of the last six years – was wiped out in a year of violent market downswings.

All of these factors contributed to the worst US recession since the Great Depression. The US unemployment rate rose from 4.9 percent in 2007 to 8.9 percent in mid 2009, representing close to 6 million lost jobs. The current recession began in December 2007, and is expected to continue to the end of 2009, with low employment levels expected to continue into 2011.

American investors, sophisticated or not, are by and large the owners of the largest firms in the USA through their stock holdings in public corporations. Are these investors able to rationally weigh 'risk and return' or are they driven mainly by greed and fear? Do investors ask appropriate questions before making important financial decisions or are they easily misled by unrealistic promises of outsized returns? Perhaps investors think and act rationally during most of the routine investment process. However, what happens when things do not go as planned and unprecedented – that is, unpredictable and uncontrollable – events occur? Does our emotional, feeling brain take over and crowd out all reason and logic? Warren Buffet, the 'Oracle of Omaha', has been quoted saying, 'I'd be a bum on the street with a tin cup if the markets were always efficient!'

LEE'S ORBITOFRONTAL CORTEX (OFC)

Richard Peterson is a psychiatrist and a former trader. He recounts the story of Lee, a 53-year-old partner in an accounting firm, who lost part of his orbitofrontal cortex (OFC) as a result of surgery to remove a tumor (Peterson, 2007). The OFC is located in the front of the brain, behind the forehead, and evaluates the relevance of emotional input – including fear of losses – to decision-making (Beer et al., 2006; Damasio, 1999). Chapters 9 and 13 of this volume discuss the functions of various regions of the brain in great detail.

After the successful operation, Lee was able to return to work and function normally except for his terrible investment decisions. He bought several expensive vacation time shares, bought penny stocks based on faxed and emailed promotional material and could not keep up with his mortgage payments. The loss of his OFC took away an important part of Lee's functional 'loss avoidance' system. Previously a conservative investor, he was now unable to feel 'risk'. Lee explained that he knew he should feel uncertain and afraid, but his highly speculative investments did not feel 'risky' to him.

The human midbrain is quite similar to that of reptiles and is the heart of the 'limbic system', the seat of animal instincts and human habits and emotions. The area that differentiates us most from others is a larger prefrontal cortex (PFC). The prefrontal cortex estimates the probability of future rewards, aids in planning for the future, is good at following rules, directs our focus and attention, does the executive decision making and is the seat of self-control and conscience. Parts of the PFC are further specialized. The OFC integrates reason and emotion and the anterior cingulate cortex (ACC) resolves conflicts between two alternative courses of action and prioritizes emotional information as either relevant or unimportant (O'Doherty et al., 2001). All of these areas are involved in financial decision-making (Peterson, 2007) (Figure 5.1).

Since the time of Aristotle in ancient Greece, scientists and philosophers have loosely hypothesized the existence of two major brain systems that are

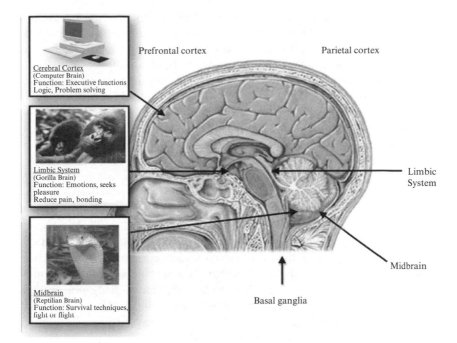

Figure 5.1   General view of brain identifying limbic system, prefrontal cortex, orbitofrontal cortex and anterior cingulate cortex

fundamental to almost all human behavior – the 'reward/approach' system (pleasure-seeking) and the 'loss/avoid' system (pain-avoidance) (Peterson, 2005). In studies of the loss-avoidance system Antonio Damasio, a neurologist at the University of Iowa, and colleagues studied patients with OFC lesions in the 1990s. These patients retained their memory, intelligence, analytical reasoning and logical thought but made poor decisions in risky situations. Damasio reported that his OFC patients, like Lee, knew when they should feel fearful, but could not experience it during risky situations. Damasio and colleagues concluded that there is a difference between what the emotional brain (the limbic system) knows about risk and the conscious awareness of the actual danger (Bechara et al., 1994, 2005).

'GREED IS GOOD' . . . GORDON GEKKO IN *WALL STREET*

'Greed and fear, greed and fear, greed and fear'. This is the mantra that appears overwhelmingly in descriptions and news accounts of investors' erratic actions in the first financial crisis of the new millennium. In support of this assertion, *The Economist* (24 January 2009) titled its special report on the future of finance, 'Greed – and fear'. In this report, *The Economist* points out that modern finance is supposed to be all about measuring risks using sophisticated computer programs. However, the massive purchases of mortgage-backed securities (CDOs) were 'just a leap in the dark' (*The Economist*, 24 January 2009, p. 13).

Despite the warnings in the Bible, Koran and other timeless sources, the human tendency to be greedy continues, especially in the financial world. However, Paul Krugman, the Princeton Nobel Laureate economist, opines, 'Greed is bad . . . a system that lavishly rewards executives for success tempts those executives, who control much of the information available to outsiders, to fabricate the appearance of success – aggressive accounting, fictitious transactions that inflate sales, whatever it takes' (Krugman, 2002).

In investing, greed results in overtrading and inadequate due diligence, and unfortunately it partners with overconfidence. Conversely, fear leads to risk aversion and inactivity. These emotions and actions lead to significantly underperforming returns. Lo and Steenbarger studied stock market day traders over five weeks (Lo and Steenbarger, 2005). These researchers monitored their emotional levels via psychosomatic instruments and then correlated emotional arousal with profitability.

> Our results are consistent with the current neuroscientific evidence that automatic emotional responses such as greed and fear (for example, responses mediated by the amygdala) often trump more controlled or 'higher level' responses (for example, responses mediated by the pre-frontal cortex). To the extent that emotional reactions 'short-circuit' more complex decision-making faculties (for example, those involved in the active management of securities) it should come as no surprise that the result is poorer performance. (Lo and Steenbarger, 2005, p. 358)

Camerer and colleagues posit that this emotional, intuitive decision-making is our 'default mode' and that our controlled processes only activate in an 'interrupt' or 'override' mode, due to an encounter with unexpected events, strong visceral sensations or novel problems (Camerer et al., 2005).

RISK AND REWARD

There is significant research supporting the view that when making decisions, people value losses as much as twice as much as they value an equivalent gain when compared to the status quo (Tversky and Kahneman,

1992). For example, people typically reject a 50/50 chance of losing money they already have unless the chance of gain is about twice as much as they might lose. In this classic example of Prospect Theory, Amos Tversky and Nobel Laureate Daniel Kahneman explain humans' tendency toward risk-aversion. Further, Kahneman, Knetsch and Thaler have shown that people overvalue items they already own (Kahneman et al., 1990). In laboratory experiments people require substantially more money when selling objects they possess than they would be willing to pay to buy those exact same objects. This is known as the 'endowment effect'. Peterson states that this is loss-aversion behavior and is the result of people forming an emotional attachment to items they own (Peterson, 2007). This behavior which, according to Peterson, affects almost two-thirds of investors, is especially easy to observe and measure in stock market decisions, where most investors hold on to losing stocks that a rational investor would dump. In contrast, Lerner and colleagues discovered that the endowment effect can be all but eliminated by 'priming' subjects with feelings of sadness or disgust (Lerner et al., 2004). The priming causes subjects to want to expel items they own and discourages the acquisition of new objects.

Another striking proof of human loss-aversion is what is known in behavioral finance as the 'equity premium puzzle' (Peterson, 2007). Consider this: the average annual inflation-adjusted return on the US stock market for the last 110 years has been approximately 7.9 percent. For the same 110 years, the corresponding real return on US Treasury bonds has been 1.0 percent. This difference in investment returns is called 'the equity premium'. The question is, why are bonds so popular when they earn so much less than stocks? It must be due to the fact that investors perceive stocks as much riskier and it appears that this is because the human brain is so sensitive to changes from the status quo. In the stock market this change is called 'volatility' and the standard deviation of the price changes of a stock is measured as the 'beta' of that stock (Shiv et al., 2005).

This hypothesis is supported by recent experiments. Mehra has shown that the more frequently performance feedback is given to individuals in investing experiments (that is, they are shown price quotes more often), the less they invest in equities versus bonds and vice versa (Mehra, 2003). This behavior appears to be caused by the fact that the more frequently investors check prices, the more they seem to see risk in the equities markets. Bernatzi and Thaler term this phenomenon 'myopic loss aversion'. These researchers have also found that this myopic loss aversion is induced by frequent feedback on stock prices (Bernatzi and Thaler, 1995). They found that the more information they gave an investor on stock price changes and the more frequently they gave the price information to their subjects, the more the investors exhibited conservative behavior,

Table 5.1   The consilience of disciplined studies of the reward-seeking system and loss-aversion system

Field of study	Positive valence	Negative valence
Financial field	Reward	Risk
Psychological science	Greed	Fear
Neuroscience	Reward-seeking system	Loss-aversion system

induced by the volatility of price moves. The investor perceived negative price moves as threatening. Bernatzi and Thaler contend that the 'equity premium' (6.9 percent as we saw above) is consistent, in their opinion, with an annual analysis of gains and losses by investors but which, consistent with Tversky and Kahneman's Prospect Theory, weighs losses approximately twice as heavily as gains.

Additionally, loss-aversion also explains behavior outside the laboratory (ibid.). More recent research shows similar loss-avoidance behavior in children as young as five and also amazingly in Capuchin monkeys, using functional resonance imaging (fMRI) (Chen and Lakshminarayanan, 2006).

Investment decisions such as buying stocks, bonds or opaque financial derivatives involve evaluating the expected reward versus the possible expected loss. In the financial sector professionals frequently employ the language of 'balancing reward versus risk' in their activities. These financial parameters of reward and risk generate positive and negative emotions, respectively, in humans – greed and fear. It is interesting that Wall Street wisdom states that 'Greed always trumps fear'. That is, when there is negative news or significant uncertainty in the markets, the stock indexes decline. This is confirmation of Prospect Theory, showing that humans feel a loss as much as twice as much as an equivalent financial gain (Tversky and Kahneman, 1992).

The assessment and comparison of expected reward and expected risk is the essential survival task of organisms. The brains of all living creatures contain a reward-seeking system and loss-avoidance system to perform this survival task and this is often the intuitive system used by investors. We present the consilience of the various disciplined studies of these two systems in Table 5.1.

HOMEOSTASIS OF BODY AND BRAIN SYSTEMS

To help us see how these systems work, it is critical to understand that the reward/loss system is a homeostatic system. It always seeks to be in balance. We possess bodily homeostatic systems that can be lethal if out of balance, such as oxygen levels in the blood or internal body temperature. When these systems are out of balance or out of 'homeostasis', there are internal cascading hormonal and chemical signals that cause physical changes to return the particular bodily system to homeostasis (for example, a rapid heartbeat and fast breathing). The human reward/loss system does have a similar homeostasis. It is in balance and endeavors to return to homeostasis when disturbed. The body's non-lethal reward/loss system homeostasis is akin to the 'fight or flight' fear system that elevates under stress but returns to balance when the danger has passed. However, under chronic stress, an imbalanced fight or flight human system becomes lethal (McEwen, 2002; Ming et al., 2004).

Paulus contends that the entire decision-making system of individuals is a homeostatic system, and he receives widespread agreement on this model from the scientific community (Camerer et al., 2005; Oswold, 1997; Paulus, 2007; Schultz and Dickinson, 2000; Shermer, 2008). According to Paulus:

> Homeostasis can be defined as a dynamic physiological, cognitive and affective state that integrates multiple bottom-up sensory afferents and top-down cognitive and affective control processes, resulting in dynamic stability (i.e., resistance to internal and external perturbations). Decisions maintain or bring individuals into a new homeostatic state. (Paulus, 2007, p. 602)

Studies of the reward/loss system in mammals and primates (including humans) show the simultaneous activation of both these neural networks until threshold activation is passed and the individual chooses the approach or avoidance action (Daw et al., 2006; De Martino et al., 2006; Koob and Le Moal, 1997; O'Doherty et al., 2004; Rietveld, 2008). This characterization of decision-making as a homeostatic system receives support from studies showing that individuals with generalized anxiety disorder exhibit intolerance of risk – their loss-avoidance system is overactive. In contrast, fMRI investigations show that subjects 'at risk' for substance abuse have higher levels of activation in the nucleus accumbens (NAcc) and exhibit high risk-taking and impulsivity (Paulus, 2007). The NAcc is an important part of the brain's expected reward system and is excited by the neurotransmitter dopamine when the brain sees an expected reward. It is what causes us to 'want' something. Further, it is located in the deep midbrain, which is an emotionally primitive part of the brain we share with reptiles and mammals (Figure 5.2). The NAcc is discussed in great detail in Chapter 9 of this volume and the reader is referred to this chapter for more details.

In support of the reward/risk system's homeostasis, Kuhnan and

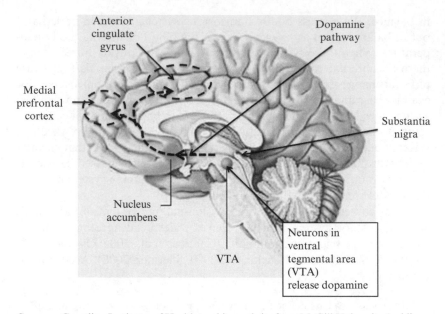

Source: Canadian Institutes of Health teaching website from McGill University (public domain), originally in color at http://thebrain.mcgill.ca/flash/i/i_03/i_03_cr/i_03_cr_que/i_03_cr_que.html.

Figure 5.2   The brain's reward system

Knutson state that their results indicate that above and beyond contributing to rational choice, anticipatory neural activation may also promote irrational choice. 'Thus, financial decision-making may require a delicate balance – recruitment of distinct circuits may be necessary for taking or avoiding risks, but the excessive activation of one mechanism or the other may lead to mistakes' (Kuhnen and Knutson, 2005, p. 767).

Camerer, Lowenstein and Prelec also characterize this reward/loss system as a homeostatic system. The actions taken by humans ('revealed preference' in standard economic theory) are only part of a complex system of internal and external cues, affects, feelings, unconscious motivations and actions (Camerer et al., 2005). When the body or the brain moves off a 'set point', the internal systems make us feel a 'wanting' and then pleasure when the bodily system again achieves homeostasis. Pleasure is only a 'homeostatic cue' or 'informational signal' that we are moving in the right direction to achieving the dual goals listed above.

An important homeostatic feature of the reward/loss system, according to Camerer and colleagues, is its sensitivity not to the absolute levels of homeostasis but to changes from those levels. That is, a constant

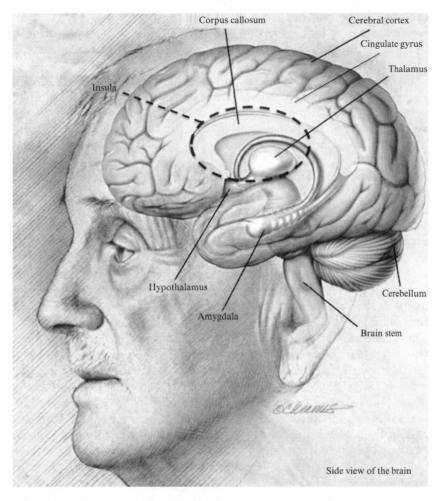

Source: National Institute on Aging, original in color at http://www.nia.nih.gov/ Alzheimers/Publications/UnravelingTheMystery.

Figure 5.3   Loss-avoidance system of the brain (the locus cereleus is a small area of neurons in the brain stem)

reinforcement reward of juice to a monkey for a specific action causes a 'strike' when the juice is removed. Similarly, humans feel acutely a change in the level of investment returns, income or wealth in relation to their 'set point', whether that set point is $60 000 per year or $600 000 per year (ibid.). Another way to frame this is that violations of expectations trigger extremely powerful emotional responses. Then depending on the genetic make-up of the individual, these emotional responses can result in pro-found feelings of loss or depression following monetary losses or result in a maladaptive alternative action, excessive risk-taking to recover those losses.

Our main hypothesis concerning the world financial crisis is that from the viewpoint of neuroeconomics the homeostasis of the reward/loss systems of the individuals involved was thrown out of balance. In the recent financial meltdown, all perception of risk was removed and there-fore untrammeled greed took control of the system with no consideration of the concomitant risk. The homeostatic balance of the brain's reward/loss system was not brought into play. The originators of the CDOs per-ceived no risk because they passed the risk of mortgage defaults on to the purchasers of the CDOs. The purchasers of the CDOs perceived no risk because the CDOs were given a superior credit rating by the bond credit rating agencies (Moody and Standard and Poor) and were insured by credit default insurance from AIG Insurance Company. AIG became insolvent and was effectively nationalized by the US government.

The anterior insula is tasked with evaluating expected risk and in loss aversion Peterson reports that patients who had lesions to their insula took monumentally higher risks than control subjects (Peterson, 2007). These laboratory experiments involved betting on a coin toss. The subject was given $20 and could bet $1 on each toss. If the subject did not bet, he did not lose anything. If the subject bet, he either lost $1 for betting wrongly or gained $2.50 for betting correctly. According to probability theory, the expected gain for each 'investment' of $1 on a toss was $1.25 versus keeping the $1 for each 'pass'. Therefore, a purely rational investor should always bet on each toss, as the simple laws of probability ensure that he will come out ahead.

However, the control subjects only invested in 57.6 percent of the total rounds and, after a loss in a round, only 40.7 percent bet on the subsequent round, showing their loss-aversion. On the other hand, the patients with insula damage bet on 91.3 percent of all rounds and 96.8 percent of the rounds following a loss. Bechara and colleagues and Chang report similar behavior in their laboratory experiments (Bechara et al., 1994; Chang, 2005).

THE NATURE OF GREED

Greed is caused by a number of factors: the desire for gain, a disregard of risk, a psychological motivation to pursue opportunities and a tendency for excess. Greed, according to Peterson, actually has deleterious effects on economic performance. In the financial world greed causes investors to chase fast-moving overpriced stocks, get caught by scams and schemes and take excessive risk in general (Peterson, 2007).

Other studies show an even further division of the brain's functions in economic decisions. The NAcc, the expected reward center of the brain, strongly activates in response to the relative size of a potential monetary reward (Knutson and Cooper, 2005; Kuhnen and Knutsen, 2005; Lerner et al., 2004; Peterson, 2005). However, the probability of actually receiving that reward – which is a more rational calculation – is evaluated or 'encoded' by the medial prefrontal cortex (MPFC) (McClure et al., 2004a). The MPFC is located at the front of the brain, behind the forehead and is the main locus of the executive function of the brain, that is, the decision to take or not take an action. We discuss the functionality of the MPFC in detail later in this chapter. Furthermore, the dopamine release in the NAcc is scaled to the size of the monetary reward – the larger the reward, the greater the NAcc activation – but the MPFC activation or excitation does not change unless the probability changes. This is the reason why when a lottery jackpot reaches a huge amount, say $10 000 000, there is a rush to buy tickets, even though the actual chance of winning is reduced by each additional ticket purchased. By way of illustration, if tickets are $1 each and 50 percent of the money taken in goes to the jackpot and 50 percent to the lottery organization, the probability of winning the jackpot of $1 000 000 is 1 out of 2 000 000. However, the probability of winning if the jackpot is $10 000 000 is 1 out of 20 000 000.

As a further refinement of their experimental work on financial risk taking (often termed 'behavioral finance') Kuhnen and Knutson have shown the separate and coordinated activation of both the NAcc versus the anterior insula ('insula') in decisions involving both risk and reward. These brain regions, respectively, elicit the emotions of 'greed and fear' (Kuhnen and Knutson, 2005). Their financial risk experiments involved rounds of choosing a bond – a riskless but lower return – versus a stock – a risky but higher return – while the subjects were being scanned using an fMRI imaging machine. The results show that NAcc activated more prior to the choice of the risky investment while the insula activated more prior to the riskless (or we might say 'loss-aversive') investment. As further confirmation of function, excessive activation in the NAcc preceded an investment error of taking on too much risk, while excessive activation in the insula preceded an investment error of taking on too little risk. These last two actions taken were suboptimal from the standpoint of a rational investor, since the subjects were provided with both the returns of the investments and their probabilities.

Another reaction of the midbrain is what Jason Zweig calls the 'prediction addiction' (Zweig, 2007). Once the human brain experiences a pattern of two or three positive monetary rewards it expects the pattern to continue. This contra-factual bias usually makes an investor euphoric about a 'hot streak' and less vigilant about risk. Porter and Smith discuss how this unconscious behavior creates 'asset market bubbles' (Porter and Smith, 1994).

THE NATURE OF FEAR

Fear is the emotion that balances greed in the normal investor's brain. The loss-aversion system, as we said above, involves the amygdala, which encodes fear and records long-term fearful memories, the hippocampus, which is the memory processing center of the brain, and the anterior insula, which processes expectation of losses (Figure 5.3). This loss-avoidance system is in homeostatic balance with the brain's reward system, and together the relative balance of the two results in approach/ avoid, invest/not invest or fight/flight behavior. For Wall Street investors, as the stock market climbs to new highs, the adage is that the market 'climbs a wall of worry' (Peterson, 2007). That is, the higher the market goes, the more fearful Wall Street traders are that it will soon crash. This is a good example of how the two systems always work in tandem.

Additionally, Hauber and Sommer show that the unconscious reward system actually performs a cost/benefit analysis on the amount of effort to expend to get a reward (Hauber and Sommer, 2009). According to their findings, the ACC, the basolateral amygdala (BLA) and the dopamine in the NAcc are part of a neural system that is critically involved in making decisions on how much effort to invest in seeking expected rewards. In their 2009 study they sought to identify functional interactions between ACC and NAcc regulating effort-based decision-making. Their research on rats shows that the unconscious reward/loss system actually performs a cost/benefit analysis to determine how much effort to invest in a particular expected reward, in a manner that is quite consistent with standard economic theory.

Finally, Westeroff, a researcher in a new field termed 'economic physics', has constructed a fully deterministic model of stock market fluctuations based simply on the contrasting emotions of greed and fear. He correctly weighted, as we have shown above, that fear motivation is twice as important as greed motivation. Although his work is of very little practical use, it is interesting that his simulation results show a credible approximation of actual historical stock market fluctuations (Westeroff, 2004).

There is an important consequence of the bifurcation of the brain systems of reward and loss. Research in the current decade has shown that because expected reward and expected loss are processed in totally different areas of the brain, humans react to them in qualitatively different ways (O'Doherty et al., 2001, 2004; Taylor et al., 2006; Xue et al., 2008). Kuhnen and Knutson have used laboratory investment experiments and fMRI to show that expected reward is processed in the NAcc area of the ventral striatum while expected loss and loss-aversion are processed in the anterior insula (Kuhnen and Knutson, 2005).

In a further refinement of our understanding of the brain's reward/loss system, Xue and colleagues contend that whereas the NAcc is sensitive to both risk and reward, the MPFC differentiates strongly between risk and reward by processing them in different brain areas. This means that both ventral and dorsal MPFC signals are predictive of risk-taking behavior. A strong reward signal in the ventral MPFC likely leads to risk-taking behavior, whereas a strong signal in the dorsal MPFC acts as a warning signal in more risk-averse individuals. This study further shows that these sensitivities are independent of one another (Xue et al., 2008).

These results suggest that the two competing forces that contend with each other in making decisions under uncertainty and risk – fear of the risk and the lure of the gain – have strong neural correlates in the MPFC. It appears that these two regions of the MPFC determine whether the risk will be taken or avoided. As we mentioned above, scientific evidence shows that there is a balance or homeostasis in this reward/loss system. On the other hand, imbalances in these forces – and the accompanying unbalanced MPFC signals – will lead to excessive reward seeking (including thrill seeking, gambling or addiction) or excessive risk aversion (the risk aversion of bankers or *in extremis* anxiety disorders and phobias).

THE NATURE OF OVERCONFIDENCE

One of our hypotheses about the causes of the global financial crisis is that overoptimism ('housing prices will never decline') and overconfidence ('hubris') played a very large part. Decisional errors of all types, but especially investment decisions, are often caused by overoptimism, which can be magnified by overconfidence. Studies have shown that students, psychologists, CIA agents, engineers, stock analysts, financial analysts, investment bankers, investors and many other categories of people tend toward irrational overconfidence in the accuracy of their decisions. Moreover, entrepreneurs, investors, stock analysts and others who have had success in their chosen fields tend to develop a sense of invulnerability,

ignoring the role that good fortune had played in their success and attrib-
uting the gains solely to their own skill (Prentice, 2007).

Similarly, people tend to believe not only that they are above average
in their occupation, but also that they are more honest and fair-minded
than both their competitors and their peers. This is especially true of those
in the financial field. Recent studies indicated that 74 percent of financial
advisors believe their ethics are higher than those of their peers – a simple
statistical impossibility – and 83 percent said that at least one half of the
people they work with would list them among the most ethical people they
know. An amazing 92 percent were satisfied with their ethics and character
(Jennings, 2005).

Irrational investing is often an excellent example of overconfidence.
Unfortunately, overconfidence is an investing bias associated with overtrading and decreased profitability (Biais et al., 2002). This type of overconfidence is more common among men than women, more common
among the young than the old. Therefore, it is important to research the
neural correlates of biases, such as overconfidence among traders and
business people, as Peterson shows that overconfidence is correlated with
subpar performance in traders and in executives' poor decision-making in
firms (Peterson, 2007).

It is a positive feedback cycle – the more money investors make, the
more money they think they can make – and their sense of all-consuming
excitement and impulsive trading often go into overdrive. This 'overdrive'
is also related to the addictive nature of day trading – an increasingly
common problem. Investors tend to overconfidently chase performance
(Peterson, 2005).

We hypothesize that a bias of overconfidence and an ignoring of risk
by the individual investors making the investment decisions in the injured
financial institutions contributed greatly to the global financial crisis. This
bias is perfectly described by Smith in *The Wealth of Nations*.

> The over-weening conceit which the greater part of man have of their own
> abilities, is an ancient evil remarked by the philosophers and moralists of all
> ages. Their absurd presumption in their own good fortune, has been less taken
> notice of. It is, however, if possible, more universal. There is no man living
> who, when in tolerable good health and spirits, has not some share of it. The
> chance of gain is by every man more or less overvalued, and the chance of loss
> is by most men undervalued, and by scarce any man, who is in tolerable health
> and spirits, valued more than it is worth. (Smith (1776) [2003], Book I, Ch. X,
> Part 1, p. 149)

We may translate Adam Smith's 'conceit' into modern language as the
observed and documented 'hubris' of today's CEOs that causes the failure
of so many mini- and mega-mergers and other business failures (Camerer

and Lovallo, 1999; Roll, 1986). This hubris is a deeply ingrained instinct from our evolutionary past (Postlewaite and Compte, 2005; Waldman, 1994). Furthermore, it has a neurological basis in the disproportionate positive affect of expected utility (as encoded by the NAcc) over actual utility (as encoded by the MPFC) (see Chapter 9 in this volume for a much more extensive treatment of the human brain's reward/loss system).

DOPAMINE AND HABIT FORMATION

Neuroeconomists who study decision-making have, through extensive research, given us great insight into the neural basis for decision processes. This also helps us to understand how the human brain can be so susceptible to overconfidence. As we show in Chapter 9, expected reward – or 'utility' – is processed in a different region of the brain than the evaluation of actual reward. The NAcc encodes expected reward but deactivates once the actual reward or loss is achieved. The MPFC, at the terminus of the brain's dopamine system, evaluates the positive or negative valence of the actual reward. If positive, it signals that the reward pursuit action was completed successfully and this is the way the brain engages in reward learning (Zweig, 2007). In particular, activation of the MPFC signals that a reward pursuit action was successfully concluded and that the organism is on track toward desired goals (Peterson, 2007).

However, there are important discoveries about the reward system that can inform our understanding of human behavior (Zweig, 2007). The dopamine system has evolved to make us willing to take risks in reward seeking. If the actual reward matches the expected reward – 'expected utility' – there is no extra kick of dopamine. The neurons return to their steady-state hum of three electrochemical bursts per second. If, on the other hand, the reward is greater than the expectation, the dopamine neurons can fire at up to 40 bursts per second. This dopamine signal is completely scalable – the bigger the unexpected reward, the faster and longer the firing. The expected reward system of the brain – the substantia nigra and NAcc – has been set up by evolution to make us take risks and seek novelty.

In support of this conclusion, Zald and colleagues found that novelty-seeking humans had less dopamine-like receptors in the substantia nigra/ventral tegmental area. These dendritic auto receptors provide an inhibitory function in the substantia nigra neurons (which release dopamine into the extracellular synapses) and control impulsive novelty-seeking behavior. The fewer auto receptors, the greater is the release of dopamine in the ventral tegmental area. Zald found that both male and female subjects with fewer of these inhibitory dendritic auto receptors scored higher on psychological tests of impulsive behavior and that this correlation was inverse and directly proportional (Zald et al., 2008). This finding is extremely important because the personality trait of novelty seeking is among the best predictors of drug use and other risky behaviors as well.

Over multiple positive outcomes of a particular action, the MPFC becomes satiated and the action can turn into a habit. If it becomes a habit, it is fixated in the basal ganglia – the site of instinct for animals – and not mediated by the dopamine reward system anymore (Choi et al., 2005). This allows the cognitive powers of the brain to be used for other avenues of exploration and attention. This also explains why habits and, worse yet, addictions are so difficult to overcome.

EXPLOITATION VERSUS EXPLORATION

Further, when a behavior is no longer rewarding (either because expectations are met or because of adaptation), it no longer elicits a dopamine release and the level of the neurotransmitter norepinephrine increases in the brain – commonly known as adrenaline. Norepinephrine increases vigilance and improved attention and focus. It induces both animals and humans to explore their environment, looking for new opportunities and causes them to shift their focus frequently. Conversely, hyperactive norepinephrine receptors are the cause of attention deficit disorder (ADD) and attention deficit hyperactivity disorder (ADHD) (Daw et al., 2006; Peterson, 2007).

McClure, Gilzenrat and Cohen have created a neural model of the neuroeconomics of exploitation versus exploration (McClure et al., 2004b). They have found that the brain has an algorithm for deciding to stay with a task or to seek a new opportunity. It rests on the difference between expected uncertainty versus unexpected uncertainty. If the unexpected uncertainty in the course of performing a reward-seeking task rises beyond a threshold relative to expected certainty in the task, the organism switches to exploration. The neural basis for this balance is the relative concentrations of acetylcholine (ACh) versus norepinephrine (NE) in the brain. Acetylcholine appears to signal expected uncertainty or prediction errors in a task and keeps us exploiting that task. Conversely, when prediction errors arise that do not meet with our expectations, NE is increasingly released by a small brainstem area called the locus ceruleus (LC) (Figure 5.3.). When the amount of NE crosses a threshold, the brain is induced to abandon the current task and exploit other alternatives. On the basis of their research, Yu and Dayan propose a Bayesian-like algorithm for the switch, that is, it is based on expected probabilities of errors and corrects itself over numerous trials (Yu and Dayan, 2005). For an excellent explanation of the human brain's Bayesian decision-making process, we refer you to Körding (2007).

Here we see again the homeostatic nature of the human brain systems. The financial implication of this research for firms is significant. Peterson asserts that after a series of successful strategies (or investments) people consider these same phenomena more predictable than they actually are and lower their vigilance of risk (Peterson, 2007).

CONCLUSIONS AND FURTHER RESEARCH

We hope that we have shown support for our hypotheses. Our main neuroeconomic hypothesis concerning the global credit crisis is that in financial markets greed and fear are balancing forces, because they have corresponding balancing emotional forces in the human brain (homeostasis). In the recent global credit crisis this homeostasis was out of balance and as a result untrammeled greed took over in investors' brains.

There are many lessons to be learned from the financial meltdown of 2008–09. The first is that all investments contain risk and the risk may be hidden. Sophisticated risk assessment models may quantify the risks that are identified, but in the old computer adage, 'garbage in, garbage out'. Experienced individual decision-makers are the best qualified to identify all the risks in a business decision and also to ask creative questions about what they might be overlooking.

Second, if you do not understand an investment vehicle, do not buy it. If you do not understand the nature of the risks in a business deal, do not do it. We may call this the 'Warren Buffet' rule or, if you prefer dark humor, the 'Bernie Madoff' rule. Buffet advised investors to stay away from the Internet stock bubble and from derivatives.

Third, from a management perspective, corporate traders need supervision as to their risk-taking. Since they are merely humans assessing risk, we have seen there is an entire spectrum of risk appetite among the various individuals and also a basket of investment biases that come with each employee. Managers need not 'run scared', but need to exercise constant benevolent vigilance over their employees.

Finally, there is a fascinating neuroeconomic and ideological vacuum that needs research. From the ideological point of view, we may frame the question, 'how free should markets be?' From the neuroeconomic perspective, 'how do we monitor the risk taking of our employees and of the institutions?' Further, 'how do we design safeguards and compensation systems that effectively motivate employees but also protect the institution?' These systems will work best if they are informed by what we know about the neuroeconomics of financial decision-making.

REFERENCES

Bechara, A., A. Damasio, H. Damasio and S. Anderson (1994), 'Insensitivity to future consequences following damage to human prefrontal cortex', *Cognition*, **50**, 7–15.

Bechara, A., H. Damasio, D. Tranel and A. Damasio (2005), 'The Iowa gambling test and the somatic marker hypothesis; some questions and answers', *Trends in Cognitive Sciences*, **9** (4), April, 159–62.

Beer, J., R. Knight and M. D'Esposito (2006), 'Controlling the integration of emotion and cognition: the role of frontal cortex in distinguishing helpful from hurtful emotional information', *Psychological Science*, **17**, May, 448–53.

Benartzi, S. and R.H. Thaler (1995), 'Myopic loss aversion and the equity premium puzzle', *Quarterly Journal of Economics*, **110** (1), February, 73–92.

Biais, B. et al. (2002), 'Psychological disposition and trading behavior', unpublished manuscript, quoted in Richard L. Peterson, 'The neuroscience of investing: fMRI of the reward system', *Brain Research Bulletin*, **67**, 391–7.

Camerer, C. and D. Lovallo (1999), 'Over-confidence and excess entry: an experimental approach,' *American Economic Review*, **89** (1), 306–18.

Camerer, C., G. Loewenstein and D. Prelec (2005), 'Neuroeconomics: how neuroscience can inform economics', *Journal of Economic Literature*, **34** (1), 9–65.

Chang, H.K. (2005), 'Emotions can negatively impact investment decisions', Stanford GSB, available at http://www.gsb.stanford.edu/news/research/finance_shiv_investmentdecisions.shtml (accessed September 2008).

Chen, M.K. and L.R. Lakshminarayanan (2006), 'How basic are behavioral biases? Evidence from capuchin monkey trading behavior', *Journal of Political Economy*, **114**, 517.

Choi, W.Y., P.D. Balsam and J.C. Horvitz (2005), 'Extended habit training reduces dopamine mediation of appetitive response expression', *Journal of Neuroscience*, **25**, 6729.

Damasio, A. (1999), *The Feeling of What Happens: Body and Emotion in the Making of Consequences*, New York: Harcourt Brace and Co.

Daw, N.D., J.P. O'Dougherty, P. Dayan, B. Seymour and R.J. Dolan (2006), 'Cortical substrates for exploratory decisions in humans', *Nature*, **441**, 15 June, 876–9.

De Martino, B., D. Kumaran, B. Seymour and R.J. Dolan (2006), 'Frames, biases and rational decision-making in the human brain', *Science*, **313** (5787), 684–7.

Economist, The (2009), 'Greed – and fear, a special report on the future of finance', 24 January, pp. 1–22.

Hauber, W. and S. Sommer (2009), 'Prefrontostriatal circuitry regulates effort-related decision making', *Cerebral Cortex*, 8 January, Advance publication online, 1–8.

Jennings, M.M. (2005), 'Ethics and investment management: true reform', *Financial Analysts Journal*, **61** (3), 45–58.

Kahneman, D., J.L. Knetsch and R.H. Thaler (1990), 'Experimental tests of the endowment effect and the Coase Theorem', *Journal of Political Economy*, **98**, 1325.

Knutson, B. and J.C. Cooper (2005), 'Functional magnetic resonance imaging of reward prediction', *Current Opinion in Neurology*, **18** (4), 411–17.

Koob, G.C. and M. Le Moal (1997), 'Drug abuse: hedonic homeostatic dysregulation', *Science*, **278** (5335), 52–8.

Körding, K. (2007), 'Decision theory: what "should" the nervous system do?', *Science*, **318** (5850), 26 October, 606–10.

Krugman, P. (2002), 'Greed is bad', *New York Times*, 4 June.

Kuhnen, C. and B. Knutson (2005), 'The neural basis of financial risk taking', *Neuron*, **47**, 1 September, 763–70.

Lerner, J., D. Small and G. Lowenstein (2004), 'Heartstrings and purse strings: carry-over effects of emotions on economic transactions', *Psychological Science*, **15**, 337–41.

Lo, A., D. Repin and B. Steenbarger (2005), 'Fear and greed in financial markets: a clinical study of day-traders', *American Economic Association Papers and Proceedings*, **95** (2), 352–9.

McEwen, B. (2002), *The End of Stress As We Know It*, Washington, DC: Joseph Henry Press.

McClure, S., D. Laibson, G. Loewenstein and J. Cohen (2004a), 'Separate neural systems value immediate and delayed monetary rewards', *Science*, **304** (5695), 503–7.

McClure, S., M. Gilzenrat and J. Cohen (2004b), 'An exploration–exploitation model based on noreprinephrine and dopamine activity', *Advances in Neural Information Processing Systems*, **18**, 867–74.

Mehra, R. (2003), 'The equity premium: why is it a puzzle?', *Financial Analysts Journal*, January/February, 54–69.

Ming, E., G. Adler, R. Kessler et al. (2004), 'Cardiovascular reactivity to work stress predicts subsequent onset of hypertension: the air traffic controller health change study', *Psychosomatic Medicine*, **66**.

O'Doherty J., M.L. Kringelbach, E.T. Rolls, J. Hornak and C. Andrews (2001), 'Abstract reward and punishment representations in the human orbitofrontal cortex', *Nature Neuroscience*, **4** (1), 95–102.

O'Doherty, J., P. Dayan, J. Schultz, R. Deichmann and K. Friston (2004), 'Dissociable roles of ventral and dorsal striatum in instrumental conditioning', *Science*, **304** (5669), 452–4.

Oswold, A. (1997), 'Happiness and economic performance', *Economic Journal*, **107**, 1815–31.

Paletta, D., D. Enrich and D. Fitzpatrick (2009), 'U.S. seeks to stem bank fears, White House plays down nationalization talks as stocks hit new bear-market low', *Wall Street Journal*, 21 February, p. A-1.

Paulus, M.P. (2007), 'Decision-making dysfunctions in psychiatry – altered homeostatic processing?', *Science*, **318** (5850), 602–6.

Peterson, R.L. (2005) 'The neuroscience of investing: fMRI of the reward system', *Brain Research Bulletin*, **67**, 391–7.

Peterson, R.L. (2007), *Inside the Investor's Brain*, Hoboken, NJ: Wiley Publishers.

Porter, D. and V. Smith (1994), 'Stock market bubbles in the laboratory', *Applied Mathematical Finance*, **1**, 111–27.

Postlewaite, A. and O. Compte (2005), 'Confidence-enhanced performance', *American Economic Review*, **94** (5), 1536–57.

Prentice, R.A. (2007), 'Ethical decision making: more needed than good intentions', *Financial Analysts Journal*, **63** (6), 17–30.

Rietveld, E. (2008), 'The skillful body as a concernful system of possible actions, phenomena and neurodynamics', *Theory and Psychology*, **18** (3), 341–63.

Roll, Richard (1986), 'The hubris hypothesis of corporate takeovers', *Journal of Business*, **59** (2), 197–216.

Schultz, W. and A. Dickinson (2000), 'Neuronal coding of prediction errors', *Annual Review of Neuroscience*, **23**, 473–500.

Shermer, M. (2008), *The Mind of the Market: How Biology and Psychology Shape Our Economic Lives*, New York, Henry Holt and Company.

Shiv, B., G. Loewenstein, A. Bechara et al. (2005), 'Investment behavior and the negative side of emotion', *Psychological Science*, **16** (6), 435–9.

Smith, A. (1776), *The Wealth of Nations*, reprinted with Introduction by A. Kruger [2003], New York: Bantam Dell Books (Random House).

Taylor, S., B. Martis, K.D. Fitzgerald et al. (2006), 'Medial frontal cortex activity and loss-related responses to errors', *Journal of Neuroscience*, **26** (15), 4063–70.

Tversky, A. and D. Kahneman (1992), 'Advances in prospect theory: cumulative representation of uncertainty', *Journal of Risk and Uncertainty*, **5**, 297–323.

Waldman, M. (1994), 'Systematic errors and the theory of natural selection', *American Economic Review*, **84** (3), 482–97.

Westeroff, F. (2004), 'Greed, fear and stock market dynamics', *Physica A*, **304**, 635–42, available at sciencedirect.com.

Xue, G., Z. Lu, I. Levin, J.A. Weller, X. Li and A. Bechara (2008), 'Functional dissociations of risk and reward processing in the medial prefrontal cortex', *Cerebral Cortex Advance Access*, published online 8 October 2008.

Yu, A. and P. Dayan (2005), 'Uncertainty, neuromodulation and attention', *Neuron*, **46**, 681–92.

Zald, D., R. Cowan, P. Riccardi et al. (2008), 'Midbrain dopamine receptor availability is inversely associated with novelty-seeking traits in humans', *Journal of Neuroscience*, **28** (53), 31 December, 14372–8.

Zweig, J. (2007), *Your Money and Your Brain, How the New Science of Neuroeconomics Can Help Make You Rich*, New York: Simon and Schuster.

PART 3

Inside the black box: decisions by hormones

This part contains four chapters, three of which visit deep inside the black box, examining the influence of hormones over decision-making. Part 3 starts with an introduction to stereotypes, a topic frequently shunned in the literature but which is taken seriously in these chapters, and is viewed in the context of the business environment inside the firm. While Chapter 6 looks at stereotypes in a more conventional way, chapters 7, 8 and 9 examine the foundation of stereotypes from the perspective of human physiology. Stereotyping is recognized by us all either consciously or unconsciously. Stereotypes are typically formed as a result of observing differing abilities, particularly in decision-making. The stereotypical differences and to what degree decisions may be swayed from staying neutral are to a large degree functions of genetic and biological sensitivity to environmental influence. How the environment may influence decision-making by activating certain hormones and how these may interfere with objective decision-making in the firm is analyzed in depth in the following chapters. The term 'stereotye' here is given a very different meaning from what the reader is familiar with.

6. In the words of Larry Summers: gender stereotypes and implicit beliefs in negotiations

Laura J. Kray, Connson C. Locke and Michael P. Haselhuhn

In January 2005 a firestorm erupted after Larry Summers, the President of Harvard University, remarked at a conference on 'Diversifying the science and engineering workforce' that men and women may differ in their 'availability of aptitude'. He put forth the admittedly controversial hypothesis that women may have less aptitude than men at the high end of the scale, which could explain women's relative absence in highly competitive scientific professions. By February 2006, Summers had abruptly resigned from the presidency, with his remarks endorsing gender stereotypes still reverberating on Harvard's campus and beyond.

The current chapter seeks to understand how the endorsement of gender stereotypes affects the performance of men and women in a stereotype-relevant domain. We explore how exposure to comments proposing innate sex differences in ability affects performance in a negotiation task requiring cooperation and competition. Building on previous research exploring the stereotype confirmation and reactance processes (Kray et al. 2001), we hypothesize that the blatant endorsement of gender stereotypes, as expressed in the words of Larry Summers, would have the ironic effect of impairing outcomes of male negotiators relative to their female counterparts. In Kray and colleagues' research, an experimenter explicitly endorsed the view that men and women differ in their negotiating abilities prior to having mixed-sex dyads engage in a quantifiable negotiation task. Doing so produced a counterintuitive effect: by gathering the wherewithal to disprove the stereotype, women actually outperformed, rather than underperformed, their male counterparts. In the current research we explored whether being reminded of Summers's comments would produce a similar pattern of results in this competitive context. We also hypothesized that how women respond to blatant stereotype endorsements, whether they react against the stereotype versus confirm it, would be moderated by their implicit beliefs about whether negotiating effective-ness is a natural talent versus a malleable skill that can be acquired (Kray and Haselhuhn, 2007). Specifically, we expected female negotiators who endorsed incremental theories, which propose negotiating ability is highly malleable, would perform better in the face of blatant stereotype endorse-ments than female negotiators who endorsed entity theories, which propose negotiating ability is highly fixed.

GENDER STEREOTYPES AND NEGOTIATION PERFORMANCE

Interest in how stereotypes impact the performance of their targets surged in the past decade, due in large part to Steele's (1997) stereotype threat theory. Steele posited that the existence of a negative stereotype about a group can produce an additional burden that members of the group shoulder when performing in stereotype-relevant domains. Regardless of whether the stereotyped group members believe the stereotype to be true, its mere existence can have a pernicious effect on their performance rela-tive to members of non-stigmatized groups.

Stereotype threat can impact negotiators (Kray et al., 2001). On average, women reap worse economic outcomes than men at the bargaining table (Kray and Thompson, 2005; Stuhlmacher and Walters, 1999; Walters et al., 1998) and the existence of a stereotype that women are less effective negotiators than men appears to contribute to this performance gap. Kray and colleagues demonstrated that men only enjoy an advantage in claim-ing resources over their female counterparts when a threat is 'in the air' That is, when the negotiation is perceived to be indicative of inherent abili-ties, women fall prey to stereotype threat. However, when the negotiation is perceived to be non-indicative of underlying abilities and instead just meant to provide an opportunity for learning, women and men divide the resources evenly.

Kray et al.'s (2001) research went beyond a simple demonstration of stereotype threat in negotiations by also demonstrating that women were not doomed to succumb to the negative stereotype concerning their nego-tiating ability. Building on Brehm's (1966) seminal work on psychological reactance, which occurs when people perceive that a limit is being placed on their freedom, Kray and colleagues showed that explicitly labeling women as inferior negotiators produced a reversal of the typical gender gap. Rather than exacerbating the typical male performance advantage, blatantly connecting gender stereotypes to expected performance led to a reversal whereby women actually outperformed their male counterparts.

'Stereotype reactance' describes the tendency to behave in a manner counter to what would be expected by a relevant stereotype. Making explicit the linkage between gender and expected performance led stereotypically disadvantaged women to set higher goals prior to the negotiation and to hold more firmly to those goals at the bargaining table. This research suggests the set of beliefs that negotiators bring with them to the bargaining table has powerful effects on performance.

The pattern of performance outcomes consistent with stereotype reactance runs counter to what would be expected by 'stereotype lift' (Walton and Cohen, 2003), which describes the performance boost resulting from the awareness of a negative stereotype concerning a group to which one does not belong. In the case of gender and negotiations, stereotype lift would suggest a performance boost for men after the endorsement of stereotypes suggesting women's inherent inferiority in this domain. In Kray et al.'s (2001) original demonstration of stereotype threat in negotiations, men did indeed experience a performance boost relative to women when the stereotype was activated subtly. However, when the stereotype was made blatant, men choked under the pressure of the positive stereotype. Instead of solidifying their identification with masculine traits suggesting a negotiation advantage, the blatant endorsement of stereotypes increased men's identification with weak traits that were stereotypically feminine, while simultaneously increasing women's identification with strong traits that were stereotypically masculine. In sum, male and female reactions to blatant stereotype endorsements accumulate to produce a reversal of the typical gender gap.

EXPERIMENT 1

Previous research has explicitly linked gender and stereotypes about negotiation ability in order to invoke stereotype reactance (Kray et al., 2001). In the current experiment we simply exposed participants to Larry Summers' s remarks concerning the abilities of men and women in science and engineering prior to the negotiation task. Even though his remarks were unrelated to negotiation, we reasoned that the endorsement of gender stereotypes in one domain would activate beliefs about gender differences in competitive contexts more generally. This activation, in turn, should impact negotiation performance between men and women.

We expected that the endorsement of gender stereotypes would improve the performance of women relative to men compared with baseline conditions. Because negotiations are mixed-motive, involving both the possibilities of cooperation and competition, we also considered the impact of stereotype endorsement on integrative negotiation performance. Because the activation of masculine stereotypes in the negotiation arena leads to more contentious behaviors and lowers joint gain (Kray et al., 2004), we also expected the more general endorsement of gender stereotypes to reduce joint outcomes.

Method

Overview and design
We included a gender stereotype endorsement and a control condition. All dyads were mixed-sex. Role assignments (candidate, recruiter) were counterbalanced across gender.

Participants
Participants were 208 undergraduate students who either received credit for a course requirement or $15. Three dyads were excluded for failing to complete all task materials, leaving 101 dyads.

Procedure
Participants were informed that they would participate in three unrelated tasks. The first task contained the stereotype endorsement manipulation, the second was an unrelated filler task and the third task was the negotiation.

Stereotype endorsement manipulation
Participants completed a 'Campus News' survey, purportedly to gauge their awareness of current events on college campuses. Participants read three news stories and indicated their degree of familiarity with each story on a seven-point Likert scale of 1 (never heard of it) to 7 (very familiar with the details) and also indicated how each story made them feel on a seven-point Likert scale from -3 (very negative) to 3 (very positive). After reading two unrelated stories, participants in the gender stereotype endorsement condition read:

> Harvard University: President Summers claims innate differences are responsible for the low number of top women scientists. At a conference in January, the President of Harvard University, Lawrence Summers, addressed the issue of the imbalance of men and women in top science and engineering jobs. In a controversial speech, he claimed one of the reasons was a difference in 'intrinsic aptitude' between men and women, making men more likely to be found in top positions in the science and engineering fields.

The control group read a paragraph of similar length regarding a dance floor built by MIT students.

Negotiation task
The negotiation task concerned an employment negotiation in which a job candidate and a recruiter negotiated eight issues relevant to both parties, such as salary and benefits. Negotiators' preferences were induced by assigning points to issues (maximum 13 200). Two issues were distributive such that the parties' preferences were completely opposed. Two issues were compatible such that the parties' preferences were identical. The remaining issues had integrative potential such that negotiators could concede on a less important issue in exchange for being granted their preference on a more highly valued issue. The dependent variables were the number of points earned individually and jointly.

Pre-negotiation measures
After reading the negotiation materials, but before learning the identity of their negotiating partner, participants indicated their intended competitiveness on a Likert scale of 1 (not at all competitive) to 9 (extremely competitive). They also indicated their mood on a Likert scale of 1 (very negative) to 9 (very positive). Upon completion of these pre-task measures, dyads were formed and they were given 20 minutes to negotiate. All procedures were approved by the university's Institutional Review Board and each participant signed a consent form before participating.

Results and Discussion

Preliminary analyses and overview of hypothesis-testing strategy
First, we determined that neither role assignment (whether the male versus the female negotiator was assigned the role of job candidate) nor the type of payment (course credit versus cash payment) influenced our dependent variables. As a result we excluded those factors from the analyses reported below. Second, we confirmed our findings using non-parametric tests. The results mirrored those from the parametric tests reported below. Below we report results of analyses of variance (*F*-ratio and *p*-value) and effect size estimates (eta-squared, η^2), in addition to descriptive information about means (*M*) and standard deviations (*SD*).

Manipulation check
Because only participants in the stereotype endorsement condition read the Larry Summers story, we conducted a one-way ANOVA comparing male and female reactions within that condition only. As expected, female participants ($M = -1.85$, $SD = 1.35$) felt significantly worse about the story than male participants ($M = -0.64$, $SD = 1.24$), $F(1, 120) = 26.70$, $p < 0.001$, $\eta^2 = 0.18$. The difference in familiarity with the story between

men ($M = 3.87$, $SD = 2.43$) and women ($M = 3.43$, $SD = 2.28$) was not statistically significant, $F(1, 120) = 1.08$, $p = 0.30$. In the control condition differences in male and female responses to the MIT story were not statistically significant, either in terms of affect (men: $M = 1.05$, $SD = 1.20$; women: $M = 1.43$, $SD = 1.11$; $F(1, 78) = 2.12$, $p = .15$) or familiarity (men: $M = 1.08$, $SD = 0.47$; women: $M = 1.00$, $SD = 0.00$; $F(1, 78) = 1.00$, $p = 0.32$).

Intended competitiveness

To analyze how competitive negotiators intended to be, we conducted a two-way ANOVA, with gender and stereotype endorsement as between-subject factors. We observed a significant Gender X Stereotype Endorsement interaction, $F(1, 198) = 6.11$, $p < 0.01$, $\eta^2 = 0.03$. Whereas men ($M = 6.80$, $SD = 1.57$) intended to be more competitive than women ($M = 5.85$, $SD = 1.89$) in the control condition ($F(1, 78) = 5.98$, $p < 0.05$, $\eta^2 = 0.07$), the difference in intended competitiveness between women ($M = 6.30$, $SD = 1.88$) and men ($M = 5.98$, $SD = 1.71$) was not statistically significant in the stereotype endorsement condition, $F(1, 120) = 0.92$, $p = 0.34$. Alternatively, men intended to be less competitive in the stereotype endorsement condition compared to the control condition ($F(1, 99) = 5.87$, $p < 0.05$, $\eta^2 = 0.06$) yet the difference in women's intentions across conditions was not statistically significant, $F(1, 99) = 1.35$, $p = 0.25$.

Mood

No effects were statistically significant.

Negotiation performance

We conducted a mixed-model ANOVA on negotiator points, with stereotype endorsement as a between-dyad factor and gender as a within-dyad factor. Consistent with our hypothesis, the two-way interaction between gender and stereotype endorsement was statistically significant, $F(1, 99) = 4.13$, $p < 0.05$, $\eta^2 = 0.04$. Women ($M = 5410$, $SD = 2471$) outperformed men ($M = 3738$, $SD = 2581$) in the stereotype endorsement condition ($F(1, 60) = 8.06$, $p < 0.01$, $\eta^2 = 0.12$), but women ($M = 4820$, $SD = 2509$) and men ($M = 5125$, $SD = 2928$) performed comparably in the control condition, $F(1, 39) = 0.15$, $p = 0.70$. Alternatively, men performed worse in the stereotype endorsement condition compared to the control condition ($F(1, 99) = 6.27$, $p < 0.01$, $\eta^2 = 0.06$), yet the difference in women's performance across conditions was not statistically significant, $F(1, 99) = 1.36$, $p = 0.25$.

Joint gain

We also examined the degree to which negotiators were able to expand the pie by examining joint gain, or the dyadic-level point total, with a one-way ANOVA. Consistent with our hypothesis, joint gain was lower in the stereotype endorsement condition ($M = 9148$, $SD = 2091$) relative to the control condition ($M = 9945$, $SD = 2074$), $F(1, 99) = 3.53$, $p = 0.06$, $\eta^2 = 0.03$. To determine the source of this difference, we examined each type of negotiation issue separately. Scores on compatible issues, where parties' preferences were identical, were significantly lower in the stereotype endorsement condition ($M = 895$, $SD = 527$) compared to the control condition ($M = 1103$, $SD = 335$), $F(1, 99) = 4.89$, $p < 0.05$, $\eta^2 = 0.05$. On the integrative issues, the two-way interaction between gender and stereotype endorsement was marginally significant, $F(1, 99) = 3.71$, $p = 0.06$, $\eta^2 = 0.04$. Women ($M = 6003$, $SD = 1527$) outperformed men ($M = 4945$, $SD = 1638$) in the stereotype endorsement condition, $F(1, 60) = 9.00$, $p < 0.001$, $\eta^2 = 0.13$, while in the control condition women ($M = 5670$, $SD = 1404$) and men ($M = 5670$, $SD = 1719$) performed comparably, $F(1, 39) = 0.00$, $p = 1.00$. On the distributive issues, no effects were statistically significant, all $F(1, 99) < 1.60$, $p > 0.21$.

Relationship between intended competitiveness and negotiation performance

We conducted an analysis to better understand the relationship between intended competitiveness and individual negotiation performance. To do so, we created scores within each dyad representing each negotiator's intended competitiveness and each negotiator's individual performance. We then examined the zero-order correlations among variables (Table 6.1). As expected, women's and men's performance were negatively related, $r(101) = -0.69$, $p < 0.001$. More importantly for understanding the relationship between gender and performance was the observation that the intended competitiveness of female negotiators was positively

Table 6.1   Experiment 1: intercorrelations between individual intended competitiveness and negotiation performance

Variable	1	2	3	4	5
1. Female competitiveness	—				
2. Male competitiveness	−0.03	—			
3. Female score	0.31**	0.07	—		
4. Male score	−0.13	0.06	−0.69***	—	
5. Joint score	0.20*	0.16	0.27**	0.51***	—

Note: $*p < 0.05$, $**p < 0.01$, $***p < 0.001$.

related to their negotiation performance, $r(101) = 0.31$, $p < 0.001$. This relationship held true in both the stereotype endorsement ($r(61) = 0.31$, $p < 0.05$) and control conditions ($r(40) = 0.29$, $p = 0.07$). For men, intended competitiveness did not predict performance, $r(101) = 0.06$, $p = 0.56$. No other effects were significant.

These results elucidate the impact of explicitly endorsing gender stereotypes on competition between the sexes. This experiment demonstrates that exposure to comments by a high status public figure endorsing gender differences in competitive contexts can trigger stereotype reactance, whereby women outperform men, rather than stereotype lift, which would predict men outperforming women. Consistent with past research (Kray et al., 2001, Experiment. 1), men and women divided the pie relatively evenly under baseline conditions, yet women outperformed men after exposure to Summers's comments.

The impact of gender stereotypes on negotiation performance is a function of both the male and female negotiator (ibid., Experiment 2), yet the current findings suggest the impact of stereotype endorsement in mixed-gender negotiations was driven largely by men's performance. Like the pattern of outcome data, men's intentions to behave competitively varied across stereotype endorsement conditions. In contrast, women's competitive intentions were stable across conditions. These data clearly suggest a greater sensitivity to Summers's message for men than women.

Although men adjusted their intentions and performance on the basis of Summers's stereotype endorsement, a greater gap between intentions and behaviors emerged for men than women. In the control condition men intended to be more competitive than women yet performed comparably; in the stereotype endorsement condition men intended to be as competitive as women yet performed worse. This disconnect could simply reflect the fact that men are more confident than women in negotiations (Kray and Thompson, 2005), leading them to underestimate their counterpart's resolve. Alternatively, it could reflect the fact that negotiators were unaware of the gender of their negotiating partner at the time at which they indicated their intended competitiveness. Once men realized their partner was the unfortunate target of Summers's comments, they may have revised their negotiating strategy to be chivalrous (Pruitt et al., 1986). Although both of these explanations address men's behavior, they do not capture the strong link between women's intentions and behaviors, particularly following exposure to Summers's comments. In this mixed-gender context women's resolve to carry out their intentions was stronger than men's. All told, the pattern of results suggests that the goals and beliefs negotiators bring with them to the bargaining table are powerful determinants of how value is claimed.

Although Larry Summers's comments had a salutary effect on women's value claiming relative to men's, this benefit was offset by a reduction in value creation achieved by dyads. Joint gain is produced through the exchange of information (Thompson, 1991) and it appears that Summers's comments reduced this behavior. Interestingly, compatible issues, those in which negotiators had identical preferences, drove the reduction in joint gain. Apparently, being reminded of the Larry Summers' controversy surrounding innate differences between men and women exacerbated the lose–lose effect (Thompson and Hrebec, 1996), whereby parties fail to realize they have the same preferences and instead settle on an outcome inferior to their alternatives.

EXPERIMENT 2

This experiment further explores the cognitive and motivational drivers of performance in mixed-gender negotiations. In particular, we identify a moderator of stereotype reactance: implicit negotiation beliefs. Building on Dweck and Leggett's (1998) exploration of implicit theories, Kray and Haselhuhn (2007) determined that negotiators' implicit beliefs about whether negotiating prowess is a skill that can be developed versus a fixed trait have powerful effects on negotiation performance. Specifically, negotiators who view negotiating ability as malleable (incremental theorists) tend to perform better than negotiators who view negotiating ability as fixed (entity theorists). Whereas incremental theorists tend to persist in the face of obstacles to success, entity theorists tend to withdraw effort in the face of challenges (Dweck and Leggett, 1988). The negotiation arena's tension between competition and cooperation creates challenges that then distinguish these different belief systems.

We extend this research by examining whether implicit negotiation beliefs influence how individuals respond to the endorsement of gender stereotypes. We hypothesized that stereotype reactance, which requires gathering the wherewithal to disprove the blatant endorsement of a negative stereotype by holding firm to one's competitive intentions, would require a belief that effort and persistence are key contributors to negotiation success. As such, we expected to see evidence of stereotype reactance only among incremental theorists. To test this hypothesis, we manipulated negotiators' implicit negotiation beliefs and then exposed negotiators to the blatant endorsement of the view that stereotypically masculine traits predict negotiation success. Kray et al. (2001) demonstrated that stereotype reactance occurs following the explicit linkage of gender to negotiation effectiveness. We examined whether this relationship is moderated by negotiators' implicit beliefs.

Method

Overview
The experiment involved a 2 (incremental verses entity implicit negotiation theory) × 2 (male verses female negotiator) mixed-model design. All dyads were mixed-sex. Role assignments (candidate, recruiter) were counterbalanced across gender.

Participants
Thirty undergraduate students participated in partial fulfillment of a class requirement, resulting in a sample of 15 dyads.

Procedure: implicit negotiation theory manipulation
Participants in all conditions were told that we were interested in how novices negotiate and how training materials can compensate for lack of experience. Following Kray and Haselhuhn's (2005) method for manipulating implicit negotiation beliefs, participants read one of two articles designed to elicit incremental or entity beliefs. Participants in the incremental condition read an article entitled 'negotiation ability is changeable and can be developed'. The article stated 'While it used to be believed that negotiating was a fixed skill that people were either born with or not, experts in the field now believe that negotiating is a dynamic skill that can be cultivated and developed over a lifetime' and 'No one's negotiation character is hard like a rock that cannot be changed.' These statements were supported by results from several fictional studies concluding negotiation ability is highly malleable. Participants in the entity ability condition read an article entitled 'Negotiation ability, like plaster, is pretty stable over time'. This article stated 'While it used to be believed that negotiating ability was a bundle of potentialities, each of which could be developed, experts in the field now believe that people possess a finite set of rather fixed negotiating skills' and 'In most of us, by the age of ten, our negotiation ability has set like plaster and will never soften again.' These statements were supported by results from several fictional studies concluding negotiation ability is very difficult to change. Both negotiators in each dyad read the same essay. After reading the essay, participants were asked, 'To what degree is negotiation a skill that can be developed?' and replied on a scale of 1 (not at all) to 7 (extremely).

After receiving the implicit negotiation theory manipulation, participants were given materials to prepare for the negotiation. Using the same procedure as Kray et al. (2001), the endorsement of gender stereotypes was embedded in the role materials. A cover sheet informed participants that the negotiation exercise is extremely challenging for novice negotiators, and as such, it allows for the experimenters to obtain a true measure of each negotiator's strengths and limitations. Participants were next told that past research had linked gender-relevant traits to success in this negotiation. Specifically, participants were told that 'The most successful negotiators in negotiations like the one that you'll do today are rational, assertive, and demonstrate a regard for their own interests. Negotiators who display these skills do better than those who are emotional, passive, and overly accommodating.' Following this information, the link between masculinity and the success-related traits was explicitly stated. Specifically, participants were told '*Because these personality characteristics tend to vary across gender, male and female students have been shown to differ in their performance on this task.*' This information was italicized to enhance the explicit communication of the stereotype endorsement.

Negotiation task
We used the same negotiation task as in Experiment 1. All procedures were approved by the university's Institutional Review Board and each participant signed a consent form before participating.

Results and Discussion

Preliminary analysis and hypothesis testing strategy
As in the previous experiment, we first confirmed that role assignment did not influence outcomes. We also confirmed that the use of non-parametric tests did not alter results obtained through parametric tests, reported below.

Implicit negotiation belief manipulation check
Individuals who read the incremental essay ($M = 6.00$, $SD = 0.82$) rated negotiation ability as significantly more developable than those who read the entity essay ($M = 4.14$, $SD = 1.92$), $F(1, 28) = 12.49$, $p < 0.001$.

Negotiation performance
To test our hypotheses concerning stereotype reactance, a mixed-model ANOVA was conducted with gender as a within-dyad variable and dyad beliefs (incremental, entity) as a between-dyad measure. Means and standard deviations are shown in Table 6.2. As predicted, the interaction between gender and dyad beliefs was significant, $F(1, 13) = 4.81$, $p < 0.05$, $\eta^2 = 0.37$. No other effects were statistically significant. Simple effect analyses revealed that females outperformed males when the dyad held incremental beliefs, $t(26) = 2.59$, $p < 0.05$; yet male and female performance did not differ when negotiators held entity beliefs, $t(26) = -1.08$, $p =$

Table 6.2   Experiment 2: means and standard deviations of negotiation performance by implicit theory and gender

Implicit theory	Gender	
	Male	Female
Entity	5057.14 (2304.24)	3857.14 (2002.38)
Incremental	3787.50 (2372.12)	6487.50 (1591.40)

0.29. To determine the source of these performance differences, we examined the effects of negotiation beliefs within each gender. Females performed significantly better when they held incremental beliefs compared to when they held entity beliefs, $t(26) = 2.44$, $p < 0.05$; male performance did not significantly differ between the incremental and entity belief conditions, $t(26) = -1.18$, $p = 0.25$.

Although the pattern of data clearly shows that incremental beliefs led to better performance for female negotiators than entity beliefs, the lack of a control condition leaves open the question of whether incremental beliefs improved performance or entity beliefs decreased performance. To aid in our establishment of baseline measures, we obtained the raw data from Kray et al. 2001, Experiment 4) and then reanalyzed the control and reactance conditions, comparing the means to the current results. Using the same negotiation task, Kray and colleagues reported that female performance improved when the gender stereotype was blatantly endorsed ($M = 5666.67$, $SD = 2138.54$) compared to a control condition ($M = 2655.56$, $SD = 2567.15$), $t(38) = 2.93$, $p < 0.01$, while male performance decreased in the presence of the negative stereotype ($M = 2525.00$, $SD = 1883.00$) compared to a control condition ($M = 5655.55$, $SD = 2845.22$), $t(38) = 3.04$, $p < 0.01$.

Mirroring this pattern, females in the incremental condition from the current study demonstrated better performance compared to Kray and colleagues' control condition, $t(30) = 3.27$, $p < 0.01$. Male performance, however, did not significantly differ between the incremental and control conditions, $t(30) = -1.59$, $p = 0.12$. When dyads held entity beliefs in the current study, neither females ($t(28) = 0.96$, $p = 0.35$) nor males ($t(28) = -0.48$, $p = 0.64$) differed from Kray and colleagues' respective control conditions. By comparing the current results to these published data, we are able to conclude that incremental beliefs did indeed promote stereotype reactance and that female negotiators primarily drove this effect. When negotiators held entity beliefs, female negotiators failed to gather the wherewithal to react against the blatant endorsement of stereotypes that reflected negatively on them.

Prior research demonstrated that explicitly endorsing gender stereotypes promotes reactance among members of the negatively stereotyped group (Kray et al., 2001, 2004). The current study demonstrates reactance depends on negotiators' implicit beliefs. Just as Kray et al. (2004) demonstrated that the ability to react is limited when women are at a power disadvantage due to a lack of viable alternatives to the current negotiation, this study suggests that women who endorse entity beliefs may be at a power disadvantage due to the doubt that this theory casts on the role of effort and persistence in negotiation success. By adopting the view that good negotiators are born that way, entity theorists failed to disprove negative stereotypes associated with their social groups.

GENERAL DISCUSSION

The current research broadens our understanding of how individuals respond to positive and negative stereotypes about the social groups to which they belong. First, we demonstrated that the blatant endorsement of gender stereotypes by a prominent figure can produce behavior that contradicts the stereotype. We observed that simply being reminded of Larry Summers's comments regarding innate differences between men and women had a powerful effect on negotiated agreements in mixed-gender dyads. Being reminded of the Summers's controversy improved women's performance relative to men's performance despite the fact that his comments referred to a different competitive context altogether. This contagion from one domain (science and engineering) to another domain (negotiations) implies the endorsement of stereotypes is powerful indeed. In addition to reversing the typical gender gap, Summers's comments reduced the joint outcomes of negotiators by causing them to fail to recognize where they had compatible interests. Conceptually, this research is important because it demonstrates that members of positively stereotyped groups do not always exhibit stereotype lift following the endorsement of an outgroup's negative stereotype.

Another contribution of this research is the observation that stereotype reactance is moderated by negotiators' implicit beliefs regarding the malleability of negotiation performance. Only female negotiators who were led to believe that negotiating effectively is a skill that can be developed reacted against the blatant endorsement of negative stereotypes about their gender. The intense motivational state characteristic of psychological reactance (Brehm, 1966) goes hand-in-hand with the incremental theorists' willingness to expend effort in the face of challenges (in this case the blatant stereotype that women are inferior negotiators).

Past research has linked implicit theories to the endorsement of stereotypes (Levy et al. 1998) with entity theorists more likely to endorse stereotypes than incremental theorists. Likewise, incremental theorists have been shown to pay greater attention to and excel at recognizing stereotype-inconsistent information compared to entity theorists (Plaks et al., 2001). The current research builds on these findings by demonstrating for the first time that incremental theorists are more likely to behave in a manner inconsistent with negative stereotypes than entity theorists. By embracing the belief that success results from hard work rather than hard-wiring, incrementalists are less constrained by societal stereotypes.

Given the different manipulations used across the two studies, a natural question to ask is whether the impact of implicit negotiation beliefs demonstrated in Experiment 2 would also occur with the stereotype endorsement manipulation employed in Experiment 1. To answer this question, we exposed a separate sample of 52 participants to the synopsis of the Larry Summers's controversy used in Experiment 1 and then had them indicate the degree to which they believed his assertions were valid before they completed a scale measuring their implicit negotiation beliefs. We found a strong relationship between endorsement of President Summers's comments and negotiators' implicit beliefs. The more valid his comments were perceived to be, the less likely individuals were to endorse the view that negotiating ability is malleable, $r(52) = -0.38, p < 0.01$. More interestingly, this pattern was driven entirely by the female respondents, $r(26) = -0.63, p < 0.001$. For male respondents, the relationship between their endorsement of Summers's comments and their implicit negotiation beliefs was not statistically significant, $r(26) = -0.23, p = 0.27$. Consistent with the findings of Experiment 2 using a different manipulation, these findings suggest that the women most likely to react against Summers's comments are those who adopt the incremental viewpoint.

Understanding the process by which individuals overcome negative stereotypes in negotiations is critical for promoting equality, as the well-documented gender gap in wages often starts at the bargaining table (Kray and Thompson, 2005). By determining that the endorsement of gender stereotypes can trigger stereotype reactance, the current research suggests that political incorrectness can have ironically positive consequences. However, this same stereotype endorsement led to a decrement in joint performance due to a failure to recognize common interests (Thompson and Hrebec, 1996). Finally, by implicating negotiators' implicit beliefs as a moderator of stereotype reactance, we provide a tool for stereotypically disadvantaged group members seeking to improve their negotiating performance: the relatively straightforward belief that improvement is possible.

REFERENCES

Brehm, J.W. (1966). *A Theory of Psychological Reactance*, New York: Academic.

Dweck, C.S. and E.L. Leggett (1988), 'A social-cognitive approach to motivation and personality', *Psychological Review*, **95**, 256–73.

Kray, L.J. and M. Haselhuhn (2005), 'Implicit negotiation theories', Academy of Management Meetings, Honolulu, HI.

Kray, L.J, and M. Haselhuhn (2007), 'Implicit negotiation beliefs and performance: longitudinal and experimental evidence', *Journal of Personality and Social Psychology*, **93**, 49–64.

Kray, L.J. and L. Thompson (2005), 'Gender stereotypes and negotiation performance: a review of theory and research', in B. Staw and R. Kramer (eds), *Research in Organizational Behavior Series*, Vol. 26, pp. 103–82.

Kray, L.J., L. Thompson and A. Galinsky (2001), 'Battle of the sexes: gender stereotype confirmation and reactance in negotiation', *Journal of Personality and Social Psychology*, **80**, 942–58.

Kray, L.J., J. Reb, A. Galinsky and L. Thompson (2004), 'Stereotype reactance at the bargaining table: the effect of stereotype activation and power on claiming and creating value', *Personality and Social Psychology Bulletin*, **30**, 399–411.

Levy, S.R., S.J. Stroessner and C.S. Dweck (1998), 'Stereotype formation and endorsement: the role of implicit theories', *Journal of Personality and Social Psychology*, **74**, 1421–36.

Plaks, J.E., S.J. Stroessner, C.S. Dweck and J.W. Sherman (2001), 'Person theories and attention allocation: preferences for stereotypic versus counter-stereotypic information', *Journal of Personality and Social Psychology*, **80**, 876–93.

Pruitt, D.G., P.J.D. Carnevale, B. Forcey and M. Van Slyck (1986), 'Gender effects in negotiation: constituent surveillance and contentious behavior', *Journal of Experimental Social Psychology*, **22**, 264–75.

Steele, C.M. (1997), 'A threat in the air: how stereotypes shape intellectual identity and performance', *American Psychologist*, **52**, 613–29.

Stuhlmacher, A.F. and A.E. Walters (1999), 'Gender differences in negotiation outcome: a meta-analysis', *Personnel Psychology*, **52**, 653–77.

Thompson, L. (1991), 'Information exchange in negotiation', *Journal of Experimental Social Psychology*, **27**, 161–79.

Thompson, L. and D. Hrebec (1996), 'Lose–lose agreements in interdependent decision making', *Psychological Bulletin*, **120**, 396–409.

Walters, A.E., A.F. Stuhlmacher and L.L. Meyer (1998), 'Gender and negotiator competitiveness: a meta-analysis', *Organizational Behavior and Human Decision Processes*, **76**, 1–29.

Walton, G.M. and G.L. Cohen (2003), 'Stereotype lift', *Journal of Experimental Social Psychology*, **39**, 456–67.

7. Ovulatory shifts in women's social motives and behaviors: implications for corporate organizations

Kristina M. Durante and Gad Saad

INTRODUCTION

More than ever before, women wield significant power and influence in today's economy as consumers, employees and/or employers. In the USA, women control nearly 80 percent of all household spending decisions and women bring in at least half or more of the income in 55 percent of households (Barletta, 2007). Further, women now hold high-ranking positions in the workforce, some equal to or higher than that of men. In US corporations women constitute 50 percent of managers and professionals (ibid.). Worldwide, the number of women employed in the workforce grew by almost 200 million over the past decade. In 2007 there were 1.2 billion women in the workforce compared to 1.8 billion men (International Labour Office, Geneva, 2008), indicating that the gap is steadily closing. In the USA, women held 14.8 percent of the corporate board-appointed officer positions at Fortune 500 companies, and 12 women held the position of CEO in 2007 (Catalyst Census, 2007; *Fortune*, 2007). Currently, female enrollment in MBA programs worldwide has reached 30 percent and will likely continue to grow (Damast, 2007).

As women's spending power and role in the workforce strengthens, marketers and corporate managers stand to benefit from a better understanding of the dynamics of female social motivations and behavior. One important determinant of women's behaviors, cognitions and emotions is the hormonal changes that occur across the menstrual cycle. Shifts in hormonal status across the cycle likely impact a woman's decision-making both in the marketplace and in organizational settings. For example, research suggests that a woman's fertility status can increase social competition with other women (Durante, 2008; Fisher, 2004). In the consumption arena a woman's menstrual cycle has a profound effect on her choice of dress (ibid.; Grammer et al., 2004; Haselton et al., 2007; Saad and Strenstrom, in preparation), her spending patterns (Durante et al., in preparation), and how much she eats and what she prefers to eat (Fessler, 2002, 2003; Saad and Stenstrom, in preparation). Other scholars have explored whether a woman's cognitive ability (Farage and Osborn, 2008), economic decision-making (Chen et al., 2007; Lucas et al., 2007; Pearson and Schipper, 2009), social judgment (Senior et al., 2007) and performance as an employee (Black and Koulis-Chitwood, 1990; Miller et al., 2007) is affected by her menstrual cycle. What is lacking is an understanding of how a woman's fertility status affects her performance in the corporate setting. In this chapter we present an evolutionary model of female social behavior to address this lacuna but more generally to explore the myriad of ways that a woman's menstrual cycle phase might affect her functioning in the business setting.

FEMALE SOCIAL BEHAVIOR: THEORETICAL BACKGROUND

In order to understand the functions of female social behavior and the variations in behavior that occur across the menstrual cycle, it is important to highlight the ancestral selection pressures that played a key role in forging women's social motivations. From an evolutionary perspective, the most important decisions that humans make are those that contribute to survival and reproduction. Those individuals who are best able to optimize their reproductive success pass on their genes to future generations.

The costs and benefits of reproduction are very different for men and women (Trivers, 1972). First, the energetic costs of ovum production are quite high, while the production of viable sperm requires little in the form of energetic expenditure (Daly and Wilson, 1983; Ellison, 2001). Post-puberty, men's fertility is not as sensitive to the age and health of the individual as is women's. Second, for women, the minimum obligatory investment in offspring survival is nine months of gestation followed by a period of nursing. Men, on the other hand, are not beholden to invest in offspring beyond the time it takes to complete the act of intercourse. However, compared to most mammals, human offspring are born relatively helpless and experience a lengthy juvenile period that requires continuous parental investment (Kaplan et al., 2000). Ancestrally, infants who received investment from the father were more likely to survive than those who received little to no paternal investment and/or care (Geary, 2000). Thus, women who were able to secure a long-term partner who invested resources in themselves and offspring obtained a colossal survival advantage.

Contemporary women are in a better position to garner material resources without the assistance of a male partner. However, the ability of a woman to bring home a paycheck equal to or greater than that of a man is a relatively new phenomenon, particularly in the context of deep evolutionary time. Although ancestral women contributed to their own subsistence and that of their kin and mates, evidence suggests that men generated a greater amount of resources (for example, food) that were subsequently allocated to women and resulting offspring (cf. Marlowe, 2001). Even today, the support of an investing male partner often confers a significant advantage to women and their children alike.

As the foregoing review indicates, compared to men, women's mating decisions often carry greater weight and the potentially high cost of reproduction impacts women's day-to-day decision-making, preferences and behaviors. Given that women's reproductive years are constrained (for example, fertility declines precipitously at age 35; Bunting and Boivin, 2008) and in light of the fact that the greatest reproductive fitness benefits that women can gain in their lifetime are limited to a brief window within the menstrual cycle (for example, approximately three days within a 28-day cycle; Eichner and Timpe, 2004), changes in fertility status should shift women's behaviors in adaptive ways. Research has unveiled various psychological adaptations in response to shifts in women's fertility status, these having a potential impact on the manner in which men and women relate to colleagues within organizations.

OVULATORY SHIFTS IN MATING MOTIVATIONS

Women with normal cycles experience certain shifts in mate preference that may have implications for workplace relations. Near ovulation, women experience increases in self-perceived attractiveness and feelings of sexiness, as well as a greater desire to attend social gatherings (Haselton and Gangestad, 2006). Women also become more flirtatious (Gangestad et al., 2002; ibid.) and experience greater sexual desire and more frequent sexual fantasies during the fertile window of the cycle (Bullivant et al., 2004). Evidence suggests that this desire is directed toward men who display indicators of good genetic fitness. For example, near ovulation women are more attracted to men with symmetrical and masculine faces (Penton-Voak and Perrett, 2000; Penton-Voak et al., 1999; Thornhill and Gangestad, 2003; Thornhill et al., 2003), those who display greater social dominance (Gangestad et al., 2004) and those possessing deeper voices (Puts, 2005). Additional evidence indicates that the ovulatory increase in preference for these traits is directed toward non-primary partners

(Gangestad et al., 2002), particularly if a woman's primary partner lacks specific indicators of genetic fitness (cf. Garver-Apgar et al., 2006). Research suggests that women prefer these dominant men for short-term relationships (Gangestad et al., 2007) and are more likely to have an affair and less likely to use contraception mid-cycle, when fertility is highest (Baker, 1996; Baker and Bellis, 1995; Bellis and Baker, 1990). Because it is difficult to obtain a partner who is both a good provider and has good genes, many women have to trade-off between having a long-term mate who provides continual material resources, or more physically attractive, short-term sexual partners possessing good genes (Gangestad and Simpson, 2000). Recent research has found that women with high levels of estradiol (a hormone critical to female reproductive viability; Lipson and Ellison, 1996) are more attracted to men with higher levels of testosterone – a marker of a man's dominance and health (Roney and Simmons, 2008), and more likely to mate outside their current romantic relationship (Durante and Li, 2009).

Workplace Implications

Social dominance and entrepreneurship are associated with high levels of testosterone (Mazur and Booth, 1998; Mehta et al., 2008; White et al., 2007) and high testosterone levels in men are associated with continued interest in sexual opportunities (McIntyre et al., 2006). Currently, corporate leadership positions are predominantly held by men (Catalyst Census, 2007). If women display differential preference to socially dominant men at high fertility, women may find themselves more attracted to men holding leadership roles within the corporation at high fertility compared to low fertility. If women are more attracted to socially dominant men and become more flirtatious at high fertility, they may unknowingly find themselves in situations that can lead to instances of sexual harassment. For example, smiling more at male co-workers, or touching a shoulder or arm during a business meeting can create intersexual discord within the workplace. Research has shown that men over-perceive a woman's sexual intent (Haselton, 2003). Because reproduction is much less costly for men, they are more open to having multiple sexual partners and engaging in sexual liaisons than are women. For a man, a smile can convey sexual interest when, for the woman, she intends only to be friendly. Thus, the slightest change in female flirtation when fertility is high can increase the likelihood that men perceive a sexual opportunity, regardless of whether or not a woman would respond to a sexual advance. Further, some women (for example, younger, single or highly fertile women) may be attracted to organizations with a significantly male-skewed upper-management sex ratio (for example, computer technology, automotive, investment banking) and, thus, may be more likely to pursue romantic relationships with male co-workers in such corporate settings. When a woman's fertility is highest within the menstrual cycle, this is precisely the time when she may be most open to engage in an intra-office romantic encounter.

Although scientists have long believed that ovulation in humans is concealed from outside observers (for example, Burt, 1992), a growing body of research has documented men's evolved capacity to identify outward cues to female fertility (Gangestad et al., 2002; Singh and Bronstad, 2001; Thornhill et al., 2003). For example, men rate women higher in facial attractiveness near ovulation (Roberts et al., 2004), which can also influence perceptions of female co-workers. Shifts in fertility status may increase the likelihood that male supervisors favor a particular female co-worker over another. This can lead to biases in the quantity and quality of assigned workload. Also, male corporate executives may be influenced by a woman's fertility status when making hiring decisions and, consequently, be more likely to hire a highly fertile woman with the subconscious agenda of pursuing a possible mating opportunity.

Accordingly, our evolutionary-based model of female social behavior would predict that, for women, instances of sexual harassment within organizations should increase at high fertility. However, if women become more flirtatious at high fertility, and the flirtation is directed toward high-status, dominant and, thus, high-quality men, the reporting of instances of sexual harassment should be lower at high fertility compared to low fertility. In other words, if women desire men of high dominance, attractiveness and/or status more so at high fertility, they should be less likely to reject or be offended by the romantic advances of such men.

The effect of fertility status on the likelihood of intra-office flirtation, sexual harassment, favoritism, biases in workload assignments and hiring can hinder, as well as improve, a woman's chance of corporate advancement. Our brains are not well equipped to shut off our penchant to solve adaptive problems (for example, finding a high-quality mate when fertility is highest) when we are in the boardroom. Much of human behavior operates without conscious awareness; albeit this does not mean that we lack the ability to control our urges, when these may be inappropriate to display. For instance, if we are insulted we may have an acute desire to retaliate harshly against the offending party. More often than not, however, we restrain ourselves as it might otherwise harm our social reputation to act out our retaliation desire. Fertility shifts in female mating motivations can operate in the same way. The hormonal imperatives are present but these can be reigned in.

OVULATORY SHIFTS IN INTRA-SEXUAL COMPETITION

Another behavioral domain that is influenced by fertility is female intra-sexual competition. When men commit time and resources to their partners and resultant offspring, they become selective about whom they choose as a long-term romantic partner. As a result, women compete amongst each other for access to the highest quality, long-term male partner available to them (Campbell, 2004).

Because ancestral women likely varied in their ability to produce offspring, men have evolved an attraction toward fertility indicators including physical beauty, which is a sign of health and fertility in women (Durante and Li, 2009; Law Smith et al., 2006). Research has found that women compete with one another by attempting to look more attractive than same-sex peers (Campbell, 2004) and by altering their appearance with make-up, tanning, anti-wrinkle creams, push-up bras and tight clothing (Saad, 2007; Saad and Peng, 2006; Tooke and Camire, 1991). In addition, women often go to extreme lengths to maintain a desirable body and facial features. According to the American Society of Plastic Surgeons Report of Procedural Statistics (2008), nearly 11.7 million cosmetic surgical and non-surgical procedures were performed in the USA in 2007. Of the 11.7 million aesthetic procedures, 10.6 million were performed on women. Further, it has been proposed that anorexia and bulimia may represent a dysfunctional form of female competition (Mealey, 2000), and that sexual selection may have favored women who were able to preserve a nubile shape, effectively signaling youth and fertility (Abed, 1998). Recently, it was found that female intra-sexual competition for mates was the driving factor behind women's perfectionism, body dissatisfaction, drive for thinness and, thus, both bulimia and anorexia (Faer et al., 2005). In addition to attractiveness-enhancing behaviors, women also stigmatize or exclude other women as a form of competition (Bjorkqvist et al., 1992), and often use gossip to derogate other women's appearance and reputation (Campbell, 2004).

Across species, fertility status predicts the intensity of intra-sexual competition for access to mates (Low, 2000; Palagi et al., 2004). That is, motivation to compete intra-sexually is especially high at the time when conception is most likely. A small but growing body of evidence suggests that fertility shifts in certain human behaviors and motivations reflect an increase in intra-sexual competition at high fertility (Durante et al., 2008; Fisher, 2004; Lucas et al., 2007). Photographs of women near ovulation are consistently rated by both men and women as 'trying to look more attractive or fashionable' compared to low-fertility points in the cycle

(Haselton et al., 2007). This suggests that women are enhancing their own attractiveness more near ovulation, possibly to increase their ability to compete with other women for a male attention. Women also select outfits that are more revealing and sexy near ovulation, particularly when preparing for a social event (Durante et al., 2008). Preliminary evidence suggests that women purchase sexier and more revealing clothing near ovulation when primed with photographs of local, attractive same-sex peers (Durante et al., in preparation). In sum, these findings suggest that women become more competitive with other women and, as a result, put more effort into enhancing their physical attractiveness when fertility within the cycle is at its highest.

On a related note, when women are most fertile, they rate photographs of other women as lower in attractiveness, suggesting that women are derogating their competitors when fertility within their cycle is highest (Fisher, 2004). In another study women were less likely to share a monetary award and more likely to reject a low offer to share a stake of the award with another woman at high fertility (Lucas et al., 2007). The authors interpreted this result as evidence that women may be prone to compete for material resources near ovulation. Taken together, research suggests that women's competitive behaviors are elevated when they are nearest to ovulation.

Workplace Implications

Ancestrally, the most physically attractive women also were the most fertile (Durante and Li, 2009) and, as a result, these women experienced greater access to the lucrative resources provided by men (for example, food, protection, shelter). Thus, although both men and women are motivated to compete to gain social status, women experience a greater desire to gain positional advantage over other women in terms of their physical attractiveness (Campbell, 2004).

Research has shown that women select sexier clothing at high fertility when they are in social situations where opposite sex socializing will take place (Durante et al., 2008). Some women may view the corporate environment as one that is fertile (pun intended) for interactions with potential mates. Without necessarily being consciously aware of their motives, women may enhance the sexiness of their workplace attire at high fertility. Increases in attractiveness can lead to greater attention from male co-workers and, in some cases, promotion (Andreoni and Petrie, 2008). However, attractiveness enhancement in the form of wearing more revealing and sexy clothing in the workplace can also stigmatize women as being unprofessional and not career-minded (Glick et al., 2005). The choice of more provocative clothing in a work environment might also incite female co-workers to spread negative gossip and possibly ruin one's reputation and opportunity for advancement.

In the corporate environment women are likely more motivated to compete with other female co-workers than they are with male co-workers. Research has found that women care more about other women's opinions than of men's (Graziano et al., 1993), and impose stringent standards of beauty and expected behaviors on one another. Recently, it was found that competition for both corporate status and mating opportunity prompted women, but not men, to indirectly attack a presumed same-sex competitor (Griskevicius et al., 2009). Men's competitive tactics, on the other hand, involved direct, face-to-face confrontations. Women were more likely to talk behind the perceived competitor's back, tell a friend an embarrassing secret about the woman, exclude the woman from a social group, or make up a lie about the woman regardless of whether the woman was a threat to a romantic or corporate goal. Further, studies have also shown that instances of competitor derogation are especially evident as women's lifespan fertility begins to peak (for example, Hess and Hagen, 2006), suggesting that younger women are more intra-sexually competitive than women who are peri-menopausal. In evolutionary terms, the ultimate goal of female intra-sexual competition is to gain access to high-quality investing males but the function is to retain a higher position relative to other women, particularly in terms of their physical attractiveness. As such, competitive behavior may be attenuated in older women who are past reproductive age or women who are mated and satisfied with their long-term partners.

Given that corporate environments are inherently social ones, the brain mechanisms that control our social and mating behaviors are operative in such settings. As such, our model would predict that women are more likely to gossip about and criticize female colleagues at high fertility. An increase in indirect competition between women can impinge upon women's work performance in various contexts. For example, indirect competition can impact the way women manage other women. Female supervisors may become overly critical of the job performance, choice of dress, hair style and etiquette of the women who report to them. This intra-sexual effect can also operate in the reverse manner. If a woman views a female supervisor as a competitor, she may spread rumors or negative gossip about her. These types of behaviors can divert focus away from corporate objectives and, moreover, lead women to be seen as divisive and disruptive to company morale.

MENSTRUAL CYCLE EFFECTS ON MOOD AND PERFORMANCE

Near ovulation, women experience elevated mood and greater sense of wellbeing (Farage et al., 2008), greater motivations to attend social gatherings (Haselton and Gangestad, 2006), and greater distances traveled by foot and fewer calories consumed (Fessler, 2003). Additionally, fMRI research has found that women experience more activation of reward-related brain areas in the mid-follicular phase of the menstrual cycle (Dreher et al., 2007). This implies that, near ovulation, women experience an increase in desire for immediate rewards.

Other neurocognitive research has found that women's short-term or working memory consolidation improves mid-cycle (Sherwin, 2003) but their performance on spatial orientation tasks declines (Hausmann et al., 2000). As estrogen levels increase, women's performance improves on tasks that have been shown to favor females (for example, verbal facility, fine motor skills) whereas performance on tasks that favor men's neurocognitive abilities declines (for example, spatial orientation, lexical decision; Sanders et al., 2002). On the other hand, during menstruation, when hormone levels decrease significantly, women perform just as well as men on mental rotation measures of spatial ability (Sherwin, 2003).

Workplace Implications

Shifts in women's mood and performance may have historically functioned to facilitate an escalation of mate-seeking behavior but, in the workplace, may impact a woman's productivity. Scant scientific research has investigated women's actual performance in the workplace across the menstrual cycle. One study examined women's typing skills to determine whether these would worsen during the premenstrual phase of the cycle (Black and Koulis-Chitwood, 1990). The researchers concluded that women's job performance (as measured by typing skills) did not decline near menses. A more recent study conducted on female lap dancers suggest that differences in occupational tasks (for example, lap dancing versus teaching) may predict whether the menstrual cycle affects job performance. Miller et al. (2007) found that lap dancers earned more tips near ovulation as compared with other cycle phases; they speculated that this effect could be mediated by an increase in facial attractiveness and more favorable body scent, among other ovulatory cues. Conversely, an increase in women's mood and feeling of sexiness at high fertility could have influenced performance level and the amount of effort the lap dancers put into procuring tips. Research has also found that, near ovulation, women took greater risks when participating in an economic bidding war in simulated auctions (Pearson and Schipper, 2009). An increase in women's risk-taking could influence performance during presentations, boardroom negotiations or creative strategy meetings. Going out on a limb can be beneficial when generating ideas for advertising campaigns or product development.

Although a gentleman's club as a place of employment and a simulated auction might appear to be radically different from a corporate setting, shifts in hormonal status across the menstrual cycle may have implications for women's performance in the boardroom. Women experience an increase in mood, sociability, verbal creativity and fluency at high fertility. Our model would predict that shifts in these emotions, cognitions and behaviors operate to facilitate mate-seeking and expand women's mating options. As such, women's performance in occupations that require significant social networking (for example, sales, public relations) should be elevated at high fertility. Research could directly test for ovulatory shifts in increases in the sale of products and services by female employees. Further, female corporate executives may experience improvement in performance level during meetings or negotiations at high fertility. Conversely, near menstruation, as hormone levels drop, women become more proficient in mathematical and spatial ability and this might translate into higher levels of accuracy in tasks, such as the statistical forecasting of sales and operational overhead. Finally, though it has been observed that women experience greater fluctuations in some areas of neurocognitive performance than do men (Farage and Osborn, 2008), shifts in hormonal status across the menstrual cycle generally do not significantly influence women's work performance, absenteeism or stress level (Hardie, 1997). In sum, the shifts in cognitions and emotions that occur in response to variation in hormone levels across the cycle need not impede a woman's productivity (contrary to widespread conjecture). Rather, with knowledge of the underlying shifts in motivation and performance, women can successfully harness these cognitions and attenuate negative effects (for example, premenstrual drop in mood) whilst capitalizing on some of the positive outcomes (for example, ovulatory increase in verbal fluency).

CONCLUSION

Women appear to be, at some level, sensitive to the varying hormones associated with ovulation, which lead to systematic changes in their social motivations, preferences and behaviors. Although men have evolved to pick up on subtle cues of female fertility (for example, cyclical changes in facial attractiveness), shifts in fertility status remain somewhat concealed from outside observers. Thus, co-workers will never be entirely privy to the fertility status of women of reproductive age and, thus, will be unable to adjust their behaviors accordingly. Modern women, on the other hand, have the luxury of estimating the time during the month when fertility is highest and accordingly of paying greater attention to workplace behaviors. By being aware of their fertility status, women can exercise some control over shifts in mate preference and, perhaps, avoid situations that may endanger their reputation within the organization and impede their ascent up the corporate ladder. Further, although women have a natural desire to compete in terms of their attractiveness, this is not the case for all women and it is not a deterministic reality that women express these behaviors in the workplace. Finally, cyclic shifts in fertility might even provide women an edge in the workplace (for example, the mid-cycle increase in verbal fluency and creativity could increase performance during corporate presentations).

Many individuals spend most of their 'active' waking hours at work. As such, the corporate setting has become an environment that is most fertile for studying human behaviors including evolutionary-based imperatives. Our goal in this chapter was to explore the effects of the menstrual cycle on women's behaviors in the workplace. The scientific work presented in this chapter hopefully provides actionable information that can be directly applied toward day-to-day corporate operations. That said, even if the practical implications are unclear, the workplace environment provides evolutionary-minded behavioral scientists with an exciting arena to further explore the richness of human behaviors.

REFERENCES

Abed, R.T. (1998), 'The sexual competition hypothesis for eating disorders', *British Journal of Medical Psychology*, **71**, 525–47.
American Society of Plastic Surgeons (2008), 'Report of the 2007 procedural statistics', http://www.plasticsurgerypractice.com/issues/articles/2008-05_08.asp (accessed 1 November 2008).
Andreoni, J. and R. Petrie (2008), 'Beauty, gender and stereotypes: evidence from laboratory experiments', *Journal of Economic Psychology*, **29**, 73–93.
Baker, R.R. (1996), *Sperm Wars: Infidelity, Sexual Conflict, and Other Bedroom Battles*, New York: Fourth Estate.
Baker, R.R. and M.A. Bellis (1995), *Human Sperm Competition*, London: Chapman and Hall.
Barletta, M. (2007), 'Big economic opportunity in marketing to women', *Advertising Age*, 7 April, available at www.adage.com (accessed 27 October 2008).
Bellis, M.A. and R.R. Baker (1990), 'Do females promote competition: data for humans', *Animal Behaviour*, **40**, 197–9.

Bjorkqvist, K., K. Lagerspetz and A. Kaukiainen (1992), 'Do girls manipulate and boys fight? Developmental trends in regard to direct and indirect aggression', *Aggressive Behavior*, **18**, 117–27.

Black, S.L. and A. Koulis-Chitwood (1990), 'The menstrual cycle and typing skill: an ecologically-valid test of the "raging hormones" hypothesis', *Canadian Journal of Behavioural Science*, **22**, 445–55.

Bullivant, S.B., S.A. Sellergren, K. Stern et al. (2004), 'Women's sexual experience during the menstrual cycle: identification of the sexual phase by noninvasive measurement of luteinizing hormone', *Journal of Sex Research*, **41**, 82–93.

Bunting, L. and A. Boivin (2008), 'Knowledge about infertility risk factors, fertility myths and illusory benefits of health habits in young people', *Human Reproduction*, **23**, 1858–64.

Burt, A. (1992), 'Concealed ovulation and sexual signals in primates', *Folia Primatologica*, **58**, 1–6.

Campbell, A. (2004), 'Female competition: causes, constraints, content, and contexts', *Journal of Sex Research*, **41**, 16–26.

Catalyst Census (2007), 'Catalyst census finds women gained ground as board committee chairs', available at http://www.imdiversity.com/villages/woman/business_finance/catalyst_boards_2007_1207.asp (accessed 20 January 2009).

Chen, Y., P. Katuscak and E. Ozdenoren (2007), 'Sealed bid auctions with ambiguity: theory and experiments', *Journal of Economic Theory*, **136**, 513–35.

Daly, M. and M. Wilson (eds) (1983), *Sex, Evolution, and Behavior*, 2nd edn, Boston, MA: Willard Grant Press.

Damast, A. (2007), 'Mommy's MBA', *BusinessWeek*, 10 May, available at http://www.businessweek.com/bschools/content/may2007/bs20070510_162993.htm (accessed 27 October 2008).

Dreher, J., P.J. Schmidt, P. Kohn, D. Furman, D. Rubinow and K.F. Berman (2007), 'Menstrual cycle phase modulates reward-related neural function in women', *Proceedings of the National Academy of Sciences of the United States of America*, **104**, 2465–70.

Durante, K.M. and N.P. Li (2009), 'Oestradiol level and opportunistic mating in women', *Proceedings of the Royal Society of London: Biology Letters*, **5**, 179–82.

Durante, K.M., N.P. Li and M.G. Haselton (2008), 'Changes in women's choice of dress across the ovulatory cycle: naturalistic and laboratory task-based evidence', *Personality and Social Psychology Bulletin*, **34**, 1451–60.

Durante, K.M., S.E. Hill, C. Perilloux and N.P. Li (in preparation), 'Fashion, rivals, and love: the effects of intrasexual competition and fertility on women's consumer behavior'.

Eichner, S.F. and E.M. Timpe (2004), 'Urinary-based ovulation and pregnancy: point-of-case testing', *Annals of Pharmacotherapy*, **38**, 325–31.

Ellison P.T. (2001), *On Fertile Ground*, Cambridge, MA: Harvard University Press.

Faer, L.M., A. Hendricks, R.T. Abed and A.J. Figueredo (2005), 'The evolutionary psychology of eating disorders: female competition for mates or for status?', *Psychology and Psychotherapy: Theory, Research, and Practice*, **78**, 397–417.

Farage, M.A. and T.W. Osborn, (2008), 'Cognitive, sensory, and emotional changes associated with the menstrual cycle: a review', *Archives of Gynecology and Obstetrics*, **278**, 299–307.

Farage, M.A. and T.W. Osborn and A.B. MacLean (2008), 'Cognitive, sensory and emotional associated with the menstural cycle: a review', *Archives of Gynecology and Obstetrics*, **278** (4), 299–307.

Fessler, D.M.T. (2002), 'Reproductive immunosuppresion and diet: an evolutionary perspective on pregnancy sickness and meat', *Current Anthropology*, **43**, 19–61.

Fessler, D.M.T. (2003), 'No time to eat: an adaptationist account of periovulatory behavioral changes', *Quarterly Review of Biology*, **78**, 3–21.

Fisher, M.L. (2004), 'Female intrasexual competition decreases female facial attractiveness', *Proceedings of the Royal Society of London, Biology Letters*, **271**, 283–5.

Fortune (2007), 'Women CEOs for FORTUNE 500 companies', 30 April, available at http://money.cnn.com/magazines/fortune/fortune500/2007/womenceos/ (accessed 27 October 2008).

Gangestad, S.W. and J.A. Simpson, (2000), 'On the evolutionary psychology of human mating: trade-offs and strategic pluralism', *Behavioral and Brain Sciences*, **23**, 573–87.

Gangestad, S.W., R. Thornhill and C.E. Garver (2002), 'Changes in women's sexual interests and their partner's mate-retention tactics across the menstrual cycle: evidence for shifting conflicts of interest', *Proceedings of the Royal Society of London B*, **269**, 975–82.

Gangestad, S.W., C.E. Garver-Apgar, J.A. Simpson and A.J. Cousins (2007), 'Changes in women's mate preferences across the ovulatory cycle', *Journal of Personality and Social Psychology*, **92**, 151–63.

Gangestad, S.W., J.A. Simpson, A.J. Cousins, C.E. Garver-Apgar and P.N. Christenson (2004), 'Women's preferences for male behavioral displays change across the menstrual cycle', *Psychological Science*, **15**, 203–7.

Garver-Apgar, C.E., S.W. Gangestad, R. Thornhill, R.D. Miller and J.J. Olp (2006), 'Major histocompatibility complex alleles, sexual responsivity, and unfaithfulness in romantic couples', *Psychological Science*, **17**, 830–35.

Geary, D. (2000), 'Evolution and proximate expression of human paternal investment', *Psychological Bulletin*, **126**, 55–77.

Glick, P., S. Larsen, C. Johnson and H. Branstiter (2005), 'Evaluations of sexy women in low- and high-status jobs', *Psychology of Women Quarterly*, **29**, 389–95.

Grammer, K., L. Renninger and B. Fischer (2004), 'Disco clothing, female sexual motivation, and relationship status: is she dressed to impress?', *Journal of Sex Research*, **41**, 66–74.

Graziano, W.G., L.A. Jensen-Campbell, L.J. Shebilske and S.R. Lundgren (1993), 'Social influence, sex differences and judgments of beauty: putting the interpersonal back into interpersonal attraction', *Journal of Personality and Social Psychology*, **65**, 522–31.

Griskevicius, V., J.M. Tybur, S.W. Gangestad, E.F. Perea, J.R. Shapiro and D.T. Kenrick (2009), 'Aggress to impress: hostility as an evolved context-dependent strategy', *Journal of Personality and Social Psychology*, **96**, 980–94.

Hardie, E.A. (1997), 'PMS in the workplace: Dispelling the myth of cyclic dysfunction', *Journal of Occupational and Organizational Psychology*, **70**, 97–102.

Haselton, M.G. (2003), 'The sexual overperception bias: evidence of a systematic bias in men from a survey of naturally occurring events', *Journal of Research in Personality*, **37**, 43–7.

Haselton, M.G. and S.W. Gangestad (2006), 'Conditional expression of women's desires and men's mate guarding across the ovulatory cycle', *Hormones and Behavior*, **49**, 509–18.

Haselton, M.G., M. Mortezaie, E.G. Pillsworth, A.E. Bleske and D.A. Frederick (2007), 'Ovulatory shifts in human female ornamentation: near ovulation, women dress to impress', *Hormones and Behavior*, **51**, 40–45.

Hausmann, M., D. Slabbekoorn, S.H. Van Goozen, P.T. Cohen-Kettenis and O. Güntürkün, (2000), 'Sex hormones affect spatial abilities during the menstrual cycle', *Behavioral Neuroscience*, **114**, 1245–50.

Hess, N.H. and E.H. Hagen (2006), 'Sex differences in indirect aggression: psychological evidence from young adults', *Evolution and Human Behavior*, **27**, 231–45.

International Labour Office, Geneva (2008), 'Global employment trends for women', available at http://www.ilo.org/global/About_the_ILO/Media_and_public_information/Press_releases/lang--en/WCMS_091102/index.htm (accessed 29 January 2009).

Kaplan, H.S., K. Hill, J.B. Lancaster and A.M. Hurtado (2000), 'A theory of human life history evolution: diet, intelligence, and longevity', *Evolutionary Anthropology*, **9**, 156–85.

Law Smith, M.J., D.I. Perrett, B.C. Jones et al. (2006), 'Facial appearance is a cue to oestrogen levels in women', *Proceedings of the Royal Society of London B*, **273**, 135–40.

Lipson, S.F. and P.T. Ellison (1996), 'Comparison of salivary steroid profiles in naturally occurring conception and non-conception cycles', *Human Reproduction*, **11**, 1090–96.

Low, B.S. (2000), *Why Sex Matters: A Darwinian Look at Human Behavior*, Princeton, NJ: Princeton University Press.

Lucas, M., F. Koff and S. Skeath (2007), 'A pilot study of relationship between fertility and bargaining', *Psychological Reports*, **101**, 302–10.

Marlowe, F. (2001), 'Male contribution to diet and female reproductive success among foragers', *Current Anthropology*, **42**, 755–60.

Mazur, A. and A. Booth (1998), 'Testosterone and dominance in men', *Behavioral and Brain Sciences*, **21**, 353–63.

McIntyre, M., S.W. Gangestad, P.B. Gray et al. (2006), 'Romantic involvement often reduces men's testosterone levels – but not always: the moderating role of extrapair sexual interest', *Journal of Personality and Social Psychology*, **91**, 642–51.

Mealey, L. (2000), 'Anorexia: a losing strategy?', *Human Nature*, **11**, 105–16.

Mehta, P.H., A.C. Jones and R.A. Josephs (2008), 'The social endocrinology of dominance: basal testosterone predicts cortisol changes and behavior following victory and defeat', *Journal of Personality and Social Psychology*, **94**, 1078–93.

Miller, G.F., J. Tybur and B. Jordan (2007), 'Ovulatory cycle effects on tip earnings by lap-dancers: economic evidence for human estrus?', *Evolution and Human Behavior*, **28**, 375–81.

Palagi, E., S. Telara and S.M. Tarli (2004), 'Reproductive strategies in *Lemur catta*: the balance among sending, receiving, and counter-marking scent signals', *International Journal of Primatology*, **25**, 1019–31.

Pearson, M. and B.C. Schipper (2009), 'Menstrual cycle and competitive bidding', unpublished manuscript, available at http://www.econ.ucdavis.edu/Graduate/pearson/Main/CV_files/cycle_and_bidding.pdf (accessed 29 January 2009).

Penton-Voak, I.S. and D.I. Perret (2000), 'Female preference for male faces changes cyclically – further evidence', *Evolution and Human Behavior*, **21**, 39–48.

Penton-Voak, I.S., D.I. Perrett, D.L. Castles et al. (1999), 'Menstrual cycle alters face preference', *Nature*, **399**, 741–2.

Puts, D.A. (2005), 'Mating context and mestrual phase affect female preferences for male voice pitch', *Evolution and Human Behavior*, **26**, 388–97.

Roberts, S.C., J. Havlicek, J. Flegr et al. (2004), 'Female facial attractiveness increases during the fertile phase of the menstrual cycle', *Proceedings of the Royal Society of London B (Suppl.)*, **271**, S270–S272.

Roney, J.R. and Z.L. Simmons (2008), 'Women's oestradiol predicts preference for facial cues of men's testosterone', *Hormones and Behaviour*, **53**, 14–19.

Saad, G. (2007), *The Evolutionary Bases of Consumption*, Mahwah, NJ: Lawrence Erlbaum.

Saad, G. and A. Peng (2006), 'Applying Darwinian principles in designing effective intervention strategies: the case of sun tanning', *Psychology and Marketing*, **23**, 617–38.

Saad, G. and E. Stenstrom (in preparation), 'The effects of the menstrual cycle on consumption phenomena'.

Sanders, G., M. Sjodin and M. de Chastelaine (2002), 'On the elusive nature of sex differences in cognition: hormonal influences contributing to within-sex variation', *Archives of Sexual Behavior*, **31**, 145–52.

Senior, C., A. Lau and M.J.R. Butler (2007), 'The effects of the menstrual cycle on social decision-making', *International Journal of Psychophysiology*, **63**, 186–91.

Sherwin, B.B. (2003), 'Estrogen and cognitive functioning in women', *Endocrinology Review*, **24**, 133–51.

Singh, D. and P.M. Bronstad (2001), 'Female body odor is a potential cue to ovulation', *Proceedings of the Royal Society of London, Biology*, **268**, 797–801.

Thornhill R. and S.W. Gangestad (2003), 'Do women have evolved adaptation for extra-pair copulation?', in K. Grammer and E. Voland (eds), *Evolutionary Aesthetics*, Berlin: Springer-Verlag, pp. 341–68.

Thornhill, R., S.W. Gangestad, R. Miller, G. Scheyd, J.K. McCollough and M. Franklin (2003), 'Major histocompatibility complex genes, symmetry, and body scent attractiveness in men and women', *Behavioral Ecology*, **14**, 668–78.

Tooke, W. and L. Camire (1991), 'Patterns of deception in intersexual and intrasexual mating strategies', *Ethology and Sociobiology*, **12**, 345–64.

Trivers, R.L. (1972), 'Parental investment and sexual selection', in B. Campbell (ed.), *Sexual Selection and the Descent of Man*, 1871–1971, Chicago, IL: Aldine-Atherton, pp. 136–79.

White, R.E., S. Thornhill and E. Hampson (2007), 'A biosocial model of entrepreneurship: the effect of testosterone and family business background', *Journal of Organizational Behavior*, **28**, 451–66.

8. Hormonal influence on male decision-making: implications for organizational management

Angela A. Stanton

INTRODUCTION

Recently, some firms have come under scrutiny for their overzealous attempts at securing success. In particular, some corporate executives have fallen from grace for their unsavory efforts to both make themselves richer and their firm more successful, at times choosing avenues that are unethical if not criminal. The underlying motives of these executives have received little attention even after some of the firms have collapsed. The most prominently held view holds executive greed responsible for the demise of the firm. In this chapter I visit some of the reasons for the actions that have come to be considered as unethical, such as the decision to spend millions on decorating an office at shareholders' expense, from a different perspective. I take on the perspective of biological, specifically hormonal, forces. Once some of the underlying biological reasons are understood, perhaps firms can prevent and proactively avoid situations in which the executive could make a decision for the detriment of the firm. Business schools teach future executives how to improve the firm's positioning in the marketplace. Business ethics courses are typically available within the curricula, but these do not address the biochemical forces an individual may have to fight within himself (or herself) to live up to general ethical values in making specific decisions. None of what is currently taught to future organizational leaders and managers incorporates how human evolutionary forces act on the organization from the perspective of the individuals within a firm and what these forces mean in terms of the decision-making of these individuals. In this chapter I address some of the hormonal forces that could make men, for example, decorate their offices with little concern for the underlying unethical component of such a decision. First, I look at male behaviors that have come to represent a partial list of the stereotypical male. These behaviors are shaped by biochemical forces and merit further analysis to understand how they affect the firm and the individuals within. I hope to illuminate how male and female hormones 'communicate' without conscious awareness of the individuals and how this communication may manifest itself in undesirable decisions in the workplace. I provide four propositions about how particular hormonal variations may cause certain behaviors, such as employee turnover, heightened stress and impaired cognitive functioning as a result of corporate structure and organization. I conclude with suggestions for future research.

WHAT DO WE MEAN BY MALE STEREOTYPICAL BEHAVIOR?

The term 'stereotype' has earned a bad reputation by its use in common language, where it refers to undesirable behaviors ad nauseum. The existence of stereotypes is viewed as a negative concept. In reality there is no such stereotypical male. What exists are behaviors that are recognizably identical in individuals who share certain characteristics. For example, all men share one characteristic: they are males. Male stereotypical actions are those that distinguish males from females and represent men uniquely in the eyes of other men and women. Although we think of stereotype as something of the past, a recent experiment showed that stereotypes are ingrained into our memories subconsciously (Eckel, 2008). Men have certain hormones whose levels predispose them to particular types of behaviors. In general, men and women are believed to differ in achievement- and communal-type traits (see, for example, Heilman, 2001). Men are assumed to be more achievement-oriented and women more concerned with community and social causes.

The stereotypical man is often characterized as aggressive, takes risks, independent, decisive, competent, better at complex tasks, good negotiator, earns higher income and possesses different ethical values from the ethical values of females (Booth and Nolen, 2009; Bowles and McGinn, 2008; Holm and Engseld, 2005; Huddy and Terkildsen, 1993; Kidwell et al., 1987; Magee and Galinsky, 2008; Stangor, 2000). The recognition of stereotypes can be confirmed by anchoring experimental subjects with statements that represent stereotypes as part of the experiment (White et al., 2009). In an experiment the word 'woman' or 'man' presented prior to a particular behavioral trait (aggressiveness, nurturing) or nontrait (nurse, engineer) word significantly primed the individual toward stereotype bias and prejudice. Participants made quicker judgments for stereotypically congruent prime–target word pairs (women:nurturing) than for incongruent word pairs (men:nurturing) (ibid., p. 5), showing that less effort is needed to recruit matching sets from memory than non-matching ones, suggesting recognition of stereotype representation.

Thus behavior that is stereotyped is recognized and associated with both males and females. The question is why did these stereotypical behaviors evolve in the first place? What are the underlying forces that create a particular behavior so consistent that it is recognized as a stereotypical behavior? What are the typical functions that may be stereotyped? Does stereotypical behavior have an evolutionary role? And, if so, what are its biological underpinnings? Whatever is associated with typical female behavior (the female stereotype) is mostly driven by her menstrual cycle, which carries with it fluctuating hormonal variations, as discussed in the previous chapter; here the focus is on the male. Research shows that just as female stereotypical behavior is driven by female hormonal shifts, so is male stereotypical behavior driven by male hormones and their variability.

TESTOSTERONE AND MEN

Testosterone is an androgen that is produced both by males and females albeit in different quantities and for different purposes (Edwards et al., 2006). In males testosterone is produced in the testes and also by the adrenal glands.

Steroids are created by the adrenal glands, of which androgens form one group of steroids. Testosterone is synthesized from androgens and it is an intermediate step in the synthesis of estrogen, which is the end product, as Figure 8.1 shows. Both men and women have testosterone and estrogen, only in different levels and for different purpose. Since estrogen is derived from testosterone, and both hormones are present in both sexes, estrogen is not the female equivalent of male testosterone. Rather, estrogen is one hormonal component influencing female behavior and testosterone is one hormonal component influencing male behavior. An individual's basal level of testosterone and its variability is genetically established (Harris et al., 1998; Kuijper et al., 2007) and further influenced by androgen exposure of the fetus in the mother's womb (Hönekopp et al., 2006a, 2006b; Lutchmaya et al., 2004; Manning et al., 2004).

Testosterone has been associated with a variety of behaviors and traits in males, in addition to its role in maintaining a libidinal drive. Testosterone has been linked to aggression (Archer, 2006; Aromaki et al., 2002; Azurmendi et al., 2006; Birger et al., 2003; Coccaro et al., 2007; Delville et al., 1996), dominance and social status (Chichinadze and Chichinadze,

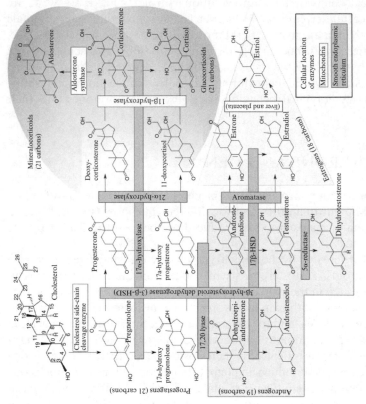

Source: Wikipedia Commons http://en.wikipedia.org/wiki/File:Steroidogenesis.png, accessed 16 November 2009. originally in color converted to black and white.

Figure 8.1   The human steroidogenesis

2008; Maner et al., 2008; Mazur, 1976; Mazur and Booth, 1998, 1999; Mehta et al., 2008), sensation seeking and competition (Aluja and Garcia, 2005; Booth et al., 1989; Coccaro et al., 2007; Gerra et al., 1999; Mazur et al., 1992; Roberti, 2004; Salvador et al., 1987, 2003; Salvador et al., 1999) and hostility (Hartgens and Kuipers, 2004). In business literature testosterone and the associated increased desire for risk taking is an often discussed topic and it is assumed to be important to entrepreneurial success (Baron, 2004; Forlani and Mullins, 2000; Keh et al., 2002; White et al., 2006). But not everyone agrees that risk-taking propensity difference exists or is important between entrepreneurs and managers, as discussed in Chapter 2 of this volume (Brockhaus Sr, 1980; Grichnik, 2008).

The stereotypical traits to which testosterone is linked in men are all related to changes in status. It is not the status per se that matters but the threat to a change in status that does. Testosterone is an ancient hormone that is homologous and has the same function in all male vertebrates (including fish) and as such influences male behaviors and motivations in similar ways across species. Thus in some cases it is appropriate to illustrate important findings of testosterone with non-human examples. Changes in status (in Arctic charr *Salvelinus alpinus*) showed that males who have recently become dominant invest less effort in sperm production than non-dominant males, and this shift from high investment in sperm to low is very rapid (Rudolfsen et al., 2006). The evolutionary reason for this might be, for example, that dominant fish may mate more often and so can afford to produce lower quality sperm in each of their copulations whereas non-dominant males need to produce more viable sperm for less frequent mating opportunities. This demonstrates how quickly males' bio-physiology responds to status change relative to the status of connected others. It also demonstrates that such behavioral response has an evolutionary role through testosterone and that behavioral response manifests itself as change in physiological as well as behavioral processes.

Specifically, testosterone levels are responsive to challenged status changes. For example, Mazur and Lamb (1980) found that in competitive events that are impersonal or have nothing to do with individual achievement, such as the luck of a random draw in the lottery or if a sports team wins by default because their competitors did not show up, testosterone does not increase. In modern hierarchical societies a change in status can alter testosterone levels in a multidirectional manner. When status is elevated, so is the level of testosterone, but when an individual is demoted in status, his testosterone levels fall (Rose et al., 1975). Furthermore, increased testosterone levels may lead to increased status and decreased testosterone levels to decreased status (Mazur and Booth, 1998; Mehta and Josephs, 2006 Mehta et al., 2008). It can be speculated that in an office environment, behavior by others that may be interpreted as a challenge to one's status, for example a disagreement in a meeting, a promotion or a larger office may elevate men's testosterone levels and influence their behavior. Alternatively, men may have a testosterone increase on their way to work (traffic jam, for example), which then influences their behavior toward more aggression and risk taking in the office. Given the nature of testosterone, one may believe that members of the prison population would have their basal testosterone levels higher than men who are not criminals, but even in prison only challenges to status and dominance show distinction in testosterone levels (Ehrenkranz et al., 1974).

Although much has been learned about status, dominance and aggression in males and the connection of these behaviors to testosterone, the fact that testosterone levels affect the cognitive and emotive abilities of both males and females is less understood. For example, women's 'reduced cognitive abilities' in terms of spatial, abstract and mathematical tasks are particularly extenuated when estrogen is high during the estrus period of the menstrual cycle and when, as a result, testosterone is low, but at other times of the month, these cognitive impairments dissolve (Josephs et al., 2003). Testosterone has significant effects on learning, memory and spatial cognition; all important factors of successful decision-making for both males and females (Janowsky, 2006a, 2006b; Janowsky et al., 2000). Recent research shows the influence of testosterone on men's cognitive ability in terms of status change. Men who have high basal testosterone suffer a cognitive decline if placed into a subordinate position (Josephs et al., 2003, 2006; Newman et al., 2005). When low basal testosterone men are placed in a dominant status role, they too suffer a cognitive impairment as a result of the stress they are ill-prepared to handle (Josephs et al., 2006). Economic decision making in finance is influenced by testosterone levels. Men of higher basal testosterone levels, or higher starting testosterone levels on a given day when comparing the same person over many days, make riskier financial decisions and earn higher returns (Apicella et al., 2008; Coates and Herbert, 2008). Testosterone levels naturally vary throughout the day diurnally (Mazur et al., 1992; Resko and Eik-nes, 1966) and are also believed to change with age (Davidson et al., 1983; Liverman and Blazer, 2004). The firm's bottom line may be affected by its aging leaders, whose testosterone levels are naturally in decline. Thus aging may reduce status confrontation but it may also reduce the willingness to take on risky projects that would otherwise be beneficial to the firm.

A man's variations in his level of testosterone are affected by his marital and parental status (Burnham et al., 2003; Byron, 2004; Mazur and Michalek, 1998). Specifically, testosterone levels decrease when a man is in a stable romantic relationship (Gray et al., 2006) but this decrease seems to only apply when the relationship is with a female partner (van Anders and Watson, 2006). Polyamorous or homosexual relationships do not yield testosterone reducing effects (van Anders et al., 2007). This phenomenon is well reflected in car insurance rates that drop when a man marries or gets older, regardless of his driving record. And finally, the type of job one holds may be predicted by a single measure of testosterone (Dabbs et al., 1990; Purifoy and Koopmans, 1979).

CORTISOL AND TESTOSTERONE

Testosterone is a major hormonal force on behavior but it does not work in isolation. Other hormones, such as cortisol, also affect decision-making but these interactive effects are less well understood. Coates and Herbert showed that whereas testosterone affects the risk-taking penchant of financial traders on the London Trading Floor, it is cortisol that responds to market volatility (Coates and Herbert, 2008). Market volatility implies lack of information (ambiguity) in the environment, whereas risk represents full information (see Chapter 2 in this volume on the definition of risk and ambiguity). Ambiguous environments likely to promote stress are very common in the everyday work life of executives and entrepreneurs. In animal studies elevated cortisol levels are indicative of stress (for a review of cortisol studies in primates and other animals, see Kikusui et al., 2006; Saltzman et al., 2009).

While male and female responses to testosterone may differ, research shows that the female stress response also manifests itself in increased cortisol, just like stress response in males (Seeman et al., 1997a, 1997b). Maternal depression increases the cortisol level of the infant (for a review, see Hill et al., 2008). Cortisol levels also increase in male gamblers (Meyer et al., 2000). Thus the connection between testosterone and cortisol appears to be representative of stressful challenges that in combination may negatively impact the health of the individual. For example, Coates and Herbert (2008) showed that although high testosterone individuals were more profitable in financial exchanges, this came at considerable health risks. Although both testosterone and cortisol are diurnal hormones with the highest level in the morning and lowest at night, financial traders who partook in the experiment ended up with significantly higher levels of both hormones in the afternoon than they started with in the morning. High cortisol and testosterone levels may be associated with trader burnout, which is suggested to be a result of long-term dealing with high volatility (Oberlechner, 2005; Taleb, 2005). High stress for longer periods of time increases the chance for various diseases, such as high blood pressure (Epel, 2009; Schneider et al., 2005).

To summarize, complex biochemical forces affect human decision-making in a subconscious manner, albeit their functions are not yet fully understood. How these biochemical forces influence communication and cooperation between men and women, and propositions about how this may impact the fate of the firm, are discussed in the following section.

POSITION AND STATUS IN THE FIRM

Changes in position have become the hallmark of corporate life. Firms promote regularly either by seniority or capability. Sometimes firms bring executives of high status into leading positions specifically to lead the firm toward new directions. But such changes often create a mismatch between individuals' position and their corresponding ability and status (Josephs et al., 2006). To clarify, a position is a title that a firm may assign whereas status is an image of power others hold of an individual. Thus, in some cases, individuals of high status may hold low level positions and in other cases individuals of low status may hold high level positions. In cases where low status individuals are promoted to higher level positions, their job becomes overly challenging and they may stall growth in the firm. In the business vernacular this is referred to as the Peter Principle. The Peter Principle suggests that in a hierarchical organization, employees are often promoted to their highest level of incompetence, and they get stuck there, unable to provide better quality of work (Peter and Hull, 1969). Testosterone levels are representative of status and not of position.

A mismatch between position and an individual's basal testosterone level can create significant personal and corporate challenges. Since low testosterone individuals placed into high status roles suffer stress and cognitive impairment, it is likely that their cortisol levels are also elevated. This is cause for concern because of the associated health implications. It is understood that, among other things, elevated cortisol levels are associated with diabetes (Chiodini et al., 2007). High basal testosterone men working in subordinate roles can also suffer stress and cognitive impairment as a result of the mismatch. The firm may experience higher health costs associated with stress-related illnesses and higher sick leave hours when mismatches exist. Since the mismatch causes both the superior and the subordinate to be uncomfortable and under stress, costly turnover may increase. And lastly, as the mismatch also comes with impaired cognitive performance, the firm's production may also suffer. This leads to the first proposition.

Proposition 1: Mismatch between the positions and an individual's basal testosterone levels in corporate promotion causes stress, contributing to personnel turnover and health-related costs.

A firm that promotes based only on seniority and not recognizing performance is likely to find basal T level mismatch as a result of promoting a low basal testosterone man into higher position and over males of high basal testosterone. Due to practical considerations, only a few unhappy workers can leave a firm. Thus, the Peter Principle's victims stay behind with negative consequences for the firm. It is my proposal that the Peter Principle is a manifestation of promoting by seniority with incompatible testosterone profile.

Proposition 2: In promoting by seniority, a firm may evoke the Peter Principle and not optimize its potential for growth.

The essence of growth in many firms is the chance for advancement for its workers, therefore an ongoing status shuffle is unavoidable. As those with high basal testosterone seek out positions of challenge and risk and those with low basal testosterone do not, it is worthwhile for the firm to invest in understanding its employees. Men who do not like challenges will not lead the firm toward increased opportunities when those opportunities require the taking of risks. I do not suggest that firms take saliva samples for testing testosterone levels during candidate interview for employment, although various tests are already routinely done, such as urine testing and personality traits tests. I do suggest the use of modified personality tests that are able to evaluate the candidate's propensity for seeking challenges, taking risks and willingness to lead. Particularly important is the use of questions that reveal what an individual will do if their status is challenged. I encourage firms to use such personal status inventory scores to help them guide their decisions in promotions as well. To avoid the high costs associated with high turnover and stress-related health problems, I propose that firms that often promote, and thereby encourage movement toward increased positions and status within the firm, formulate specifically tailored tests to guide promotional decisions. These tests should be able to identify those individuals who possess the physiological qualities that predispose them to seek challenges and avoid frustration when promoted.

Proposition 3: The use of appropriate personality traits tests will guide promotional decisions to the benefit of the individuals as well as the firm.

The reality of a hierarchical firm is ongoing change. It is beneficial to the employees and to the firm to consider biological and physiological factors in addition to knowledge, experience and seniority when considering the promotion of an individual to a new role.

TESTOSTERONE MEETS ESTROGEN IN THE FIRM

The previous chapter in this volume discussed in detail how women's ovulatory cycles affect their cognitive and emotive abilities at different times of the month. In this section I discuss how men's testosterone levels are vulnerable to and are affected by the presence of these cycles in young and beautiful women (Baker Jr and Maner, 2008). Facial and body symmetry is a crucially important factor in the eyes of both men and women (O'Doherty et al., 2003; Rhodes et al., 2001; Tovee et al., 1999, 2000). Symmetry is understood to reflect health and well-being and is thus suggestive of fitness in terms of mate selection (Rhodes et al., 2003, 2007). During the follicular phase of the ovulatory cycle women's faces and bodies become their most symmetric (Manning et al., 1996). Men and women are affected by 'beauty' but in different ways, using different brain regions to evaluate what beauty means (Cela-Conde et al., 2009). Different parts of the brain are activated by hormones to influence preference toward different representations of beauty (Rupp et al., 2009b). Women also show increased sexual interest at the follicular phase of their menstrual cycle (Rupp et al., 2009a, 2009b). Cela-Conde and colleagues suggests that 'the different strategies used by men and women in assessing aesthetic preference may reflect differences in the strategies associated with the division of labor between our male and female hunter-gatherer hominin ancestors' (Cela-Conde et al., 2009, p. 3847). Thus cyclical variations in beauty and the associated hormonal changes are likely to have implications for the firm.

Economic games are frequently used to test human decision-making to confirm economic theories or evaluate departures from the axioms of rational choice. Economic games have recently been used to test male decision-making when men can see young women casually passing by or are shown photographs of young women. Does female presence change male decision-making? And if it does, is there a difference between high or low basal testosterone males in how they change their decisions? A favorite game to test this type of decision-making is the ultimatum game (UG). The UG is particularly appropriate to test the necessary give and take dependence and reciprocity represented in the corporate environment. Two players are paired randomly, and typically anonymously, playing through the computer with one another in an experimental laboratory – although in a modified version the game has been carried to field experiments as well (Henrich et al., 2005). One of the two players (proposer) is given a sum of money, say $10, and is told to share this sum with the other player (responder), in any fashion. Any amount between $0 and $10 may be offered to the responder, including $0 and $10. The caveat in this game is that the responder may accept or reject the offer. If the responder accepts, each player takes their respective split but if he rejects, both players receive nothing. In thousands of experiments, both in laboratories and field experiments around the world, UG results show that the majority of people share the money evenly. In general, offers of $2 or less are usually rejected and actually are very seldom offered, whereas $3 and larger sums are typically accepted (Camerer, 2003). How does the presence of women affect men's sharing and rejecting in this game?

Economic theories suggest that the proposers should send the smallest possible amount ($1 in this case) because the responder should, according to the axiom of income maximization, accept any positive amount that is greater than zero. However, experiments have shown that most players send greater amounts than the economic theory suggests. And on those rare occasions when the rational amount of $1 is sent (rational in terms of rational choice theory), that offer is routinely rejected (ibid.). Some researchers have suggested that rejection in the UG is altruistic punishment, implying that the responder rejects at a cost to himself in order to 'teach a lesson' to the proposer for the future (de Quervain et al., 2004; Fehr and Gachter, 2002). First, if the rejection is an altruistic act, the presence of women should not affect the amount rejected by men. If there is a difference in the rejection rates between high and low basal T level males in the presence of women, basal T levels cannot be indicative of altruistic behavior.

An experiment comparing rejection amounts (without women present) showed no difference between high and low basal T level men (Millet and Dewitte, 2008). In the same experiment, when subjects' status was artificially changed to either dominant or subordinate (still no women present), significant differences emerged in the rejection levels of high and low basal T level men. High T men placed into subordinate levels discounted their future earnings, but low T level men in subordinate status or high T men in dominant status did not (ibid.). And finally, when women were present (actually photographs were shown), men of high basal testosterone discounted their earnings, accepting a smaller amount as responders but not men of low basal T (Wilson and Daly, 2004). Another point of interest is that in the same experiment pictures of cars were also shown and women also partook in the experiment. While men discounted their future earnings when they were presented images of women, they did not discount so when they were shown images of cars. However, women did not discount their future earnings when they were presented with images of men's or women's faces but they did so when they were shown images of 'hot' cars (ibid.). These differences in earnings discounting highlighted a division between the sexes that has traditionally been associated with stereotypes. We can see that the difference between what men and women consider important in their interactions is strongly influenced by hormonal differences within and between the sexes.

The level of testosterone in humans manifests itself in a morphological trait that can be measured by the digit ratio of the second and the fourth finger (typically referred to as 2D:4D) of the hand (Bailey and Hurd, 2005; Benderlioglu and Nelson, 2004; Coates et al., 2009). In an experiment with the UG, Van den Bergh and Dewitte (2006) showed that 2D:4D in males impacts rejection rates when females are present. Men of low 2D:4D ratio (high basal testosterone) became impatient and more impulsive by choosing a less desired financial outcome (accepted smaller financial amount) but ensured that they were going to receive a share of the stash in the game. Not all men are sensitive to the presence of young women in their decision making the same way. Men with high 2D:4D ratio (low basal testosterone marker) did not change their behavior as a result of female presence, only high basal testosterone men did (ibid.).

Evolutionary forces on females during their monthly hormonal cycles change female preferences based on fitness requirements of their possible progeny, as discussed in the previous chapter in this volume on female hormonal cycles. As female faces become most attractive, their bodies most symmetrical and sexy, and as they feel sexier and dress sexier (Broder and Hohmann, 2003; Chavannea and Gallup Jr, 1998) and they temporarily also change their preferences in men to higher testosterone men in the firm (Little et al., 2007; Pawlowski and Jasienska, 2005; Penton-Voak and Perrett, 2000; Penton-Voak et al., 1999; Peters et al., 2009; Puts, 2005), these hormonal changes are unconsciously acted upon by hormones of the other sex. An evolutionary role of testosterone level variability is to detect subtle changes in the follicular status of nearby women and to adjust immediately in order to elicit mating opportunity. Similarly, an evolutionary role of estrogen is to detect testosterone levels in males and to help the female to choose a male who will provide healthy progeny and high status to provide generously in support of that child. It is thus not surprising that the presence of young women makes men impatient and impulsive. It is also not surprising that since females prefer high testosterone males during their time of estrus, men evolved their ability to change their testosterone levels in response to nearby fertile women.

Proposition 4: High basal testosterone men might become shortsighted and impulsive in the presence of young female co-workers, and this may impact the bottom line of the firm.

Although men and women both change their preferences when an appropriate stimulus is present, not all men and women are equal in terms of what those stimuli are. More research is needed to understand the differences in hormonal variability between and within men and women in the workplace. For men of high basal testosterone the external stimulus that affects their decision-making seems to be sexual and for women the stimulus of changed decision is associated with status. For low basal testosterone men, research has so far come up empty handed. Low basal T level men's decision-making is not affected by the types of stimulus so far presented to them. The take-home message for the firm is that in a situation of negotiation, selling or buying, and interviewing new employees it matters who the participants are. Placing a high testosterone man in negotiation with a young woman may mean that the firm will leave money on the table. The opposite might be true if the firm places a young woman into a negotiation role with a high testosterone male. It should also be questioned if hiring is influenced by these hormonal factors. For example, if there are two men being interviewed for a position and the person conducting the interview is a young woman, will the man with the higher testosterone level get the offer? By contrast, if a man conducts the interview and two women are interviewed for the job, will the one in estrus get the job?

Men and women are fluent in the language of their hormonal communication. In an experiment women and men were shown photographs of other women and men. The women's perceptions of photographs of men were sensitive to and predicted correctly by two variables: men's scores on the interest in infants and how much they liked children, and the men's testosterone levels as expressed by the masculinity of their faces (Roney and Simmons, 2008; Roney et al., 2006). Furthermore, how much the men liked children was predictive of the women's long-term mate attractiveness to the men, and each man's testosterone level and perceived masculinity predicted how attractive the women judged him as a short-term mate. Thus women and men read facial cues of each other's hormone concentration. Reading and understanding hormonal concentrations and their meaning in terms of evolutionary fitness is part of human daily life. This hormonal communication does not stop at the front door of the firm but continues into the everyday working lives of all employees.

CONCLUDING THOUGHTS

Of the many issues this chapter addressed, the first, and most important one, is that human decision-making has a hormonal base. It is important to understand what influences hormonal variations so that a firm does not inadvertently introduce factors into the work environment that negatively impact the employees and the firm. Knowing about the importance of hormonal communications at a subconscious level between and within the sexes is important. The firm should be aware what factors may activate, promote or prevent influences that initiate hormone level changes, which can negatively impact employees – such as stress hormones for longer periods or stress hormones in employees who are predisposed to not perform well under high stress. Since some men perform better and have a preference for high stress environments but others do not, the task for the firm is to find work environments for both types of men. A firm that understands hormonal shifts and what they mean in terms of human wellbeing and working ability stands a better chance for success. There are privacy and ethical issues that a firm must consider in its plight to understand and support its human resources better. I believe that education is key to success.

Much more research needs to be done to understand human behavior in organizational environments. The propositions reflect some immediately accessible areas for future research. It is important to conduct empirical research into whether corporate promotion of low testosterone men to higher status over high testosterone men leads to the undesired consequences firms often deal with, such as high health costs as a result of a high stress environment, increased turnover and reduced performance. Should the firm find this to be the case, measures may be taken to change promotional policies as well as educate employees about some of these newly understood behavioral forces. Since high basal testosterone men might become shortsighted and impulsive in the presence of female co-workers, when key decisions need to be made, a decision team made of several men and women is more beneficial to the firm. And finally, we know much about the influence of hormonal variation on the decision-making of high basal testosterone men but little about what influences the decision-making of low basal testosterone men. As undoubtedly firms employ both low and high (and in between) basal testosterone men, it is imperative to understand all types of men.

REFERENCES

Aluja, A. and L.F. Garcia (2005), 'Sensation seeking, sexual curiosity and testosterone in inmates', *Neuropsychobiology*, **51** (1), 28–33.
Apicella, C.L., A. Dreber, B. Campbell, P.B. Gray, M. Hoffman and A.C. Little (2008), 'Testosterone and financial risk preferences', *Evolution and Human Behavior*, **29**, 384–90.

Archer, J. (2006), 'Testosterone and human aggression: an evaluation of the challenge hypothesis', *Neuroscience and Biobehavioral Reviews*, **30** (3), 319–45.

Aromaki, A.S., R.E. Lindman and C.J. Eriksson (2002), 'Testosterone, sexuality and antisocial personality in rapists and child molesters: a pilot study', *Psychiatry Research*, **110** (3), 239–47.

Azurmendi, A., F. Braza, A. Garcia, P. Braza, J.M. Munoz and J.R. Sanchez-Martin (2006), 'Aggression, dominance, and affiliation: their relationships with androgen levels and intelligence in 5-year-old children', *Hormones and Behavior*, **50** (1), 132–40.

Bailey, A.A. and P.L. Hurd (2005), 'Finger length ratio (2D:4D) correlates with physical aggression in men but not in women', *Biological Psychology*, **68** (3), 215–22.

Baker Jr, M.D. and J.K. Maner (2008), 'Risk-taking as a situationally sensitive male mating strategy', *Evolution and Human Behavior*, **29**, 391–5.

Baron, R.A. (2004), 'The cognitive perspective: a valuable tool for answering entrepreneurship's basic "why" questions', *Journal of Business Venturing*, **19**, 221–39.

Benderlioglu, Z. and R.J. Nelson (2004), 'Digit length ratios predict reactive aggression in women, but not in men', *Hormones and Behavior*, **46** (5), 558–64.

Birger, M., M. Swartz, D. Cohen, Y. Alesh, C. Grishpan and M. Kotelr (2003), 'Aggression: the testosterone–serotonin link', *Israel Medical Association Journal*, **5** (9), 653–8.

Booth, A., G. Shelley, A. Mazur, G. Tharp and R. Kittok (1989), 'Testosterone, and winning and losing in human competition', *Hormones and Behavior*, **23** (4), 556–71.

Booth, A.L. and P.J. Nolen (2009), 'Gender differences in risk behavior: does nurture matter?', IZA, Discussion paper no. 4026.

Bowles, H.R. and K.L. McGinn (2008), 'Chapter 2: untapped potential in the study of negotiation and gender inequality in organizations', *Academy of Management Annals*, **2**, 99–32.

Brockhaus Sr, R.H. (1980), 'Risk taking propensity of entrepreneurs', *Academy of Management Journal*, **23** (3), 509–20.

Broder, A. and N. Hohmann (2003), 'Variations in risk taking behavior over the menstrual cycle: an improved replication', *Evolution and Human Behavior*, **24** (6), 391–8.

Burnham, T.C., J.F. Chapman, P.B. Gray, M.H. McIntyre, S.F. Lipson and P.T. Ellison (2003), 'Men in committed, romantic relationships have lower testosterone', *Hormones and Behavior*, **44** (2), 119–22.

Byron, C. (2004), *Testosterone inc*, Elektronisk udgave (edn), Hoboken, NJ: John Wiley and Sons.

Camerer, C. (2003), *Behavioral Game Theory: Experiments in Strategic Interaction*, New York: Russell Sage Foundation.

Cela-Conde, C.J., F.J. Ayala, E. Munar, F. Maestu, M. Nadal and Miguel A. Capo et al. (2009), 'Sex-related similarities and differences in the neural correlates of beauty', *Proceedings of the National Academy of Sciences*, **106**, 3847–52.

Chavannea, T.J. and G.G. Gallup Jr (1998), 'Variation in risk taking behavior among female college students as a function of the menstrual cycle', *Evolution and Human Behavior*, **19** (1), 27–32.

Chichinadze, K. and N. Chichinadze (2008), 'Stress-induced increase of testosterone:

contributions of social status and sympathetic reactivity', *Physiology and Behavior*, **94** (4), 595–603.

Chiodini, I., G. Adda, A. Scillitani et al. (2007), 'Cortisol secretion in patients with type 2 diabetes: relationship with chronic complications', *Diabetes Care*, **30** (1), 83–8.

Coates, J.M. and J. Herbert (2008), 'Endogenous steroids and financial risk taking on a London trading floor', *Proceedings of the National Academy of Sciences of the United States of America*, **105** (16), 6167–72.

Coates, J.M., M. Gurnell and A. Rustichini (2009), 'Second-to-fourth digit ratio predicts success among high-frequency financial traders', *Proceedings of the National Academy of Sciencesof the United States of America*, **106** (2), 623–8.

Coccaro, E.F., B. Beresford, P. Minar, J. Kaskow and T. Geracioti (2007), 'CSF testosterone: relationship to aggression, impulsivity, and venturesomeness in adult males with personality disorder', *Journal of Psychiatric Resarch*, **41** (6), 488–92.

Dabbs, J.M.J., D. de La Rue and P.M. Williams (1990), 'Testosterone and occupational choice: actors, ministers, and other men', *Journal of Personality and Social Psychology*, **59** (6), 1261–5.

Davidson, J.M., J.J. Chen, L. Crapo, G.D. Gray, W.J. Greenleaf and J.A. Catania (1983), 'Hormonal changes and sexual function in aging men', *Journal of Clinical Endocrinology and Metabolism*, **57** (1), 71–7.

Delville, Y., K.M. Mansour and C.F. Ferris (1996), 'Testosterone facilitates aggression by modulating vasopressin receptors in the hypothalamus', *Physiology and Behavior*, **60** (1), 25–9.

De Quervain, D.J.-F., U. Fischbacher, V. Treyer et al. (2004), 'The neural basis of altruistic punishment', *Science*, **305** (1254), 1258.

Eckel, C., A.C.M. de Oliveira and P.J. Grossman (2008), 'Gender and negotiation in the small: are women (perceived to be) more cooperative than men?', *Negotiation Journal*, **24** (4), 429–45.

Edwards, D.A., K. Wetzel and D.R. Wyner (2006), 'Intercollegiate soccer: saliva cortisol and testosterone are elevated during competition, and testosterone is related to status and social connectedness with team mates', *Physiology and Behavior*, **87** (1), 135–43.

Ehrenkranz, J., E. Bliss and M.H. Sheard (1974), 'Plasma testosterone: correlation with aggressive behavior and social dominance in man', *Psychosomatic Medicine*, **36** (6), 469–75.

Epel, E.S. (2009), 'Psychological and metabolic stress: a recipe for accelerated cellular aging?', *Hormones (Athens)*, **8** (1), 7–22.

Fehr, E. and S. Gachter (2002), 'Altruistic punishment in humans', *Nature*, **415**, 137–40.

Forlani, D. and J.W. Mullins (2000), 'Perceived risks and choices in entrepreneur's new venture decision', *Journal of Business Venturning*, **15** (4), 305–22.

Gerra, G., P. Avanzini, A. Zaimovic et al. (1999), 'Neurotransmitters, neuroendocrine correlates of sensation-seeking temperament in normal humans', *Neuropsychobiology*, **39** (4), 207–13.

Gray, P.B., C.-F. Jeffrey Yang and H.G. Pope (2006), 'Fathers have lower salivary testosterone levels than unmarried men and married non-fathers in Beijing, China', *Proceedings of the Royal Society B: Biological Sciences*, **273** (1584), 333–9.

Grichnik, D. (2008), 'Risky choices in new venture decisions–experimental evidence from Germany and the United States', *Journal of International Entrepreneurship*, **6**, 22–47.

Harris, J.A., P.A. Vernon and D.I. Boomsma (1998), 'The heritability of testosterone: a study of Dutch adolescent twins and their parents', *Behavioral Genetics*, **28** (3), 165–71.

Hartgens, F. and H. Kuipers (2004), 'Effects of androgenic-anabolic steroids in athletes', *Sports Medicine*, **34**, 513–54.

Heilman, M.E. (2001), 'Description and prescription: how gender stereotypes prevent women's ascent up the organizational ladder', *Journal of Social Issues*, **57** (4), 657–74.

Henrich, J.P., R. Boyd, S. Bowles et al. (2005), '"Economic man" in cross-cultural perspective: behavioral experiments in 15 small-scale societies', *Behavioral and Brain Sciences*, **28**, 795–855.

Hill, J., L. Murray, V. Leidecker and H. Sharp (2008), 'The dynamics of threat, fear and intentionality in the conduct disorders: longitudinal findings in the children of women with post-natal depression', *Philosophical Transactions of the Royal Society B: Biological Sciences*, **363** (1503), 2529–41.

Holm, H. and P. Engseld (2005), 'Choosing bargaining partners – an experimental study on the impact of information about income, status and gender', *Experimental Economics*, **8** (3), 183–216.

Hönekopp, J., J.T. Manning and C. Müller (2006a), 'Digit ratio (2D:4D) and physical fitness in males and females: evidence for effects of prenatal androgens on sexually selected traits', *Hormones and Behavior*, **49** (4), 545–9.

Hönekopp, J., M. Voracek and J.T. Manning (2006b), '2nd to 4th digit ratio (2D:4D) and number of sex partners: evidence for effects of prenatal testosterone in men', *Psychoneuroendocrinology*, **31** (1), 30–37.

Huddy, L. and N. Terkildsen (1993), 'Gender stereotypes and perception of male and female candidates', *American Journal of Political Science*, **37** (1), 119–47.

Janowsky, J.S. (2006a), 'The role of androgens in cognition and brain aging in men', *Neuroscience*, **138** (3), 1015–20.

Janowsky, J.S. (2006b), 'Thinking with your gonads: testosterone and cognition', *Trends in Cognitive Sciences*, **10** (2), 77–82.

Janowsky, J.S., B. Chavez and E. Orwoll (2000), 'Sex steroids modify working memory', *Journal of Cognitive Neuroscience*, **12** (3), 407–14.

Josephs, R.A., M.L. Newman, R.P. Brown and J.M. Beer (2003), 'Status, testosterone, and human intellectual performance: stereotype threat as status concern', *Psychological Science*, **14** (2), 158–63.

Josephs, R.A., J.G. Sellers, M.L. Newman and P.H. Mehta (2006), 'The mismatch effect: when testosterone and status are at odds', *Journal of Personality and Social Psychology*, **90** (6), 999–1013.

Keh, H.D.F., M.D. Foo and B.C. Lim (2002), 'Opportunity evaluation under risky conditions: the cognitive processes of entrepreneurs', *Entrepreneurial Theory and Practice*, **27** (2), Winter, 125–48.

Kidwell, J.M., R.E. Stevens and A.L. Bethke (1987), 'Differences in ethical perceptions between male and female managers: myth or reality?', *Journal of Business Ethics*, **6** (6), 489–93.

Kikusui, T., J.T. Winslow and Y. Mori (2006), 'Social buffering: relief from stress and anxiety', *Philosophical Transactions of the Royal Society B: Biological Sciences*, **361** (1476), 2215–28.

Kuijper, E.A., C.B. Lambalk, D.I. Boomsma et al. (2007), 'Heritability of reproductive hormones in adult male twins', *Human Reproduction*, **22** (8), 2153–9.

Little, A.C., B.C. Jones and R.P. Burriss (2007), 'Preferences for masculinity in male bodies change across the menstrual cycle', *Hormones and Behavior*, **51**, 633–9.

Liverman, C.T. and D.G. Blazer (2004), *Testosterone and Aging*, Elektronisk udgave edn, Palo Alto, CA: ebrary.

Lutchmaya, S., S. Baron-Cohen, P. Raggatt, R. Knickmeyer and J.T. Manning (2004), '2nd to 4th digit ratios, fetal testosterone and estradiol', *Early Human Development*, **77** (1–2), 23–8.

Magee, J.C. and A.D. Galinsky (2008), 'Social hierarchy: the self-reinforcing nature of power and status', *The Academy of Management Annals*, **2**, 351 –98.

Maner, J.K., S.L. Miller, N.B. Schmidt and L.A. Eckel (2008), 'Submitting to defeat: social anxiety, dominance threat, and decrements in testosterone', *Psychological Science*, **19** (8), 764–8.

Manning, J.T., D. Scutt, G.H. Whitehouse, S.J. Leinster and J.M. Walton (1996), 'Asymmetry and the menstrual cycle in women', *Ethology and Sociobiology*, **17** (2), 129–43.

Manning, J.T., S. Wood, E. Vang et al. (2004), 'Second to fourth digit ratio (2D:4D) and testosterone in men', *Asian Journal of Andrology*, **6** (3), 211–15.

Mazur, A. (1976), 'Effects of testosterone on status in primate groups', *Folia Primatology (Basel)*, **26** (3), 214–26.

Mazur, A. and A. Booth (1998), 'Testosterone and dominance in men', *Behavior and Brain Sciences*, **21** (3), 353–63; discussion 363–97.

Mazur, A. and A. Booth (1999), 'The biosociology of testosterone in men', *Social Perspectives on Emotion*, **5**, 311–38.

Mazur, A. and T.A. Lamb (1980), 'Testosterone, status, and mood in human males', *Hormones and Behavior*, **14**, 236–46.

Mazur, A. and J. Michalek (1998), 'Marriage, divorce and male testosterone', *Social Forces*, **77**, 315–30.

Mazur, A., A. Booth and J.M. Dabbs Jr (1992), 'Testosterone and chess competition', *Social Psychology Quarterly*, **55** (1), 70–7.

Mehta, P.H. and R.A. Josephs (2006), 'Testosterone change after losing predicts the decision to compete again', *Hormones and Behavior*, **50** (5), 684–92.

Mehta, P.H., A.C. Jones and R.A. Josephs (2008), 'The social endocrinology of dominance: basal testosterone predicts cortisol changes and behavior following victory and defeat', *Journal of Personal and Social Psychology*, **94** (6), 1078–93.

Meyer, G., B.P. Hauffa, M. Schedlowski, C. Pawlak, M.A. Stadler and M.S. Exton (2000), 'Casino gambling increases heart rate and salivary cortisol in regular gamblers', *Biological Psychiatry*, **48** (9), 948–53.

Millet, K. and S. Dewitte (2008), 'A subordinate status position increases the present value of financial resources for low 2D:4D men', *American Journal of Human Biology*, **20** (1), 110–15.

Newman, M.L., J.G. Sellers and R.A. Josephs (2005), 'Testosterone, cognition, and social status', *Hormones and Behavior*, **47** (2), 205–11.

O'Doherty, J., J. Winston, H. Critchley, D. Perrett, D.M. Burt and R.J. Dolan (2003), 'Beauty in a smile: the role of medial orbitofrontal cortex in facial attractiveness', *Neuropsychologia*, **41** (2), 147–55.

Oberlechner, T.A.N. (2005), 'Work stress and performance among financial traders', *Stress and Health*, **21** (5), 285–93.

Pawlowski, B. and G. Jasienska (2005), 'Women's preferences for secual dimorphism in height depend on menstrual cycle phase and expected duration of relationship', *Biological Psychology*, **70**, 38–43.

Penton-Voak, I.S. and D.I. Perrett (2000), 'Female preference for male faces changes cyclically: further evidence', *Evolution and Human Behavior*, **21**, 39–48.

Penton-Voak, I.S., D.I. Perrett, D.L. Castles et al. (1999), 'Menstrual cycle alters face preference', *Nature*, **399** (6738), 741–2.

Peter, L.J. and R. Hull (1969), *The Peter Principle*, New York: W. Morrow.

Peters, M., L.W. Simmons and G. Rhodes (2009), 'Preferences across the menstrual cycle for masculinity and symmetry in photographs of male faces and bodies', *PLoS ONE*, **4** (1), e4138.

Purifoy, F.E. and L.H. Koopmans (1979), 'Androstenedione, testosterone, and free testosterone concentration in women of various occupations', *Social Biology*, **26** (3), 179–88.

Puts, D.A, (2005), 'Mating context and menstrual phase affect women's preferences for male voice pitch', *Evolution and Human Behavior*, **26**(5), 388–97.

Resko, J.A. and K.B. Eik-nes (1966), 'Diurnal testosterone levels in peripheral plasma of human male subjects', *Journal of Clinical Endocrinology and Metabolism*, **26** (5), 573–6.

Rhodes, G., S. Yoshikawa, A. Clark, K. Lee, R. McKay and S. Akamatsu (2001), 'Attractiveness of facial averageness and symmetry in non-western cultures: in search of biologically based standards of beauty', *Perception*, **30** (5), 611–25.

Rhodes, G., J. Chan, L.A. Zebrowitz and L.W. Simmons (2003), 'Does sexual dimorphism in human faces signal health?', *Proceedings of the Royal Society of London, Series B: Biological Sciences*, **270** (Suppl.1), S93–S95.

Rhodes, G., S. Yoshikawa, R. Palermo et al. (2007), 'Perceived health contributes to the attractiveness of facial symmetry, averageness, and sexual dimorphism', *Perception*, **36** (8), 1244–52.

Roberti, J.W. (2004), 'A review of behavioral and biological correlates of sensation seeking', *Journal of Research in Personality*, **38** (3), 256–79.

Roney, J.R. and Z.L. Simmons (2008), 'Women's estradiol predicts preference for facial cues of men's testosterone', *Hormones and Behavior*, **53** (1), 14–19.

Roney, J.R., K.N. Hanson, K.M. Durante and D. Maestripieri (2006), 'Reading men's faces: women's mate attractiveness judgments track men's testosterone and interest in infants', *Proceedings of the Royal Society Biological Sciences*, **273** (1598), 2169–75.

Rose, R., I. Bernstein and T. Gordon (1975), 'Consequences of social conflict on plasma testosterone levels in rhesus monkeys', *Psychosomatic Medicine*, **37**, 50–61.

Rudolfsen, G., L. Figenschou, I. Folstad, H. Tveiten and M. Figenschou (2006), 'Rapid adjustments of sperm characteristics in relation to social status', *Proceedings of the Royal Society Biological Sciences*, **273** (1584), 325–32.

Rupp, H.A., T.W. James, E.D. Ketterson, D.R. Sengelaub, E. Janssen and J.R. Heiman (2009a), 'Neural activation in the orbitofrontal cortex in response to male faces increases during the follicular phase', *Hormones and Behavior*, **56** (1), 66–72.

Rupp, H.A., T.W. James, E.D. Ketterson, D.R. Sengelaub, E. Janssen and J.R. Heiman (2009b), 'Neural activation in women in response to masculinized male faces: mediation by hormones and psychosexual factors', *Evolution and Human Behavior*, **30** (1), 1–10.

Saltzman, W., L.J. Digby and D.H. Abbott (2009), 'Reproductive skew in female common marmosets: what can proximate mechanisms tell us about ultimate causes?', *Proceedings of the Royal Society B: Biological Sciences*, **276** (1656), 389–99.

Salvador, A., V. Simon, F. Suay and L. Llorens (1987), 'Testosterone and cortisol responses to competitive fighting in human males: a pilot study', *Aggressive Behavior*, **13**, 9–13.

Salvador, A., F. Suay, E. Gonzalez-Bono and M.A. Serrano (2003), 'Anticipatory cortisol, testosterone and psychologocal responses to judo competition in young men', *Psychoneuroendocrinology*, **28**, 364–75.

Salvador, A., F. Suay, S. Martinez-Sanchis, V.M. Simon and P.F. Brain (1999), 'Correlating testosterone and fighting in male participants in judo contests', *Physiology and Behavior*, **68** (1–2), 205–9.

Schneider, R.H., C.N. Alexander, F. Staggers et al. (2005), 'Long-term effects of stress reduction on mortality in persons > or = 55 years of age with systemic hypertension', *American Journal of Cardiology*, **95** (9), 1060–64.

Seeman, T.E., B.S. McEwen, B.H. Singer, M.S. Albert and J.W. Rowe (1997), 'Increase in urinary cortisol excretion and memory declines: MacArthur studies of successful aging', *Journal of Clinical Endocrinology and Metabolism*, **82** (8), 2458–65.

Seeman, T.E., B.H. Singer, J.W. Rowe, R.I. Horwitz and B.S. McEwen (1997), 'Price of adaptation – allostatic load and its health consequences. MacArthur studies of successful aging', *Archiveis of Internal Medicine*, **157** (19), 2259–68.

Stangor, C. (2000), *Stereotypes and Prejudice: Essential Readings*, Philadelphia, PA: Psychology Press.

Taleb, N. (2005), *Fooled by Randomness: The Hidden Role of Chance in Life and in the Markets*, 2nd edn, New York: Random House.

Tovee, M.J., D.S. Maisey, J.L. Emery and P.L. Cornelissen (1999), 'Visual cues to female physical attractiveness', *Proceedings of the Royal Society of London, Series B: Biological Sciences*, **266** (1415), 211–18.

Tovee, M.J., K. Tasker and P.J. Benson (2000), 'Is symmetry a visual cue to attractiveness in the human female body?', *Evolution and Human Behavior*, **21** (3), 191–200.

van Anders, S.M. and N.V. Watson (2006), 'Relationship status and testosterone in North American heterosexual and non-heterosexual men and women: cross-sectional and longitudinal data', *Psychoneuroendocrinology*, **31** (6), 715–23.

van Anders, S.M., L.D. Hamilton and N.V. Watson (2007), 'Multiple partners are associated with higher testosterone in North American men and women', *Hormones and Behavior*, **51** (3), 454–9.

Van den Bergh, B. and S. Dewitte (2006), 'Digit ratio (2D:4D) moderates the impact of sexual cues on men's decisions in ultimatum games', *Proceedings of the Royal Society B: Biological Sciences*, **273** (1597), 2091–5.

White, K.R., S.L. Crites Jr, J.H. Taylor and G. Corral (2009), 'Wait, what? Assessing stereotype incongruities using the N400 ERP component', *Social Cognitive and Affective Neuroscience*, published online 6 March.

White, R.E., S. Thornhill and E. Hampson (2006), 'Entrepreneurs and evolutionary biology: the relationship between testosterone and new venture creation', *Organizational Behavior and Human Decision Processes*, **100**, 21–34.

Wilson, M. and M. Daly (2004), 'Do pretty women inspire men to discount the future?', *Proceedings of the Royal Society of London Series B*, **271** (Suppl.), S177–S179.

9. Dopamine, expected utility and decision-making in the firm

Donald T. Wargo, Norman A. Baglini and Katherine A. Nelson

INTRODUCTION

The lessons to be learned from understanding the mechanisms underlying expected utility (the economic model of decision-making) and the dopamine-mediated reward system (the neurological correlate of decision-making) are quite profound for understanding decision-making in the firm. The current research from neuroeconomics, psychology and neuroscience has shown that there are three interconnected but nevertheless distinct decision-making systems in the human brain: (1) an unconscious, intuitive and emotional system mediated mainly by midbrain regions such as the ventral striatum, the insula and the amygdala; (2) a conscious, rational system or 'executive function', mediated principally in the orbitofrontal cortex; (3) a system of habitual behavior that is either preprogrammed genetically or developed into habits over time.

Dopamine is the principal neurotransmitter that is involved in these three systems, so analyzing its role in individual decision-making in the firm is critical. As a prime example of a system gone haywire, we can see a disastrous case study of conflicts among these three systems by looking at the causes of the 2008 global credit crisis. As an example with serious consequences, the major investment banks saw little risk in the massive leverage they exposed their companies, their stockholders and their clients to during the years from 2004 to 2007. Further, the US Securities Exchange Commission, even while worried about the risks, removed the borrowing limits of the largest Wall Street investment banks. These investment banks borrowed massive amounts of money for their investments and also sold massive amounts of collateralized debt obligations (CDOs) to their clients with the promise that they were 'risk-free'.

EXPECTED UTILITY AND THE DOPAMINE REWARD SYSTEM

Classical economic decision theory says that we make decisions based on 'expected utility', or 'satisfaction', that we receive from the things we want. The best decision strategy over time maximizes our expected utility function, which specifies the utility we receive from all possible outcomes of our decisions.

However, the neurological structure underlying this economic theory is the human brain's processing of expected rewards. The human brain, from an evolutionary point of view, is organized to efficiently interpret information necessary to our survival, navigate our clan's social hierarchy and direct actions to achieve goals and avoid danger. Despite our elevated opinion of our human brain, it evolved mostly in the stone age where rewards, dangers and social interactions were all within a stone's throw. The human brain is still evolving today, although the pace of technological advance may give it challenges that it is not quite yet prepared for. That is why some cognitive scientists contend that the human brain may not be exactly acclimated to our modern world (Peterson, 2005).

The brain, which is composed of 100 billion neurons with 100 trillion connections, can be conceptualized as an integrated organism having three divisions: the 'triune brain' (Peterson, 2007). Neuroscientists have come to understand more about the functioning of the parts of the human brain through four major methods. The first is functional magnetic resonance imaging (fMRI), which measures the oxygen use in specific parts of the brain. The neurons of the brain that are activated in a specific task use more energy, which requires increased amounts of oxygen. Thus, we can see each area's functionality in specific brain activities during specific tasks. The second method of understanding the brain's function is through testing the cognitive deficiencies of humans or animals that have suffered brain injury or damage, either through injury or experimental manipulation. Third, scientists can measure in the blood or urine levels of certain hormones and cell signaling transmitters under specific experiments. For example, the standard scientific measure of the level of stress of an animal or human is the amount of cortisol, the stress hormone, released in the blood or urine. The fourth method is by inserting micro wires into the brains of laboratory animals (mostly rats and monkeys) and also in humans undergoing surgery for epilepsy. Some experiments electrically stimulate areas of the brain while others measure the electrical firing of neurons during certain activities. The information we present in this chapter has been garnered by all of these methods.

THE STRUCTURE OF THE BRAIN

The most primitive division of the human brain is the brainstem, which contains the basal ganglia and cerebellum (see Figure 5.1 in Chapter 5). The midbrain is commonly referred to as the 'reptilian brain'. This is the locus of a primitive level of consciousness, certain instincts and the management of the body's autonomic system, such as respiration and pulse rate. It is the locus of human actions that have become habits after repetition.

The second division is the midbrain or limbic system – the emotional center of the brain. We refer to this division as the 'gorilla brain'. The word emotion means a feeling that moves us to action, and accordingly this division activates approach or avoidance behavior. The two major circuits of the limbic system are the reward approach and loss/avoidance systems. Our brain's reward/approach system and the complementary loss/avoidance system are fundamentally the same systems that reptiles and mammals are endowed with.

The reward system, which governs our valuation of expected rewards, is mediated by the neurotransmitter dopamine and has been well studied (Knutson and Cooper, 2005). It governs the expectations as well as the pleasures of eating and drinking, investment behavior, mate seeking, the value coding of goals and the search for novelty. From an evolutionary point of view, the reward system makes us want to acquire things or perform actions that are positive for our maintenance as organisms. More importantly, the wanting feeling is scalable according to the functional proximity of the positive action and the potential for reproduction as an example. Thus, the pleasure of a cold drink of water when we are thirsty is nowhere near the pleasure of sex (ibid.; O'Doherty et al., 2004). On the other hand, dysfunction of this system or excessive activation of this system can cause thrill seeking, excessive risk taking, greed or addiction.

This finding is especially supported by the research of Pecina and colleagues (Pecina et al., 2003). These researchers genetically manipulated mice to have a deficient dopamine reuptake system, thereby increasing the amount of dopamine remaining in the synapses of the nucleus accumbens neurons by 70 percent. The mice in the trial had to learn an experimental run to find a sweet water-dispensing machine. The hyperdopaminergic mice experienced significantly more wanting behavior but not more liking behavior. The altered mice left the start box more quickly, required fewer trials to learn the run, were distracted less often and proceeded more directly to the reward. However, they showed no higher liking of the reward than control group mice.

The second motivational circuit in the limbic system motivates us to avoid loss and is triggered by perceived threats or danger (Taylor et al.,

2006). The structures in this system include the anterior insula, which registers pain and disgust; the amygdale, which processes emotions; the hippocampus, the center of memory processing and fixating; and the hypothalamus, which secretes hormones to activate physiological responses (see Figure 5.3 in Chapter 5). Anxiety, fear and panic are all triggered in the loss/avoidance system. These emotions have correlating cognitive thoughts of pessimism and worry.

Behavioral economics has shown through innumerable experiments that humans are loss-averse. The difference of valence between the reward/pursuit system and the loss/avoidance system is enormous. Economic games using real money show that humans feel a loss more or less twice as much as an equivalent gain (Kahneman and Tversky, 1979, 1991; Tversky and Kahneman, 1992).

The neoclassical model of homo economicus states that we make decisions as a rational utility maximizer, with expected utility being defined as the 'satisfaction' we expect to receive from the consumption or possession of goods and services. Further, economics as a science observes the outcomes of economic decisions by individuals and not the actual decision process in the human brain. It states that we cannot know nor interpersonally compare the actual preferences of individuals, but only observe the 'revealed preferences', so the outcomes are all that matters. In effect, neoclassical economics treats the human brain as a black box.

Neuroeconomics shows that this neoclassical model is incorrect. Real humans make decisions by internally maximizing dopamine and other hormones that make them feel good, rather than maximizing the outcome. Real humans are focused (either unconsciously or consciously) on the process in the brain, rather than the outcome by itself. This different decision-making model is the subject of this chapter, so we discuss it in detail below. However, we point out here that the difference is highlighted by this issue of addiction. Neoclassical economics struggles with trying to explain how addicts maximize utility, as the addiction is self-destructive. Paulus, on the other hand, shows how neuroeconomics can easily explain the decision-making process of the addict as dopamine-maximizing behavior (Paulus, 2007).

When confronted with a threat or danger, the loss/avoidance system activates the entire body. Neurotransmitters prepare the brain to focus on the danger. Further, the hypothalamus-pituitary-adrenal axis (HPA axis) floods the bloodstream with stress hormones and epinephrine. Then, the sympathetic nervous system prepares the entire body for the 'fight or flight' response. Of course, when this system is overactivated, it causes panic attacks and when it is chronically activated under stress, it can cause high blood pressure, arteriosclerosis and heart attacks and strokes.

The third division in the triune brain model is the cortex (see Figure 5.1

in Chapter 5). We refer to this as the 'computer brain'. Humans, along with primates, have a large cortex, but humans have an expanded prefrontal cortex. The prefrontal cortex is the area of learning from rewards and losses, abstract thinking, impulse control, planning, calculation and executive function. More specifically, the orbitofrontal cortex (OFC) integrates reason and emotion, while the anterior cingulate cortex (ACC) resolves decision conflicts and evaluates emotional information as either relevant or unimportant (Peterson, 2007).

Although neuronal networks integrate these three divisions, the fact that they are evolutionarily and physically distinct has important consequences. The most important consequence for neuroeconomists is that in contrast to the neoclassical economic assumption that homo economicus is a rational maximizer of expected utility; the economic and scientific literature is full of examples of the seemingly 'irrational' decision-making behavior in humans (Camerer, 2003; Tversky and Kahneman, 1981, 1992). Neuroeconomics appears to be the most successful discipline to date in reconciling these contrasting behaviors (Glimcher and Rustichini, 2004; Sanfey, 2007).

THE SOCIETY OF MINDS

The most successful theoretical model of the brain, which explains 'irrational' judgments, is that proposed by Jonathan Cohen (2005). Borrowing a term first used by Minsky, Cohen posits that although the parts of the human brain are all interconnected and work together, the brain is best not thought of as a homogeneous unit, but as a 'society of minds', with each part allocated a specific task or tasks (Minsky, 1986). Thus there is competition among the faster and unconscious 'emotional brain', whose neurological correlates are the ventral striatum, the brainstem and the amygdale, and the slower, deliberate 'conscious brain'. This latter system enables the person to consider and act on abstract goals and principles and has the capability of impulse control, but which thinks in words, can only focus on and compare two items at one time and is located in the prefrontal cortex (Koechlin and Hyafil, 2007).

Further, the decision-making, moral psychology and neuroeconomic literatures group the 'society of minds' into two general mechanisms: system 1 is for automatic processing and decisions. It works quickly and results in intuitive solutions to problems. System 2 corresponds to the conscious and controlled processes of our mind, rational thought, logic and rumination. It monitors the correctness of the System 1 answers and sometimes overrides them. 'Free will' resides in the prefrontal cortex – the seat of abstract ideas and actions based on abstract ideas, impulse control and transcendence.

Since we have introduced the concept of free will, it is important to discuss the current controversy surrounding its existence. The concept of free will is, of course, fundamental to philosophers and religions. However, in a series of famous experiments, Benjamin Libet (Libet et al., 1983; Libet 1985), using MRI scanning, found that a freely voluntary act was preceded by about 550 milliseconds by a readiness potential to act in the brains of his subjects (ibid.). However, the subject was only consciously aware of the wish or intention to act approximately 200 milliseconds before the act. In other words, the brain was initiating the process unconsciously, about 350 milliseconds before the subjects were aware of wanting to act!

The critiques and sometimes attacks on Libet's research and its implications are extensive. The most serious worry is that his experiments disprove the existence of free will. However, over the course of the current decade, Libet has been both vociferous and prolific in answering all his critics, insisting that his findings do not negate free will (Libet, 2002, 2003, 2006).

'We had also found (Libet et al., 1983) that the brain exhibits a preparatory process (the "readiness potential," RP) that begins about 400 ms before the subject is consciously aware of the urge or intention to produce a voluntary act.' Pockett (2004) cites the view that this 'seems to negate the idea that we have free will.' Pockett does not give our full story. Our findings only indicated that free will could not initiate the volitional process. Since awareness of intention to act does precede the actual act by about 150 ms, it is still possible for conscious will to control the final outcome of the process; it could potentially provide a necessary trigger for the process to go to completion; and/or it could block or veto the intention to act, so that no action occurs (Libet, 1985, 1999). 'Our findings, therefore, would allow free will as a control agent rather than as an initiator of the volitional process. Free will might then be called "free won't," as also noted by some other commentators' (Libet, 2006).

Cohen contends that the seemingly 'irrational' behavior or decisions of individuals is explained by the outcome of the competition of these two systems with each presenting solutions to the problem; the outcome is not always economically optimal (Cohen, 2005). If we agree with the universally accepted assumption of economic theory, that people make decisions that maximize their utility, then we must posit that people always act rationally in accord with their long-term goals. Clearly they do not, which begs a crucial question: why?

The answer, according to Cohen, is that people seek to optimize their utility subject to constraints. These constraints include limited information, specific existential circumstances, limited ability to learn from mistakes, limited ability to focus on the problem, limited ability to control one's own behavior and selfish versus altruistic orientation to name a few. As a result, our neural decision-making systems produce decisions that are locally optimal but not universally optimal. In the case of hominins, the environment that encouraged the development of the human brain has changed radically in the last 300 years. Some of the decision systems (as well as biological systems) that we still possess are maladapted to our current circumstances. A good example of a maladapted biological system is our body's stress response. It works for acute emergencies but the allostatic load that modern life's stressors put on our 'fight or flight' system can cause heart attacks, type II diabetes, immune system deficiencies, reproductive problems and a host of other ailments (Sapolsky, 2004).

This is not to say that the rational brain is optimal either in making economic decisions. We will see that the conscious, 'rational' brain also has constraints. It thinks in words, it can only focus on one problem at a time limited by being able to only compare two competing solutions to the problem at one time (Koechlin and Hyafil, 2007). These limitations, we believe, are the cause of the artificial creation by philosophers from Aristotle to the present day of the 'ethical dilemmas' so popular in moral philosophical thought.

System 1 and System 2 have localized regions that perform their functions in the architecture of the human brain. The reaction to rewarding events or the anticipation of them is localized in the brainstem, which releases the neurotransmitter dopamine, and the striatum which reacts to the receipt of the released dopamine. These are the sites affected by drugs of abuse (Paulus, 2007).

Other subcortical structures respond to valenced events – positive and negative utility. These include the medial prefrontal cortex, the orbitoprefrontal cortex, the insular cortex, the amygdala and the striatum. All of these structures have neuronal connections to areas associated with higher cognitive processing, primarily the anterior prefrontal cortex, the dorsolateral prefrontal cortex and the temporal lobe. The prefrontal cortex comprises one-third of the volume of the neocortex and is the area that has expanded the most over our primate relatives during evolution. The separateness yet interconnectedness of these structures also has profound effects on how humans perceive reward and risk and make decisions based on those valuations.

INSTINCTUAL BRAIN SYSTEMS

At the deepest level of brain organization, cognitive neuroscientists have identified four basic instinctual brain systems (Bloom, 2007): (1) the seeking/reward system that pursues pleasure (or what is its equivalent in economic theory to the value associated with the expected utility); (2) the anger/rage system which governs angry aggression (but not predatory aggression); (3) the fear/anxiety system, which causes avoidance; (4) the panic system which creates the fight or flight reaction but also assists more complex functions, such as social bonding.

Further, there is ongoing scientific research to suggest that a fifth brain system, the 'play system', is just as important an evolutionary survival system as the above four (Pelligrini and Smith, 2005). G. Stanley Hall, the father of child and development psychology in the USA, formulated this postulate: 'Ontogeny recapitulates phylogeny.' In the case of humans, this means that the stages of development of an individual member of our species replicate the evolutionary history of *Homo sapiens* (ibid.). While behavioral anthropologists do not rigidly accept this dictum today, it is widely accepted that individuals actively engage in their own development, spontaneously seeking experiences that prepare them for adult life. Play is critically important in learning one's own strengths and weaknesses, rules of behavior and survival skills by mimicking adult activities (Bateson, 2005).

Malfunctions of these systems can occur either by nature (genetic) or nurture (environmental). At the basic level, these aberrations include: seeking/reward system: addiction to drugs, alcohol, gambling and so on; anger-rage system: violent crime, child and wife abuse and so on; fear-anxiety system: depression, anxiety disorders, and so on; panic system: panic attacks, claustrophobia, agoraphobia and so on.

The neurological correlate of the decision mechanism that maximizes this expected utility is the brain's dopamine reward system. In the ventral striatum and its associated brain areas, dopamine encodes the expected rewards of a contemplated action (eating, drinking, sex, generosity, revenge, punishment of cheaters). Further, when the action is taken, it also reliably and proportionately judges the actual outcome compared to the expected outcome by releasing dopamine scaled to the magnitude of the outcome's reward to bind to the dopamine reward receptors (D_1 ... D_5), thereby reinforcing a correct decision. Conversely, if the action taken does not meet expectations, there is no similar dopamine release. Dopamine also mediates the medial prefrontal cortex's 'executive function', which decides between two competing anticipated actions. Finally, dopamine also mediates the buildup of habits. It rewards repeated actions in the ventral striatum (but in diminishing magnitude), as the action becomes more and more rote. When the action becomes a habit, it is no longer mediated by dopamine, but actually is now controlled and is mediated by the basal ganglia, the same brainstem area that governs animal instincts (Choi et al., 2005; Wickens et al., 2007).

HOMEOSTASIS OF BODY AND BRAIN SYSTEMS

Another crucially important but often overlooked characteristic of the human body and brain is their need to achieve homeostasis. This is the organism's need to maintain a steady internal state. Human body examples include temperature (98.6°C) and the blood and brain oxygen levels. If these levels change by much, we get sick and may die. However, not all body systems' homeostasis is so critical. Certain body systems such as the stress response system or the reward system can, through external or internal stimuli, become chronically elevated. McEwen and Lasley (2002) refers to this capacity of certain systems to remain at elevated levels as allostasis. Chronic elevation of the stress system causes heart disease, diabetes, colitis, fibromyalgia and so on (ibid.). This is also true for other members of the animal kingdom (Sapolsky, 2005).

Paulus contends that the entire decision-making system of individuals is a homeostatic system, and he receives widespread agreement on this model from the scientific community (Camerer et al., 2005; Oswold, 1997; Paulus, 2007; Schultz and Dickinson, 2000; Shermer, 2008). See further details on homeostasis in Chapter 5 in this volume.

It is quite helpful in the case of the reward/loss system to view it as a homeostatic system. Studies show the simultaneous activation of both these neural networks until threshold activation is passed and the individual chooses the approach or avoidance action (Daw et al., 2006; De Martino et al., 2006; Koob and Le Moal, 1997; Rietveld, 2008). This characterization of decision-making as a homeostatic system receives support from studies showing that individuals with generalized anxiety disorder exhibit intolerance of risk. Additionally, fMRI investigations show that subjects 'at risk' for substance abuse have higher levels of activation in the nucleus accumbens and exhibit high risk taking and impulsivity (Paulus, 2007).

THE DOPAMINE REWARD SYSTEM

In looking at Figure 9.1, we see that the reward system is composed of neurons in the ventral tegmental area (VTA) of each brain half, which release the neurotransmitter dopamine. The dopamine then binds to dopamine receptors in the nucleus accumbens (NAcc), the medial prefrontal cortex (MFPC) and the anterior cingulate gyrus. When the brain perceives an expected reward via visual and/or auditory stimulus, the release of dopamine in the synapses between the VTA neurons and the NAcc neurons stimulates the organism to seek or want the reward and to take appropriate action to acquire that reward. After the expected reward is acquired, the MFPC records the actual 'utility' or 'satisfaction' of the reward. The MPFC also learns how to obtain rewards and learns from successes and mistakes.

The manner in which dopamine neurons in the VTA not only predict rewards but also learn from errors is well known. Schultz (2002) has shown from brain-wired monkeys that the resting firing of dopamine neurons is three times per second (ibid.). If the expected reward is exactly what was anticipated, the neurons do not increase the firing rate. However, if the reward is better than expected the firing rate goes to 40 times per second and the intensity of the firing increases. However, if the reward does not meet expectations (no valenced reward) the firing of the dopamine neurons is depressed. D'Ardenne and colleagues have replicated these results in human subjects using fMRI imaging (D'Ardenne et al., 2008).

DOPAMINE AND ADDICTION, INCLUDING ADDICTION TO MONEY

As to the psychological consequences of money, Lea and Webley characterize money as both a 'tool' – an interest in money for what it can be exchanged for – and a 'drug' – an interest in money for itself – a maladaptive function (Lea and Webley, 2006). This theory further emphasizes that although the standard model states that people value money for its instrumentality – that is, money enables people to achieve goals without aid from others –there are many actions that humans take related to money that are not explained by instrumentality. For example, Price and colleagues show that physical and mental illness after financial strain due to job loss is triggered by reduced feelings of personal control (Price et al., 2002).

Lea and Webley explain many behaviors concerning money as an addiction to its drug properties. This aspect of money is reinforced by clinical psychologists Klontz and colleagues in their paper, 'The treatment of disordered money behaviors', which documents the widespread aberrant and pathological disorders that involve money (Klontz et al., 2008). Klontz states that, 'Disordered money behaviors are not caused by lack of money. It is a seemingly logical conclusion for many that problems with money and related stress can be cured by having more money. However, research consistently shows that this is not the case' (ibid., p. 296).

Therefore, we believe it is critical to understand how addiction can high-jack the brain's dopamine reward system. This is especially true of money addiction, which is a possible cause of aberrant individual behavior in the firm. Thus, we explain addiction below.

We can learn a lot about the dopamine reward system from its aberrations, such as drug abuse. All drugs of abuse (alcohol, cocaine, nicotine, amphetamines) act primarily on dopamine transmission. As a result of the war on drugs and the enormous social cost of addiction, much research money has been directed to studying drug addiction. Consequently, the molecular biology and the neurological interactions of these drugs of abuse are well known (Nestler and Malenka, 2004; Paulus, 2007; Paulus et al., 2004; Rajadhyaksha and Kosofsky, 2005; Sergo, 2008). Unfortunately, despite all the research no effective treatment for addiction has yet been found (Carey, 2008).

Like all neurotransmitters, once the dopamine is released into the synapses between the dopamine-producing neurons (about 15 000 on each hemisphere of the brain in the VTA) and the dopamine-receiving neurons (in the NAcc,) it is reabsorbed ('reuptake') by a protein transporter on the VTA neurons. It is then processed for reuse and stored in vesicles in the VTA neurons (Figure 9.1). All drugs of abuse interfere with the normal working of this system with the result that the amount of dopamine remaining in the synapses is significantly increased, up to ten times. This is where the high comes from.

Cocaine and related stimulants (amphetamines) increase dopamine by blocking the reuptake process, binding to the dopamine transporter proteins (Figure 9.2). Alcohol and opiates enhance dopamine release by quieting another set of neurons in the VTA that regulate and inhibit the dopamine-releasing neurons. Nicotine directly stimulates the VTA dopamine neurons to overexpress.

Unfortunately, there are other pernicious chemical effects of drugs of abuse that permanently alter the neurons and cause the addiction. The same typical addictive behavior can also be replicated in laboratory animals (rats, mice and monkeys.) These animals are connected to an intravenous line that can dispense saline solution or a drug. They are given three levers to push, one for the saline, one for the drug and one for a food pellet. In a few days they are addicted and will constantly preferentially administer the drug, often dying of exhaustion or malnutrition (Nestler and Malenka, 2004).

When the drug is taken away, the animals will cease working to get the drug, however, the addiction memory remains. Even rats that have been 'clean' for months will immediately repeat the bar-pressing behavior when given a little taste of cocaine or even placed in a cage that they associate with a drug high. This reaction is replicated in humans, where recovering addicts will relapse upon contact with stress, low doses of the drug ('I'll just have one glass of wine') or drug-associated cues, such as the sight of a crack pipe. This is because dopamine not only creates a high but also

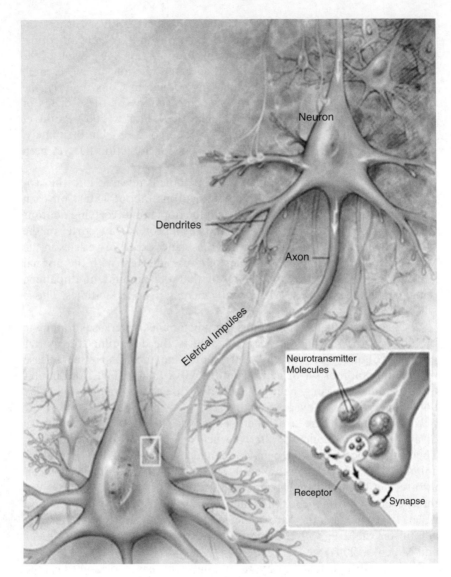

Source: National Institute on Aging, http://www.nia.nih.gov/NR/rdonlyres/9AE77333-
CC65-456E-AA7A-6FF465BE3109/0/NEURONS_HIGH.JPG.

Figure 9.1   *Dopamine neurons in the ventral tegmental area (VTA) and
the nucleus accumbens (NAcc)*

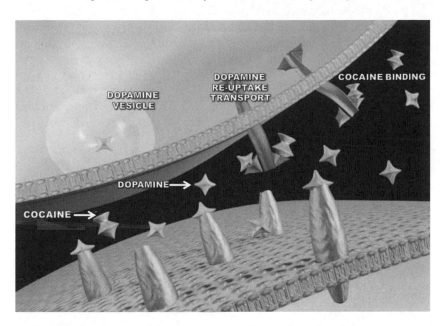

Source: National Institute on Drug Abuse, originally in color, at http://www.drugabuse.gov/pubs/teaching/teaching3/largegifs/slide-8.gif.

Figure 9.2 Cocaine blocks dopamine reuptake

actually activates specific genes in the NAcc neurons that 'learn' the high and thus makes the reward system sensitized to drugs and drug cues. As an evolutionary mechanism, remembering the reward of food or sex is adaptive. However, this also makes it so difficult to cure addiction (ibid.; Rajadhyaksha and Kosofsky, 2005). Recent research has shown that the mechanism of the learned relapse in rodent models is excess dopamine signaling in the extended amygdala, which causes a cortisol cascade – the stress hormone (Kash et al., 2008).

DOPAMINE AND PATHOLOGICAL GAMBLING

Further insights into the dopamine reward system can be garnered from research on pathological gamblers. The literature and experiments overwhelmingly conclude that gambling addicts have desensitized dopamine reward systems. Their NAcc neurons have decreased concentrations of dopamine receptors, so they are less sensitive to rewards and everyday novelties as compared to normal subjects. Additionally, gambling addicts exhibit significantly less neural and somatic response to losses (Peterson, 2007). Further, Goudrian and colleagues measured the psychophysiological responses (heartbeat, skin conductance, that is, measure of autonomic sympathetic arousal, stress levels) of addicted gamblers versus control groups experiencing wins and losses. They concluded that gamblers exhibited deficient responses to both wins and losses. These findings point to both impaired risk assessment and decreased reward sensitivity (Goudriaan et al., 2006).

The current scientific hypothesis states that gamblers are deficient in their dopamine-mediated response to reward and thus self-stimulate with games of chance that temporarily overstimulate dopamine production. The research of Reuter and colleagues describes fMRI scans of pathological gamblers while playing games of chance showed decreased activation in their brain's ventral striatum region and ventromedial prefrontal cortex. Reuter and colleagues found that the activation of these areas in addicted gamblers was scalable and negatively proportional to the severity of their gambling habit. This links hypo-activation – that is, deficient responsiveness – of these areas to the severity of the gambling addiction (Reuter et al., 2005).

An unusual confirmation of the workings of the dopamine system is reported by Dodd. Parkinson's disease, caused by a deficiency in the dopamine system, is primarily treated by drugs that restore or improve dopaminergic neurotransmission. In as much as 30 percent of Parkinson's disease cases, pathological gambling is induced in the patients by the dopamine-enhancing drugs. According to Dodd, administering an antagonist that removes dopamine cures the pathological gambling (Dodd et al., 2005).

REWARD/LOSS AND THE PREFRONTAL CORTEX

Thus, the brain's dopamine system includes the encoding of the 'expected utility' of a reward, the acquisition of that reward, and the encoding of the value of the 'actual utility' or 'satisfaction' derived from that reward. As a further understanding of the role of the MPFC in the reward system, we present the recent work of Xue. Xue and colleagues used fMRI imaging on subjects in standard laboratory experiments replicating gains and losses (Xue et al., 2008).

These neuroscientists found that different regions of the MPFC evaluate the experienced risk level of the possible decision options and the valenced magnitude (positive or negative) of the outcome. The dorsal MFPC activity was scaled to the experienced risk by each participant and was negatively correlated and proportional to the risk preference of the subject. That is, those with a high risk-taking personality profile had decreased activity in the dorsal MPFC and vice versa. On the other hand, the ventral MPFC registered the actual gain/loss and was proportionately activated by the actual gain or loss and its signal was positively correlated with the individual's risk preference. Thus, the dorsal MPFC conveys a risk signal whereas the ventral MPFC conveys a reward signal.

Xue and colleagues contend that whereas the NAcc is sensitive to both risk and reward, the MPFC differentiates strongly between the two by processing them in different areas. This means that both ventral and dorsal MPFC signals are predictive of risk-taking behavior. A strong reward signal in the ventral MPFC likely leads to risk-taking behavior, whereas a strong signal in the dorsal MPFC acts as a warning signal in more risk-averse individuals. The study further shows that these sensitivities are independent of one another.

These results suggest that the two competing forces that contend with each other in making decisions under uncertainty and risk – fear of the risk and the lure of the gain – have strong neural correlates in the MPFC. It appears that these two regions of the MPFC determine whether the risk will be taken or avoided. As we mentioned above, there is strong evidence of a homeostasis mechanism in this reward/loss system that keeps it in balance. On the other hand, imbalances in these forces – and the accompanying MPFC signals – will lead to excessive reward seeking (including thrill seeking, gambling or addiction) or excessive risk aversion (risk-averse bankers, or *in extremis* anxiety disorders).

IMPLICATIONS FOR ORGANIZATIONAL BEHAVIOR IN THE FIRM

Individuals have different risk preferences. Thus, it is important to have a system to monitor their risk taking in firms that take risks, such as investment and stock trading. Examples of traders and financial institutions taking on risk far beyond their firm's capabilities are plentiful in the recent financial credit crisis. However, there are particular individuals who ignored or skirted those risk controls and brought the companies huge losses or bankruptcy. Jerome Kerviel, a trader at the French bank Société Générale, was only authorized to take positions up to 125 million euros but lost 4.9 billion euros for the bank (*The Economist*, 2008). Joseph Cassano, who headed AIG's tiny Financial Products Unit in London, brought this largest insurance company in the world into insolvency by overexposing it to credit-default swaps (*Wall Street Journal*, 31 October 2008).

Zweig reports that two aspects of the dopamine reward system give us insights into these aberrant behaviors. The first is that the unconscious brain is extremely sensitive to the size of the reward and much less sensitive to the changes in the probability of receiving that reward. Thus, the bigger the expected gain, the more active the NAcc regardless of how poor the odds are of actually receiving the prize. This is because the size of the reward is processed unconsciously while probabilities must be processed in the rational brain – actually in the MFPC (Zweig, 2007). Second, the reward system is the locus of addiction. The fMRI brain scan of someone who is about to make money is identical to that of a cocaine addict. Further, there is an addiction memory akin to that of drugs. The expectation of making money becomes more rewarding than the actual making of money (ibid.).

It is critically important to take the power of money explicitly into account when thinking about business ethics. Pessiglione and colleagues performed experiments to show how the brain translates money into a force. The researchers had their subjects view pictures of money (a penny or a pound) and were told they could keep the amount shown depending on how hard they squeezed a handgrip. The subjects received feedback in the form of a visual thermometer and the researchers also measured subjects' skin conductance response and brain activity. Not surprisingly, the larger the amount shown, the stronger the grip force exercised by the subjects.

The brain scans showed activity in a specific basal forebrain area that includes the ventral striatum – the reward center of the brain (the dopamine processing brain facility), ventral pallidum and extended amygdala (Pessiglione et al., 2007). This research supports the view that this region created the motivational effect of the money and is a key node in brain circuitry that enables expected rewards to energize behavior. More specifically, other research has shown that ventral striatum activity has been linked to reward prediction and reward prediction error during learning (O'Doherty et al., 2004; Pessiglione et al., 2006).

However, the amazing results from this experiment occurred when the subjects were shown the money amounts in display times that were subliminal (17 and 50 ms) and therefore below the conscious perception of the subjects. The grip force, SCR and brain activity were similar even when the subjects could not consciously see the monetary display. Thus, expected rewards energize behavior without the need for the subjects' awareness.

Vohs and colleagues hypothesized that when people were reminded of money they would feel more self-sufficient and would want to be free from dependency on other people and conversely not want people to depend on them. The researchers devised nine experiments to test that theory.

An amazing aspect of this experiment was that the subjects were mentally primed with money or neutral concepts subliminally. They then were ordered to perform certain tasks, some of which were actually impossible.

The researchers found that participants who were primed with the concept of money preferred to work alone, play alone and put more physical distance between themselves and a new acquaintance. Reminders of money led to reduced requests for help and reduced helpfulness towards others. These researchers conclude that the self-sufficiency pattern they found helps explain why people view money both as a great good and a great evil. As societies developed, they contend, the acquisition of money allowed people to pursue their goals with diminished reliance on friends and family (Vohs et al., 2006). That is, money enhanced individualism but diminished communal motivations, as it still does so today. Grouzet shows that across 15 different cultures, 'financial success' as a goal is in direct opposition to goals concerning 'community' – although less so for less developed areas of the world (Grouzet et al., 2005).

Finally, Fliessbach and colleagues show that even though money triggers dopamine reactions in the brain's ventral striatum, it is the relative reward rather than the absolute reward that matters in social comparisons. These experimenters used side-by-side brain imaging scanners and a behavioral task in which equal performance was rewarded inequitably. Blood oxygen levels were elevated in the ventral striatum, a brain area that has a central role in responding to and predicting rewards, and showed that this region was indeed sensitive to the relative amount of money that was paid. More importantly, this ventral striatum response occurred when no decisions were made, suggesting that the calculation of social standing – as indexed by payment – may be automatic (Fliessbach et al., 2007).

Like the stress system, the reward system was not evolved to cope with constant activation of modern society. Therefore, in jobs where there are constant reward/risk decisions, the NAcc can become desensitized and, like a drug addict, the individual needs more activation of the NAcc to feel normal. This is known as 'hedonic adaptation' and can cause the investor/trader/decision-maker to lose interest in all other human pursuits, such as friends, family and love (Peterson, 2007). More research into the reward system is essential to help create appropriate incentive systems for companies.

REFERENCES

Bateson, P. (2005), 'The role of play in the evolution of great apes and humans', in A.D. Pellegrini and P.K. Smith (eds) (2005), *The Nature of Play, Great Apes and Humans*, New York: The Guilford Press.

Bloom, F.E. (ed.) (2007), *Best of the Brain from Scientific American*, New York and Washinghton, DC: Dana Press.

Camerer, C. (2003), *Behavioral Game Theory*, Princeton, NJ: Princeton University Press.

Camerer, C., G. Loewenstein and D. Prelec (2005), 'Neuroeconomics: how neuroscience can inform economics', *Journal of Economic Literature*, **34** (1), 9–65.

Carey, B. (2008), 'The evidence gap: drug rehabilitation or revolving door?' *New York Times*, Science Times, 23 December, D-1.

Choi, W.Y., P.D. Balsam and J.C. Horvitz (2005), 'Extended habit training reduces dopamine mediation of appetitive response expression', *Journal of Neuroscience*, **25** 6729.

Cohen, J.D. (2005), 'The vulcanization of the human brain: a neural perspective on interactions between cognition and emotion', *Journal of Economic Perspectives*, **19** (4), 3–24.

D'Ardenne, K., S.M. McClure, L.E. Nystrom and J.D. Cohen (2008), 'Responses reflecting dopaminergic signals in the human ventral tegmental area', *Science*, **319** (5867), 1264–87.

Daw, N.D., J.P. O'Doherty, P. Dayan, B. Seymour and R.J. Dolan (2006), 'Cortical substrates for exploratory decisions in humans', *Nature*, **441**, 15 June, 876–9.

De Martino, B., D. Kumaran, B. Seymour and R.J. Dolan (2006), 'Frames, biases and rational decision-making in the human brain', *Science*, **313** (5787), 684–7.

Dodd, M.L., K.J. Klos, J.H. Bower, Y.E. Geda, K.A. Josephs and J.E. Ahlskog (2005), 'Pathological gambling caused by drugs used to treat Parkinsons disease', *Archives of Neurology*, **62**, September, 1377–81.

Economist, The (2008), 'The rogue rebuttal, not only Jerome Kerviel is pointing an accusing finger at the French bank', 7 February.

Fliessbach, K., B. Weber, P. Trautner et al. (2007), 'Social comparison affects reward-related brain activity in the human ventral striatum', *Science*, **318**, 1305.

Glimcher, P.W. and A. Rustichini (2004), 'Neuroeconomics: the consilience of brain and decision', *Science*, **306**, 447–52.

Goudriaan, A.E., J. Oosterlaan, E. deBeurs and W. van den Brink (2006), 'Psychophysiological determinants and concomitants of deficient decision making in pathological gamblers', *Drug and Alcohol Dependence*, **84** (3), 231–9.

Grouzet, F.M., A. Ahuvia, Y. Kim et al. (2005), 'The structure of goal contents across 15 cultures', *Journal of Personality and Social Psychology*, **89** (5), 800.

Kahneman, D. and A. Tversky (1979), 'Prospect Theory: an analysis of decision under risk', *Econometrica*, **4**, 263–91.

Kahneman, D. and A. Tversky (1991), 'Loss-aversion in riskless choice: a reference-dependent model', *Quarterly Journal of Economics*, **106**, 1039–61.

Kash, T.L., W.P. Nobis, R.T. Matthews and D.G. Winder (2008), 'Dopamine enhances fast excitatory synaptic transmission in the extended amygdala by a CRF-R1-dependent process', *Journal of Neuroscience*, **28** (51), 13856–65.

Klontz, B., A. Bivens, P. Klontz, J. Wada and R. Kahler (2008), 'The treatment of disordered money behaviors: results of an open clinical trial', *Psychological Services*, **8** (3), 295–308.

Knutson, B. and J.C. Cooper (2005), 'Functional magnetic resonance imaging of reward prediction', *Current Opinion in Neurology*, **18** (4), 411–17.

Koechlin, E. and A. Hyafil (2007), 'Anterior prefrontal function and the limits of human decision-making', *Science*, **318**, 26 October, 594–8.

Koob, G.C. and M. Le Moal (1997), 'Drug abuse: hedonic homeostastic dysregulation', *Science*, **278** (5335), 52–8.

Lea, S.E.G. and P. Webley (2006), 'Money as a tool and a drug', *Behavioral Brain Science*, **29**, 161.

Libet, B. (1985), 'Unconscious cerebral initiative and the role of conscious will in voluntary action', *Behavioral and Brain Sciences*, **8** (4), 529–66.

Libet, B. (1999), 'Do we have free will?', *Journal of Consciousness Studies*, **6**, 47–57.

Libet, B. (2002), 'The timing of mental events: Libet's findings and their implications', *Consciousness and Cognition*, **11**, 291–9.

Libet, B. (2003), 'Timing of conscious experience: Reply to the 2002 commentaries on Libet's findings', *Consciousness and Cognition*, **12**, 321–31.

Libet, B. (2006), 'The timing of brain events: reply to the "Special Section" in this journal of September 2004, edited by Susan Pockett', *Consciousness and Cognition*, **15**, 540–47.

Libet, B., C. Gleason, F. Wright and D. Pearl (1983), 'Time of conscious intention to act is relation to onset of cerebral activities (readiness-potential). The unconscious initiation of a freely voluntary act', *Brain*, **106**, 623–42.

McEwen, B. and E.N. Lasley (2002), *The End of Stress As We Know It*, Washington, DC: Joseph Henry Press.

Minsky, M. (1986), *The Society of Mind*, New York: Simon and Schuster.

Nestler, E.J. and R.C. Malenka (2004), 'The addicted brain', *Scientific American*, **290** (3), March, 78–85.

O'Doherty, J., P. Dayan, J. Schultz, R. Deichmann and K. Friston (2004), 'Dissociable roles of ventral and dorsal striatum in instrumental conditioning', *Science*, **304** (5669), 452–4.

Oswold, A. (1997), 'Happiness and economic performance', *Economic Journal*, **107**, 1815–31.

Paulus, M.P. (2007), 'Decision-making dysfunctions in psychiatry – altered homeostatic processing?', *Science*, **318**, 603ff.

Paulus, M.P., J.S. Feinstein, A. Simmons and M.B. Stein (2004), 'Anterior cingulate activiation in high-trait anxious subjects is related to altered error processing during decision-making', *Biological Psychiatry*, **55**, 1179.

Pecina, S., B. Caginard, K.C. Berridge, J.W. Aldridge and X. Zhuang (2003), 'Hyperdopaminergic mice have higher "wanting" but not "liking" for sweet rewards', *The Journal of Neuroscience*, **28** (28), 9395–402.

Pellegrini, A.D. and P.K. Smith (eds) (2005), *The Nature of Play, Great Apes and Humans*, New York: The Guilford Press.

Pessiglioni, M., B. Seymour, G. Flandrin et al. (2006), 'Dopamine-dependent prediction errors underpin reward-seeking behavior in humans', *Nature*, **442** (August), 1042.

Pessiglioni, M., L. Schmidt, B. Draganski et al. (2007), 'How the brain translates money into force: a neuroimaging study of subliminal motivation', *Science*, **316** (5826), 904–6.

Peterson, R.L. (2005), 'The neuroscience of investing: FMRI of the reward system', *Brain Research Bulletin*, **67**, 391.

Peterson, R.L. (2007), *Inside the Investor's Brain, The Power of Mind Over Money*, Hoboken, NJ: John Wiley and Sons.

Pockett, S. (2004), 'Hypnosis and the death of "subjective backwards referral"', *Consciousness and Cognition*, **13**, 621–5.

Price, R.H., J.N. Choi and A.D. Vinokur (2002), 'Links in the chain of adversity following job loss', *Journal of Occupational Health and Psychology*, 7, 302.

Rajadhyaksha, A.M. and B.E. Kosofsky(2005), 'Psychostimulants, protein phosphorylation and gene expression: a growing role of L-type calcium channels', *Cellscience*, 2 (1).

Reuter, J., T. Raedler, M. Rose et al. (2005), 'Pathological gambling is linked to reduced activation of the mesolimbic reward system', *Nature Neuroscience*, 8 (2), February, 147–8.

Rietveld, E. (2008), 'The skillfull body as a concernful system of possible actions, phenomena and neurodynamics', *Theory and Psychology*, 18 (3), 341–63.

Sanfey, A. (2007), 'Social decision-making: insights for game theory and neuroscience', *Science*, 318, 598–602.

Sapolsky, R.M. (2004), *Why Zebras Don't Get Ulcers*, New York: Henry Holt and Company.

Sapolsky, R.M (2005), 'The influence of social hierarchy on primate health', *Science*, 308 (5722), 648–52.

Schultz, W. (2002), 'Getting formal with dopamine and reward', *Neuron*, 36, 241–63.

Schultz, W. and A. Dickinson (2000), 'Neuronal coding of prediction errors', *Annual Review of Neuroscience*, 23, 473–500.

Sergo, P. (2008), 'New weapons against cocaine addiction', *Scientific American Mind*, April/May, 53–7.

Shermer, M. (2008), *The Mind of the Market: How Biology and Psychology Shape Our Economic Lives*, New York, Henry Holt and Company.

Taylor, S., B. Martis, K.D. Fitzgerald et al. (2006), 'Medial frontal cortex activity and loss-related responses to errors', *Journal of Neuroscience*, 26 (15), 4063–70.

Tversky, A. and D. Kahneman (1981), 'The framing of decisions and the psychology of choice', *Science*, 211, 453.

Tversky, A. and D. Kahneman (1992), 'Advances in Prospect Theory: cumulative representation of uncertainty', *Journal of Risk and Uncertainty*, 5, 297–323.

Vohs, K.D., N.L. Mead and M.R. Goode (2006), 'The psychological consequences of money', *Science*, 314 (5802), 1154–6.

Wickens, J.R., J.C. Horvitz, R.M. Costa and S. Killcross (2007), 'Dopaminergic mechanisms in actions and habits', *Journal of Neuroscience*, 27 (31), 8181.

Xue, G., Z. Lu, I. Levin, J.A. Weller, X. Li and A. Bechara (2008), 'Functional dissociations of risk and reward processing in the medial prefrontal cortex', *Cerebral Cortex Advance Access*, published online 8 October.

Zweig, J. (2007), *Your Money and Your Brain: How the New Science of Neuroeconomics Can Help Make You Rich*, New York: Simon and Schuster.

PART 4

Entrepreneurial propensity

Entrepreneurial firms come in all sizes, from the sole proprietor of an innovative entrepreneur to very large firms. The definition of what we mean by an entrepreneur is not detailed in this part, since that in itself is a grand topic worthy of a book on its own. However, entrepreneurs are understood to be endowed with various skills that differentiate them from managers and other people. In Part 4, three chapters detail various entrepreneurial talents and capabilities under various conditions, including the political arena. Each of the chapters looks inside the black box to various degrees in search of what might be important in the determination of who might make a successful entrepreneur.

10. An economic and neuroscientific comparison of strategic decision-making

Theresa Michl and Stefan Taing[1]

INTRODUCTION

Economic decision-making is traditionally based on the assumptions of the predominant existence of *Homo economicus* (Latin: economic human being). The framework of this theory is known as the Rational Choice Theory (RC Theory). It includes assumptions such as utility maximization, opportunism, bounded rationality, complete information and rational facts. Thus, everything that can be measured is integrated into the decisions of homo economicus, and the decision is rationally made. But the decision model of the homo economicus is subject to criticism by many economists as this agent's decisions are supposed to be based on comprehensiveness and quantitative factors (Camerer et al., 2005). What is missing in this decision model are soft factors such as motivations and emotions as well as context and interdependencies between the factors of decision-making. The need to improve the decisive power of the homo economicus is reflected in the different derivates coming from various fields, for example, *Homo sapiens, Homo sociologicus, Homo ludens, Homo reciprocans, Homo politicus, Homo religiousus, Homo europaeus* and many more. Still even these derivatives are criticized as not being satisfyingly adequate and comprehensive for decision models. One basic reason for this is that behavioral models are harder to develop than traditional economic models; building models of rational, unemotional agents is easier than building models of quasi-rational emotional humans.

Neuroeconomics is a newly recognized field of interest that aims to open the 'black box' of economic decision-making and might help to formulate new economic models of decision-making that are more realistic compared to traditional models, thus making them more efficient (Fehr et al., 2005; Zak, 2004). In this chapter we focus on strategic decision-making and two of its important aspects and ask the following research question:

can results of neuroscientific research help to better manage aspects of uncertainty and reward in strategic decision-making?

In order to answer this question, we first compare strategic decision-making in economics with strategic decision-making in neuroscience regarding uncertainty and reward. Second, we integrate these results and show how they accord (or do not) with each other. Lastly, we give implications on how strategic decisions can be made more efficient by integrating results from neuroeconomics and give propositions for future research.

STRATEGIC DECISION-MAKING IN ECONOMIC THEORY

Strategic decisions in companies are typically made by higher delegates and follow long-term goals. Strategic decisions are, for example, research and development investment, outsourcing/offshoring, spin-offs, make-or-buy decisions, business models or pricing. As strategic decisions seek to optimize long-term goals, incorporating time factors in intertemporal choice also plays an important role. As intertemporal choice is a large research field of its own, it lies beyond the scope of this chapter to go into further detail.

Boulding et al. (1994) describes strategic decisions as messy, that is, they occur in a complex environment, are difficult or expensive to reverse and the outcomes are, to a greater extent, contingent on other individuals' or organizations' behavior. Boulding concludes that uncertainty, as an external variable, needs to be decomposed to increase the overall quality of decisions. Rajagopalan et al. (1993) built an integrative framework of the strategic decision-making process, including seven variables: environmental factors (uncertainty, complexity, munificence), organizational factors (for example, organization structure, power distribution, top management team characteristics), decision-specific factors (for example, decision urgency, outcome uncertainty/risk, decision complexity), decision process characteristics (comprehensiveness, extent of rationality, duration/length), process outcomes (for example, decision quality, speed, organizational learning), and economic outcomes (for example, return on investment/return on asset, growth in sales/profit, market share). Thus, uncertainty is seen as an environmental factor whereas outcome uncertainty/risk is regarded as a decision-specific factor.

Elbanna and Child (2007) decode strategic decision-making effectiveness into strategic decision-making process dimensions (intuition, rationality, political behavior), strategic decision-specific characteristics (decision importance, decision uncertainty, decision motive), external environmental characteristics (environmental uncertainty, munificence/hostility), and

Table 10.1   Overview of uncertainty and reward in economic and business literature

Authors	Research Focus	Uncertainty	Reward
Boulding et al. (1994)	Decision-making process	External variable to be dealt via decomposition	(−)
Rajagopalan et al. (1993)	Strategic decision processes	Environmental attribute	(−)
Elbanna and Child (2007)	Strategic decision-making process	Internal variable moderating decision efficiency	(−)
Papadakis et al. (1998)	Decision-making framework	Both external and internal factor	(−)
Hitt and Tyler (1991)	Strategic decision-making models	External factor managed through internal processes where individuals cognitive abilities are crucial	Reward, i.e. reward systems as strategic choice
Eisenhardt (1989)	Decision-making of executive teams in high-velocity industries	Uncertainty leads to difficulties in deciding, confidence and relating to past decisions are possible solutions	(−)
Tversky and Kahneman (1992)	Decision-making process	Source dependence variable	(−)

internal firm characteristics (firm performance, company size). Therefore, for strategic decision effectiveness, uncertainty is also part of decision-specific as well as of environmental characteristics. Papadakis et al. (1998) describe further factors influencing the strategic decision-making process, such as the top management (CEO and top management team), the nature of strategic decision (generic characteristics and type of strategic decision), decision process characteristics (for example, rationality/comprehensiveness, financial reporting, formalization) and broader context (external environment and internal context). They conclude that decision-specific characteristics appear to have the most important influence on the strategic decision-making process, as decisions with different decision-specific characteristics are dealt with in different processes.

In the next sections we focus on aspects of uncertainty and reward in decision-making within the economic literature. Table 10.1 shows a basic overview of economic and business literature concerned with aspects of uncertainty and reward.

STRATEGIC DECISIONS UNDER UNCERTAINTY IN ECONOMIC THEORY

In economics uncertain decisions are typically treated in two ways; they are either reduced to decisions under risk or they are solved using decision rules, such as maximin (choose the decision with the maximum of the minimum payoff), minimax regret (choose the decision with the minimum of regrets for each alternative), maximax criteria (choose the decision with the maximum of the maximum payoff), Hurwicz criterion (choose decision in which payoffs are weighted by a coefficient of optimism) or equal likelihood (Laplace) criterion (choose decision in which each state of nature is weighted equally).

Different perspectives of strategic decision-making and choice-outcomes have been advanced in the literature. The above-mentioned stream of literature (Elbanna and Child, 2007; Papadakis et al., 1998; Rajagopalan et al., 1993) deals with uncertainty as an external environmental and context-specific internal variable. Another stream of literature extends the term uncertainty and considers it as an individual-specific variable. Hitt and Tyler (1991) examined hypothesized effects of factors associated with three perspectives: rational normative, external control and strategic choice models on strategic acquisition decisions. They found strong support for the rational normative perspective explaining the greatest amount of total variance in target firms (ibid.). They explicitly state that the individual's cognitive abilities are crucial in assessing uncertainty.

Eisenhardt (1989) investigated the speed of strategic decision-making and found that fast decision-makers use more information than slow decision-makers. In addition, fast decision-makers develop more alternatives and use a two-tiered advice process and this type of decision-making leads to superior performance. Uncertainty is considered to always be present in strategic decisions, especially in high-velocity environments. In order to overcome decision difficulties due to uncertainty, the use of a counselor and past experience is suggested.

Tversky and Kahneman (1992) extended their original Prospect Theory (cf. Kahneman and Tversky, 1979) to formulate the Cumulative Prospect Theory which allows for cumulative decision weights to apply to uncertain and risky decisions. They differentiate between biases towards uncertainty depending on the source of the bias. They found that 'individuals consistently preferred bets on uncertain events in their area of expertise over matched bets on chance devices, although the former are ambiguous and the latter are not' (Tversky and Kahneman, 1992, p. 317).

In the following section we focus on the rewards of strategic decisions. As shown in Table 10.1, this is often a neglected topic in economic research.

REWARD OF STRATEGIC DECISION-MAKING IN ECONOMIC THEORY

In general, when talking about rewards in economics, one typically only thinks of monetary reward. Even if it is not defined directly as monetary, in the end it will somehow convert to and pay off in money. Monetary rewards refer to increased salaries, bonuses, company cars, presents or other material things.

In our sample of the economic decision-making literature only Hitt and Tyler (1991) mention non-monetary reward as a variable in their model. They consider reward as a strategic choice in terms of implementation of a reward system as part of a process of interpreting the environment and responding to unfixed elements.

Social rewards of strategic decision-making, such as praise, apprecia-tion, responsibility or other immaterial attentions, do not play a promi-nent part in economic decision-making literature. We could assume that social or monetary rewards provide utilities that might be achieved with a certain probability. Social rewards are hard to express in utility, which is probably the reason why traditional economics does not model social reward as part of its utility models.

STRATEGIC DECISION-MAKING IN NEUROSCIENCE

In the following two sections we examine neuroscientific studies regard-ing uncertainty and reward in decision-making. Table 10.2 shows a basic overview of neuroscientific studies concerned with aspects of uncertainty and reward.

It seems that in neuroscience, decisions under uncertainty and decisions with reward are not clearly differentiated, as they are often investigated together. This is because decision-making under uncertainty always pro-vides (or is expected to provide) at least some reward. Thus, neuroscience in general investigates decision-making in certain situations under spe-cifically given circumstances. However, as far as we are aware, there is no neuroscientific decision model so far, but this field is of course a very young one.

Human decision-making from the neuroscientific point of view is generally based on the interaction of different brain areas. Hereby, an evolutionarily older area of the brain, noting that the oldest area is the brainstem, is made up of the limbic system (amygdala, mesolimbic system). Consciousness is processed in the cerebral cortex. One part

Table 10.2   Overview of uncertainty and reward in neuroscientific literature

Author	Uncertainty	Reward
Hsu et al. (2005)	Ambiguity	(−)
Kuhnen and Knutson (2005); Trepel et al. (2005)	Risk	(−)
Preuschoff et al. (2008)	Risk prediction	(−)
Zink et al. (2004); Delgado et al. (2000); Knutson et al. (2001a, 2001b); O'Doherty et al. (2001); Elliot et al. (2000)	(−)	Monetary reward
McClure et al. (2004); Rilling et al. (2004); Paulus et al. (2002); Fliessbach et al. (2007)	(−)	Reward
McClure et al. (2007)	(−)	Reward and intertemporal choice
McClure et al. (2003)	(−)	Primary reward (prediction)
Erk et al. (2002); Aharon et al. (2001); Kawabata and Zeki (2004); Aron et al. (2005); Bartels and Zeki (2004); Azim et al. (2005); Menon and Levitin (2005); Mobbs et al. (2003)	(−)	Social reward
Decety et al. (2004); Rilling et al. (2002)	(−)	Cooperation reward
De Quervain et al. (2004); Montague and Berns (2002)	(−)	Reward and punishment
Nieuwenhuis et al. (2005); Preuschoff et al. (2006)	Risk	Reward
Tom et al. (2007); Breiter et al. (2001); Smith et al. (2002)	Risk	Gains and losses

of the cortex is concerned with rational and emotional considerations of behavioral consequences (orbitofrontal cortex (OFC), ventromedial cortex). Other parts of consciousness are the dorsolateral prefrontal cortex (DLPFC), the working memory and the posterior parietal cortex (PPC), which is involved in precise planning of spatial orientation (Lehmann-Waffenschmidt et al., 2008). Some parts of unconsciousness also play important roles in the strategic decision-making process as successful action patterns, which formulate attitudes and instincts, and are especially stored in the striatum.

A frequently used game to examine economic decisions in neuroscience is the Ultimatum Game (UG). In the UG two players receive a certain amount of money and have to decide how they distribute this amount. The first player suggests an offer and the second player can accept or reject this offer. When the second player accepts the offer, the money is distributed as suggested. But when the second player rejects the offer neither player receives any money. Thus, it is obvious that the second player – the responder – as a rational individual should accept any offer that will give a positive payoff, even if it is very small, because he will always be better off than rejecting a positive offer. Hence, it should be possible for the first player – the proposer – as a rational individual to offer only a marginal amount of the money and keep the rest of the money for herself (Güth et al., 1982). In many studies (Roth, 1991), however, it is shown that most of the proposers offer 40–50 percent of the total amount, and that more than half of the responders reject an offer when it is fewer than 30 percent of the total amount. This deviation from standard theory is explained with altruistic punishment (Fehr and Fischbacher, 2006) and status-protecting behavior (Nowak et al., 2000).

STRATEGIC DECISIONS UNDER UNCERTAINTY IN NEUROSCIENCE

There are numerous studies in neuroscience which investigate how individuals make decisions under uncertainty. In opposition to the field of business, there is a distinction between uncertain decisions in risk and ambiguity in neuroscience and economics (Schultz et al., 2008). Whereas risk in economics is defined as having full information about all possible outcomes and their associated probability distribution, ambiguity is defined as having full information about all possible outcomes but incomplete information about their associated probability distribution (see also Chapter 2 in this volume).

Hsu et al. (2005) suggest a general neural circuit responding to degrees of uncertainty, which is contrary to decision theory. They found that the level of ambiguity in choices correlates positively with an activation in the amygdala and the OFC, and negatively with a striatal system. However, the striatal activity correlates positively with expected reward. They found that subjects with orbitofrontal lesions were insensitive to the level of ambiguity and risk in behavioral choices. Their results suggest a unified treatment of ambiguity and risk as limiting cases of a general system evaluating uncertainty.

Regarding individuals' risk propensity in decisions, Kuhnen and Knutson (2005) demonstrate that choices among gamblers are correlated with blood oxygen level dependent (BOLD) responses in the nucleus accumbens (NAcc) and the anterior insula (AI), and that activations in these areas could be used to predict the probability of making subsequent choices. Hence, differential activation in these regions may lead to either risk-seeking or risk-averse behavior. As anticipation of rewards activates the NAcc, this may lead to an increase in the likelihood of individuals switching from risk-averse to risk-seeking behavior.

Trepel et al. (2005) examined the possible neural bases of the components of Prospect Theory and suggest that focused studies of decision-making in the context of quantitative models may provide substantial leverage towards a fuller understanding of the cognitive neuroscience of decision-making. Preuschoff et al. (2008) further found that an early-onset activation in the human insula correlates significantly with risk prediction error and that its time course is consistent with a role in rapid updating. Thus, they argue that our understanding of the neural basis of reward anticipation under uncertainty needs to be expanded to include risk prediction.

In economics risk refers to the probability of losses whereas in the field of business risk is equated with the variation of outcomes, both positive and negative. Yet neuroeconomic research has shown that risk, ambiguity and uncertainty are related to different activities in the insula.

REWARDS OF STRATEGIC DECISIONS IN NEUROSCIENCE

Brain areas that play important roles in reward processing are the prefrontal cortex (PFC), NAcc, striatum, thalamus cores, amygdala and ventral tegmental area (VTA). Recent functional magnetic resonance imaging (fMRI) studies postulate that different types of rewarding stimuli consistently increase activity in a common set of neural structures, including the OFC, the amygdala and the NAcc. Other current neuroscientific studies have shown that non-monetary rewards like primary rewards such as fruit juice and water (McClure et al., 2003, 2004; O'Doherty et al., 2003), social rewards such as attractive faces (Aharon et al., 2001), romantic love (Bartels and Zeki, 2004), cultural objects (Erk et al., 2002), humor (Mobbs et al., 2005), music (Menon and Levitin, 2005) and cooperation rewards (Decety et al., 2004; Rilling et al. 2002) activate the same coterie of neural structures as commonly used monetary rewards do (Delgado et al., 2000; Elliott et al., 2000; Knutson et al., 2001a, 2001b; Paulus et al., 2002). Erk et al. (2002) claim that products symbolizing wealth and status lead to increased activity in reward-related brain areas as they found significantly more activation in the ventral striatum (VStr), OFC, anterior cingulate and occipital regions for sports cars than for other categories of cars. In general, individuals are more aroused by rewards they actively earn than by rewards they passively acquire (Zink et al., 2004).

Furthermore, the results of Knutson et al. (2001b) indicated that while anticipation of reward and non-reward activated foci in the VStr, actual reward and non-reward outcomes activated foci in the ventromedial frontal cortex. These findings suggest that reward anticipation and outcomes differentially recruit distinct regions that lie along the trajectory of ascending dopamine projections. Further, Knutson et al. (2001a) showed that activity in the striatum is correlated with the magnitude of the monetary reward individuals earn during lotteries. Therefore, it can be concluded that the striatum plays an important role in the reward system.

Rilling et al. (2004) confirmed that mesencephalic dopamine projection sites carry information about errors in reward prediction that allow individuals to learn who can and who cannot be trusted to reciprocate favors. O'Doherty et al. (2001) showed that distinct areas of the OFC were activated by monetary rewards and punishments. Moreover, in these areas they found a correlation between the magnitude of the brain activation and the magnitude of the rewards and punishments received. These findings indicate that one emotional involvement of the OFC is its representation of the magnitudes of abstract rewards and punishments, such as receiving or losing money. This study proves that monetary reward is processed in the same region as social and primary rewards.

In contrast, the results of Elliott et al. (2003) indicate that the premotor cortex shows a linear increase with increasing reward value. Additionally, they found that the medial and lateral foci of the OFC respond non-linearly; the response is enhanced for the lowest and highest reward values relative to the mid-range. Thus, these results of Ellis and colleagues suggest a functional distinction in response patterns within a distributed reward system. In addition, these findings demonstrate dissociable neural responses to rewards and penalties that are dependent on the psychological context in which they are experienced.

Considering the time factor in decision-making, McClure et al. (2007) found that the lateral prefrontal cortex (LPFC) and the PPC responded similarly whether choices were between an immediate and a delayed reward or between two delayed rewards, whereas short-term delays were discounted hyperbolically and long-term delays exponentially. This study supports a dual process model in accounting for intertemporal choices. Besides, McClure et al. (2003) showed that positive and negative prediction errors in reward delivery time correlate with BOLD changes in human striatum, with the strongest activation lateralized to the left putamen.

They found that for negative prediction error, the brain response was elicited only by expectations and not by the stimuli presented.

Fliessbach et al. (2007) showed that individuals' brain activity in the VStr is strongly influenced by the reward they receive relative to what other individuals receive, demonstrating that social comparison of the reward levels affect individuals' wellbeing differently than an absolute reward level. In addition, the VStr is able to integrate contextual information. There is no evidence for the involvement of other brain regions in this comparison process, especially not the medial and dorsolateral PFC, important in social cognition. Thus, it is differently rewarding to win a competition or to earn more money than a rival earns. Whether social comparison affects individual well-being is of central importance for understanding behavior in social environments. Traditional economic theories focus on the role of absolute rewards, whereas behavioral evidence suggests that social comparisons influence decisions.

Montague and Berns (2002) developed a computational model, the predictor-valuation model (PVM), and composed a specific relationship between the value of a predictor and the future rewards or punishments that it promises. The PVM suggests anticipating a class of single-unit neural responses in orbitofrontal and striatal regions and proposes how these neural responses in the orbitofrontal-striatal circuit may support the conversion of disparate types of future rewards into a kind of internal currency, a common scale used to compare the valuation of future behavioral acts or stimuli. As such, dopaminergic neurons detect the discrepancy between predicted and experienced utility.

Nieuwenhuis et al. (2005) also observed reward-sensitive activity in a number of brain areas previously implicated in reward processing, including the striatum, PFC, posterior cingulate (PC) and inferior parietal lobule. They noted that activity in a number of reward-sensitive areas in the brain was highly sensitive to the range of possible outcomes available for choice. In line with these findings, Breiter et al. (2001) found that responses to prospects and outcomes could generally, but not always, be observed in the same regions. Tom et al. (2007) further showed that potential losses are represented by decreasing activity in gain-responsive regions rather than by increasing activity in regions associated with expected and experienced negative outcomes. These two studies of Breiter et al. (2001) and Tom et al. (2007) reinforce the importance of distinguishing between different types of utilities in economic theories of choice.

In addition, Smith et al. (2002) showed that individuals are risk averse in gains, risk seeking in losses and do not seek ambiguity in gains or losses, by identifying two neural substrates in the interaction between attitudes and beliefs: dorsomedial neocortical and ventromedial systems. Interactions between attitudes and beliefs trigger neural activation changes in dorso-medial and ventromedial brain areas. In other words, there is not a single executive decision-making mechanism, but two systems in the brain: deliberative and emotional. Deliberative systems (also referred to as calculation areas) utilize parts of the brain related to mathematics and rational decisions. Emotional systems utilize older, more primal parts of the brain. The authors argue that individual behavior is affected by attitudes about payoffs – such as gains and losses – in addition to beliefs about outcomes such as risk and ambiguity.

Smith et al. (2002) found that risky losses are not processed by the part of the brain that responds to fear; rather they are dealt with in a fairly rational manner. Also, the deliberative areas of the brain did not show high activation with decisions relating to risky gains. These results suggest that emotional areas may overwhelm rational areas.

Preuschoff et al. (2006) showed that during reward anticipation, initial activation in VStr and other subcortical dopaminoceptive structures varied with expected reward, whereas subsequent activation in VStr varied with risk. In this way, neuroscientific methods can offer researchers an opportunity to identify neural substrates that support the computation of financial parameters and predict financial choices from brain activation. Finally, Peterson (2005) argues that the appraisal of uncertainty and reward plays a crucial role in the process of decision-making and that this appraisal process is strongly correlated with overconfidence. It can be concluded that different types of (primary, social, monetary) reward stimuli activate the same neural structures: the OFC, amygdala and the NAcc. This activation with different stimuli leads to the assumption that brains process rewards along a common pathway. In the following section we derive practical implications for a more efficient decision-making process and give propositions for future research.

IMPLICATIONS FOR STRATEGIC DECISION-MAKING IN NEUROECONOMICS

Economic theory was constructed ignoring the details about the functioning of the brain, treating it as an unknown 'black box' (Bruni and Sugden, 2007). Because of this, traditional economic research is restricted to the level of describing decision outcomes, leaving the cognitive mechanisms behind them unknown. Consequently, traditional economic theory often fails to predict decision outcomes under real circumstances.

The field of neuroeconomics aims at understanding how decisions are made by using neuroscientific methods, focusing on the processes of the brain while making a decision. Thus, neuroeconomics tries to open the 'black box' of decision-making by combining neuroscience and economics to uncover the underlying mental and neural processes of economic decision-making. Based on the data collected through this process, neuroeconomics serves to aid economic decision models that are able to predict human decision-making more accurately than traditional economic models. If we regard behavioral economics as a subfield of neuroeconomics, it can not only give neuroscientific evidence for economic theories, such as Prospect Theory, Regret Theory or Game Theory, but also foundations for more comprehensive and powerful prediction of economic decision models. However, the main field of conflict between neuroeconomic and traditional economic research remains the neoclassical theoretical and methodological choice of economists to ignore the mind and focus on the narrow axiomatic assumptions of what a rational decision-maker is. This is questioned and contested by many neuroeconomists (for example, Camerer, 2007; Camerer et al., 2005).

Based on results discussed earlier, uncertainty in economics cannot be merely considered as external, but should be considered as a complex internal decision-specific variable, as it is already regarded in neuroscience. Many neuroscientific studies (for example, Kuhnen and Knutson, 2005; Trepel et al., 2005) showed that risk propensity is not a stable construct, since it is context- and situation-specific. As such, neuroscience considers preferences as unstable (Stanton, 2009). This has crucial implications for the understanding of strategic decision-making processes and the corresponding decisions as they are understood to be highly dependent on the individuals' risk propensity and preferences. Therefore, we can derive the first proposition regarding the (un)stability and the external/internal causes of these constructs:

Proposition 1: Managers' risk propensity will be strongly influenced by situational circumstances: in times of economic downturn managers will be more risk seeking than in times of economic recovery.

Besides situational circumstances influencing managers' risk propensity, studies from entrepreneurship demonstrate that emotions influence individuals' risk propensity. It has been shown that positive emotions (for example, happiness, joy and so on) often increase entrepreneurs' willingness to take risks, because they feel more optimistic and capable of dealing with potential problems (Weiss, 2002) and expect positive outcomes (Busenitz and Barney, 1997). On the other hand, potentially negative emotions (for example, fear, shame and so on) might have the opposite effect on entrepreneurs' risk taking. When Higgins (2005) and Brockner et al. (2004) speak of a 'prevention focus', they speak of entrepreneurs who avoid entrepreneurial action even if it could be beneficial. However, some entrepreneurship researchers (Koh, 1996; Sagie and Elizur, 1999; Shaver and Scott, 1991; Stewart and Roth, 2001) argue that entrepreneurs are constitutionally more willing to take risk than are non-entrepreneurs, while others (Busenitz and Barney, 1997; Norton and Moore, 2006; Palich and Bagby, 1995; Sexton and Bowman, 1985) showed that entrepreneurs are moderate risk takers and do not significantly differ from managers or other non-entrepreneurs. These results are in conflict with each other and differ from neuroscientific findings. While risk measurement in the brain is in the PFC and OFC areas and not tied to emotions, ambiguities are strongly tied to emotions and activate the fear center, the amygdala.

Closely related to this is the overconfidence bias. Overconfidence is a known decision bias especially discussed in the psychology and finance literature. Camerer and Lovallo (1999) describe the effects of overconfidence as 'most people are overconfident about their own relative abilities and unreasonably optimistic' (p. 306). In the finance literature Malmendier and Tate (2005) have empirically tested the effects of overconfidence on corporate investment decisions of CEOs, finding evidence that overconfidence leads to overinvestment when funds are abundant and curtailed investment when funds are restricted. Ben-David et al. (2007) showed that CEOs systematically miscalibrate because of overconfidence. Generally, overconfidence is considered as stable across people and domains (Glaser and Weber, 2005; Klayman et al., 1999; Jonsson and Allwood, 2003). Peterson et al. (2005) examined investment decisions from a neuroscientific viewpoint and suggested that overconfidence, like other biases such as narrow framing of optimism, is not a stable effect. They suggest correlations in collective behavior and non-rational decisions. Following this, we expect that managers postpone strategic decisions in times of crisis because of overconfidence. As their interval estimation of the likelihood of future outcomes is too high, this leads them to underinvest, even if the investment would lead to beneficial business opportunities. Using more objective input variables that are not based on the individual's opinion would enable the successful exploitation of business opportunities even in times of crisis. We conclude this in the following proposition.

Proposition 2: In times of crisis higher overconfidence intervals will lead managers to postpone related strategic decisions.

It is intuitive to understand that gains produce neural rewards, whereas losses provoke emotional responses associated with fear or regret (Zak, 2004). What might be surprising, however, is that individuals do not feel rewarded if they received less than what they expected or if what they received was exactly what they expected to receive. This leads to the distinction between hormonal reward and the reward that the good itself causes. In the first case individuals receive a reward from dopamine, which is a feedback of how far off individuals were with their prediction of not expecting to win. In the second case individuals receive the reward of some good, like money. The variation of the type of reward, hormonal or monetary, both make individuals feel rewarded. Additionally, we argue that the type of reward (hormonal or the object received) does not matter for the feeling of the reward, as hormonal or monetary reward stimuli activate the same neural structures. Social reward that shows wealth and status (Erk et al., 2002) and reward that is relatively higher compared to other individuals (Fliessbach et al., 2007) both make individuals feel more rewarded.

Another important aspect associated with strategic decision-making is fairness. Managers are often accused of taking unfair offers, for example, bonuses they receive for their decisions in bad economic times. However, Knoch et al. (2006) showed that the disruption of the right DLPFC by low-frequency repetitive transcranial magnetic stimulation (TMS) substantially reduces subjects' willingness to reject their partners' intentionally unfair offers. Knoch et al. (2006) interpret this finding by suggesting that TMS systems renders subjects less able to resist the economic temptation to accept these offers. Tabibnia et al. (2008) showed that receiving a fair offer in an UG is associated with brain regions activation that are involved in reward processing, including the VStr. This was also the case after controlling for monetary payoff. Reciprocating cooperation in the trust game or receiving a fair offer in an UG are both associated with activation in brain regions implicated in reward processing, including the VStr. In contrast to this, Sanfey et al. (2003) argue that receiving an unfair offer is associated with both negative emotions and activation of the AI. The significant high activity in AI for rejecting unfair offers further underlines the important role for emotions in decision-making (ibid.). The brain reacts with higher activity of the AI, from which we can conclude that its function is to serve someone's selfish advantage. In other words, unfair offers of individuals mainly activate regions (AI) which are associated with negative emotions and these activations are clearly weaker when those unfair offers are made by computers.

Moreover, Zink et al. (2004) found that individuals are more aroused by rewards they actively earn than by rewards they passively gain. This has crucial implications considering that the type and the amount of reward elicit emotions and that emotions strongly and continuously influence decision-making. Decision-making is a process that often involves others and hence we also need to speak of social decision-making (Rilling et al.,

2008). Decisions with strategic social elements can be described mathematically, using Game Theory. A game-theoretic model of behavior requires a description of the players in the game, the information each has or can obtain, the actions available to each player and the payoff expected from each strategy. Nash equilibrium identifies the optimal strategy that is conditional on everyone else's optimal behavior in the game. Game Theory models of social decisions are more complex than isolated utility maximization and its predictive record is more mixed (Camerer, 2003).

CONCLUSION

Neuroeconomics, the integrated field of neuroscience and economics, certainly brings helpful contributions to traditional economic theories about decision-making. However, we should not expect neuroscience to completely clear the blind spot of assumed rationality in economics, but its results will influence economic theories and models. As we have seen how complex the strategic decision-making process is, the integration of more than two fields is necessary to help in understanding how the strategic decision can be made efficient and how the process can best be managed.

The integration of more than two fields is given in the entrepreneurship literature where researchers from different fields contribute to the explanation and prediction of entrepreneurial behavior as well as entrepreneurial and strategic decision-making. As it is argued (Dess et al., 2003; Hitt et al., 2001; McGrath and MacMillan, 2000), strategic and entrepreneurship literature should be integrated as both fields have strategic decisions in entrepreneurial opportunities as key research areas in common.

NOTE

1. Special thanks go to Josef Schützeichel from the Ludwig-Maximilians-University, Department of Economics, for his great contributions to our neuroscience section.

REFERENCES

Aharon, I., N. Etcoff, D. Ariely, C.F. Chabris, E. O'Connor and H.C. Brieter (2001), 'Beautiful faces have variable reward value: fMRI and behavioral evidence', *Neuron*, **32** (3), 537–51.
Aron, A., H. Fisher, D.J. Mashek, G. Strong, H.F. Li and L.L. Brown (2005), 'Reward, motivation and emotion systems associated with early-stage intense romantic love: an fMRI study', *Journal of Neurophysiology*, **94** (1), 327–37.

Azim, E., D. Mobbs, J. Booil, V. Menon and A.L. Reiss (2005), 'Sex differences in brain activation elicited by humor', *Proceedings of the National Academy of Sciences of the United States of America*, **102** (45), 16496–501.

Bartels, A. and S. Zeki (2004), 'The neural correlates of maternal and romantic love', *Neuroimage*, **21** (3), 1155–66.

Ben-David, I., J.R. Graham and C.R. Harvey (2007), 'Managerial overconfidence and corporate policies', NBER Working paper no. 13711, December.

Boulding, W., M.C. Moore, R. Staelin et al. (1994), 'Understanding managers' strategic decision-making process', *Marketing Letters*, **5** (4), 413–26.

Breiter, H.C., I. Aharon, D. Kahneman, A. Dale and P. Shizgal (2001), 'Functional imaging of neural responses to expectancy and experience of monetary gains and losses', *Neuron*, **30**, 619–39.

Brockner, J., E.T. Higgins and M.B. Low (2004), 'Regulatory focus theory and the entrepreneurial process', *Journal of Business Venturing*, **19**, 203–21.

Bruni, L. and R. Sugden (2007), 'The road not taken: how psychology was removed from economics, and how it might be brought back', *Economic Journal*, **117** (516), 146–73.

Busenitz, L.W. and J.B. Barney (1997), 'Differences between entrepreneurs and managers in large organizations: biases and heuristics in strategic decision-making', *Journal of Business Venturing*, **12** (1), 9–30.

Camerer, C.F. (2003), 'Strategizing in the brain', *Science*, **300** (13), 1673–5.

Camerer, C.F. (2007), 'Using neuroscience to make economic predictions', *Economic Journal*, **117** (519), C26–C42.

Camerer, C. and D. Lovallo (1999), 'Overconfidence and excess entry: an experimental approach', *American Economic Review*, **89** (91), 306–18.

Camerer, C., G. Loewenstein and D. Prelec (2005), 'Neuroeconomics: how neuroscience can inform economics', *Journal of Economic Literature*, **43**, 9–64.

Decety, J., P.L. Jackson, J.A. Sommerville, T. Chaminade and A.N. Meltzoff (2004), 'The neural bases of cooperation and competition: an fMRI investigation', *Neuroimage*, **23** (2), 744–51.

Delgado, M.R., L. Nystrom, C. Fissell, D. Noll and J.A. Fiez (2000), 'Tracking the hemodynamic responses to reward and punishment in the striatum', *Journal of Neurophysiology*, **84**, 3072–7.

De Quervain, D.J.-F., U. Fischbacher, V. Treyer et al. (2004), 'The neural basis of altruistic punishment', *Science*, **305**, 1254–8.

Dess, G.G., R.D. Ireland, Z.A. Shaker, S.W. Floyd, J.J. Janney and P.J. Lane (2003), 'Emerging issues in corporate entrepreneurship', *Journal of Management*, **29** (3), 351–78.

Eisenhardt, K.M. (1989), 'Making fast strategic decisions in high-velocity environments', *Academy of Management Journal*, **32** (3), 543–76.

Elbanna, S. and J. Child (2007), 'Influences on strategic decision effectiveness: development and test of an integrative model', *Strategic Management Journal*, **28** (4), 431–53.

Elliott, R., K.J. Friston and R.J. Dolan (2000), 'Dissociable neural responses in human reward systems', *Journal of Neuroscience*, **20** (16), 6159–65.

Elliott, R., J.L. Newman, O.A. Longe and J.F. Deakin (2003), 'Differential response patterns in the striatum and orbitofrontal cortex to financial reward in humans: a parametric functional magnetic resonance imaging study', *Journal of Neuroscience*, **23** (1), 303–7.

Erk, S., M. Spitzer, A. Wunderlich, L. Galley and H. Walter (2002), 'Cultural objects modulate reward circuitry', *Neuroreport*, **13** (18), 2499–503.

Fehr, E. and U. Fischbacher (2006), 'The nature of human altruism', *Nature*, **425**, 785–91.

Fehr, E., U. Fischbacher and M. Kosfeld (2005), 'Neuroeconomic foundations of trust and social preferences: initial evidence', *American Economic Review Papers and Proceedings*, **95**, 346–51.

Fliessbach, K., B. Weber, P. Trautner et al. (2007), 'Social comparison affects reward-related brain activity in the human ventral striatum', *Science*, **318** (5854), 1305–8.

Glaser, M., T. Langer and M. Weber (2005), 'Overconfidence of professionals and lay men: individual differences within and between tasks?', Working paper, http://www.sfb504.uni-mannheim.de/puplications/dp05-25.pdf.

Güth, W., R. Schmittberger and B. Schwarze (1982), 'An experimental analysis of ultimatum bargaining', *Journal of Economic Behavior and Organization*, **3** (4), 367–88.

Higgins, E.T. (2005), 'Value from regulatory fit', *Current Directions in Psychological Science*, **14**, 209–13.

Hitt, M. and B.B. Tyler (1991), 'Strategic decision models: integrated different perspectives', *Strategic Management Journal*, **12**, 327–51.

Hitt, M.A., R.D. Ireland, M.S. Camp and D.L. Sexton (2001), 'Strategic entrepreneurship: entrepreneurial strategies for creating wealth', *Strategic Management Journal*, **22** (6/7), 479–91.

Hsu, M., M. Bhatt, R. Adolphs, D. Tranel and C.F. Camerer (2005), 'Neural systems responding to degrees of uncertainty in human decision-making', *Science*, **310** (5754), 1680–83.

Jonsson, A.C. and C.M. Allwood (2003), 'Stability and variability in the realism of confidence judgments over time, content domain, and gender', *Personality and Individual Differences*, **34** (4), 559–74.

Kahneman, D. and A. Tversky (1979), 'Prospect theory: an analysis of decisions under risk', *Econometrica*, **47**, 313–27.

Kawabata, H. and S. Zeki (2004), 'Neural correlates of beauty', *Journal of Neurophysiology*, **91**, 1699–705.

Klayman, J., J.B. Soll, C. Gonzales-Vallejo and S. Barlas (1999), 'Overconfidence: it depends on how, what, and whom you ask', *Organizational Behavior and Human Decision Processes*, **79** (3), 216–47.

Knoch, D., A. Pascual-Leone, K. Meyer, V. Treyer and E. Fehr (2006), 'Diminishing reciprocal fairness by disrupting the right prefrontal cortex', *Science*, **314** (5800), 829–32.

Knutson, B., C.M. Adams, G.W. Fong and D. Hommer (2001a), 'Anticipation of increasing monetary reward selectively recruits nucleus accumbens', *Journal of Neuroscience*, **21**, 1–5.

Knutson, B., G.W. Fong, C.M. Adams, J.L. Varner and D. Hommer (2001b), 'Dissociation of reward anticipation and outcome with event-related fMRI', *Neuroreport*, **12** (17), 3683–7.

Koh, H.C. (1996), 'Testing hypotheses of entrepreneurial characteristics: a study of Hong Kong MBA students', *Journal of Managerial Psychology*, **11** (3), 12–25.

Kuhnen, C.M. and B. Knutson (2005), 'The neural basis of financial risk taking', *Neuron*, **47** (5), 763–70.

Lehmann-Waffenschmidt, M., G. Roth and F. Thießen (2008), 'Die (innere) Logik des Entscheidens', unpublished paper, Dresden Discussion Paper Series in Economics, available at: http://rcswww.urz.tu-dresden.de/~wpeconom/seiten/pdf/2009/DDPE200911_a.pdf.

Malmendier, U. and G. Tate (2005), 'CEO overconfidence and corporate investment', *Journal of Finance*, **60** (6), 2661–700.

McClure, S.M., G.S. Berns and P.R. Montague (2003), 'Temporal prediction errors in a passive learning task activate human striatum', *Neuron*, **38**, 339–46.

McClure, S.M., D. Laibson, G. Loewenstein and J.D. Cohen (2004), 'Separate neural systems value immediate and delayed monetary rewards', *Science*, **306**, 503–7.

McClure, S.M., K.M. Ericson, D. Laibson, G. Loewenstein and J.D. Cohen (2007), 'Time discounting for primary rewards', *Journal of Neuroscience*, **27** (21), 5796–804.

McGrath, R.G. and I.C. MacMillan (2000), *The Entrepreneurial Mindset*, Boston, MA: Business School Press.

Menon, V. and D.J. Levitin (2005), 'The rewards of music listening: response and physiological connectivity of the mesolimbic system', *Neuroimage*, **28** (1), 175–84.

Mobbs, D., M.D. Greicius, E. Abdel-Azim, V. Menon and A.L. Reiss (2003), 'Humor modulates the mesolimbic reward centers', *Neuron*, **40** (5), 1041–8.

Mobbs, D., C.C. Hagan, E. Azim, V. Menon and A.L. Reiss (2005), 'Personality predicts activity in reward and emotional regions associated with humor', *Proceedings of the National Academy of Sciences of the United States of America*, **102** (45), 16502–6.

Montague, P.R. and G.S. Berns (2002), 'Neural economics and the biological substrates of valuation', *Neuron*, **36** (2), 265–84.

Nieuwenhuis, S., D. Heslenfeld, N.J. Alting von Geusau, R.B. Mars, C.B. Holroyd and N. Yeung (2005), 'Activity in human reward-sensitive brain areas is strongly context dependent', *Neuroimage*, **25**, 1302–9.

Norton, W.I. and W.T. Moore (2006), 'The influence of entrepreneurial risk assessment on venture launch or growth decisions', *Small Business Economics*, **26** (3), 215–26.

Nowak, M.A., K.M. Page and K. Sigmund (2000), 'Fairness versus reason in the Ultimatum Game', *Science*, **289**, 1773–5.

O'Doherty, J., M.L. Kringelbach, E.T. Rolls, J. Hornak and C. Andrews (2001), 'Abstract reward and punishment representations in the human orbitofrontal cortex', *Nature*, **4** (1), 95–102.

O'Doherty, J., P. Dayan, K.J. Friston, H.D. Critchley and R.J. Dolan (2003), 'Temporal difference models and reward-related learning in the human brain', *Neuron*, **38** (2), 329–37.

Palich, L.E. and D.R. Bagby (1995), 'Using cognitive theory to explain entrepreneurial risk-taking: challenging conventional wisdom', *Journal of Business Venturing*, **10** (6) 425–38.

Papadakis, M.V., S. Lioukas and D. Chambers (1998), 'Strategic decision-making process: the role of management and context', *Strategic Management Journal*, **19** (2), 115–47.

Paulus, M.P., N. Hozack, B. Zauscher et al. (2002), 'Parietal dysfunction is associated with increased outcome-related decision-making in schizophrenia', *Biological Psychiatry*, **51**, 995–1004.

Peterson, R.L. (2005), 'The neuroscience of investing: fMRI of the reward system', *Brain Research Bulletin*, **67** (5), 391–7.
Preuschoff, K., P. Bossaerts and S.R. Quartz (2006), 'Neural differentiation of expected reward and risk in human subcortical structures', *Neuron*, **51** (3), 381–90.
Preuschoff, H.K., S.R. Quartz and P. Bossaerts (2008), 'Human insula activation reflects risk predictions errors as well as risk', *Journal of Neuroscience*, **28** (11), 2745–52.
Rajagopalan, N., A. Rasheed and D.K. Datta (1993), 'Strategic decision processes: critical review and future directions', *Journal of Management*, **19** (2), 349–84.
Rilling, J.K., D.A. Gutman, T.R. Zeh, G. Pagnoni, G.S. Berns and C.D. Kilts (2002), 'A neural basis for social cooperation', *Neuron*, **35** (2), 395–405.
Rilling, J.K., A.G. Sanfey, J.A. Aronson, L.E. Nystrom and J.D. Cohen (2004), 'Opposing BOLD responses to reciprocated and unreciprocated altruism in putative reward pathways', *Neuroreport*, **15** (16), 2539–43.
Rilling, J.K., B. King-Casas and A.G. Sanfey (2008), 'The neurobiology of social decision-making', *Current Opinion in Neurobiology*, **18** (2), 159–65.
Roth, A. (1991), 'Bargaining and market behavior in Jerusalem, Ljubljana, Pittsburgh, and Tokyo: an experimental study', *American Economic Review*, **81**, 1068–95.
Sagie, A. and D. Elizur (1999), 'Achievement motive and entrepreneurial orientation: a structural analysis', *Journal of Organizational Behavior*, **20** (3), 375–87.
Sanfey, A.G., J.K. Rilling, J.A. Aronson, L.E. Nystrom and J.D. Cohen (2003), 'The neural basis of economic decision making in the Ultimatum Game', *Science*, **300** (5626), 1755–8.
Schultz, W., K. Preuschoff, C. Camerer et al. (2008), 'Review. Explicit neural signals reflecting reward uncertainty', *Philosophical Transactions of the Royal Society B: Biological Sciences*, **363** (1511), 3801–11.
Sexton, D. and N. Bowman (1985), 'The entrepreneur: a capable executive and more', *Journal of Business Venturing*, **1** (1), 129–40.
Shaver, K.G. and L.R. Scott (1991), 'Person, process, choice: the psychology of new venture creation', *Entrepreneurship and Regional Development*, **16** (2), 23–45.
Smith, K., J. Dickhaut, K. McCabe and J. Pardo (2002), 'Neuronal substrates for choice under ambiguity, risk, gains, and losses', *Management Science*, **48** (6), 711–18.
Stanton, A.A. (2009), 'Neuroeconomics: a critique of neuroeconomics: A critical reconsideration', *SSRN eJournal Neuroeconomics*, **1** (2)
Stewart, W.H. and P.L. Roth (2001), 'Risk propensity differences between entrepreneurs and managers: a meta-analytic review', *Journal of Applied Psychology*, **86** (1), 145–53.
Tabibnia, G., A.B. Satpute and M.D. Lieberman (2008), 'The sunny side of fairness: preference for fairness activates reward circuitry (and disregarding unfairness activates self-control circuitry', *Psychological Science*, **19** (4), 339–47
Tom, S., C.R. Fox, C. Trepel and R.A. Poldrack (2007), 'The neural basis of loss aversion in decision making under risk', *Science*, **315** (5811), 515–18.
Trepel, C., C.R. Fox and R.A. Poldrack (2005), 'Prospect theory on the brain? Toward a cognitive neuroscience of decision under risk', *Cognitive Brain Research*, **23** (1), 34–50.
Tversky, A. and D. Kahneman (1992), 'Advances in prospect theory: cumulative representation of uncertainty', *Journal of Risk and Uncertainty*, **5** (4), 297–323.

Weiss, H.M. (2002), 'Deconstructing job satisfaction: separating evaluations, beliefs and affective experiences', *Human Resource Management Review*, **12**, 173–94.

Zak, P.J. (2004), 'Neuroeconomics', *Philosophical Transactions of the Royal Society B*, **359** (1451), 1737–48.

Zink, C.F., G. Pagnoni, M.E. Martin-Skurski, J.C. Chappelow and G.S. Berns (2004), 'Human striatal response to monetary reward depends on saliency', *Neuron*, **42** (3), 509–17.

11. Mapping neurological drivers to entrepreneurial proclivity

Robert Smith

INTRODUCTION

The topic of this chapter is interesting both from a theoretical and practical perspective because our understanding of the intricacies and nuances of neurobiological and endocrinal influences upon entrepreneurial proclivity, and thus behavior, are in their infancy. From a theoretical perspective many exciting possibilities for explaining entrepreneurial behavior abound. New theories, models and frameworks will undoubtedly emerge. These may well have practical applications in terms of how we seek to explain entrepreneurial behavior. This particular chapter contributes by combining many strands of neurobiological research and synthesizing them with entrepreneurship research. As such, the chapter will be of interest to entrepreneurship scholars and those in the scientific community interested in neurobiology but who may have a sketchy notion of what entrepreneurship is or is not. It may also be of interest to a broad range of social scientists because it relates to the practical application of cross-disciplinary theory.

As a new(ish) academic discipline, entrepreneurship has been said to suffer from science envy. As entrepreneurship research continues to mature, it is self-evident that its frontiers will require constant remapping as we continue to learn more and more about this societally eulogized cognitive behavior. Despite the fact that trait research has been somewhat disparaged of late in the social sciences, our knowledge of behaviorism continues to expand since trait researchers first began to chart the visible manifestations of entrepreneurial behavior in the form of trait and personality theories. Trait research operates at the level of what Shane (2003) refers to as the 'individual-opportunity nexus' exploring the interactions, or fit, between the individual(s) and the opportunity. Scholars such as Shane (2003, 2008) and Zhao and Seibert (2006) have been at the forefront of a revival in the use of trait research in entrepreneurial studies. In particular, Shane and colleagues (Shane et al., 2003) have mapped the links between traits and motivations.

As scholars, we learned not to package our research as being trait-based and instead we have turned to research the psychological, the sociological and the philosophical elements of being and thus we concern ourselves with the abstract issues of ontology, epistemology, narrative and identity. We hope that this imbues our research with a more scientific aura but nevertheless I, for one, continue to be drawn back to the simplicity of traits as narrative descriptors for the complex human behavior that is entrepreneurship. This is so because traits (and states) form the basis of many storylines in entrepreneur stories and thus in our research quest to understand the nuances of entrepreneurial behavior we have turned to heuristics such as narrative or identity. However, biology and in particular the neurological–endocrinal nexus remains a relatively uncharted territory in relation to developing a deeper understanding of entrepreneurial behavior. Nevertheless, there is a growing appreciation that trait research in entrepreneurship is currently seeing a revival because previous research had neglected to control for the size of the opportunities that entrepreneurs perceive.

Consequentially, this chapter attempts to map recent breakthroughs in the field which suggest that there may be a neurobiological underpinning to such behavior. This is a complex area of study for social scientists without a medical background because whilst traits were frustratingly difficult to isolate and research despite allegedly being relatively constant, the same cannot be said for ephemeral biological underpinnings such as states, moods, drives, urges, ergs and appetites. In discussing neurological and endocrinal influences such as thyroxine, testosterone and adrenalin on entrepreneurial behavior as a discipline, I am perhaps researching at the edge of my knowledge base. It is this quest for '*verstehen*' which drives me. This loose 'conceptual mapping' methodology is useful in helping determine the biological basis of business by plotting biological bases into an understandable format which illustrates that entrepreneurship has a biological basis, albeit a proto-entrepreneurial one.

The purpose of this chapter is therefore to seek to understand how we can take advantage of the emerging area of neuroeconomics to inform how we view organizations by providing an overview of the literature. In doing so, I seek to map and understand the complex causal relationships and biological drivers which combine to inform concepts such as beliefs, opportunity recognition, risk-aversion or risk-seeking and personal motivation of individuals within the organization, but in particular amongst members of the entrepreneurial community who set up and manage firms. This overview will permit the mapping of pre-decisional dynamics of the human brain and in the process achieve important new insights into how we as humans organize our work allowing others to challenge classic economic models and their implicit assumptions relating to the ascendancy of rationality as the key organizing principle.

Whilst I agree with the editors of this volume that complex organizational decision-making requires the understanding of human cognition and incentive evaluation using modern economic tools and rigorous experimental methodologies, it should not be forgotten that there is also a role to be played by qualitative research methodologies. Neuroscience may well give economics new ways to conceptualize and measure important facets of decision-making but these can be triangulated by existing research methods such as in-depth interviews, observational techniques, self-reflective action research and by shadowing entrepreneurs and key organizational players. Scientific tools of neuroeconomics can highlight the role of neural substrates in the 'decision making' processes of entrepreneurs but it still requires a qualitative approach to articulate their behavioral consequences in organizational terms.

Accordingly, this review highlights sound theoretical and empirical contributions and in particular how the literature on neuroeconomics facilitates our understanding of organizational processes and of entrepreneurship. In the process it collates extant work being carried out in the neuroeconomics, neuroentrepreneurship and neuroscience literature, pointing to how an understanding of neuroscience can inform organizational theory and research methodologies. In particular, this chapter seeks to (1) identify how neuroscientific tools can help to identify the drivers of opportunity perception of the entrepreneur and (2) demonstrate how neuroscientific tools can help us visualize the opportunity analysis of the entrepreneur. This sets up other questions which beg to be answered. For instance, are certain people genetically and psychologically hardwired to become successful entrepreneurs? Do hormones such as testosterone and adrenaline influence human drives? The third aim of this chapter is to (3) map the pre-decisional dynamics of the entrepreneurial process.

The remainder of this chapter is divided into five further sections. The following section, conducts the literature review and is subdivided into sections on (1) the entrepreneur as driven – in search of entrepreneurial proclivity, which seeks to understand what forces drive entrepreneurial proclivity; (2) the biological basis for this proclivity; (3) mapping genetic influences on entrepreneurial proclivity; (4) the cognitive basis of entrepreneurial proclivity; (5) the neurological basis of dyslexia and other learning deficits; (6) mapping endocrinal influences upon entrepreneurial proclivity; (7) linking testosterone research and entrepreneurial behavior. The main thrust of this section is to consider the neurobiological basis of entrepreneurial behavior by linking these disparate research outputs together. In the third section we analyze the above and develop a conceptual map of the research terrain. In the fourth section we discuss the material assembled and consider other human internal drives such as the theological and libido. The final section assesses the theoretical contributions of the research drawing out conclusions and implications. In seeking to address these issues the chapter will also address the following research questions: do neurobiological and endocrinal factors influence entrepreneurial proclivity? And if so, what are the implications for society?

REVIEWING THE LITERATURE

This section conducts a review of the literature, identifying area of research activity which will be mapped and analyzed in later sections. One of the issues which remains problematic is that there is no one literature which one can draw upon but numerous including, entrepreneurship, psychology and medicine. Issues which impinge upon and may indeed underpin the behavior of Carland et al.'s (2000) 'indefatigable entrepreneur' include the role of genetic factors in leadership, neural circuits, the effect of hormones on occupational choice, decision-making, risk-taking, the drive for power and reputation which are all relevant to the practice of entrepreneurship as a behavioral output. We begin by considering the entrepreneur as driven and, in particular, entrepreneurial proclivity.

The Entrepreneur as Driven – in Search of Entrepreneurial Proclivity

Entrepreneurs as individuals are often said to be driven, but many of the questions as to what drives them remains unanswered. This is perhaps not surprising given that we as a research community have yet to develop an accepted universal definition of what constitutes entrepreneurship. For this reason the subject of entrepreneurial proclivity is one which continues to fascinate me. It is a subject which fascinates other entrepreneurship researchers, such as Covin and Slevin (1991), Matsuno et al. (2002), Carland et al. (2000), Griffith et al. (2005) and Dess and Lumpkin (2005), all of whom have researched the antecedents of entrepreneurial drive. Griffith et al. (2005) refer to entrepreneurial proclivity as being a dynamic capability. A proclivity is defined as a natural or habitual inclination or tendency, or a propensity or predisposition towards pursuing a particular behavior. This is frustratingly vague and it is also described as a bent. It is connected to a quest for learning. Perhaps the key to decoding its mysteries lies in taking cognizance of the words 'natural' and 'habitual'. This vagueness extends into the literature on entrepreneurship where different phrases are used to refer to the same concept. For example, Covin and

Slevin (1991) refer to 'entrepreneurial posture', Dess and Lumpkin (2005) refer to 'entrepreneurial orientation' and Matsuno et al. (2002) refer to 'entrepreneurial proclivity' despite clearly referring to the same predisposition for the masculine cult of risk taking (McCarthy, 2000). Indeed, McCarthy links risk taking to innate personality traits and cognition and suggests that an entrepreneur's perceptions of risk, and capacity to bear risk, evolve over time perhaps indicating that risk taking is not just a static personality trait forged by nature or nurture, reflecting learning in a business context.

The 'nature versus nurture' and 'born versus made' debates have long been familiar to students of entrepreneurial proclivity and one burning question has always been whether certain people are genetically and psychologically hardwired to become successful entrepreneurs. This brings cognitive and neurological factors into play but underlying biological influences are also important.

Shane and Venkatraman (2000), in calling for new approaches to the study of entrepreneurship, describe it as the nexus of two phenomena, namely the presence of lucrative opportunities and enterprising individuals (ibid., p. 218). Nevertheless, this does not explain what drives enterprising individuals to succeed where others fail. However, socio-biological approaches such as those discussed in this chapter do have the potential to provide answers to such questions. Significantly, such approaches align themselves with existing psychological approaches (Kets de Vries, 1985; Shaver and Scott, 1991) which possess an established scientific basis and thus credibility. In the following we look at several interconnected strands in the emerging debate including genetics, cognition, the neurological basis for dyslexia and endocrinal influences such as testosterone, adrenalin and thyroxin. We begin by considering the biological basis for entrepreneurial proclivity.

Considering the Biological Basis for Entrepreneurial Proclivity

In general terms, there is a broad acceptance of the influence of biology on business and, in particular, success (Arnot, 2000; Clippinger, 1999; Sahtouris, 2005). Indeed, biological approaches to entrepreneurship are becoming more common, for example, Aldrich and Martinez (2001), Horide (2001), Mitchell et al. (2002b), McKelvey (2003), Mitchell (2004), Shane (2008), Nicolaou and Shane (forthcoming) and Nicolaou et al. (2008a). Incisively, Arnot (2000) refers to mental energy as being the basic foundation of success and in his book details many biological influences upon success. Mention of biological approaches brings the nature/nurture argument into play but as Ridley (2003) has asserted, nature and nurture often work together. Entrepreneurship spans psychological and cognitive aspects of organizational behavior such as perception, cognition, judgment, attitudes, emotion, well-being, motivation, choice and performance. These topics are inherently integrative, given that perceptions, attitudes and emotions are rooted in cognition and judgment, and motivation and performance are inextricably linked to choice. The practice of entrepreneurship revolves around the performance of sound judgment and decision-making, which positions it very much as a product of cognitive human forces.

The idea that entrepreneurs are somehow by the process of evolution designated as 'chosen ones' (Aldrich and Martinez, 2001) is not particularly helpful, making it necessary to map the biological precursor to entrepreneurial proclivity, which may well be influenced by such considerations as character and personality type, not to mention specific life themes (Bolton and Thompson, 2000; Nardi, 2000). However, the human body is more than just a biological vessel through which entrepreneurial behavior is channeled, which entails consideration of genetic influences upon such behavior.

Mapping Genetic Influences on Entrepreneurial Proclivity

Genetics is a discipline within biology and is the science dealing with heredity and variation in living organisms (Griffith et al. 2000). The study of genetics entails consideration of DNA, genes and chromosomes. Nicolaou et al. (2008a) define a gene as a piece of DNA passed from parents to their biological children during reproduction and which influences an observed (and unobserved) characteristic of an individual, referred to as a phenotype. Nicolaou et al. (2008a) quite rightly point out that any findings that are seen in empirical work might not survive the test of replication.

A detailed consideration of genetics is not in the scope of this chapter but genetics are nevertheless important because they influence human development and cognition. Until recently consideration of the genetic influences upon entrepreneurial proclivity were confined to the realms of speculation. Indeed, Newton and Shreeves (2002) reported on suggestions and deeply held beliefs by business leaders, such as Rebecca Smith of A.D. Morgan, that entrepreneurial ability is genetic.

However, the recent study of Nicolaou et al. (2008a) has provided a skeletal framework upon which further research can build. Indeed, they suggest that a significant portion of the variance in who becomes an entrepreneur is accounted for by genetic factors. Thus Nicolaou et al. (2008a) sought to link personality to extraversion and introversion, paying particular attention to the traits of agreeableness, conscientiousness, emotional stability and openness to experience. In particular, they noted that people who are agreeable are less likely to become entrepreneurs, thus positioning entrepreneurs, as likely to be of a disagreeable disposition. The final point they make is that such entrepreneurs are prone to the trait of sensation seeking. To reach these conclusions Nicolaou and colleagues used quantitative genetics techniques to compare the entrepreneurial activity of 870 pairs of monozygotic and 857 pairs of (mainly female) same-sex dizygotic twins in the UK. Their findings indicate relatively high heritabilities for entrepreneurship across different operationalizations, suggesting that family environment and upbringing have little effect upon entrepreneurial proclivity. Therefore genetic factors may influence people's tendency to become entrepreneurs because our genes may predispose us to develop traits such as being sociable and extroverted. This, in turn, may facilitate skills such as salesmanship, vital to entrepreneurial success. Nicolaou and colleagues are confident about their predictions because identical twins share 100 percent of their genetic composition, while fraternal twins share about 50 percent, on average. Therefore differences in the rates at which pairs of identical twins both become entrepreneurs and the rates at which both members of fraternal twins both become entrepreneurs can be attributed to genetics. Indeed, such points of concordance (the numbers of pairs of twins in which both members are or are not entrepreneurs) make it possible to infer that genetic factors account for the differences. This consideration of genetic factors in explaining why people engage in entrepreneurial activity is an exciting contribution to the literature, albeit their assertion that up to 50 percent of someone's propensity to become self-employed could be attributed to genetic factors is quite frankly mind blowing. Although this seminal study does not suggest there in an entrepreneurial gene, it has nevertheless laid the groundwork for future research on what specific genes affect entrepreneurship.

There has been a significant rise in research into the genetics of entrepreneurial cognition and behavior, for example, Nicolaou et al. (2008a, 2008b; Nicolaou and Shane, forthcoming). We are also seeing the rise of a new, more scientific rhetoric in which research questions are replaced by hypotheses, theories with pheonotypes and the introduction of methodologies such as genetic etiology, bivariate genetics techniques and quantitative genetics. Nevertheless, it is wise to exercise a few words of caution because few behavioral traits can be directly attributed to a particular gene. Toates (2005) discusses the emergence of evolutionary psychology (EP) and the theory of dual-layered behavioral control involving an integration of behavior, cognition and complex human information processing capabilities. We thus now turn to consider cognition and its part in the entrepreneurial process.

Examining the Cognitive Basis of Entrepreneurial Proclivity

Entrepreneurship occurs at the conjunction of opportunities and individuals (Shane and Venkatraman, 2000). Moreover, Baron (2000) argues that cognitive and social factors influence success in entrepreneurial venturing. For Baron, successful entrepreneurs appear to think differently than other persons in several respects and have more direct thought processes and high levels of social competence but may be prone to overconfidence. Entrepreneurship scholars such as Stewart et al. (1999) have long wondered whether entrepreneurial proclivity influences ones' occupation and whether there are physiological differences between entrepreneurs and/or managers and the rest of the population. Entrepreneurship is first and foremost a cognitively driven human behavior and as such cognitive studies have much to contribute to our understanding because cognition links behavior to emotions, attitudes, moods and states, creativity and intuition (Tomasino, 2007), not to mention thought process intentions (Shepherd and Krueger, 2002).

Research into cognitive aspects of entrepreneurial behavior is a fruitful area of research. For example, Krueger and Brazeal (1994) researched entrepreneurial potential, Shane and Venkatraman (2000) researched timidy and boldness, Shepherd and Krueger (2002) examined entrepreneurial intention, whilst Goss (2007) considered entrepreneurial emotion. Krueger (2008) has considered biases and heuristics. For Tomasino (2007) entrepreneurial behavior is informed by a high degree of creativity and intuition – capacities which remain scientific enigmas. Therefore Tomasino considers that creativity may be a distinct bodily state or psychophysiological coherence influenced by positive emotions. In a similar vein, Schindehutte et al. (2006) examined the cognitive and emotional experiences of entrepreneurs. However, cognition is influenced by hormones. Hampson (in press) further argues that endocrine levels can contribute to sex differences in visio-spatial perception and cognition, and Becker et al. (2005) accept that there are sex differences in brain and behavior influenced by the endocrine system. Indeed, Eckel et al. (in press) accept that behavioral differences between the sexes are influenced by hormones linking genetics to the biological discipline of endocrinology, to which we will turn in a later section, but first we will consider the neurological basis of dyslexia and other learning deficits.

Considering the Neurological Basis of Dyslexia and Other Learning Deficits

Consideration of the effects of learning difficulties such as dyslexia, attention deficit hyperactivity disorder (ADHD), attention deficit disorder

(ADD) and so on is another emerging area of entrepreneurship research which has great potential. Studies include those of Logan (2001), Mannuzza et al. (1993), Gilbertson (2003) and Smith (2008). What is significant is the mathematics of negative attrition in that whether one is studying incidences of dyslexia, ADD, ADHD, criminality, drug addiction or even delinquency is struck by the 4 plus to 1 ratio frequently encountered in such studies, indicating that boys are more likely than girls to be represented in those behavioral categories. For example, ADHD adults are nearly four times as likely to be entrepreneurs as their non-ADHD counterparts (Mannuzza et al., 1993) and ADHD is considered to be present in 2–5 percent of the population (Goodyear and Hynd, 1992). According to Gilbertson (2003) ADD is highly hereditary. These factors suggest that there may be an underlying biological or neurological underpinning to these conditions and testosterone is one plausible explanation. For Habib (2000) up to 10 percent of school-age children fail to learn to read in spite of normal intelligence, adequate environment and educational opportunities because of developmental dyslexia. Habib argues that there is a neurological basis to dyslexia which has been tentatively corroborated by brain scans. Such neuropsychological studies have provided considerable evidence that the main mechanism leading to these children's learning difficulties is phonological in nature. Cohen (2003) suggests that high levels of testosterone in the womb can lead to incidences of autism and Asperger's syndrome in boys. These conditions can influence entrepreneurial proclivity. Moreover, Gilbertson (2003) identifies a tentative link between ADHD and adrenalin.

Mapping Endocrinal Influences upon Entrepreneurial Proclivity

Hampson and Moffat (2004) refer to the psychobiology of gender and explored the effects of reproductive hormones on the adult nervous system. The human endocrine system is an integrated system of small organs that secrete hormones and regulates metabolism, energy levels and also our moods. The endocrinal glands of interest to us are the thyroid, the adrenal gland and the sexual organs (testes and ovaries). In this study we are primarily interested in testosterone, adrenalin and thyroxine because of their potential to influence entrepreneurial proclivity via the mechanism of adrenalin or testosterone rushes. To date, the only study which the author could locate which specifically links adrenalin to entrepreneurial behavior is that of Derr (1982/2006). See Table 11.1 for an overview of their function and how they relate to entrepreneurial behavior.

It is necessary to concentrate upon the linkages between testosterone,

Table 11.1   Endocrinal influences upon entrepreneurial behavior

Endocrinal Hormone	A Description of How the Hormone Affects Behavior
Testosterone	Testosterone influences energy levels, libido and strength. It is an androgenous based steroid hormone produced in the testes of men and in the ovaries of women. However, it is found in small quantities in the adrenal glands. It is normally associated with masculinity and aggressiveness but studies suggest that aggressiveness is associated with low testosterone levels, whereas risk-taking behavior is associated with high levels. The literature suggests that attention, memory and spatial ability are key cognitive functions affected by testosterone. These of course are all cognitive elements of entrepreneurial proclivity. In adult males testosterone is produced at a level of 40 to 60 times higher than in females, therefore males who exhibit e-behavior are statistically more likely to have high testosterone levels. However, females are more responsive to its effects and there is a wide range of levels across the population. Testosterone levels are not static and are subject to biological rhythms and the effects of aging on its production. Testosterone is said to be a 'virilizing agent' and is often regarded as a rejuvenating elixir. This opens up possibilities for further research and the possibility of a cure for flagging (entrepreneurial) libido by prescribing testosterone replacements to prospective entrepreneurs at the new venture stage.
Adrenalin	Adrenalin boosts the supply of oxygen to our brain and muscles and increases our heart rate to enable us to sustain high energy levels. Despite the fact that there has to date been little research into the influence of adrenalin on e-behavior, journalistic accounts often describe entrepreneurs as 'adrenalin junkies'. Indeed, entrepreneurial adventures are fraught with dangers and exhilarations during which adrenalin freely flows and there is the possibility that entrepreneurial behavior may become addictive and engaged in for fun.
Thyroxine	The thyroid plays a part in regulating energy levels and metabolic rate. It is perhaps one of the least appreciated of the endocrine secretions in relation to e-behavior, but too much thyroxine can lead to hyperactivity and increased energy levels. Likewise too little can lead to lethargy and inactivity. It can thus be a behavioral suppressant. It may also have a role to play in communicational difficulties such as dyslexia and dyspraxia. It is worthy of further research.
Dopamine	Dopamine increases heart rate, influences motivation for physical activity and the need for sensory variety and therefore may also play a significant part in e-behavior. However, there are no known studies relating to dopamine.

adrenalin and thyroxin because collectively such endocrinal secretions influence mental and physical energy and have the potential to influence entrepreneurial behavior. Frustratingly for researchers because it is a system, all are interrelated, thus Hampson (2004) links reproductive hormones to cognition.

Linking Testosterone Research and Entrepreneurial Behavior

Testosterone drives male aggression and sexual interest. We know more about testosterone than many other hormones (Dabbs, 2000). White et al. (2006) argue that entrepreneurs have higher levels of testosterone than other men in the population. Using saliva swabs White and colleagues tested 31 male business students who had previously invested in and managed their own business. These males had significantly higher testosterone levels than 79 of their male classmates who had no entrepreneurial experience. For White et al. (2006) colleagues, as a specific heritable characteristic one's testosterone level 'explains something about the likelihood of that individual being significantly involved in creating a new venture'. They argue that although entrepreneurs may not be born, one's biological inheritance may influence one's likelihood of engaging in entrepreneurial activities. Thus they argue that biological evolutionary processes select for heritable behaviors providing advantages in terms of survival and reproductive advantage; therefore how we behave is, at least in part, affected by the evolutionary history of our species. Building upon this, White et al. (2007) argue for a biosocial model of entrepreneurship reiterating the message that new venture creation is more likely among those individuals having a higher testosterone level in combination with a family business background. O'Boyle (1994), taking a biological perspective, considered the effects of testosterone on the development of men and ultimately linked it to the work of entrepreneurs. This discussion on testosterone obviously precludes female entrepreneurs. It is well understood that females are not driven to many things by testosterone, nevertheless there are growing numbers of female entrepreneurs. This suggests that there is a weakness in the biological argument for the influence of testosterone on entrepreneurial proclivity. This points to the pressing need for further research. Furthermore, testosterone changes every minute (or fraction of a minute) and so any experiment that takes one or two samples for measurement is suspect for measurement errors.

In books and films financial-market traders are often dramatized as macho gamblers. It is thus significant that Coates and Herbert (2008) conducted research into the effects of testosterone on trading activity on the stock exchange taking saliva samples in the morning and evening and found that the levels of two hormones, testosterone and cortisol, affected traders. Interestingly, cortisol is linked to uncertainty, novelty and unpredictability. Their findings indicate that testosterone can be equated to commercial success. If traders have high levels of testosterone in the morning, then the amount of money they earn per day increases. However, Coates and Herbert stress that traders with moderate base levels of testosterone do better than those with higher base levels. High base levels can lean one towards over risky, bullish behavior. The best traders do not have an ego and approach trading with an attitude of humbleness. Coates and Herbert (2008) were careful to stress that the traders they tested were operating in high pressure trading situations with little opportunity to reflect and that their findings would not be applicable to trading where one has time to reflect before making decisions. Coates and Herbert (2008) suggest that it would be good for both banks and the financial system to employ more women and older men in the markets. Men and women may thus have different biological trajectories. Such a change would produce a much more stable financial system. Coates and Herbert (2008) conclude that cortisol appears to rise in a market crash and increases risk aversion, thus exaggerating the market's downward movement. They suggest that testosterone appears to rise in a bubble effect increasing risk taking, thereby exaggerating the market's upward movement. This explains why people caught in bubbles and crashes may find it difficult to make rational choices.

For Kuhnen and Knutson (2005) there is a neurological basis to such financial risk taking. Indeed research by Knutson et al. (2008) suggests that young men shown erotic pictures were more likely to make a larger financial gamble than if they were shown non-erotic images, indicating that money and women may trigger the same brain area in men. It falls short of proving a causal link between testosterone and profitability. Coates, an ex Wall Street trader himself, suggests that some trading activity does not make sense in terms of economic or game theory and that it is more akin to them being on a drug-induced high. The above research is in keeping with the research of Barber and Odean (2001) who argue that theoretical models predict that overconfident investors trade excessively. Barber and Odean (2001) suggest 'Boys will be boys'. What is significant is that they reached this conclusion by examining 35 000 trading records over a significant time frame. Hormone research certainly suggests that there is a winner model in which competitors have rising testosterone levels. Eventually this leads to overreach and poor decision making. Cooper et al. (1988) have noticed a similar propensity for often illogical risk taking in entrepreneurs.

What is interesting about T-research in relation to occupation is that, for example, male trial lawyers have been found to have higher average T-levels than male non-trial lawyers (Dabbs et al., 1995). This pattern is the same for female lawyers suggesting that competitive or combative behavior raises levels of testosterone and increases energy levels. Adrenalin and testosterone make a heady cocktail. Dabbs et al. (1990a) have studied the effects of testosterone on occupational choice. According to White et al. (2003 and 2006), individuals with low testosterone levels are less likely to exhibit entrepreneurial behavior. However, it is not as simple as to argue that T-behaviors equate to 'e-behaviors'. Harris (1999) reviewed the studies investigating the possible correlation between testosterone and aggression and how testosterone is related to various personality dimensions, suggesting that testosterone may have a relationship with sexually dimorphic behaviors and in particular aggression (which can be counter-productive to entrepreneurial proclivity).

Testosterone can be linked to destructive anti-social behavior. Indeed, Stålenheim et al. (1998) examined testosterone as a biological marker in psychopathy and alcoholism. In fact, Sulivan (2000, pp. 94–8) considers testosterone to be a metaphor for manhood correlated with risk and physicality (and criminality) explaining why boys are action orientated and why the ideologies of masculinity and heroism fuse together in heroic narratives. Dabbs et al. (1995) examined testosterone, crime and prison behavior among 692 adult male prison inmates, measuring testosterone from saliva samples. The behaviors were then coded from prison system records. Inmates who had committed personal crimes of sex and violence had higher testosterone levels than inmates who had committed property crimes of burglary, theft and drugs. Interestingly, inmates with higher testosterone levels also violated more rules in prison, especially rules involving overt confrontation. The findings indicate differences between low and high testosterone individuals in the amount and pattern of their misbehavior. In another study Dabbs et al. (1990b) examined the personalities of college students and compared them with military veterans, suggesting that it is likely that testosterone has innate effects that are socially undesirable and can lead to anti-social behavior, delinquency and criminal behavior particularly in the working classes. Dabbs et al. (1990b) also suggest that such behavior can be attenuated by fostering (pro-social) bonds between the individual and society. Entrepreneurship is a potentially pro-social behavior.

Having considered the above biological elements of entrepreneurial behavior in isolation, it is now incumbent upon us to consider how such themes combine. Thus in the following sector we analyze what the review of the literature tells us in research terms whilst developing a conceptual map of the research terrain.

ANALYZING THE ABOVE AND DEVELOPING A CONCEPTUAL MAP OF THE RESEARCH TERRAIN

The material reviewed above investigates both at individual and collective levels how human drives and forces influence entrepreneurial behavior. When one begins to assemble the material and concepts in relation to an existing level of knowledge of entrepreneurship theory, one begins to see linkages to existing entrepreneurship theory and behaviors, such as charisma, creativity and innovation. In this respect the literature review forms the basis of an empirical framework backed up by methodological approaches, such as observation and field-based studies. An interesting picture emerges, which is illustrated in Figure 11.1.

The assembled model considers three stages – socio-biological, bio-logical and behavioral. Socio-biological influences can affect ingrained neurobiological disturbances such as dyslexia. In the biological model issues such as physiognomy, ethnicity, fitness levels, stamina and physical and mental wellbeing play a part, as does character and personality. Behavioral typologies such as introversion versus extroversion and morality versus criminality may have biological underpinnings. One of the problems with researching states, moods, urges, ergs, appetites and rushes is that these are often proto-cognitional, never mind proto-entrepreneurial and as such cannot be directly observed. Phan et al. (2002) researched such pre-entrepreneurial states of being. Like hedonistic dispositions and playfulness, they must be inferred from other observable behaviors. The pictorial model developed has a cross-disciplinary utility because of the broad spread of its knowledge base and because visually it arranges a staggering amount of material and concepts in an understandable format which would require several thousand words more to articulate clearly.

CONSIDERING OTHER INTERNAL DRIVING FORCES

One of the most difficult issues to research in this complex area is that of the interlinked nature of many of the concepts discussed and how many drives, urges and states flow into one another leading to linked human drives. In reflecting and theorizing about human drives which influence entrepreneurial proclivity, one of the most obvious and most well researched is that of theological drive and in particular the influence of religious belief upon the formation of the Weberian Protestant work ethic. This is so well documented that it is not the place of such a review here to regurgitate the work. Instead, we will briefly consider the subject of sex

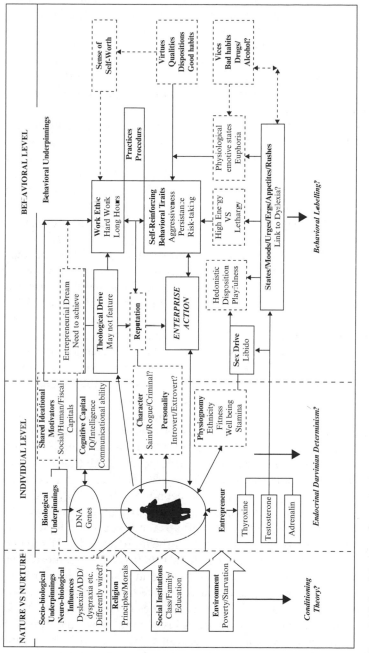

Figure 11.1   Mapping neurobiological precursors to entrepreneurial proclivity

drive or libido. These (like sex drive) are notoriously difficult to research. However, sex drives and other human impulses ebb and flow with the passing of time and can be subjugated by other drives and impulses and the other pressing priorities of life. As men mature, their sex drives can, and do, wane but the embedded behaviors which result from such earlier conditioning and programming often remain constant. In this ontological process other invisible endocrinal chemicals can influence our competitive behavior and thus perhaps entrepreneurial proclivity.

In this chapter, libido and sex drive are considered in the wider Jungian sense of being free creative or psychic energies and not in its narrowest base sense. For Cannon (1991, p. 223) enterprise is akin to a life force feeding on energy, drive and creativity. Taken at this level, it could be argued that entrepreneurial proclivity and behavior could well be influenced by latent or subjugated drives and states such as the human sex drive which in turn is shaped by hormones such as testosterone, adrenalin and thyroxin (discussed above).

This may strike readers as being a bizarre theoretical lens but the title of the study by Dabbs (2000), 'Heroes, rogues, and lovers', into the linkages between such behaviors and testosterone strike the author as being an apt descriptor of some entrepreneurs. The psychologist Richard Webster bemoans the lack of a systematic theory which seeks to explain 'the exceptionally violent nature of our own species, the extraordinary range and complexity of our non-sexual reproductive behavior or the depth and power of the most ordinary human emotions' (Webster, 1996, p. 2). According to Webster (1996), the history of science is full of such tentative hypotheses, later validated by advances in science.

Economists are also contributing to the emerging argument. Indeed, Dostaler and Morris (1999, p. 247) link psyche and physiology to economics by discussing the works of Freud and Keynes in relation to money and capitalism. They echo the words of Keynes that sexual drive or libido is a major component of the animal spirit, as are also the closely linked behaviors of aggression and sadism. The economist John Maynard Keynes (Keynes, 1936, p. 161), in trying to articulate the animal spirit which animates the entrepreneur, was thus perhaps the first economist to envisage entrepreneurial activity as a diversion of the human sex drive from normal sex. Keynes remarked 'It is better that a man should tyrannise over his bank balance than over his fellow citizens and whilst the former is sometimes denounced as being but a means to the latter, sometimes at least it is an alternative' (ibid., p. 374). Thus Keynes (1936), in laying the foundation stones of macro-economics in his seminal work the *The General Theory of Employment, Interest and Money*, was perhaps also laying the foundations of macho-economics in unleashing the animal spirit that is entrepreneurship. Certainly, for Dostaler and Morris (1999, p. 248) Keynes was suggesting that entrepreneurial speculation and capital accumulation constitute excellent outlets and stimulation for the abundant libido of certain individuals. Indeed, Dostaler and Morris (1999, p. 251) remark that 'Moreover, dangerous human proclivities can be canalized into comparatively harmless channels by the existence of opportunities for money making and private wealth.' With these sobering words of advice, we now consider how this chapter has contributed to our theoretical understanding of the neurobiological basis for entrepreneurial proclivity.

ASSESSING THE THEORETICAL CONTRIBUTIONS OF THIS REVIEW

Having considered the literature and mapped some neurobiological precursors to entrepreneurial proclivity, it is now time to return to the research questions. In relation to the first question regarding identifying how neuroscientific tools can help to identify the drivers of opportunity perception of the entrepreneur, the mapping exercise illustrated the breadth of potential topics and research areas to be embraced. This would best be done by forming research alliances between social and pure scientists as is already occurring in the USA between Professor Scott Shane and others (Nicolaou and Shane, forthcoming and Nicolaou et al., 2008a). It would be difficult for us as researchers to routinely ask respondents about their sex life or their emotional states, but clearly we need to overcome our hang-ups and design ethically bounded research agendas which permit us to do so.

In relation to the second research question regarding neuroscientific tools that can help us visualize the opportunity analysis of the entrepreneur, the conceptual map has proven how this can be achieved. We now consider whether certain people are genetically and psychologically hardwired to become successful entrepreneurs and whether hormones such as testosterone and adrenaline influence human drives. The research of Nicolaou et al. (2008c) into genetic and endocrinal influences certainly indicates that this may well be the case. The work of Smith (2008) on dyslexia also suggests that there may be a neurological element to entrepreneurial proclivity. However, these studies are a long way from providing conclusive proof of the supposition. Collectively, the work of White et al. (2006, 2007) and the studies by Nicolaou et al. (2008d) and Coates and Herbert (2008) provides tentative corroboration that hormones such as testosterone and adrenaline influence human drives, thus answering the second research question. Together, these studies illustrate the part played by biological underpinning in the entrepreneurial process.

The work of Shane et al. (2003) is both erudite and impressive and it sees the scientification of trait theory. Indeed, it is difficult to argue against and is strangely compelling. In this respect it is far removed from early non-scientific trait research in which proof of trait was provided by case studies, examples, narratives and consensus. When entrepreneurship theory is merged with quantitative and scientific verification it becomes very powerful as an explanatory tool. It almost sees the birth of a new breed of entrepreneurship theorists and researchers. It is far removed from the qualitatively inclined social constructionist scholarship with its narrative and philosophical underpinnings which this author is comfortable with. I can see it, I can feel it and I can believe in it but I cannot read nor verify the data. It is beyond my pail. We are perhaps entering a new era of experimental entrepreneurship in which more rigorous scientific controls can be introduced. According to Krueger (2008), understanding entrepreneurial behavior requires that we focus at the deepest, most fundamental levels through the lenses of cognitive and developmental psychology. Interestingly, Norris Krueger recently participated in an interdisciplinary workshop focusing on the experimental investigation of entrepreneurial behavior from the perspectives of economics, cognitive, social and developmental psychology, neuroscience, philosophy and evolutionary anthropology. One of the areas of interest was in biological/neurological bases of entrepreneurial behavior. This is an example of deep cognitive research. Krueger welcomes such research as a way to escape the limitations of observational research.

This chapter makes a tentative contribution to the literature of entrepreneurship by mapping and therefore aligning several interrelated neurobiological precursors to entrepreneurial behavior. Although it stops short of developing and testing new theory, it does, nevertheless, highlight possible avenues of future research. Moreover, it makes a minor theoretical contribution to the fields of applied psychology and entrepreneurship being anchored as it is in phenomena relevant to organizations. This work integrates different theories, propositions or research streams into a unified framework and potential behavioral model. This study should be evaluated on how the marshaled data and narratives resonate with readers and whether it has indeed yielded valid answers to the important research questions set. This work breaks new ground and has the potential to make a lasting impact providing that ethical empirical research can be conducted to test the hypothesis that sex drive influences entrepreneurial proclivity. Consideration of entrepreneurship as being a manifestation of sexual drive is to date an untested hypothesis. It may well be a theory whose time has yet to come. However, without a public airing and a rigorous debate this protean theory may remain in the cognitive realm of wishful thinking.

Nevertheless, as a student of entrepreneurship, I find the emerging arguments, implications and conclusions of this debate on the biological determination of entrepreneurial proclivity mildly disconcerting, because if we ever arrive at a stage where instead of writing a business plan to acquire startup capital for an entrepreneurial venture, we are forced to submit a laboratory sample to be tested for our testosterone levels – or perhaps even tested to see if we possess a gene which determines whether we are likely to be dyslexic or not – then the fun and excitement of entrepreneurship may well wane. What will become of the proverbial poor boy or bright girl deemed to be merely 'normal'. Professor Tim Spector's assertion (in Nicolaou et al. 2008c) that in the future business schools and employers could identify ways of selecting those who were most likely to succeed is not so benign a statement as it first appears.

Another flaw is introduced by the possibility that in the future parental choice may be exerted in selecting breeding stock which is high in heritable entrepreneurial capital. Producing and cloning genetically predisposed entrepreneurs is the stuff from which science fiction is written. In addition, it has been suggested that genes have been shown to affect the level of education an individual receives, and thus by (bio)logical extension more highly educated people are more likely to become entrepreneurs because they are better able to recognize new business opportunities when they arise. This is at variance with the mythology of entrepreneurs being high school dropouts.

Thus by paying too much attention to biological determination we are perhaps in danger of creating a new entrepreneurial caste that, like the privileged Jedi in George Lucas's *Star Wars*, are deemed to have extraordinary powers. It is akin to ascribing certain individuals with the theological status of an elect.

In this respect I concur with the sentiment of Baumol (1991) who, in referring to the limits on observing mega-entrepreneurial events of the kind that create new industries, remarked, 'Each one is unique. If you could describe it completely you could replicate it, and it would become management instead of entrepreneurship.' Nevertheless, Coates and Herbert (2008) scoff at suggestions that scientists and business owners can use science to recruit genetically modified employees with entrepreneurial traits or even supplement the testosterone levels of employees because it takes time to develop trading mentality. It is all fair and well to seek to understand human behavior in its entirety and point out to individuals with certain conditions (such as dyslexia) that there is reason for their difference and that this may predispose them towards an entrepreneurial trajectory, but to deliberately select them for such a proclivity is perhaps a step too far. In this respect we must beware of being seduced by the scientific nature of such research because, although biology creates a pre-disposition or potential for certain behaviors, it cannot fully determine complex behaviors such as entrepreneurial proclivity.

REFERENCES

Aldrich, H.E., and M. Martinez (2001), 'Many are called, but few are chosen: an evolutionary perspective for the study of entrepreneurship', *Entrepreneurship Theory and Practice*, **25**, 41–56.

Arnot, R.B. (2000), *The Biology of Success*, Boston, MA: Little, Brown and Company.

Barber, B.M. and T. Odean (2001), 'Boys will be boys: gender, overconfidence and common stock investment', *Quarterly Journal of Economics*, **116** (1), 261–92.

Baron, R.A. (2000), 'Psychological perspectives on entrepreneurship: cognitive and social factors in entrepreneurs' success', *Current Directions in Psychological Science*, **9** (1), February, 15–18.

Baumol, W.J. (1991), 'Entrepreneurship theory: existence and inherent bounds', paper presented at the Conference on Entrepreneurship Theory, University of Illinois at Urbana-Champaign, 18–19 October.

Becker, J.B., A.P. Arnold, K.J. Berkley et al. (2005), 'Strategies and methods for research on sex differences in brain and behavior', *Endocrinology*, **146**, 1650–73.

Bolton, B. and J. Thompson (2000), *Entrepreneurs, Temperament, Talent, Technique*, Oxford: Butterworth-Heinemann.

Cannon, T. (1991), *Enterprise Creation, Development and Growth*, London: Butterworth-Heinemann.

Carland, J.A., J.W. Carland and W.H. Stewart, Jr (2000), 'The indefatigable entrepreneur: a study of the dispositions of multiple venture founders', *Journal of Business and Entrepreneurship*, **12** (1), 1–16.

Clippinger, J.H. (ed.) (1999), *The Biology of Business: Decoding the Natural Laws of Enterprise*, New York: Jossey Bass.

Coates, J.M. and J. Herbert (2008), 'Endogenous steroids and financial risk taking on a London trading floor', *Proceeding of the Academy of Sciences of the United States of America*, **104**, 6167–72.

Cohen, S.B. (2003), *The Essential Difference: The Truth About the Male and Female Brain*, New York: Perseus Publishing.

Cooper, A.C., C.Y. Woo and W.C. Dunkelberg (1988), 'Entrepreneurs' perceived chances for success', *Journal of Business Venturing*, **3**, 97–108.

Covin, J. and D.P. Slevin (1991), 'A conceptual model of entrepreneurship as firm behavior', *Entrepreneurship Theory and Practice*, **16** (1), 7–24.

Dabbs, J.M. Jr (2000), *Heroes, Rogues, and Lovers: Testosterone and Behavior*, New York: McGraw-Hill.

Dabbs, J.M. Jr, D. de La Rue and P.M. Williams (1990a), 'Testosterone and occupational choice: actors, ministers, and other men', *Journal of Personality and Social Psychology*, **59**, 1261–5.

Dabbs, J.M. Jr, C.H. Hopper and J. Gregory (1990b), 'Testosterone and personality among college students and military veterans', *Personality and Individual Differences*, **11** (12), 1263–9.

Dabbs J.M., T.S. Carr, R.L. Frady and J.K. Riad (1995), 'Testosterone, crime, and misbehavior among 692 male prison inmates', *Personality and Individual Differences*, **18** (5), May, 627–33.

Derr, C.B. (1982/2006), 'Living on adrenalin: the adventurer entrepreneur', *Human Resource Management*, **21** (2–3), 6–12.

Dess, G.G. and G.T. Lumpkin (2005), 'The role of entrepreneurial orientation in stimulating effective corporate entrepreneurship', *Academy of Management Executive*, **19** (1), 147–56.

Dostaler, G. and B. Morris (1999), 'Dr Freud and Mr Keynes on money and capitalism', in J.N. Smithin (ed.), *What is Money*, London: Routledge.

Eckel, L., A.P. Arnold, E. Hampson, J.B. Becker, J. Blaustein and J.P. Herman (in press), 'Research and methodological issues in the study of sex differences and hormone-behavior relations', in J.B. Becker, K.J. Berkley, N. Geary, E. Hampson, J.P. Herman and E. Young (eds), *Sex on the Brain: From Genes to Behavior*, New York: Oxford University Press.

Gilbertson, D. (2003), '"ADHD" or "Latent Entrepreneur Personality Type"?', available at http://www.windeaters.co.nz/publications/innovation_entrepreneurship/Adhd2_web.pdf (accessed 5 April 2008).

Goodyear, P. and G.W. Hynd (1992), 'Attention-deficit disorder with (ADD/H) and without (ADD/WO) hyperactivity: behavioural and neuropsychological dilterentiation', *Journal of Clinical Child Psychology*, **21** (3).

Goss, D. (2007), 'Enterprise ritual: a theory of entrepreneurial emotion and exchange', *British Journal of Management*, doi:10.1111/j.1467-8551.2006.00518.x.

Griffith, D.A., S.A. Noble and Q. Chen (2005), 'The performance implications of entrepreneurial proclivity: a dynamic capabilties approach', *Journal of Retailing*, **82** (1), 51–62.

Griffiths, A.J.F., J.H. Miller, D.T. Suzuki, R.C. Lewontin and W.M. Gelbart (2000), *An Introduction to Genetic Analysis*, New York: W.H. Freeman and Company.

Habib, M. (2000), 'The neurological basis of developmental dyslexia: an overview and working hypothesis', *Brain*, **123** (12), 2373–99.

Hampson, E. (2004), 'Cognitive function: sex differences and hormonal influences', in G. Adelman and B.H. Smith (eds), *Encyclopedia of Neuroscience*, 3rd edn (CD-ROM), New York: Elsevier Science B.V.

Hampson, E. (in press), 'Endocrine contributions to sex differences in visuospatial perception and cognition', in J.B. Becker, K.J. Berkley, N. Geary, E. Hampson, J.P. Herman and E. Young (eds), *Sex on the Brain: From Genes to Behavior*, New York: Oxford University Press.

Hampson, E. and S.D. Moffat (2004), 'The psychobiology of gender: cognitive effects of reproductive hormones in the adult nervous system', in A.H. Eagly, A.E. Beall and R.J. Steinberg (eds), *The Psychology of Gender*, 2nd edn, New York: Guilford Press, pp. 38–64.

Harris, J.A. (1999), 'Aggression and violent behavior', **4** (3), Autumn, 273–91.

Horide, I. (2001), 'The rise and fall of the firm: an application of biology into the theory of the firm', *International Journal of Economic Studies*, **9** (1), March.

Kets de Vries, M.F.R. (1985), 'The dark side of entrepreneurship', *Harvard Business Review*, November–December, 160–66.

Keynes, J.M. (1936), *The General Theory of Employment, Interest and Money*, London: Macmillan (reprinted 2007).

Knutson, B.A., G. Wimmer, A. Elliott, C.M. Kuhnen and P.B. Winkielman (2008), 'Nucleus accumbens activation mediates the influence of reward cues on financial risk taking: brain imaging', *Neuroreport*, **19** (5), 26 March, 509–13.

Krueger, N. (2008), 'Experimental entrepreneurship: a research prospectus and workshop', paper presented at the 2008 USASBE Conference, San Antonio, Texas.

Krueger, N.F. and D.V. Brazeal (1994), 'Entrepreneurial potential and potential entrepreneurs', *Entrepreneurship Theory and Practice*, **18**, 91–104.

Kuhnen, C. and B. Knutson (2005), 'The neural basis of financial risk-taking', *Neuron*, **47**, 763–70.

Logan, J. (2001), 'Entrepreneurial success: a study of the incidence of dyslexia in the entrepreneurial population and the influence of dyslexia on success', PhD thesis, University of Bristol.

Mannuzza, S., R.G. Klein, A. Bessler, P. Malloy and M. LaPadula (1993), 'Adult outcome of hyperactive boys: education achievement, occupational rank, and psychiatric status', *Archives of General Psychiatry*, **49**, 565–76.

Matsuno, K., J.T. Mentzer and A. Özsomer (2002), 'The effects of entrepreneurial proclivity and market orientation on business performance', *Journal of Marketing*, **66** (7), 18–32.

McCarthy, B. (2000), 'The cult of risk taking and social learning: a study of Irish entrepreneurs', *Management Decision*, **38** (8), 563–75.

McKelvey, B. (2003), 'Toward a complexity science of entrepreneurship', *Journal of Business Venturing*, **19** (3), May, 313–41.

Mitchell, R.K. (2004), 'Evolutionary biology research, entrepreneurship, and the morality of security-seeking behavior in an imperfect economy', *Business Ethics Quarterly*, **4**, 263–87.

Mitchell, R.K., L. Busenitz, T. Lant, P.P. McDougall, E.A. Morse and J.B. Smith (2002), 'Are entrepreneurial cognitions universal? Assessing entrepreneurial cognitions across cultures', *Entrepreneurship Theory and Practice*, **26** (4), Summer, 9–32.

Nardi, D. (2000), 'Character and Personality Type', Telos Publications, www. telospublications.com.

Newton, J. and D.G. Shreeves (2002), 'An investigation into the relationships between characteristics and life experiences of entrepreneurs', *Journal of Research in Marketing and Entrepreneurship*, **4** (1), 16–36.

Nicolaou, N. and S. Shane (forthcoming), 'Born entrepreneurs? The genetic foundations of entrepreneurship,' *Journal of Business Venturing*.

Nicolaou, N., S. Shane, L. Cherkas and T. Spector (2008), 'The behavioral genetics of opportunity recognition and opportunity exploitation', *Management Science*, **54** (1), January, 167–79.

Nicolaou, N., S. Shane, L. Cherkas and T. Spector (2008b), 'Openness to experience and opportunity recognition: evidence of a common genetic etiology', working paper, available at http://wsomfaculty.cwru.edu.

Nicolaou, N., S. Shane, L. Cherkas, J. Hunkin and T.D. Spector (2008c), 'Is the tendency to engage in entrepreneurship genetic?', *Management Science*, **54** (1), January, 167–79.

Nicolaou, N., S. Shane, L. Cherkas and T. Spector (2008d), 'The influence of sensation seeking in the heritability of entrepreneurship', *Strategic Entrepreneurship Journal*, **2**, 7–21.

O'Boyle, E.J. (1994), 'On the person and the work of the entrepreneur', *Review of Social Economy*, **52** (4), Winter, 315–37, available at http://www.informaworld.com/smpp/title~content=t713708792~db=all~tab=issueslist~branches=52-v5252.

Phan, P.H., P.K. Wong and C.K. Wang (2002), 'Antecedents to entrepreneurship among university students in Singapore: beliefs, attitudes, and backgrounds', *Journal of Enterprise Culture*, **10** (2), June, 151–74.

Ridley, M. (2003), *Nature versus Nurture: Genes, Experience and what makes us Human*, London: Fourth Estate/Harper Collins.

Sahtouris, E. (2005), 'The biology of business: new laws of nature reveal a better way for business', available at http://www.via-visioninaction.org/via-li/articles/Sahtouris_BiologyOfBusiness-full_version.pdf (accessed 5 April 2008).

Schindehutte, M., M. Morris and J. Allen (2006), 'Beyond achievement: entrepreneurship as extreme experience', *Small Business Economics*, **27** (4–5), December, 349–68.

Shane, S. (2003), *A General Theory of Entrepreneurship: The Individual-Opportunity Nexus*, Cheltenham, UK and Northampton, MA, USA: Edward Elgar Publishing.

Shane, S. (2008), 'Entrepreneurship and the big five personality traits: a behavioral genetics perspective', working paper, available at http://wsomfaculty.cwru.edu.

Shane, S. and S. Venkatraman (2000), 'The promise of entrepreneurship as a field of research', *Academy of Management Review*, **25**, 217–26.

Shane, S., E. Locke and C. Collins (2003), 'Entrepreneurial motivation', *Human Resource Management Review*, **13** (2), 257–79.

Shaver, K.G. and L.R. Scott (1991), 'Person, process, choice: the psychology of new venture creation', *Entrepreneurship: Theory and Practice*, **16**, 23–45.

Shepherd, D.A. and N.F. Krueger (2002), 'An intentions-based model of entrepreneurial teams' social cognition', *Entrepreneurship Theory and Practice*, **27** (2), 167–85.

Smith, R. (2008), 'Being differently abled: learning lessons from dyslexic entrepreneurs', in R.T. Harrison and C.M. Leitch (eds), *Entrepreneurial Learning*, London: Routledge, 291–312.

Stålenheim, E.G., E. Eriksson, L. von Knorring and L. Wide (1998), 'Testosterone as a biological marker in psychopathy and alcoholism', *Psychiatry Research*, **77** (2), 79–88.

Stewart, W.H. Jr, W.E. Watson, J.C. Carland and J.W. Carland (1999), 'A proclivity for entrepreneurship: a comparison of entrepreneurs, small business owners, and corporate managers', *Journal of Business Venturing*, **14** (2), 189–214.

Sulivan, A. (2000), 'Why men act the way they do: don't blame them, it's the testosterone', *Readers Digest*, 192–99.

Toates, F. (2005), 'Evolutionary psychology – towards a more integrative model', *Biology and Philosophy*, **20** (2–3), March, 305–28.

Tomasino, D. (2007), 'The psychophysiological basis of creativity and intuition: accessing "the zone" of entrepreneurship', *International Journal of Entrepreneurship and Small Business*, **4** (5), 528–42.

Webster, R. (1996), *Why Freud was Wrong: Sin, Science and Psychoanalysis*, London: Harper Collins.

White, R.E., S. Thornhill and E. Hampson (2003), 'Entrepreneurs and evolutionary biology: the relationship between testosterone and new venture creation', Frontiers of Entrepreneurship Research, Proceedings of the 23rd Annual Babson-Kauffman Entrepreneurship Research Conference, 201–15.

White, R.E., S. Thornhill and E. Hampson (2006), 'Entrepreneurs and evolutionary biology: the relationship between testosterone and new venture creation', *Organizational Behavior and Human Decision Processes*, **100**, 21–34.
White, R.E., S. Thornhill and E. Hampson (2007), 'A biosocial model of entrepreneurship: the effect of testosterone and family business background', *Journal of Organizational Behavior*, **28**, 451–66.
Zhao, H. and S.E. Seibert (2006), 'The big five personality dimensions and entrepreneurial status: a meta-analytical review', *Journal of Applied Psychology*, **91** (2), March, 259–71.

12. Embodied entrepreneurship: a sensory theory of value

Frédéric Basso, Laurent Guillou and Olivier Oullier

INTRODUCTION

'I am drawing the line between outer and inner environment not at the firm's boundary but at the skin of the entrepreneur, so that the factory is part of the external technology; the brain, perhaps assisted by computers, is the internal' (Simon, 1996, p. 25). One could see in Herbert Simon's words an invitation to consider neuroscientific advances (and the advent of neuroeconomics) in the economy of the firm to better understand the behavior of the entrepreneur. Simply put, neuroeconomics can be defined as the use of cognitive and brain sciences to uncover the dynamics underlying economic decision making (for example, Zak, 2004). Over the past decade cognitive neuroscientists interested in the neural foundations of the states of mind at stake in economic decisions have taken note of and used the strong body of results coming from well-controlled empirical and theoretical paradigms that experimental economics has been offering. Combining the concept and methods of (social) neuroscience and experimental economics has therefore provided original insights that could lead to a better understanding of the processes underlying preferences, investments and economic exchanges between two (or more) individuals.

Here we propose to build on Friedrich Hayek's pioneer book *The Sensory Order* (Hayek, 1952a), not only to specify Simon's views but also to expand them in order to design neuroeconomic paradigms that would be useful to understand the economy of the firm. To do so, we consider the connections between the skin and the brain of the entrepreneur by including the role of his entire body, that is, not only his brain, in determining the value of the goods he produces. Hence, one of our claims is to understand the behavior of the entrepreneur on the market, whereby neuroeconomics has to consider a sensory theory of value (STV; Basso and Oullier, 2009).

Of particular interest with STV is to consider the role of the human body as a whole, that is, by including its shared coordination dynamics occurring at many levels of description between the brain, the body, the individual and collective behaviors as well as the physical and social environments (Kelso, 1995). Those embodied aspects have too often been neglected when studying the behavior of the entrepreneur. By taking them into account STV offers means to refine the understanding of the entrepreneur's innovator status on the market in considering the individual as a key component of an actor–environment system that cannot be considered separately (Gibson, 1979; Herrmann-Pillath, 1992). As suggested by Hayek's definition of the entrepreneur, his innovative qualities entice others into copying or mimicking him. Thus, STV offers a novel angle to the theoretical field of entrepreneurship by considering the role played by imitative actions on the market.

In this chapter we therefore explain how STV can be applied to the concept of cost by exploring the links between this theory of value and entrepreneurship. Ultimately, it will arise that the application of STV to the behavior of the entrepreneur lies with the interdependence between innovation and imitation on the market as a discovery procedure.

INDIVIDUAL ENTREPRENEUR: INNOVATION IN CATALLAXY

Many contemporary authors have addressed entrepreneurship and the behavior of the entrepreneur (for example, Casson et al., 2006). Although our approach is deeply rooted in Hayek's work, one should bear in mind that he did not make a systematic study of the entrepreneurship the way other authors of the Austrian school did (for example, Mises or Kirzner). Nevertheless, the topicality of Hayek's views on neurophysiology is a strong motivation to further appreciate his contributions, under the scope of social neuroscience and neuroeconomics. In his latest book to date, Nobel laureate Vernon Smith wrote: 'Hayek (1952) was a pioneer in developing a theory of perception, which anticipated recent contributions to the neuroscience of perception and is particularly helpful in understanding why context is important' (Smith, 2008, p. 206). Needless to say that we concur with this statement. It is in the context of the market that we approach Hayek's views on perception.

Hence, according to Hayek, the entrepreneur is:

- an individual since he belongs to the 'separate individuals' category, unlike organizations (Hayek, 1979, p. 96);
- an innovator in the market thanks to opportunities that he creates and uses as well as by the innovative features of the products and methods he brings to the competition (Hayek, 1988, p. 89).

Thus, the entrepreneur carries out experiences that participate in the functioning of the market. He discovers new processes (and/or new products) and allows others to benefit from them. As such, 'the entrepreneur must in his activities probe beyond known uses and ends if he is to provide means for producing yet other means which in turn serve still others, and so on – that is, if he is to serve a multiplicity of ultimate ends' (ibid., p. 104).

In the following sections we call 'hypothesis' testable propositions made from our interpretation of Hayek's writings, and 'proposal' conclusions we draw.

Hypothesis 1: Competition is a discovery process.

Taking part in the competition that occurs on the market brings the entrepreneurial endeavor to a level that goes beyond the sole selfish interest of separate individuals. It allows the entrepreneur to participate in a discovery process inherent to the market which happens to be a spontaneous order, a catallaxy, that cannot be rationally planned as a defined goal (Hayek, 1967).

Hypothesis 2: Prices have a cognitive function, they convey information and allow anticipation on the market.

It is through the mechanism of prices that information is conveyed on a decentralized market and anticipation for economic actors is allowed (Hayek, 1937; Smith, 1982).

Hypothesis 3: Rationality is acquired thanks to imitation processes.

Competition on the market (and elsewhere) is a trial-and-error process and catallaxy, as a component of praxeology, deals with the homo agents rather than the homo economicus (Mises, 1944, p. 534). In other words, heir to both Scottish Enlightment and Austrian economics (for example, Menger or Mises), Hayek refuses to root his analysis of the entrepreneur's behavior on the market in terms of rationality of the actors. To the contrary, according to him, any kind of rationality that could be found on the market is rather a consequence of competition. Therefore, the only form of rationality to be found there is through imitation processes. Similar conclusion can be drawn regarding the behavior of the entrepreneur: when his peers imitate him, they somewhat rationalize his actions.

Proposal 1: The diffusion of an entrepreneurial innovation is conveyed by a form of imitation of the entrepreneur's behavior.

Indeed, if one confronts this first quote: 'In a society in which rational behavior confers an advantage on the individual, rational methods will progressively be spread by imitation' (Hayek, 1979, p. 75) with this second one: 'in highly developed economies, competition is important primarily as a discovery procedure whereby entrepreneurs constantly search for unexploited opportunities that can also be taken advantage of by others' (Hayek, 2002, p. 18), one finds even more reasons to support the idea that entrepreneurial innovation is carried out by imitation. In line with Hayek's view, James Gibson stated that: 'Behavior affords behavior . . . what the buyer affords the seller cannot be separated from what the seller affords the buyer, and so on' (Gibson, 1979, p. 135). We can therefore conclude that the entrepreneur constitutes an affordance for the imitator.

Hypothesis 4: The intentions of an individual (as constitutive opinions) are not accessible to the other actors on the market.

In the context of radical ignorance inherent to the spontaneous order of the market, the subjectivity of each individual makes his mental states inaccessible to others. It is here where the theory of mind is to be considered. For instance, the only way other actors on the market could have access to the mental states of their peers would be by inferring, guessing or speculating about them (for example, thoughts, beliefs, feelings; Frith and Singer, 2008). In addition, every individual has not only beliefs but also a strong tendency to assume that others share those beliefs.

Proposal 2: The intentions of an actor are deduced from the observation and the interpretation (speculative opinions) of his behavior.

Moreover, with the lack of possibility to directly reach reliable and usable information regarding the mental states of our peers, we infer them from the only information that is available: the one that can be observed. From this, behavior is interpreted and supposed to reveal the intentions and preferences of the entrepreneur. This interpretation mechanism of the behavior of others on the market is therefore to be related to the concept of speculative opinion and contrasted with that of constitutive opinion. Any belief which causes a social phenomenon is to be considered as a constitutive opinion whereas a speculative opinion is a belief formed about this phenomenon (Hayek, 1952b, p. 62).

Hypothesis 5: The producer is a price-maker.

Applied to price determining, Hayek deducted from this distinction that:

The changes in the [constitutive] opinions which people hold about a particular commodity and which we recognize as the cause of a change in the price of that commodity stand clearly in a different class from the ideas which the same people may have formed about the 'nature of value' in general [speculative opinions]. (ibid., p. 63)

Applied to the cost of a good, a speculative opinion justifies that another participant on the market could not determine objectively the difference between the price of this good set by the entrepreneur and its actual opportunity cost. The cost illustrates the entrepreneur's opinion on the renunciation (or not) of awaited events on the market:

It is, therefore, generally also not possible for an outsider to establish objectively whether a large excess of price over costs, manifesting itself in high profits and due to some improvement in technique or organization, is merely an 'adequate' return on investment. 'Adequate' in this connection must mean a return the expectation of which was sufficient to justify the risk incurred. In technologically advanced production the cost of a particular product will quite generally not be an objective ascertainable fact, but will in large measure depend on the opinion of the producer about probable future developments. The success of an individual enterprise and its long-run efficiency will depend on the degree of correctness of the expectations which are reflected in the entrepreneur's estimate costs. (Hayek, 1979, pp. 70–1)

Proposal 3: The price determined by the entrepreneur reflects his constitutive opinion about the value of a good he produces according to the anticipations on the market (opportunity cost).

The opinion of the producer is constitutive of the future value of the good he produces. This way of reasoning implies breaking with the model of the producer as a price taker. The entrepreneur has the capacity to fix the price or the quality of the product thanks to private property rights (ibid., p. 72). The constitutive opinion of the value of the good, as determined by an entrepreneur, is therefore a function of information that he is the only one to possess. In so far as entrepreneurship is based on experimenting new processes, the entrepreneur himself is an innovator on the market. Such private information can be sustained by the process of innovation per se or by the 'mysteries of the trades' as Hayek put it (Hayek, 1988, p. 91). The other players intervening on the market do not have access to this information. They are only able to make inferences about it, their opinion being purely speculative, inductive at the most. This step is built in any form of competition because the market is, at the same time, a discovery process and one that allows subjective opinion formation: 'Competition is essentially a process of the formation of opinion' (Hayek, 1946, p. 106).

Hypothesis 6: The reasons why the entrepreneur is innovative cannot be verbalized and rely on the mysteries of trade.

In other words, some of the actors of the market (including entrepreneurs themselves) have access to information that others do not have. Those who are in possession of this information will never be able to explain how they managed to acquire such a knowledge because 'so much knowledge of particular circumstances is unarticulated, and hardly even articulable (for example, an entrepreneur's hunch that a new product will be successful) that it would prove impossible to make it "public" quite apart from considerations of motivation' (Hayek, 1988, p. 89). The entrepreneur has a tacit knowledge of the market. When he changes his behavior with respect to a given good, he provides the other actors of the market with information that they did not have access to because of what Hayek (ibid.) refers to as 'the mysterious world of trade'. According to him, this information about the good of interest is specific to the competition and any modification of the good (for example, its quality) is reflected in its price (Hayek, 1940, p. 192). As such the price is also a clear indicator of the entrepreneur's behavior.

The hypotheses and proposals previously introduced lead to a particular model of reasoning. The entrepreneur is an individual innovator who owns information and a knowledge that are different from the ones of the other actors (Hypothesis 6). He is often imitated (Proposal 1).

Given that the market overinforms every person involved (Hypotheses 1 and 2), the genuine information that the entrepreneur is the only one to own forms his constitutive opinion (Proposal 3). This constitutive opinion and the information it conveys are inaccessible to the other actors who therefore speculate on his behavior to find the reasons motivating the entrepreneur's acts (speculative opinion; Hypothesis 4 and Proposal 2). Hence, others rationalize the behavior of the entrepreneur and, from there, tend to imitate it (Hypothesis 3). His competitors will also imitate his modus operandi whereas his customers will adopt the value he has allotted the goods he produced (Proposal 1 and Hypothesis 5). As such, imitation is a form of rationality (or rather a rationalization of the entrepreneur's behavior by his peers) on the market. The opinion of the other actors regarding the value of the good determined by the entrepreneur is of a speculative nature. Actors on the market concur with the judgment of the entrepreneur by finding reasons to explain (rationally) his choices, strategies and moves. This rationalization process entice them into revising their own beliefs and leads to an imitation of the behavior of the entrepreneur on the market. The imitation on the market can thus be explained by the recourse to a subjective theory of value (Hypothesis 4).

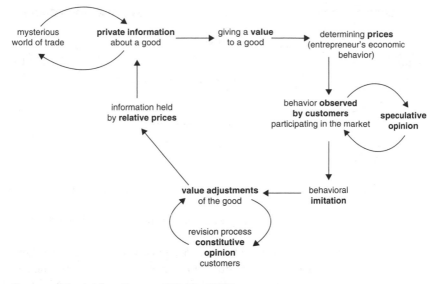

Source: Adapted from Basso and Oullier (2009).

Figure 12.1   Reciprocal imitation dynamics of entrepreneurs on the market

In summary, economic actors not directly having access to the mental states of their peers on the market (subjectivism) are inclined to interpret directly the behavior they observe (revealed preferences). This means that each and every one of them has speculative opinions on the constitutive opinions of others and revises his own beliefs by imitating the behavior of the entrepreneur as illustrated in Figure 12.1. This applies also to customers and shows how entrepreneur's private information becomes common knowledge thanks to prices and through imitation by the revision process of constitutive opinions.

EMBODIED VALUE IN SPONTANEOUS ORDER

In the previous section we discussed how discoveries and innovation resulting from entrepreneurship are spread throughout the market thanks to imitation. In order to start building a (social) neuroscience approach of the imitation of the entrepreneur's behavior on the market, we transform the usual subjective theory of value into our STV. Ultimately, we will be able to provide hypotheses regarding a 'neuroeconomic' analysis of the entrepreneur's behavior by bringing together studies addressing bodily

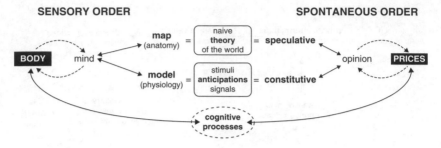

Source: Adapted from Basso and Oullier (2009).

Figure 12.2   Connections between sensory and spontaneous orders

information, sensorimotor coordination dynamics and studies on prices dynamics.

As the reader must have noticed, our approach is firmly rooted in a novel reading of Friedrich Hayek's writings. Our goal is to gather the neuro-physiological developments of the *The Sensory Order* (Hayek, 1952a) with another side of his work devoted to the spontaneous order of the market. Of particular interest to us are the links between the concepts of map and model introduced in *The Sensory Order* with those of speculative and con-stitutive opinion from *The Counter-revolution of Science* (Hayek, 1952b). Connecting the sensory order of the mind and the spontaneous order of the market enables us to consider the subjective theory of value in sensory terms as depicted in Figure 12.2.

We have already discussed the right-hand part of Figure 12.2 by expos-ing the role of speculative and constitutive opinions in determining prices of a good in the spontaneous order of the market (Proposal 3). Let us now address the sensory order, that is, an apparatus of classification of the environmental signals that are perceived (Hayek 1952a, p. 167). These signals (referred to as impulses by Hayek) are conveyed by the model as a representation of the physical world (physical order) and make sense accord-ing to their position within the map, the latter summarizing our past experi-ences: 'The pattern of impulses which is traced at any moment within the given network of semi-permanent channels [map] may be regarded as a kind of model of the particular environment in which the organism finds itself at the moment and which will enable to take account of that environment in all its movements' (ibid., pp. 114–15). Simply put, the map is structural, static and refers to fixed anatomical structures of the brain. It forms 'a theory of how the world works rather than a picture of it' (ibid., p. 131) whereas the model is functional and dynamic. On the other hand, the model refers to the topicality of the world and relies on physiological process (ibid., p. 51).

Hypothesis 7: Anticipations are carried out as a function of the position of the model in the map.

Hayek gives an account of the anticipations carried out by each individual by the position of the model within the map. The sensory order, as a classification process, carries out anticipations according to the stimuli from the physical order that reach it (ibid., pp. 130–1).

Proposal 4: Prices allow anticipations to be achieved and are thus processed like sensory data.

Applied to the case of the entrepreneur, these stimuli/impulses originate in the market. They allow for the anticipations of the entrepreneur to become effective: 'In some sense, what entrepreneurs do is to deploy smaller, more localized, versions of Hayek's "map" and "model" in anticipating future constellations of prices (concretized in the budget) and allowing them to make changes as their economic "sensory data", in the form of profits and losses, illustrate their degree of accuracy' (Horwitz, 2000, p. 33). When the brain of the entrepreneur (his sensory order) processes and coordinates signals resulting from the spontaneous order of the market, anticipations can be achieved. Thus, these price signals become, de facto, sensory data processed by the model.

For the understanding of the entrepreneur in the marginalist theory, one should keep in mind that prices are the reverse of costs. Subjective in nature, costs are opportunity costs relying on a subtle trade-off between profits and losses. Moreover, in his distinction between a firm's internal and external environments, Herbert Simon points out that: 'The goal (maximizing the difference between income and expenditure) fully defines the firm's inner environment' (Simon, 1996, p. 25). It therefore makes sense to consider the cerebral level to understand how prices are determined in the firm.

The computation of opportunity costs results from brain activity: the determination of the value is the product of a choice which depends on the subjective preferences of each one and of (his) anticipations on the market (Proposal 3). When an entrepreneur decides the value of goods he has produced, the sensory order is at stake: the map refers to his subjective preferences and the model to the anticipations he carried out.

Hypothesis 8: The body modulates the sensory order.

At this point in our development, Simon's views meet Hayek's and neuroscience can be brought into the discussion. Considering the influences of the body in economic decision making is therefore not vain: the sensory order deals with the body because the body and its components are constitutive elements of the sensory order:

> The higher centres will in consequence at any one time receive reports not only of given external stimuli but also of the body's spontaneous reaction to those stimuli. . . . it is true that the sensory order with which we are concerned is both a result and a cause of the motor activities of the body. Behavior has to be seen in a double role: it is both the input and output of the activities of the high nervous centres. (Hayek, 1952a, pp. 89–90)

Thus, according to Hayek, our perceptions of the environment are mediated by our body. Furthermore, Hayek supports the idea that our perception of the environment is built with respect to our body:

> Our tendency to personify (to interpret in anthropomorphic or animistic terms) the events we observe is probably the result of such applications of schemata which our own bodily movements provide. It is they which make, though not yet intelligible, at least perceivable (comprehensible or meaningful) complexes of events which without such perceptual schemata would have no coherence or character as wholes. (Hayek, 1962, p. 52)

The Hayekian analysis of the body goes beyond the interoceptive influences. It precedes contemporary work on the metaphor and considers the anthropomorphism in the language of economic actors: 'All people, whether primitive or civilized, organize what they perceive partly by means of attributes that language has taught them to attach to groups of sensory characteristics' (Hayek 1988, p. 106). Our body influences both our perception and our reasoning (Frith and Singer, 2008). Decision making and imitation of peers cannot escape the influence of the body (Hayek, 1962, pp. 47–8; Oullier and Basso, forthcoming). To some extent one can see an anticipation of the concepts of the perception-action cycle (Gibson, 1979; Herrmann-Pillath, 1992) and of the mirror system (Rizzolatti and Craighero, 2004).

Proposal 5: The map is a translation, in the sensory order, of our speculative opinion. The model is the translation, in the sensory order, of our constitutive opinion.

This sensory reading of the behavior of the entrepreneur enables us to consider differently his behavior on the market. Indeed, the map, as defined by Hayek, is to be seen as a pre-sensory experience and mostly the product of our genetic evolution, contrary to the model that integrates environmental stimuli. For this reason, the map provides an account for the similarity of the mind of the individuals given that we tend to attribute beliefs and intentions to other actors on the market (mentalizing). This is known as the principle of similarity of the mind (Hayek, 1952a, pp. 23, 110), a consequence of the pre-sensory experience represented by the map (ibid., p. 165). The map, as an anatomical substrate of our individual theories on how the world functions (ibid., p. 131), is to be considered together with the concept of speculative opinion. The model, on the other hand, is more of a physiological process that underlies the achievement of our actions and is therefore related to the constitutive opinions of the actors. Thus, both speculative and constitutive opinions in the spontaneous order of the market have their counterparts in the sensory order (Hypothesis 7). The map and the model are the neurophysiological underpinning of the behavioral mechanisms involved on the market (Proposal 5).

This approach is revived by neuroeconomic studies since this new field offers the opportunity of considering the role of the body (and its movements as far as we are concerned) in economic analysis by taking into account its influences in decision making (Hypothesis 8; Basso and Oullier, 2009; Oullier and Basso, forthcoming; Oullier et al., 2008b). Furthermore, there is now the possibility to complement the analysis of prices on the market with neuroeconomic games that consider the bodily aspects (emotional contagion and movement dynamics, for example) of interpersonal coordination (Oullier et al., 2008a). In such a context, prices would be considered (and processed) as sensory data (Proposal 4). For Hayek, the (human) body and the prices are both cognitive mechanisms: they are useful to convey a tacit knowledge, not verbalizable between the individuals (Basso and Oullier, 2009).

Given that the body and the prices illustrate a kind of behavior (a social one for the body and an economic one for the prices), and that both consider imitation in Hayekian theory, one should consider a neuroeconomic game where the analysis of physical interactions and the process of imitation would make it possible to describe the revision of beliefs taking place on the market.

PHYSICAL INFLUENCES: IMITATION AND BODILY DIMENSION IN THE MARKETPLACE

We argue that prices are sensory data; neuroscientific measuring tools should come handy to better understand the role of imitation in their dynamics. However, even when neuroscientific paradigms are used, the analysis of the behavior of economic actors on the market has, to date, essentially been confined to situations in which individuals are not influenced by the physical presence of their partners (or competitors). This leaves few 'observable behaviors' to feed the imagination of the peers and allow them to speculate about the intentions of the entrepreneur. Thus, interactions should be considered not only as a mental process but also as one involving exchanges and influences through sensory/physical signals.

Some might argue that this need for giving a sensorimotor dimension to economic studies is fulfilled by the involvement of brain sciences. This is partly true. A brain is not an entire body and what a body does is a lot more than just being the structure that is moved by the brain (Oullier and Basso, forthcoming).

So why have physical presence and movement of self and others – as well as their influence on economic decisions – so far received such little treatment in the field of economics? Maybe because of the belief that the way we move does not influence the way we make economic decisions. What about the strong unintended responses to people's actions, such as adopting a similar posture, a speech rhythm during a conversation, a common gait pace when walking next to someone or even yawning (Barsalou et al., 2003)? Imitation and mimicry are facilitators of social interactions as demonstrated by the works of Chartrand and Bargh (1999, see also Sommerville and Decety, 2006). They showed that the more gestures and posture were matching, the more people tend to like each other and exhibit better social cooperation. Given recent developments in motor cognition (Jeannerod, 2006), there is no reason why economic decisions should be immune from sensorimotor influences, at the individual and/or social levels (see Oullier and Basso, forthcoming, for an extensive treatment).

A first reason could be the historical dichotomy between 'high-level' cognitive processes that are distinguished from 'low-level' motor ones in neuroscience. However, this tendency has been challenged in the past decade with the discovery of the mirror system (for example, Rizzolatti and Craighero, 2004). A second, and more pragmatic, reason might lie at the technical level given that methods used to record brain activity usually require subjects' immobility. Such a methodological constraint logically precludes further investigation of how physical interactions between individuals affect social decisions in their daily lives. However, recent findings in the context of social coordination dynamics might offer new directions (Oullier and Kelso, 2009). Methods to quantify online formation (and dissolution) of physical bonds between humans have been developed at the behavioral (Oullier et al., 2005) and neural levels (Tognoli et al., 2007). It is now possible to measure the impact of mutual bodily influences during and even after a social encounter to quantify social motor memory and correlate it with economic decisions (Oullier et al., 2008a, 2008b). These methods can now be used to make neuroeconomics more genuinely social, and by extension 'human'. Findings such as the neuromarkers of social coordination (Tognoli et al., 2007) could lead to a better and more realistic understanding of why decisions to like/trust or imitate someone on the market are not based solely on mental processes but also on the way bodies interact with each other at the sensorimotor level (Oullier et al. 2008b).

ENTREPRENEURSHIP AND THE COORDINATION DYNAMICS OF DECISION-MAKING IN A VIRTUAL NEUROECONOMIC GAME

One problem still remains. How does one manage to connect the multiple levels of analysis (and interest) and their non-linear coordination dynamics when behavioral and brain processes are to be investigated jointly? In light of the shared dynamics that have been revealed between the brain and the behavioral levels, one good candidate would be metastable coordination dynamics (Kelso, 1995; Oullier and Kelso, 2006). In that conceptual and empirical framework one could propose a new game to address the issues discussed either.

Hayek considered the game as a metaphor of the market: 'The practices that led to the formation of the spontaneous order have much in common with rules observed in playing a game' (Hayek, 1988, p. 154). We therefore introduce a new game to test for our hypotheses and proposals in the context of entrepreneurship. The so-called 'Innovator Game' (IG; Basso and Oullier, 2009) allows us to measure the extent to which the entrepreneur is imitated and what kind of factors participate (or not) in this process. In order to concur with the theoretical framework depicted in Figure 12.1, the IG offers a novel way to investigate how consumers revise their constitutive opinion when they are exposed to innovation on the market. This revision process illustrates the dynamics of imitation by which a player–consumer adopts the value defined by the entrepreneur for a good he produced and launched on the market. Throughout multiple rounds, two players (a consumer and an innovator) have to carry out anticipations on a virtual market. The innovator's behavior is driven by an algorithm – materialized by a computer-generated avatar (see Schilbach et al., 2006) – against which the consumer plays. The task of the consumer is to predict better than the innovator evolutions of market, given a slight twist: the innovation provided by the entrepreneur is actually his faculty to anticipate! In other words, the good of interest that is evolving is the actual propensity to anticipate well per se. The only feedback given to the consumer is through facial expressions displayed on the face of the avatar following Ekman and Friesen's (1978) typology. The IG offers insights on how speculative opinions of the consumer regarding the behavior of the innovator are generated. This speculative opinion is modulated by information that is available to everyone on the market: the evolution of prices. If this game is crossed with the social coordination dynamics paradigm (Oullier et al., 2008a), one could replace the computer-generated innovator with a real human and measure what signals in his bodily actions influence the behavior of the consumer. Therefore, we can find out to what extent the mirror system and neuromarkers of social coordination are at stake during the game.

CONCLUSIONS

Henry Greely (2007, p. 533) recently reminded us that 'Human society is the society of human brains. Of course those brains are encased in, affected by, and dependent on the rest of the body, but our most important interactions are with other people's brains, as manifested through their bodies.' Decades later, these words somewhat echoed Hayek and Simon's pioneering views on the role of the body and sensorimotor processes in the behavior of the entrepreneur. Tacit knowledge in innovation needs physical interactions between entrepreneurs, as elegantly put by Alfred Marshall: 'the secrets of industry are in the air' (cited in Madiès and Prager, 2008, p. 38). Our sensory theory of value intends to follow in their footsteps.

ACKNOWLEDGMENTS

The writing of this chapter has been supported by the French Ministère de l'Enseignement Supérieur et de la Recherche (O.O. and F.B.) and the Centre National de la Recherche Scientifique's 'Programme CNRS Neuroinformatique' (O.O.). The authors would like to thank M. Mandard (Université de Rennes 1) for fruitful discussions and Ch. Norris for his unorthodox views on competition.

REFERENCES

Basso, F. and O. Oullier (2009), *Le corps et les prix – Esquisse d'une théorie sensorielle de la valeur*, Paris: Hermann.
Barsalou, L.W., P.M. Niedenthal, A. Barbey and J. Ruppert (2003), 'Social embodiment', in B. Ross (ed.), *The Psychology of Learning and Motivation*, Vol. 43, San Diego, CA: Academic Press, pp. 43–92.

Casson M., B. Yeung, A. Basu and N. Wadeson (2006), *The Oxford Handbook of Entrepreneurship*, Oxford: Oxford University Press.

Chartrand, T.L. and J.A. Bargh (1999), 'The chameleon effect: the perception–behavior link and social interaction', *Journal of Personality and Social Psychology*, **76** (6), 893–910.

Ekman, P. and W. Friesen (1978), *Facial Action Coding System: A Technique for the Measurement of Facial Movement*, Palo Alto, CA: Consulting Psychologists Press.

Frith, C.D. and T. Singer (2008), 'The role of social cognition in decision making', *Philosophical Transactions of the Royal Society B: Biological Sciences*, **363** (1511), 3875–86.

Gibson, J.J. (1979), *The Ecological Approach to Visual Perception*, Hillsdale, NJ: Lawrence Erlbaum.

Greely, H. (2007), 'On neuroethics', *Science*, **318** (5850), 533.

Hayek, F.A. (1937), 'Economics and knowledge', *Economica*, **4**, 33–54.

Hayek, F.A. (1940), 'Socialist calculation III: the comptetitive solution', in F.A. Hayek (1948), *Individualism and Economic Order*, Chicago, IL: University of Chicago Press, pp. 181–208.

Hayek, F.A. (1946), 'The meaning of competition', in F.A. Hayek (1948), *Individualism and Economic Order*, Chicago, IL: University of Chicago Press, pp. 92–106.

Hayek, F.A. (1952a), *The Sensory Order – An Inquiry into the Foundations of Theoretical Psychology*, Chicago, IL: University of Chicago Press.

Hayek, F.A. (1952b), *The Counter-revolution of Science*, Indianapolis: Liberty Fund.

Hayek, F.A. (1962), 'Rules, perception and intelligibility', in F.A. Hayek (1967), *Studies in Philosophy, Politics and Economics*, London: Routledge and Kegan Paul, pp. 43–65.

Hayek, F.A. (1967), 'The results of human action but not of human design', in F.A. Hayek (1967), *Studies in Philosophy, Politics and Economics*, London: Routledge and Kegan Paul, pp. 96–105.

Hayek, F.A. (1979), *Law, Legislation and Liberty, Volume 3: The Political Order of a Free People*, London: Routledge and Kegan Paul.

Hayek, F.A. (1988), *The Fatal Conceit. The Errors of Socialism*, Chicago, IL: University of Chicago Press.

Hayek, F.A. (2002), 'Competition as a discovery procedure', *Quarterly Journal of Austrian Economics*, **5** (3), 9–23 (translated by Marcellus Snow).

Herrmann-Pillath, C. (1992), 'The brain, its sensory order, and the evolutionary concept of mind: on Hayek's contribution to evolutionary epistemology', *Journal of Social and Evolutionary Systems*, **15** (2), 145–86.

Horwitz, S. (2000), 'From the sensory order to the liberal order: Hayek's non-rationalist liberalism', *Review of Austrian Economics*, **13**, 23–40.

Jeannerod, M. (2006), *Motor Cognition: What Actions Tell the Self*, Oxford: Oxford Press.

Kelso, J.A.S. (1995), *Dynamic Patterns: The Self-organization of Brain and Behavior*, Cambridge, MA: MIT Press.

Madiès, T. and J.C. Prager (2008), *Innovation et compétitivité des régions. Rapport du Conseil d'Analyse Economique du 27 août 2008*, Paris: La documentation française.

Mises, L. (von) (1944), 'The treatment of "irrationality" in the social sciences', *Philosophy and Phenomenological Research*, **4** (4), 527–46.

232   *Neuroeconomics and the firm*

Oullier, O. and F. Basso (forthcoming), 'Embodied economics: how bodily information shapes the social coordination dynamics of decision making', *Philosophical Transactions of the Royal Society B: Biological Sciences*.
Oullier, O. and J.A.S. Kelso (2006), 'Neuroeconomics and the metastable brain', *Trends in Cognitive Science*, **10** (8), 353–4.
Oullier, O. and J.A.S. Kelso (2009), 'Coordination from the perspective of social coordination dynamics', in R. Meyers (ed.), *Encyclopedia of Complexity and Systems Science*, Berlin: Springer-Verlag.
Oullier, O., G.C. de Guzman, K.J. Jantzen, J. Lagarde and J.A.S. Kelso (2005), 'Spontaneous interpersonal synchronization', in C. Peham, W.I. Schöllhorn and W. Verwey (eds), *European Workshop on Movement Sciences: Mechanics–Physiology–Psychology*, Köln: Sportverlag, pp. 34–5.
Oullier, O., G.C. de Guzman, K.J. Jantzen, J. Lagarde and J.A.S. Kelso (2008a), 'Social coordination dynamics: measuring human bonding', *Social Neuroscience*, **3** (2), 178–92.
Oullier, O., A.P. Kirman and J.A.S. Kelso (2008b), 'The coordination dynamics of economic decision making: a multi-level approach to social neuroeconomics', *IEEE Transactions on Neural Rehabilitation Systems Engineering*, **16** (6), 557–71.
Rizzolatti, G. and L. Craighero (2004), 'The mirror-neuron system', *Annual Review of Neuroscience*, **27**, 169–92.
Schilbach, L., A.M. Wohlschlaeger, N.C. Kraemer et al. (2006), 'Being with virtual others: neural correlates of social interaction', *Neuropsychologia*, **44** (5), 718–30.
Simon, H.A. (1996), *The Sciences of the Artificial*, Cambridge, MA: MIT Press.
Smith, V.L. (1982), 'Markets as economizers of information: experimental examination of the "Hayek Hypothesis"', *Economic Inquiry*, **20**, 165–79.
Smith, V.L. (2008), *Rationality in Economics – Constructivist and Ecological Forms*, Cambridge: Cambridge University Press.
Sommerville, S.J. and J. Decety (2006), 'Weaving the fabric of social interaction: articulating developmental psychology and cognitive neuroscience in the domain of motor cognition', *Psychonomic Bulletin Review*, **13** (2), 179–200.
Tognoli, E., J. Lagarde, G.C. de Guzman and J.A.S. Kelso (2007), 'The phi complex as a neuromarker of human social coordination', *Proceedings of the National Academy of Sciences of the United States of America*, **104**, 8190–95.
Zak, P.J. (2004), 'Neuroeconomics', *Philosophical Transactions of the Royal Society B: Biological Sciences*, **359** (1451), 1737–48.

PART 5

Organizational culture and ethics

Whenever we experience an economic crisis, such as the crash of the high-tech bubble at the turn of the twentieth century, the fall of Enron and other giants, and most recently the global financial crisis, the blame falls on the lack of moral and ethical values of those responsible. It is very easy to claim that those responsible acted without ethical considerations; it is much harder to understand what we actually mean by ethical considerations and where such considerations come from. In Part 5 three chapters discuss various components of ethical and moral decisions, and what ethical and moral responsibility really means in terms of the organization.

13. What neuroeconomics informs us about making real-world ethical decisions in organizations

Donald T. Wargo, Norman A. Baglini and Katherine A. Nelson

The financial collapse of 2008 and 2009 shows clearly what can happen to world economic markets when trust evaporates. In general, the public perceives that ethical lapses and personal greed – in myriad institutions and firms – are the root cause of the global collapse. It is also clear that we cannot restore confidence in governments, regulatory bodies and businesses until the public trusts them. However, the public will not trust them until they see that these governing bodies are behaving ethically and making ethical decisions. It is evident that even if ethics training was provided to the individuals in these institutions at some time in the past, it failed miserably.

Why did it fail? We believe that the training in vogue in institutional settings is not designed to take the entire human being into account with all of the complexity of the human brain and the situations under which most people make critical decisions. Corporate ethics training is overly rational and does not take into account the real world, its threats, coercions and risks.

Recent research on how the human brain makes decisions and thinks about ethics is not only interesting, but it also provides important clues for organizational development professionals – and for many others – about how people in organizations make ethical decisions and what factors influence them. Recent neuroeconomics research has important implications for individual decision-making, and also highlights the effect that organizational culture can have on the decision-making process.

In addition, recent research in the areas of moral psychology, biological anthropology, neuroscience, economic game theory, behavioral economics, neuroeconomics and institutional theory presents overwhelming evidence that ethical decisions are not exclusively rational and may not be

235

principally conscious decisions. They are also emotional and almost all the time made under some stress or at least pressure that is institutional or personal in nature.

Ethics in the real world is often enacted as contextual and relational, carried out in the context of the institution or in relation to a superior or colleague. Additionally, there can be serious individual and institutional impediments to making ethical decisions. The pressure can come from any of the relevant stakeholders in the decisions. In the case of government, this may come from corporate interests or in the case of business from the stockholders' pressure to 'maximize earnings per share'.

DECISION-MAKING UNDER RISK AND UNCERTAINTY

There is much research supporting the view that when making decisions, people value losses as much as twice the amount they value gains when compared to the status quo (Tversky and Kahneman, 1992). For example, people typically reject a 50/50 chance of losing money to one where the chance of gain is about twice as much as the possible loss. In this classic example of Prospect Theory, Tversky and Kahneman explain humans' tendency toward risk-aversion. Further, Kahneman and colleagues have shown that people require substantially more money when selling objects they possess than what they would pay to buy those same objects. This is known as the 'endowment' affect (Kahneman et al., 1990).

In business and governments, individuals have different risk preferences. That is, their decisions are influenced by whether they are risk-takers or loss-averters – a condition that may vary in different situations or over different subjective affect states but can also change over time. Political decisions frequently are heavily influenced by the decision-makers' differing intuition for 'playing it safe with our constituents' or 'the future is in our hands, we must act swiftly and decisively!'

HOW RATIONAL ARE MOST BUSINESS AND GOVERNMENT DECISIONS?

Much research has supported the view that some choice phenomena affect the standard decision-making model of rationality. These are discussed below.

Framing Issues

The standard model of rational decision-making assumes that the choices made are complete and consistent. However, evidence supports the view that the framing or reframing of the options, in terms of gains or losses and so on, often leads to different preferences within the same types of options. Also, the risk preferences of decision-makers change significantly when the options are framed in terms of potential losses as opposed to potential gains (Tversky and Kahneman, 1981, 1992). How government and business leaders 'frame' the questions they pose to their constituents have an enormous impact on how the issue is perceived and therefore processed in the brain. Further, marketing research on consumer behavior demonstrates the power of framing. Consumers greatly prefer to buy foods that are '95 percent fat free' rather than 'only 5 percent fat content'.

While there is much evidence that framing greatly influences buying habits, there is also evidence that framing exerts much influence on ethical decision-making (Tversky and Kahneman, 1992). When issues are framed by focusing almost exclusively on one overriding factor, such as national security or survival of the organization, other relevant factors are minimized or eliminated from consideration. When business decisions are driven by one all-consuming value, for example, the increase in the price of the corporation's stock, other key factors often can be totally disregarded.

The Power of Authority

The power of authority plays a key role in government and business every day, including those decisions, actions and behaviors that are morally questionable. Psychologist Stanley Milgram's experiments directed people to administer shocks at increasingly higher levels to unseen subjects who failed to answer questions correctly. In reality, the subjects were actors. Despite cries of pain and pleadings for mercy, 65 percent obeyed the researchers' orders to shock the subjects due to people's tendency to obey those in positions of authority. The mantle of authority in this case was white lab coats (Milgram, 1974). Hierarchies in government and business are vulnerable for this abuse of authority by those in power who use others for their own purposes. How much stronger than a lab coat is the charisma of an elected official or key cabinet minister? How much stronger than a lab coat is the influence of a powerful business leader who promises to promote those who are loyal to them – an ethical value?

Decision-Making and Neuroeconomics

Social decision-making is the context in which we do ethics – not the laboratory nor the philosopher's armchair. Unfortunately, most work on decision-making – the study of our fundamental ability to process multiple alternatives and to choose the optimal course of action – is in fragmented and not integrated studies (Sanfey, 2007). The interdisciplinary science of neuroeconomics, however, shows the most promise in modeling real-world decisions among multiple alternatives is in complex social interactions, according to Sanfey. It uses the precision and mathematical models of game theory in economics along with the findings of neuroscience and brain scanning.

Economic game theory has as its assumptions the classical fundamentals of economics – that individuals are rational maximizers of utility – but the real-world results of game theory experiments show that individuals are generally less selfish and less strategic than the standard model predicts and also temper their decisions by social factors such as reciprocity and equity (Camerer, 2003). The fundamental experiments of game theory are actually quite simple – the Prisoners' Dilemma, the Ultimatum Game and so on – yet they elicit profound and useful conclusions from observations of the behavior of the participants.

In the realm of ethical decision-making, neuroeconomics has already begun to focus on the broad research themes of (1) social reward, (2) competition, cooperation and coordination and (3) strategic reasoning.

Social reward
Researchers have shown that in the human brain the ventral striatum (composed of the caudate, the putamen and the nucleus accumbens) appears to be centrally involved in social decisions. This is also called the mesolimbic dopamine system, since dopamine release and its effects are central to all brain reward mechanisms. This is the basis of decision theory – maximizing reward or 'utility', which is defined in neoclassical economics as the 'satisfaction' one receives from the consumption of objects or services. More precisely, Cromwell and Schultz have shown that neural responses of dopamine cells scale reliably with the magnitude of each reward. The amount of dopamine released is consistent with the differential feelings of all activities (Cromwell and Schultz, 2003) (Figure 13.1).

Furthermore, Knutson and Cooper and O'Doherty and colleagues have shown that activity changes in the striatum scale directly proportionally to the magnitude of monetary reward or punishment (Knutson and Cooper, 2005; O'Doherty et al., 2004). More importantly for ethics, the human striatum encodes the value of a social partner's decision to

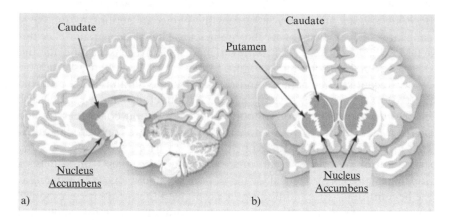

Source: Sanfey (2007), reprinted with permission from AAAS.

Figure 13.1   The subcomponents of the striatum involved in the processing of reward

reciprocate or not reciprocate cooperation, regardless of the magnitude of the monetary reward. Reciprocated cooperation increases activity in the striatum and eventually leads to the build-up of trust. On the other hand, non-reciprocated cooperation leads to decreased activity in the striatum (Rilling et al., 2002).

The hallmarks of ethics, as identified by many researchers, are empathy, cooperation, reciprocity, altruism and costly punishment (Dawkins, 1989; de Waal, 2005, 2007/2008; Dugatkin, 2006; Gürerk et al., 2006; Hauert et al., 2007; Nowak, 2006; Sanfey, 2007). Earlier, we discussed how the striatum is activated in both social cooperation and punishment. Further, understanding the brain when the individual is performing altruistic acts is also critical to our study of ethics.

Since the dopamine limbic system is fundamentally important to goal-directed performance and the creation of habits, Wickens and colleagues reviewed the current research and reported findings with important implications for ethical training (Wickens et al., 2007). In the early stages of learning the neurotransmitter dopamine plays an essential role. The corresponding brain area in this brain cell signaling loop is the neostriatum, which is the primary recipient of glutamate input from almost all the regions of the cerebral cortex and also the primary recipient of the major dopamine inputs from the midbrain dopamine neurons involved in reward processing. Thus, information processing in this reward – and loss – circuit is controlled by dopamine. Dopamine creates synaptic plasticity in the corticostriatal pathway and also actually changes the neurons in the brain's striatum. It thereby influences the choice of actions by the basal ganglia, which is also called the brainstem. The basal ganglia executes actions decided upon and it is also the seat of instincts in animals and established habits in humans (Figure 13.4).

Two recent studies on mice and rats have helped illuminate the importance of the dopamine system in our goal-directed behavior. In classic Skinnerian stimulus-response conditioning, Choi and colleagues trained rats to poke their heads into a hole to get food that was delivered immediately after the researchers rang a bell. Then, at various time periods during the conditioning of individual rats, Choi and colleagues administered a dopamine-blocking chemical. If the dopamine block was administered at the beginning of the conditioning, it suppressed the head-entry response. However, as the conditioning continued, the dopamine antagonist resulted in less and less suppression until, when the habit was completely formed, the dopamine antagonist did not suppress the head-entry response at all. This behavior occurred even when the rats were deprived of food and therefore hungry. The conclusion, according to Choi, is that as an activity is in the process of becoming a reality the role of dopamine diminishes in motivating that activity. In fact, the action becomes dopamine independent with extended training (Choi et al., 2005). This actually means that well-established (habitual) behavior becomes no longer outcome mediated. Although it is not within the scope of this chapter to explore this further, it is clear to us that the implications of this research for habit formation and habit suppression – including addiction – should be studied.

Experiments by Pecina and colleagues also underscore the importance of the dopamine expected reward system. After the neurotransmitter dopamine is released into the neuron synapse, a dopamine transporter molecule binds to the dopamine and reuptakes it back into the nerve cell that released it, where it is reprocessed and stored for future release into the synapse. These researchers bred genetically-mutated mice that lacked the normal level of dopamine reuptake transporter molecules. As a result, the amount of dopamine in the neuron synapses of these mice was continuously elevated by 70 percent above the normal levels. In a runway test these mutant mice navigated to the sweet reward faster and learned the run more quickly than wild mice. The researchers state that their 'wanting' was significantly elevated. However, the elevated dopamine levels did not increase their 'liking' of the sweet reward once it was taken. This was measured by the accepted experimental standard of oro-facial reactions in an affective taste reactivity test. As Chapter 9 in this volume explains, this divergence is because 'expected reward' and 'actual reward' are evaluated in different parts of the brain (Pecina et al., 2003).

The reward value of money presents a special challenge to creating ethical habits. A recent study of how the brain translates money into a motivational force used monetary rewards to motivate subjects to squeeze a handgrip (Pessiglione et al., 2007). In addition, the experimenters also measured skin conductance and imaged the reward centers of the brain with functional magnetic resonance imaging (fMRI). The amazing results in this study are that even when the monetary reward (English pound versus penny) was flashed so quickly that the subjects' perception was subliminal the results were the same in the tests as when the subjects could consciously perceive the reward. Activation was seen in the reward and motivational structures of the brain, including the ventral striatum, ventral palladium and amygdala.

The implications of all these studies for ethical decision-making are important and pretty straightforward. Both social rewards – which actually means 'ethics' – and monetary rewards activate the same reward circuits in the brain, so they are competing in the decision-making process. Even more important, the activation of the brain and the force exerted by the subjects was directly proportional to the amount of the monetary reward, whether it was subliminal or conscious!

Competition, cooperation and coordination
The areas associated with emotional processing play a predominant role in cooperation and fairness. These are the striatum, the ventromedial prefrontal cortex (VMPC), the orbitofrontal cortex and anterior cingulate cortex, as well as the insula. These areas also react negatively to both inequitable and unreciprocated actions in games (Pillutla and Murnighan, 1996). It is likely that they evolved to encourage reciprocal cooperation, to make reputation important in the social group and to encourage the punishment of cheaters (Nowak et al., 2000; Nowak and Sigmund, 2005).

These reactions to inequity are even seen in capuchin monkeys (Brosnan and de Waal, 2003). The anterior insula seems to be particularly important to judgment of inequity as its activation has been shown to be directly proportional to the magnitude of the unfairness (Sanfey et al., 2003). The anterior insula is also associated with physically painful and disgusting stimuli and in mapping visceral sensations of autonomic arousal. Its role may be to create a sense of disgust at inequity and therefore future distrust of the unfair player (Sanfey, 2007).

The dorsolateral prefrontal cortex also plays a role in the value coding of unfair offers. This is evidenced by the fact that transcranial magnetic inactivation of this region caused the subject to accept unfair offers, compared to the control group (Knoch et al., 2006). Finally, it is clear that the neurotransmitter oxytocin enhances feelings of trust in the brain. In one trust experiment involving investments it was administered intranasally and it led to increased trust by investors (Kosfeld et al., 2005).

Strategic thinking: theory of mind
An important aspect to social decision-making – and therefore ethics – is the brain's processing of the actions and intentions of others. This is collectively known as 'Theory of Mind' (ToM). ToM is crucial to strategy and response in social interactions but also to empathic responses, one of the hallmarks of ethics. The areas associated with ToM are primarily the medial prefrontal cortex and the anterior paracingulate cortex (Frith and Frith 2003; Gallagher and Frith, 2003). Autistic individuals and some psychiatric patients exhibit severe ToM deficits and this hampers their social abilities.

THE NEUROECONOMIC BASIS OF DECISION-MAKING UNDER THREAT AND STRESS

We all are well aware of the 'fight or flight' response of the human psyche and autonomic/limbic system of the human body. Scientists have been able, with virtual reality projectors and fMRI scanners, to pinpoint the exact locations of these responses in the brain. Mobbs et al. set up subjects to perceive and feel both a distant and a proximate threat from an intelligent predator – a wolf (Mobbs et al., 2007). In the distant threat, part of the prefrontal cortex and the lateral amygdala responded to the threat. The authors interpret this as the brain trying to come up with a strategy to evade the distant predator. On the other hand, when the virtual predator was up close – 'proximate' – the logical brain was completely shut down and the only activity was in the central amygdala and the basal ganglia. These are areas of unconscious mental processing (Figure 13.2).

The implications of this are significant for making ethical decisions. Since many business-related ethical decisions are made under stress, the stress triggers the 'fight or flight' response. This turns off the logical, conscious brain. In business ethics classes we use the analogy that the IQ of a person under stress drops 20 points. Since IQ scores are normalized on 100 and the 'mentally challenged' have IQs of 70 or below, we say that the effect of making a decision under stress is like making a decision in a mentally challenged state.

ETHICAL DECISIONS CAN BE RATIONAL, EMOTIONAL AND/OR UNCONSCIOUS

Hauser, borrowing an idea from Noam Chomsky, the Harvard linguist, states decisively that humans have a moral instinct that is designed to

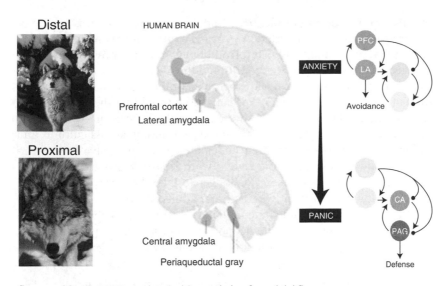

Source: Maren (2007), reprinted with permission from AAAS.

Figure 13.2   Topography of fear: as predatory threat approaches, neural activity in the human brain shifts from the forebrain to the midbrain

generate rapid judgments about moral matters (Hauser, 2006). It includes some universal principles such as: (1) killing is wrong, (2) helping is good, (3) breaking promises is bad and (4) gratuitously harming someone is evil. Hauser posits that this fundamental moral instinct is innate but is developed, over time, through social systems and learning environments. Thus, his view is pluralistic and not deterministic.

The moral system creates expectations of norms of behavior and consequences, according to Hauser, such as obligations, promises and commitments. When an expectation is met, we react positively and these positive emotions are rewarding and reinforcing. When expectations are violated, negative emotions are the reaction. These are aversive and can cause us to shun or punish the violator.

The neurobiological correlates of these behaviors have received lots of scientific attention recently. From the standpoint of biological anthropology, ethics can be seen as encompassing empathy, cooperation, reciprocity, altruism – altruism here is defined in the biological sense, that is, giving up some of your individual desires/fitness to receive the benefits of living in a group – and punishment of cheaters, even if it is costly to the punisher. Each of these requires the ability of the individual to control their selfish impulses and to delay gratification. Impulse control is the provenance of the prefrontal cortex's interaction with and control of the amygdala (especially the ventromedial and orbitofrontal regions of the prefrontal cortex, referred to respectively as the VMPC and the OPC.

Classic delay-of-gratification experiments offer marshmallows to children or money to adolescents. The subjects are told that they may choose to have the reward now or, when the researcher returns in a while (time not specified), a larger reward. The consistent finding across cultures and economic classes is that children under the age of four have little or no patience and choose the immediate reward (ibid.). However, those preschoolers who wait a few seconds longer to take the larger reward grow up to be more successful adolescents and adults. On the other hand, adolescents who take the immediate monetary reward are likely to end up as youthful cheaters and juvenile delinquents and as adults, job losers and abusers of their partners in romantic relationships.

> The number of seconds a two-year-old waits is like a crystal ball that predicts her future moral behavior; her ethical style, if you will. Longitudinal studies suggest that impatience or impulsivity on the delayed gratification task is an excellent predictor of who will transgress the mores of the culture. (Ibid., p. 216)

In order to test his ideas concerning innate moral universals, Hauser created a web-based questionnaire called the 'Harvard Moral Sense Test' (http://www.moral.wjh.harvard.edu/index2.html). Hauser reports that during the first year, 60 000 people took the test from 120 countries and from all walks of life. The vast majority of those participating agreed on what was moral and immoral concerning certain forms of harm. However, less than 10 percent were able to articulate a correct rational justification for their opinions (Hauser, 2006).

In subsequent work Hauser and colleagues analyze the purported rational justifications of the participants in the Harvard Moral Sense Test (Cushman et al., 2006; Hauser et al., 2007). The results show that some moral principles are intuitive and generally not available to the conscious, while some are.

While these moral intuitions have the force of habits/instincts, in practice there are three main ways that we can actually override our initial intuitions, according to Haidt (Haidt and Graham, 2007). (1) We can use conscious verbal reasoning, as in considering the costs and benefits of various courses of action. (2) We can reframe the situation, thereby triggering a new moral intuition. (3) We can talk to people whom we trust, who can raise new framing perspectives or raise new arguments, thereby triggering new moral intuitions. Haidt reports that the first two are rarely used and that most moral changes of thought and action come about by social interaction.

WHAT MAKES US WANT TO BE GOOD?

Pinker points out that morality is close to our conception of the meaning of life and carries so much weight in all human societies that it is 'bigger than any of us and outside all of us'. It also defines us as an acceptable human. Like Hauser and Haidt, Pinker also delineates a difference between human moral intuition and human rational ethical reasoning. The two hallmarks of moral intuition are that the rules it invokes are felt to be universal and that people feel those who commit immoral acts – that is, break the intuitive moral rules – deserve to be punished. Even further, they need to be punished (Pinker, 2008).

However, an interesting twist to Pinker's discussion of rational moral faculty is his observation that rational moralization is a separate faculty of the brain, a different psychological mindset that we can turn on and off, so there is variability to the rational moralizing side. For example, moral vegetarians as opposed to health vegetarians consider eating meat immoral in that they refuse to be complicit in the suffering of animals. Lately, smoking in public has become a moral issue, due to the recognition of the dangers of second-hand smoke. On the other hand, divorce and having illegitimate children have been removed from the list of moral failings in the USA and redefined as lifestyle choices. Further, homosexuality is in the process of being 'demoralized', as evidenced by the enactment of same-sex marriage laws in multiple states.

Pinker points out, as others have done, that we have both an innate moral intuition and a rational moral cognitive facility. Nowhere is this more evident in the thought experiment than the affectionately called 'trolleyology'. This is the Trolley Problem experiment extensively tested on subjects by Hauser and Mikhail (Hauser, 2006). In short, you see a runaway trolley heading toward five workers on the tracks, you can throw the switch that will divert the trolley to the alternative track where it will kill one man instead of the five. Hauser and Mickail found that almost universally everyone said it was moral to throw the switch. By everyone we mean over 200 000 people from 100 countries and of all religions who took the Harvard Moral Sense Test online.

Alternatively, if you are on a bridge above the tracks and have the opportunity to push a fat man off in front of the trolley to save the five men, almost everyone said this was not moral, even though from a

Scenario	Schematic	Description	% 'Yes'
1	Denise	Denise is a passenger on a train whose driver has fainted. On the main track ahead are 5 people. The main track has a side track leading off to the left, and Denise can turn the train on to it. There is 1 person on the left hand track. Denise can turn the train, killing the 1; or she can refrain from turning the train, letting the 5 die.	Is it morally permissible for Denise to turn the train? 85%
2	Frank	Frank is on a footbridge over the train tracks. He sees a train approaching the bridge out of control. There are 5 people on the track. Frank knows that the only way to stop the train is to drop a heavy weight into its path. But the only available, sufficiently heavy weight is 1 large man, also watching the train from the footbridge. Frank can shove the 1 man onto the track in the path of the train, killing him; or he can refrain from doing this, letting the 5 die.	Is it morally permissible for Frank to shove the man? 12%
3	Ned	Ned is walking near the train tracks when he notices a train approaching out of control. Up ahead on the track are 5 people. Ned is standing next to a switch, which he can throw to turn the train on to aside track. There is a heavy object on the side track. If the train hits the object, the object will slow the train down, giving the men time to escape. The heavy object is 1 man, standing on the side track. Ned can throw the switch, preventing the train from killing the 5 people, but killing the 1 man. Or he can refrain from doing this, letting the 5 die.	Is it morally permissible for Ned to throw the switch? 56%
4	Oscar	Oscar is walking near the train tracks when he notices a train approaching out of control. Up ahead on the track are 5 people. Oscar is standing next to a switch, which he can throw to turn the train on to aside track. There is a heavy object on the side track. If the train hits the object, the object will slow the train down, giving the 5 people time to escape. There is 1 man standing on the side track infront of the heavy object. Oscar can throw the switch, preventing the train from killing the 5 people, but killing the 1 man. Or he can refrain from doing this, letting the five die.	Is it morally permissible for Oscar to throw the switch? 72%

Source: Hauser et al. (2007), reprinted with permission from Marc Hauser, http://www3.interscience.wiley.com/journal/117998132/abstract.

Figure 13.3   The Trolley Problem experiment

rational, utilitarian basis it is an indistinguishable act from that of throwing the switch. Also, when fMRI was used on subjects contemplating these different dilemmas, different brain areas were activated in the two different dilemmas (Figure 13.3).

COGNITION AND EMOTION

The most successful theoretical model of the brain we have seen thus far – that is, it integrates and explains the seemingly contradictory moral judgments we have heretofore discussed – is that proposed by Jonathan Cohen (Cohen, 2005). Borrowing a term first used by Minsky, Cohen posits that although the parts of the human brain are all interconnected and work together, the brain is best thought of not as a homogeneous unit, but as a 'society of minds', with each part allocated a specific task or tasks (Minsky, 1986). Thus there is competition among the faster and unconscious 'emotional brain', whose neurological correlates are the ventral striatum, the brainstem and the amygdala, and the slower, conscious, deliberate 'conscious brain'. This latter system enables the person to consider and act on abstract goals and principles and has the capability of impulse control – with emphasis on the word 'capability'.

Further, the decision-making, moral psychology and economic literatures group the 'society of minds' into two general mechanisms: System 1 is for automatic processing and decisions. It works quickly and results in intuitive solutions to problems. System 2 corresponds to the conscious and controlled processes of our mind, rational thought, logic and rumination. It monitors the correctness of the System 1 answers and sometimes overrides them. In this System 2 mechanism resides what philosophers call 'free will' and it resides in the neocortex and the prefrontal cortex, which is the seat of abstract ideas and actions based upon abstract ideas. It is also the seat of impulse control over the amygdala and the seat of transcendence.

Cohen contends that the seemingly 'irrational' behavior or decisions of individuals is explained by the outcome of the competition of these two systems with each presenting solutions to the problem given to them and unfortunately, the outcome is not always optimal. If we accept the universally accepted assumption of economic theory – people make decisions that maximize their utility – which is a central concept of modern decision theory, then we must posit that people always act rationally. Clearly they do not choose to do so and a crucial question in decision theory is 'why not?'

The answer, according to Cohen, is that people seek to optimize their utility subject to constraints. These constraints include limited information, specific existential circumstances, limited ability to learn from mistakes, limited ability to focus on the problem, limited ability to control one's own behavior, selfish versus altruistic orientation and so on. All of these constraints are impediments to ethical decision-making. The conscious, 'rational' brain has severe constraints. It thinks in words, it can only focus on one problem at a time and it is limited to only being able to

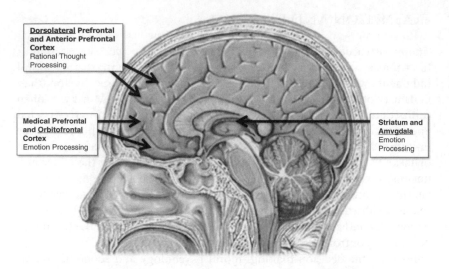

Dorsolateral Prefrontal
and Anterior Prefrontal
Cortex
Rational Thought
Processing

Medical Prefrontal
and Orbitofrontal
Cortex
Emotion Processing

Striatum and
Amygdala
Emotion
Processing

Source: National Institute on Aging.

*Figure 13.4   Areas of the human brain associated with decision-making,
            some with higher level cognitive processing and others
            associated with emotional processing*

compare two competing solutions to the problem at one time (Koechlin
and Hyafil, 2007).

System 1 and System 2 have specific localized regions that perform their
functions in the architecture of the human brain. The reaction to rewarding events or the anticipation of them are localized in the midbrain (which
releases the neurotransmitter dopamine) and the striatum (which reacts
to the receipt of the released dopamine). These, by the way, are the sites
affected by drugs of abuse (Paulus, 2007).

Other subcortical structures also respond to valenced events – that is,
positive and negative utility. These include the medial prefrontal cortex,
the orbito-prefrontal cortex, the insular cortex, the amygdala and the striatum. All of these structures have neuronal connections to areas associated
with higher cognitive processing, primarily the anterior prefrontal cortex,
the dorsolateral prefrontal cortex and the temporal lobe. The prefrontal
cortex comprises one-third of the volume of the neocortex (Figure 13.4).

Greene and colleagues provide strong evidence that different brain areas
are involved in the two different 'trolleyology' moral challenges (Greene et
al., 2001). Using fMRI, they showed that in the switch-throwing scenario
the dorsolateral prefrontal cortex was the most active. This area has been
consistently shown to be involved in working memory, abstract reasoning

and problem solving, but not emotional processing. This area also deals with all non-moral rational problem solving. Further, Greene shows that in moral reasoning tasks, activity in the prefrontal cortex precedes and is directly associated with utilitarian moral judgments (Greene and Haidt, 2002; Greene et al., 2004).

In our review of the research in this field, it appears that there is a distinct difference between moral decisions that are moral personal (MP) and those that are moral impersonal (MI). In the trolley example pulling the switch is MI whereas pushing the fat man off the bridge is a MP dilemma. These two types of problems are resolved in different parts of the brain such that the MI does not bear on the emotional but the MP does. The studies also support the 'society of minds' hypothesis in that subjects who make the most utilitarian responses (the 'ends' versus the 'means') are shown in the fMRI studies to be overriding the emotional decision of their ventromedial prefrontal cortex (VMPC) with activation of their anterior cingulate and dorsolateral prefrontal cortex, brain areas associated with cognitive conflict and abstract reasoning.

This conclusion is supported by multiple studies of patients who have damage (or 'lesions') to the areas principally involved in emotional processing, collectively known as the VMPC. Patients with damage to this area are overwhelmingly utilitarian in their moral judgments in the case studies presented to them – trolleyology and many others.

Finally, Young and Koenigs remind us that psychological and neurological studies of moral reasoning are descriptive and not normative. That is, science cannot tell us what is moral and what is not (Young and Koenigs, 2007). This is the domain of philosophers – Kant, Hume, Bentham and Mill.

THE FIVE HALLMARK BEHAVIORS OF ETHICS

As discussed above, from the viewpoint of biological anthropology – formerly termed 'sociobiology' – ethics is characterized by five hallmark behaviors, which are presented in Table 13.1.

Figure 13.5 shows the neurological correlates associated with ethical behaviors.

Empathy

Empathy is the beginning of ethics and is an essential capacity if we are able to behave ethically. We must be able to feel for another person or imagine what they must be feeling in order to take them into account.

Table 13.1   The five hallmark behaviors of ethics

Hallmark	Psychological Correlate	Brain Correlate
Empathy	Theory of Mind	Mirror neurons
Cooperation	Perception of community	Spindle neurons (social cognition)
Reciprocity/fairness	Sensitivity to fairness	Right dorsolateral prefrontal cortex
Altruism	Kin selection or 'Virtual' kinship	Mirror neurons (reciprocal) Ventral striatum (non-reciprocal)
Punishment of cheaters ('free-riders')	Disgust or anger	Ventral striatum (dopamine reward)

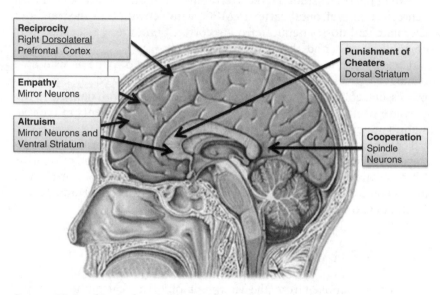

Source: National Institute on Aging.

Figure 13.5   The five hallmark behaviors of ethical decision-making

This is called 'Theory of Mind' or 'ToM'. Needless to say, psychopaths find this impossible and autistic individuals find this very difficult. 'Mirror neurons' are what makes us capable of empathy, but they also perform a great number of other important and related functions.

One of the most salient capabilities of mirror neurons is to allow us to have empathy, without which ethics would be impossible! People use one region of the MPFC to consider the mental state of someone they perceive as similar to themselves and a completely different area of the MPFC to consider someone perceived as dissimilar (Mobbs et al., 2007). This is obviously an evolutionarily adaptive trait, as it is a matter of life or death to distinguish friend from foe; however, it is also an interesting area for future exploration, as this mechanism likely plays a role in prejudice.

Cooperation

The emergence of cooperation via natural selection is nothing short of a miracle. This is because cooperation has a cost to it and therefore reduces the 'fitness' of the cooperator, while 'cheating' or more specifically 'free-riding' has no associated cost. Nowak summarizes the evolutionary rules for cooperation (Nowak, 2006). A cooperator pays a cost and deals out a benefit to another individual. A defector does not pay a cost and does not deal out a benefit. Therefore, in any random population, defectors have a higher average fitness than cooperators and thus natural selection acts to increase the number of defectors in a mixed population. However, the payoffs in terms of fitness to a group of cooperators is the highest and the payoffs to a group of defectors is the lowest. Thus, there is some incentive to cooperate. However, we have to ask the question, 'how did cooperation evolve?'

Nowak sets forth the five mechanisms by which cooperation evolved via natural selection. These are: (1) kin selection (according to Hamilton's Law); (2) direct reciprocity; (3) indirect reciprocity; (4) network reciprocity and (5) group selection.

Each of these mechanisms works to identify and shun defectors, thereby establishing groups of cooperators (or, more specifically, cooperators and reciprocators), who will over time out-populate the cheaters (ibid.).

The exclusive home of the spindle neurons are the anterior cingulate cortex and the frontoinsular cortex. They enable us to unconsciously and rapidly make social judgments that allow us to navigate in our group, tribe, pack or social surroundings.

Reciprocity and Costly Punishment of Free-riders/Cheaters

The dorsolateral prefrontal cortex, along with the amygdala, are the most important brain areas that react to fairness and unfairness. It is the area that lights up under fMRI scans in Ultimatum Games and when offers are rejected. Also, when it is disrupted by transcranial interruption in subjects playing Ultimatum Games, the subjects complain that the offer is unfair but accept it anyway (Knoch et al., 2006).

When we perceive an unfair situation, such as the non-reciprocation of an altruistic act or free-riding, we punish the cheater. Groups that punish or expel free-riders stabilize cooperative behavior and outperform groups that do not (Gürerk et al., 2006). The brain area that manages this punishment is the same reward area that is rewarded with dopamine when we cooperate or do altruistic acts. De Quervain and colleagues show that the ventral striatum gets a shot of dopamine when we punish cheaters – 'Revenge is sweet' (de Quervain et al., 2004).

Altruism

Altruism is the giving of a benefit to another or to your group without receiving an immediate, corresponding benefit. It is different from cooperation in that there is a time delay involved. In most social situations we expect 'reciprocal altruism', which means we expect the receivers of the benefit to pay us back at some future time (Trivers, 1971). If they do not, they are 'free-riders' and we punish them or institutions set up by the society punish them (Gurerk et al., 2006). However, there is also 'non-reciprocal altruism', in which one does not expect a payback. We do this to our kin, according to 'Hamilton's Law', which says that we are willing to give non-reciprocal altruism to an individual in direct relation to the number of genes (equals closeness of kinship) that we share with them. We can also mentally create 'virtual kinship' via our perceptual mechanisms (Dugatkin, 2006). This is the basis of the commandments of most religions, urging us to see that 'all men are brothers'. This creates a virtual kinship and brings forth an unconscious 'kin selection' and therefore intuitive altruistic feelings.

IMPEDIMENTS TO ETHICAL DECISION-MAKING – INDIVIDUAL AND INSTITUTIONAL

Individual Impediments

In economic game theory significant advances have been made in accurately predicting cooperative behavior in groups by examining the individual characteristics of the group members (Kurzban and Houser, 2005). It is thought that there are both individual and institutional impediments that interfere with correct ethical decision-making and that by examining and understanding these impediments and counteracting them, we can significantly improve group cooperation and team work. First, let us examine the most important individual impediments.

Status and Hierarchical Influence

A social comparison of self to community expectations is consistent with what is found in primates. Primates are genetically predisposed to focus on status and social hierarchy. The underpinnings of this concept is an evolutionarily adaptive behavior in a group setting. As humans, a similar tendency shows up in our obsession with the rich and powerful members of our society. It also is the unconscious basis for our desire to 'keep up with the Joneses'.

A fascinating experiment at Duke University Medical School titled 'Monkeys Pay-Per-View' shows that primates are hard-wired to pay close attention to high-status individuals. This is the first experimental evidence showing that primates automatically discriminate among images of other monkeys based on social status (Deaner et al., 2005).

A favorite treat for rhesus macaque monkeys is a slurp of sweet cherry juice. Males were given the choice of pressing a lever to get a reward of the juice or to view images on a computer screen, either of the face of the high-status monkey in their troop, the face of a low-status monkey also in their troop or the rears of female monkeys in estrus. The authors report that, despite the fact the monkeys were purposely made thirsty before the experiment, monkey subjects always gave up the cherry juice to view the faces of high-status monkeys or female rumps in estrus. However, the same monkeys had to be bribed with juice payment to view the faces of low-status monkeys. The authors strongly believe that similar mental processes are at work in human primates due to the fact that we have evolved in the same kinds of social conditions.

Time Stress and Pressure

Everyone knows that people are less willing to help other people when they are under time stress. A broken-down motorist will get virtually no help at rush hour but likely will on a Sunday afternoon. One of the classic social psychology experiments in this area is the 'Good Samaritan' experiment on seminary students at Princeton Theological Seminary in 1973 (Darley and Batson, 1973). The seminarian volunteers in the experiment were variously prepared by the researchers to give a speech on the 'jobs that seminary students would be good at' or a talk on the Parable of the Good Samarian. Each group was given the relevant written material to read. Next, the seminarians were sent to an adjacent building to give the prepared speech; some were told they were late, some that they were expected immediately and some that they were early but that they might as well go over. On the way, the student encountered an actor moaning and clearly in distress. Only 10 percent of the high-hurry students offered help, but 45 percent of the intermediate-hurry students helped and 63 percent of the low-hurry students helped. The subject they had studied, that is, the jobs or the Good Samaritan Parable, had no correlation at all with their aid to the victim.

The implications of this and other time-stressed research should be clear to us all. In our quest for productivity, in our statistical monitoring of output performance and in our over-scheduled lives, there is a diminishment of altruism and even good neighborliness. This is an important but overlooked impediment in ethical decision-making.

Cheater Types in Society: Evidence from Economic Game Theory

Recent research in economic game theory has emphasized the polymorphic nature of the make-up of the human population and the importance of individual differences in modeling group behavior and dynamics in economic games and decisions problems. In an important seminal article, Kurzban and Houser detail experiments they performed that were designed to identify and analyse these differences. They find that human subjects fall into three types: reciprocators, cooperators and free-riders (Kurzban and Houser, 2005).

Reciprocators, who make up 63 percent of the population, contribute to the public good as a positive function of their beliefs about others' contributions – in game theory parlance, they use a conditional strategy called 'tit-for-tat'. Cooperators, who make up 13 percent of the human population, always contribute to the public good at a cost to themselves whether others do or not – in game theory parlance, they play the absolute strategy of 'always cooperate'. Free-riders, who make up 20 percent of the human population, do not contribute to the public good but take from it – again, in game theory parlance, these agents employ the absolute strategy of 'always cheat.'

The make-up of the members of an institution or corporation can be a serious impediment to (or conversely an aid to) ethical behavior of the individual. More importantly, since institutions and corporations are not democracies but rather dictatorships, the ethical culture is always created from the top down so the behavioral type of the CEO is critically important to the ethics of the entire organization. Enron is a prime example.

The Neuroeconomic and Psychological Consequences of Money

Many philosophers and religions hold that 'Money, or the love of money is the root of all evil.' Certainly, it is a powerful force and it is critically important to take the power of money explicitly into account when thinking about business ethics. Pessiglione and colleagues devised experiments to show how the brain translates money into a force (Pessiglione et al., 2007). The researchers had their subjects view pictures of money (a penny or a pound) and were told they could keep the amount shown depending on how hard they squeezed a hand-grip. The subjects received feedback in the form of a visual thermometer and the researchers also measured subjects' skin conductance response (SCR) – to measure autonomic sympathetic arousal) and brain activity. Not surprisingly, the larger the amount shown, the stronger the grip force exercised by the subjects.

The brain scans showed activity in a specific basal forebrain area that includes the ventral striatum – the reward center of the brain (the dopamine processing brain facility), ventral pallidum and extended amygdala. This research supports what other studies have found, namely, that this region created the motivational effect of the money and is a key node in brain circuitry that enables expected rewards to energize behavior.

Resistance to Change

Unfortunately for teachers and trainers in business ethics, the resistance of people to change is huge. Arkowitz and colleagues report that the Centers for Disease Control and Prevention have established that 20 percent of American adults continue to smoke, more than 30 percent are significantly overweight and 15 percent are binge drinkers (Arkowitz and Engle, 2006; Arkowitz and Lilienfeld, 2007). Further, over 50 percent of medical patients do not follow their doctor-prescribed regimens, even in situations where non-compliance could end in amputation (a result of diabetes) or blindness (a result of glaucoma).

Why don't people change? Arkowitz and Lilienfeld (2007) cite the following reasons: 'diablos conocidos' (The devils you know are better than the devils you don't know); the status quo is familiar, comfortable and predictable even though it may be extremely painful; change is unpredictable and anxiety-producing; fear of failure: if they fail, people fear they will feel worse; faulty beliefs: some feel they are failures if not 100 percent successful, some feel a push to change by another person as a threat and unconsciously resist it (called 'reactance'); reward of the undesirable behavior: the individual clearly derives some reward from the undesirable behavior (for example, the alcoholic drinks to relieve their anxiety) and this coping behavior may be the only thing the person knows.

THE LIMITS OF THE HUMAN BRAIN: THE FRONTOPOLAR CORTEX AND EXECUTIVE

Function

The rational facilities of our neocortex suffer from extreme limitations that not only bias but actually hamper our ability to do complex thought. For example, Dijksterhuis and colleagues interviewed subjects choosing between kitchen accessories at a department store and another group who were choosing furniture at IKEA. For the accessory shoppers, the ones who consciously deliberated more were happier with their purchase. For the IKEA shoppers, those who deliberated more were less happy with their purchase than those who 'went with their gut'. Dijksterhuis and colleagues conclude this was due to the limits of the conscious mind and its ability to consider only a few variables at a time. This limitation may seem surprising, given that humans do make complex decisions (Dijksterhuis et al., 2006). However, Koechlin and Hyafil (2007) hypothesize that learned or trained expertise allows spatial navigation of memorized cognitive branching map sets, which are performed by the parietal cortex and hippocampus.

The Influence of Organizational Culture and Executives on Individuals

Available literature provides clear indications that individuals are strongly influenced by the cultures of the organizations to which they belong and by the executives and managers they report to and/or observe. To summarize, here is what we know about individuals that might be within their organization's ability to influence: individuals look to executives and managers for cues on how to behave; when they are in the midst of an ethical dilemma and under extreme stress, people are likely to be irrational and instead rely on emotions or ingrained patterns of behavior; the threat of punishment – losing a job, for example – has a profound influence on how people behave in organizations – in fact, the notion of loss may have significantly more impact on individuals than any possibility of gain; people resist change – 'diablos conocidos' (Arkowitz and Lilienfeld, 2007); framing – or how people rationalize a situation – can have profound implications on the ethics of their decisions; culture can have a profound effect on how we behave if the culture creates a sense of kinship among colleagues – this kind of close 'bonding' behavior has been exhibited in a number of organizations where a kind of 'artificial' or 'virtual' kinship has been encouraged and developed among members, such as the military, police departments, fire departments, medical staff and so on; gossip within an organization – the 'grapevine' effect – is how employees judge the credibility of an organization – members unconsciously compare 'formal' messages (what an organization says it stands for) with 'informal' messages (what an organization demonstrates in the way of values; in other words, what it really stands for). If there is a match, the organization is judged to be credible; if not, the organization is judged to be not credible. This phenomenon has a critical impact on behavior (Dunbar, 2004).

While these realities might seem daunting to executives who are charged with building an ethical culture within their organizations, there are steps they can take to improve the odds that people will do the right thing under pressure. The following are some of the most important institutional issues to consider.

Executives and managers need to understand their critical role in building ethical culture
Organizational behavioralists have long understood that people joining an organization look for clues from their orientation process, initial work experience, and what they are told about the culture by peers and managers. New hires quickly deduce what is expected of them from what they hear and observe.

Studies have shown that executives need to do much more than think ethically to have the desired effect on employees (Trevino, 2000). Being a moral person is in fact only half of the equation. In addition, executives and managers need to actively 'manage morally' in order for employees to perceive that they are ethical. This means that executives need to first communicate openly about the importance of ethics and values to the organization role model, about the desired behavior, and finally executives must hold people accountable for their behavior. An effective way to do this across an employee population is through a performance management system, which integrates ethical behavior competencies into its metrics.

Ethics and integrity need to be strategically and holistically built into a culture as core values
It is not enough for an organization to intend to be ethical and demonstrate integrity. Organizational cultures will not reflect integrity and ethics until those values are articulated and integrated into the spectrum of organizational life. Studies indicate that organizations which try to build value-based compliance cultures are likely to be significantly more effective at growing ethical cultures than organizations where a strict 'check-the-box' compliance effort is in place (Trevino, 1999, 2000). Specifically,

research indicates that a holistic ethics culture is one that is rooted in the organization's culture and values, is proactive, involves executives in strategic ways and is integrated into the organization's performance management system. In such a culture employees are more likely to be aware of and report unethical and illegal activities they observe, seek help inside the organization, support decision-making across the board, be committed to the organization and finally they are more likely to be ethical themselves.

Ethics programs need to recognize the importance of repetition in influencing employee behavior

It is important that various elements in an organizational culture repeat the themes of ethics and integrity and that these themes are reinforced constantly. Only this kind of repetition – making ethics and integrity a 'habit' – can override the emotional, irrational response of an individual employee who feels pressured in an ethical dilemma. It is only when employees feel that non-compliance is riskier than compliance that they will be able to override their emotional response to 'go along to get along'.

People resist change ('diablos conocidos')

We know from recent studies that people resist change and that peer pressure is highly influential in encouraging people to change. This is another factor that could be used to an organization's advantage with the creation of an ethical culture. If 'how business is done here' – the culture of an organization – is rooted in ethics and integrity, the peer pressure will drive individuals in that direction.

Time constraints can result in pressure that profoundly influences even the most well-meaning individual (Princeton Divinity School's 'Good Samaritan' experiment)

We know that time pressures can encourage workers to make inappropriate decisions, and yet the issue of time is one that organizations can do little to alleviate. What organizations can do, however, is to train employees to ask for additional time if possible when making complex decisions. It is almost never necessary in business to make an instant decision, and often just a little extra time can have a significant impact on outcomes.

Framing – or how people rationalize a situation – can have profound implications on the ethics of their decisions

Skilled executives and co-workers with distinct 'agendas' can easily frame issues in ways that might significantly influence individuals to respond – and decide – in a particular way. This is difficult for organizations to address, although perhaps training could help workers understand that this framing phenomenon exists and how they can reframe a problem or issue as part of their decision-making process.

Gossip
Organizational grapevines are how most information in the workplace is communicated and the news that travels on the grapevine greatly influences employee attitudes and behavior. Nevertheless, organizations can greatly influence what the grapevine contains by training its managers to communicate often and well with individuals.

CONCLUSION

A Chinese wish expresses the desire that we may always 'live in interesting times'. Clearly, the advent of medical technology to examine the inner workings of the brain has greatly affected how we view ethical decision-making – resulting in very interesting times indeed. No longer do researchers need to guess at a subject's reasoning; we are able to see how a subject evaluates a dilemma and how emotions and reason work together to produce a decision. Improvements in technology and added research into the brain will no doubt explain other cognitive and emotional processes that now are mysterious. These discoveries are not just fascinating forays into how humans 'work', but they also provide important clues to how organizations and societies might be able to influence individual decisions.

REFERENCES

Arkowitz, H. and D. Engle (2006), *Ambivalence in Psychotherapy, Facilitating Readiness to Change*, New York: Guilford Press.

Arkowitz, H. and S.O. Lilienfeld (2007), 'Why don't people change?', *Scientific American Mind*, **18**, 81–82.

Brosnan, S.F. and F.B.M. de Waal (2003), 'Monkeys reject unequal pay', *Nature*, **425**, 297–9.

Camerer, C. (2003), *Behavioral Game Theory*, Princeton, NJ: Princeton University Press.

Choi, W.Y., P.D. Balsam and J.C. Horvitz (2005), 'Extended habit training reduces dopamine mediation of appetitive response expression', *Journal of Neuroscience*, **25** (29), 6729–33.

Cohen, J.D. (2005), 'The vulcanization of the human brain: a neural perspective on interactions between cognition and emotion', *Journal of Economic Perspectives*, **19**, 3–24.

Cromwell, H.C. and W. Schultz (2003), 'Effects of expectations for different reward magnitudes on neuronal activity in primate striatum', *Journal of Neurophysiology*, **89**, 2823–38.

Cushman, F., L. Young and M. Hauser (2006), 'The role of conscious reasoning and intuition in moral judgment', *Psychological Science*, **17**, 1082–9.

Darley, J.M. and D. Batson (1973), 'From Jerusalem to Jericho: a study of situational and dispositional variables in helping behavior', *Journal of Personality and Social Psychology*, **27**, 100–108.

Dawkins, R. (1989), *The Selfish Gene*, Oxford: Oxford University Press.

Deaner, R.O., A.V. Khera and M.L. Platt (2005), 'Monkeys pay per view: adaptive valuation of social images by rhesus macaques', *Current Biology*, **15**, 543–8.

De Quervain, D.J.-F., U. Fischbacher, V. Treyer et al. (2004), 'The neural basis of altruistic punishment', *Science*, **305** (5688), 1254–8.

de Waal, F. (2005), *Our Inner Ape*, London: Penguin Books.

de Waal, F. (2007/2008), 'Do animals feel empathy?', *Scientific American Mind*, **18**, 28.

Dijksterhuis, A., M.W. Bos, L.F. Nordgren and R.B. van Baaren (2006), 'On making the right choice: the deliberation-without-attention effect', *Science*, **311**, 1005–7.

Dugatkin, L.A. (2006), *The Altruism Equation: Seven Scientists Search for the Origins of Goodness*, Princeton, NJ: Princeton University Press.

Dunbar, R.I.M. (2004), 'Gossip in evolutionary perspective', *Review of General Psychology*, **8**, 100–110.

Frith, U. and C.D. Frith (2003), 'Development and neurophysiology of mentalizing', *Philosophical Transactions of the Royal Society of London Series B*, **358**, 459–73.

Gallagher, H.L. and C.D. Frith (2003) 'Functional imaging of "Theory of Mind"', *Trends in Cognitive Science*, **7**, 77–83.

Greene, J. and J. Haidt (2002), 'How and where does moral judgment work?', *Trends in Cognitive Science*, **6**, 517–23.

Greene, J.D., R.B. Sommerville, L.E. Nystrom, J.M. Darley and J.D. Cohen (2001), 'An fMRI investigation of emotional engagement in moral judgment', *Science*, **293**, 2105–8.

Greene, J.D., L.E. Nystrom, A.D. Engell, J.M. Darley and J.D. Cohen (2004), 'The neural basis of cognitive conflict and control in moral judgment', *Neuron*, **44**, 389–400.

Gürerk, O., B. Irlenbusch and B. Rockenbach (2006), 'The competitive advantage of sanctioning institutions', *Science*, **312** (5770), 7 April, 108–11.

Haidt, J. and J. Graham (2007), 'When morality opposes justice: conservatives have moral intuitions that liberals may not recognize', *Social Justice Research*, **20**, 98–116.

Hauert, C., A. Traulsen, H. Brandt, M. Nowak and K. Sigmund (2007), 'Via freedom to coercion: the emergence of costly punishment', *Science*, **316**, 1905–7.

Hauser, M.D. (2006), *Moral Minds*, New York: Harper Collins.

Hauser, M., F. Cushman, L. Young, R.K. Jin and J. Mikhail (2007), 'A dissociation between moral judgments and justifications', *Mind and Language*, **22** (1), 1–21.

Kahneman, D., J.L. Knetsch and R.H. Thaler (1990), 'Experimental tests of the endowment effect and the Coase Theorem', *Journal of Political Economy*, **98**, 1325–48.

Knoch, D., A. Pascual-Leone, K. Meyer, V. Treyer, and E. Fehr (2006), 'Diminishing reciprocal fairness by disrupting the right prefrontal cortex', *Science*, **314**, 329–32.
Knutson, B. and J.C. Cooper (2005), 'Functional magnetic resonance imaging of reward prediction', *Current Opinion in Neurology*, **18**, 411–17.
Koechlin, E. and A. Hyafil (2007), 'Anterior prefrontal function and the limits of human decision-making', *Science*, **318**, 594–8.
Kurzban, R. and D. Houser (2005), 'Experiments investigating cooperative types in humans', *Proceedings of the National Academy of Sciences of the United States of America*, **102**, 1803–7.
Milgram, S. (1974), *Obedience to Authority: An Experimental View*, New York: HarperCollins.
Maren, S. (2007), 'The threatened brain', *Science*, **307**, 1043–4.
Minsky, M. (1986), *The Society of Mind*, New York: Simon and Schuster.
Mobbs, D., P. Petrovic, J.L. Marchant et al. (2007), 'When fear is near, threat imminence elicits prefrontal-periaqueductal gray shifts in humans', *Science*, **317**, 1079–83.
Nowak, M.A. (2006), 'Five rules for the evolution of cooperation', *Science*, **314**, 1560–63.
Nowak, M.A. and K. Sigmund (2005), 'The evolution of indirect reciprocity', *Nature*, **437**, 1291–8.
Nowak, M.A., K.M. Page and K. Sigmund (2000), 'Fairness vs. reason in the Ultimatum Game', *Science*, **289**, 1773–5.
O'Doherty J., P. Dayan, J. Schultz, R. Deichmann and K. Friston (2004), 'Dissociable roles of ventral and dorsal striatum in instrumental conditioning', *Science*, **304** (5669), 452–4.
Paulus, M.P. (2007), 'Decision-making dysfunctions in psychiatry – altered homeostatic processing?', *Science*, **318**, 602–6.
Pecina, S., B. Cagniard, K.C. Berridge, J.W. Aldridge and X. Zhuang (2003), 'Hyperdopaminergic mutant mice have higher "wanting" but not "liking" for sweet rewards', *Journal of Neuroscience*, **23** (28), 9395–402.
Pessiglioni, M., L. Schmidt, B. Draganski et al. (2007), 'How the brain translates money into force: a neuroimaging study of subliminal motivation', *Science*, **316**, 904–6.
Pillutla, M.M. and J.K. Murninghan (1996), 'Unfairness, anger and spite: emotional rejections of ultimatum offers', *Organizational Behavior and Human Decision Process*, **68**, 208–24.
Pinker, S. (2008), 'The moral instinct', *New York Times Magazine*, 13 January, p. 32.
Rilling, J.K., D.A. Gutman, J.R. Zeh et al. (2002), 'A neural basis for social cooperation', *Neuron*, **35**, 395–405.
Sanfey, A. (2007), 'Social decision-making: insights from game theory and neuroscience', *Science*, **318**, 598–602.
Sanfey, A.G., J.K. Rilling, J.A. Aronson, L.E. Nystrom and J.D. Cohen (2003), 'The neural basis of economic decision-making in the Ultimatum Game', *Science*, **300** (5626), 1755–8.
Treviño, L., L. Klebe, L.P. Hartman and M. Brown (2000), 'Moral person and moral manager', *California Management Review*, **42** (4), 128–42.
Trivers, R.L. (1971), 'The evolution of reciprocal altruism', *Quarterly Review of Biology*, **46**, 35–57.

Tversky, A. and D. Kahneman (1981), 'The framing of decisions and the psychology of choice', *Science*, **211**, 453–8.
Tversky, A. and D. Kahneman (1992), 'Advances in prospect theory: cumulative representation of uncertainty', *Journal of Risk and Uncertainty*, **5**, 297–323.
Wickens, J.R., J.C. Horvitz, R.M. Costa and S. Killcross (2007), 'Dopaminergic mechanisms in actions and habits', *Journal of Neuroscience*, **27** (31), 8181–3.
Young, L. and M. Koenigs (2007), 'Investigating emotion in moral cognition: a review of evidence from functional neuroimaging and neuropsychology', *British Medical Bulletin*, **84**, 69–79.

14. Culture, cognition and conflict: how neuroscience can help to explain cultural differences in negotiation and conflict management

John F. McCarthy, Carl A. Scheraga and Donald E. Gibson

Today, in our world of global markets and accelerating, cross-cultural exchanges, we all live in one another's world, a world of collisions and confrontations that emerge not only from struggles for power but from blurred images of one another.

Weiss (1992, p. 6)

Because some negotiation processes are also culture specific, negotiating with someone from another culture requires understanding the other party's communication and interaction norms.

Adair and Brett (2005, p. 46)

INTRODUCTION

With an ever-more globalized world, understanding cultural differences and how these cultural differences get played out in organizational processes is becoming increasingly important. Large-scale research has established the basic dimensions on which cultures can be differentiated (for example, Gelfand et al., 2007; Hampden-Turner and Trompenaars, 1993; Hofstede, 1980). However, applying these broad dimensions to actual individual behavior has not been as fruitful, since these broad dimensions tend to cloak innumerable individual differences. It is precisely at the level of micro-interactions, however, where cross-cultural differences play out. For example, in negotiation and conflict management situations understanding cultural patterns and tendencies is critical to whether a negotiation will accomplish the goals of the involved parties (Adair and Brett, 2005; Gelfand and Dyer, 2000; Tinsley, 1998).

Some of these cultural patterns have been identified and usefully applied to negotiation situations (for example, Gelfand and Dyer, 2000); however, researchers hasten to point out that cultural patterns do not explain all of the variations found (Tinsley, 2001). Finding that German negotiators, for example, are higher in power distance than Americans (meaning that they are likely to more readily accept that power will be distributed unequally between people) has not helped much to explain differences in actual negotiation styles. What is needed is a more fine-grained approach that examines differences below the level of behavioral norms. Drawing on recent social neuroscience approaches (for example, Cacioppo and Bernston, 1992; Cacioppo et al., 2007), we argue that these differing negotiating styles may not only be related to differing cultural norms, but to differences in underlying language processing strategies in the brain (see Nisbett et al., 2001). In this chapter we discuss the results of two studies in which we hypothesize that due to syntactical differences, native German-speaking individuals will develop a more deliberative cognitive style than native English-speaking individuals, resulting in a longer comprehension reaction time. The factors being proposed in these studies are related to how culture is internalized through language and subsequently how it affects thinking through embedded processing mechanisms in the brain, which we measure through neuroscience techniques. We argue that discovering these processing strategies at the level of cerebral activity may help us to understand more completely the basis of differences in negotiation and conflict management style.

Current research has focused on how different cultures address their perceptions and frames of the negotiation process (that is, Tinsley, 1998, 2001). The assumption is that cognitive processing is identical across people, but that cultures add a layer of behavioral norms creating differences in the understanding of negotiation and conflict management processes and practices. The metaphor is the computer: 'Brain equals hardware, inferential rules and data processing procedures equal the universal software, and output equals belief and behavior, which can, of course, be radically different given the different inputs possible for different individuals and groups' (Nisbett et al., 2001, p. 291). Hall and Hall (1990, pp. 3–4) also refer to culture as a 'computer program', comparing it to 'a giant, extraordinarily complex subtle computer'. Hofstede (1991, p. 5) calls culture 'the collective programming of the mind'. Using this metaphor, however, the brain is considered a black box in which, it is assumed, cognitive processing at the level of neuroscience is largely universal, or etic. In this chapter we argue that, in fact, cultural differences may influence neuropsychological processes (see Kotik-Friedgut, 2006). If this is the case, we would expect that individuals from different cultures will exhibit different neuropsychological tendencies, and that these tendencies have implications for negotiation and conflict management processes.

CONFLICT BEHAVIOR AND CULTURE

While practicing negotiators have long observed cultural differences in negotiation behavior, empirical study of the influence of culture on negotiation behavior has only been developed in the last 25 years (Gelfand and Brett, 2004). Research on cross-cultural differences was dramatically advanced by approaches arguing that culture is based on shared meanings defined by patterns of thinking, feeling and acting that individuals acquire from their social environment and collected life experiences (Hofstede, 1991). Conceiving of culture as shared meaning structures suggests that different collectives, organized by national cultures, would share particular group values. This perspective allowed researchers such as Hofstede (1991) to differentiate national cultures by the degree to which they were characterized by relatively few dimensions, such as individualism/ collectivism, power distance, uncertainty avoidance, masculinity/femininity and Confucian dynamism (Hofstede, 1980, 1991; Hofstede and Bond, 1988; see also dimensional models of Hampden-Turner and Trompenaars, 1993; Schwarz, 1992, 1994). Following this line of reasoning, people located in a culture characterized as individualistic (for example, the USA) should behave differently in negotiation situations than those located in a culture characterized as collectivistic (such as Japan).

While it is clear that behavioral differences exist based on dimensional classification systems such as Hofstede's (Brett, 2001), demonstrating consistent culturally-differentiated behavioral patterns in negotiation settings has been difficult. The primary approach in early studies was to use laboratory simulations to examine whether people located in different nations (typically represented by geographical area) use different negotiation tactics or conflict styles. Overall, cultural differences in preferred forms of handling conflict have been found in numerous studies (see Adler and Graham, 1987; Adler et al., 1987; Allerheiligen et al., 1985; Chua and Gudykunst, 1987; Graham, 1985; Graham et al., 1993; Pearson and Stephan, 1998; Ting-Toomey, 1986; Ting-Toomey et al., 1991). However, these studies often reveal inconsistent and conflicting results. For example, as summarized by Gelfand and Dyer (2000), Adler and Graham (1987) and Adler et al. (1987) found that French-speaking Canadians used fewer cooperative tactics than Americans, English-speaking Canadians or Mexicans in a simulated negotiation. These results were opposite to the authors' prediction that French-Canadians would engage in more cooperation. In a different study Adler et al. (1992) found that Americans used fewer cooperative tactics (that is, questions and self-disclosure) and more instrumental tactics (such as threats and commitments to positions) in comparison with Chinese negotiators. Graham (1985) found no

differences in the degree to which American, Japanese and Brazilian subjects used instrumental tactics, though American negotiators were found
to use aggressive tactics sooner than Japanese or Brazilian subjects.

Gelfand and Dyer, in a review of 20 years of cross-cultural negotiation
research, lament that 'For the most part, there is an abundance of conflicting and unexpected patterns in the literature, making it difficult to make
any generalizations' (Gelfand and Dyer, 2000, p. 68). They argue that the
reason for this inconsistency is that the theoretical mechanisms for cross-
cultural effects were not well developed, pointing to three major pitfalls.
First, much research to that point used geographical location as a sur-
rogate for culture, rather than measuring cultural dimensions at the individual level; second, research tended to ignore the psychological processes
– such as motives and information processing – underlying negotiation
behaviors; and third, few moderating effects of culture had been examined,
taking into account more specific situational variables.

A further complication in empirically linking cultural dimensions to specific conflict management behaviors is that the same dimensions may cause
different conflict behaviors, depending on culture. In one study, while
American participants did not differ from their German counterparts in
their levels of individualism, hierarchy or polychronicity, their specific
negotiation behaviors differed substantially (Tinsley, 2001). This research
suggests that, while observed conflict management behaviors may differ
depending on culture, using macro classification systems with relatively
few dimensions has not led to a theoretically or empirically satisfying
explanation for cultural differences in conflict management behaviors.

CONFLICT COGNITION AND CULTURE

One explanation for the lack of compelling results in research focusing
on conflict management behaviors is that insufficient attention has been
paid to the underlying cognitive processes of negotiators. While studies
observed that negotiation behavior appears to differ depending on culture,
there was little theoretical or empirical investigation of why behaviors
might differ. The general assumption of previous research is that while
culture may affect behavior, cognitive processes are likely to be universal
– and, as such, these processes were initially unexamined, treated as something of a 'black box' (Gelfand and Dyer, 2000). However, a substantial
tradition exists characterizing negotiation and conflict management as
cognitive decision-making tasks, in which negotiators construct mental
representations of the conflict situation, issues and their opponents
(Bazerman and Neale, 1983; Gelfand et al., 2001; Thompson, 1990). Thus,

the processes and outcomes of a negotiation have been shown to be substantially affected by the interactants' cognitive frames, that is, the aspects of the conflict that are attended to and interpreted as important (Pinkley, 1990). Pinkley (1990) showed that conflict frames tend to fall into one of three independent dimensions: compromise versus win, intellectual versus emotional or relationship versus task.

A developing line of research demonstrates that culture affects these cognitive processes. For example, evidence suggests that the culture dimension of individualism/collectivism affects an individual's concept of self-identity, and thus information processing (Gelfand et al., 2001; Markus and Kitayama, 1991). Additional support that culture affects cognitive processes is exhibited in research showing that cognitive biases are affected by culture. Substantial research examines the degree to which negotiators are subject to judgment biases in the way they make decisions and act in conflict management situations (Bazerman and Carroll, 1987; Pruitt and Carnevale, 1993; Thompson, 1990). Biases result from mental shortcuts humans unconsciously use when facing otherwise overwhelming information-processing demands (Morris and Gelfand, 2004). While support exists for a range of cognitive biases in processing conflict situations, this support is almost exclusively from studies in the USA and other culturally similar Western countries (ibid.). However, when different cultures are included in investigations, there is evidence that these biases are at least partially culturally determined (Gelfand and Christakopoulou, 1999). Gelfand et al. (2001) found that Japanese negotiators were more likely than US negotiators to construe conflicts in terms of a compromise frame rather than win–lose (Pinkley, 1990), suggesting the difference in prevalence of the fixed-pie errors. Other biases such as the egocentric bias (the tendency to view one's own behavior as more fair than others) and the disposition versus situation bias (the tendency to misattribute behaviors as being trait as opposed to situation-related) also have shown cultural effects (Morris and Gelfand, 2004).

LANGUAGE AND CULTURE

There is substantial support for the notion that culture affects individual negotiators' cognitive processes, and these cognitive processes, in turn, affect conflict management behavior (Figure 14.1). What has not been addressed in the conflict management literature, however, is how culture affects cognitive processes. Yet exploring this link is critical to answering the question of why culture affects conflict management behavior.

One avenue for examining the linkage between culture and cognitive

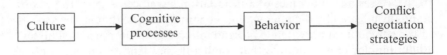

Figure 14.1   The linkage path from culture to conflict negotiation
strategies

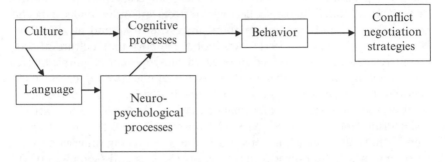

Figure 14.2   The linkage path from culture to conflict negotiation
strategies incorporating language and neuro-psychological
processes

processes draws on the effect of culture on language, and in turn, the effect
of language on cognitive processing (Figure 14.2). The notion that culture
shapes language that shapes cognitive processes finds its theoretical underpinning in the work of Lev Vygotsky (1986), who contended that language is the internalization of culture. Language, he argued, shapes how
we represent internally the external world, and our language-processing
strategies shape how we think. As Vygotsky (1987, p. 285) put it, 'The
word is the most direct manifestation of the historical nature of human
consciousness.' Vygotsky suggested that individuals bring culturally determined 'tools of thought' to their problem-solving tasks. These tools, or
'higher psychological functions' are only acquired through socio-historical
means; that is, they are transmitted from one person to another by jointly
solving the problems of everyday existence. In this way, individuals' cognitive processes are shaped by the transmission of a culture through the
child's socialization process. Inherent to that process is language, which
represents and exemplifies the culture (Rogoff, 1990). If Vygotsky's ideas
and supporting studies hold, we would expect that individuals from different cultures with different languages will develop different language-
processing strategies which will shape their approach to thinking and,
subsequently, their behavior.

THE ROLE OF NEUROSCIENCE

Recently it has become possible to measure, rather than speculate about, differing language processing strategies. As is evident in the research on conflict management behavior, such behavior is determined by myriad factors. What this means is that the expression of a specific conflict behavior may say little about the specific antecedent condition or cause, and may not provide much information about underlying cognitive processing. Relevant to the quest to understand the cognitive antecedents of social behavior has been the dramatic increase in cognitive neuroscience research, which uses functional brain imaging to study social cognition and social behavior (Adolphs, 2003; Cacioppo et al., 2003, 2007). This research has fostered a marked increase in our understanding of the neural bases of human social behavior, including the areas of judgment, decision-making, self-perception, self-regulation, group processes and economics (Cacioppo et al., 2007; Sanfey, 2007).

The role played by the brain in language has been of interest to researchers for many years. However, much of what was known about the relationship came from the study of brain-injured persons or invasive techniques. The data provided by these sources has been referred to as the classical model. The model states that Broca's area, which is a small cortical area in the ventro-caudal part of the frontal lobe, specialized in expressive and articulatory speech and language. Also, Wernicke's area, which is a larger postero-dorsal region in the temporal lobe, was believed to be involved with the receptive features of language and auditory comprehension (Damasio, 1999).

However, it is questionable whether data from such sources can be generalized to non-brain-injured individuals. The development of a number of scanning techniques (position emission tomography (PET), event-related potential (ERP) and functional magnetic resonance imaging (fMRI) shed light on the relationship between brain functioning and language – and the possibility of generalizing findings – by allowing the use of healthy subjects. The synthesis of more recent computational technology with longer-used techniques such as electroencephalography (EEG) has given rise to a particular form of brain wave data recordings, called event-related potentials (Kutas and Van Petten, 1994). Event related potential (ERP) recordings arise as a result of brain wave recordings averaged across a number of trials of presented stimuli from routine measures of EEG. By averaging multiple trials of similar stimuli, extraneous background waveforms are neutralized. The resulting waveform pattern presents a clearer and more precise correlation between the presented stimulus and the measurable changes elicited by the stimulus (Reinvang, 1999). ERPs have thus served as a vital tool in uncovering the physiological changes resulting from specific stimuli.

Only in the last 20 years has ERP recording found a place in language research. It embodies the characteristic procedure of presenting trial after trial of stimuli, averaging these trials together and labeling the respective components, identical to earlier studies on attention and memory processing. In this case, however, the stimuli come in the form of simple (words) or complex (sentences) language components that are systematically manipulated in order to be correlated to ERP components which are advanced to explain processes involved in language cognition (Friederici and Frisch, 2000; Hagoort et al., 1993; Knight et al., 1993; Kutas and Van Petten, 1994; Nobre and McCarthy, 1995).

STUDY 1: COMPREHENSION TIME DIFFERENCES BETWEEN NATIVE ENGLISH AND GERMAN-SPEAKERS

To examine the effect of language on cognitive processes in conflict management, this research focuses on differences between native English-speakers and native German-speakers. The reason for comparing English and German is based on major syntactical differences that exist between the two languages (Table 14.1). Specifically, in terms of syntactical differences, English is an action language that usually follows a subject–verb–predicate structure. German syntax, on the other hand, is more intricate and complex. German syntax includes separable prefix verbs, auxiliary verbs in relation to infinitives and the placement of verbs in dependent clauses.

This syntax, which frequently requires waiting until the end of the sentence for the verbal information necessary for comprehension, would lead one to hypothesize that cognitive processes would be affected and result in a more deliberative cognitive style. In the first of two studies, an auditory listening comprehension task was used to investigate the hypothesis that due to syntactical differences native German-speaking individuals will develop a more deliberative cognitive style than native English-speaking individuals, resulting in a longer comprehension reaction time.

Addressing cultural differences at the level of neuroscience helps to address two of the pitfalls identified above (Gelfand and Dyer, 2000). First, it avoids basing predicted cultural differences on an individual's geographical location, but rather, focuses on the more precise measure of the individual's use of a particular language. Second, it begins to answer the call for a more fine-grained investigation of the psychological

Table 14.1   Syntactic differences between German and English

	German	English
Basic Structure	1. Intricate and complex syntax. 2. Auxiliary verbs' relation to infinitives, placement of verbs in dependent clauses and separable prefix verbs.	1. Action language. 2. Subject–Verb–Predicate.
Auxiliary Verb Example	*Möchtest* du lieber den französischen oder den deutschen Film *sehen?*	*Would* you prefer *to watch* the French movie or the German movie?
Dependent Clause Example	Er hat gesagt daß er gestern abend mit seinem Chef in einem italienischen Restaurant zu viel *getrunken hat.*	He said that he and his boss *drank* too much in an Italian restaurant last night.
Separable Prefix Verb Example	Ich *stieg* ohne mein Gepäck in Hamburg ins Flugzeug *ein.*	I *got into* the plane in Hamburg without my luggage.

processes underlying observed differences in negotiation behavior. The use of neuroscience techniques allows a more precise view of why differences in behavior occur.

While there have been many studies of language using brain imaging techniques, fewer studies have investigated how language at the level of sentences is comprehended. In research using brain imaging techniques to study language comprehension, Hald et al. (2006) specifically used EEG to study theta and gamma responses to semantic violations in online sentence processing. EEG was used to compare subjects' brain activity when listening to systematically congruent and incongruent sentences. One difference occurred when subjects were listening to systematically congruent sentences. In this situation the subjects had increased gamma activity in the frontal areas. This gamma activity, referring to brain wave oscillations around 40 Hz, did not occur when subjects were listening to systematically incongruent sentences. This finding proposes that activity in the gamma frequency range is part of the neural pattern of activity that occurs during normal language processing (ibid.), suggesting that gamma activity could reflect time of comprehension.

In past studies gamma activity has been seen as playing a key role in understanding the physiological process of binding in sensory perception (Crick and Koch, 1997; Llinas and Pare, 1996). Forty hertz has appeared to be the most likely frequency range involved in indicating the point at which all signals used to process a given stimulus are integrated into one

(Haig et al., 2000). A study of neurophysiologic functioning of the brain during language processing could reveal more information on how humans comprehend auditory information. Based on the role of 40 Hz frequency in sensory binding, it would be reasonable to assume that 40 Hz is an indicator of the point at which the separate discrete signals caused by the onset of the language stimuli come together as a meaningful sentence. Thus, 40 Hz could be used not only as a measure of perceptual recognition but also as a measure of linguistic comprehension (McCarthy et al., 2002).

Having a stable marker for timing of comprehension would be particularly relevant when trying to study and compare different languages and their neurophysiologic similarities and differences. Looking at 40 Hz activity specifically, time-frequency representations of power changes in the gamma range can be used. These representations are referred to as wavelets and have been used for analyzing localized variations of power within a time series (Torrence and Compo, 1998). The fact that these representations use time and frequency makes them the analysis of choice for this study.

In this first study native German-speaking subjects listened to a series of sentences in their native language and clicked a mouse when they understood each sentence. EEG data were collected as subjects listened and responded. It was hypothesized that because of the previously mentioned syntactical differences, native German-speakers have developed a language processing style that displays a more deliberative cognitive style than native English-speakers. This deliberative cognitive style in native German-speakers would be reflected in a longer reaction time indicating comprehension as well as a later onset of 40 Hz when compared to native English-speakers on simple sentences (subject–verb–predicate).

Method

A total of 11 native English-speaking people and 10 native German-speaking people participated in the study. The German subjects were local 'au pairs' who had recently arrived from Germany. All subjects were right-handed college-aged women (19–22 years) who were enrolled in classes at a university.

Presentation software was used to present a series of 86 sentences, which were a randomized combination of sentences having both simple and complex syntax. All sentences were originally written in English and were then translated by a native German-speaker into German. Sentences with simple syntax were defined as following the structure of subject–verb–predicate. A variety of sentences with complex syntax were used to create an alternate set of sentences. Since only sentences using simple syntax could be equated for length and position of verb between the two language groups, only the reaction time recorded for the sentences with simple syntax (45 in total) were used in the analysis of the two language groups. A statistical analysis showed that any differences in the length of simple sentence between the two languages were not significant (t = 1.21, p = 0.23). The sentences on average lasted 2.67 seconds and were separated by a gap of 4 seconds.

When subjects arrived, they filled out a questionnaire and signed a consent form. The questionnaire asked them to identify their name, age, handedness (if subjects were left-handed they were not used in the study), where they were born and where their parents were born. Subjects were then seated in a comfortable leather recliner, and the EEG setup was completed. They viewed instructions on a monitor directly in front of them, instructing them to remain as still as possible during the experiment and to click the mouse when they understood a sentence. In order to reduce eye movement, the subjects were also told to look towards the monitor, which had a simple fixation cross displayed in the center, during the presentation of the sentences. The lights were turned off and the experiment began. Presentation software recorded the experiment from beginning to end on a millisecond time scale, and each response made by a subject was recorded by the presentation system. Later analysis was done to determine the average length of time that transpired between when a sentence ended and when comprehension was reported. At the end of the experiment subjects received monetary compensation for participating, were debriefed on the nature of the experiment and were thanked for their participation.

EEG data were collected using products by Bio Semi including a 64-channel ActiveTwo EEG/ERP acquisition system that had an AD box with battery and a USB2 Receiver. The acquisition system was controlled by a Dell personal computer with a Pentium 4 processor using the program Acti-View, which monitored and collected EEG signals. EEG data were analyzed, segmented and averaged using Brain Vision Analyzer version 1.0. The stimulus of the 86 sentences created through the presentation program contained markers indicating key events essential to the experiment. These markers were translated into the Brain Vision Analyzer program and provided corresponding EEG data occurring at the key events. These key events were the beginning of each sentence, the occurrence of each verb, the end of each sentence and the response click to each sentence. The markers included EEG data that occurred at some time before the key event and at some time after the key event. For the markers indicating the beginning of a sentence and the occurrence of a verb, EEG data were marked 100 ms before the marker and 900 ms after the marker. For the markers indicating the end of a sentence and a response click,

EEG data were marked 500 ms before the marker and 500 ms after the marker. The EEG data collected for each marker, on each sentence and for each subject were averaged to create a grand average for that key event for each language group. This data collection method allowed for comparative analysis between groups for each key event.

The averaged and filtered data were transformed into wavelets to compute the gamma power change between 30 Hz and 50 Hz. A wavelet was created for the markers at the verb, 100 ms pre-stimulus to 920 ms post-stimulus; at the end of sentence, 500 ms pre-stimulus to 500 ms post-stimulus; and at the response, 500 ms pre-stimulus to 500 ms post-stimulus. This procedure was followed for each region of the brain. To ensure that the two studies safeguarded human subjects and followed federal guidelines, Fairfield University's Institutional Review Board reviewed the protocols for each. The board ruled that regulations were met and approved the studies.

Results

Both parametric and non-parametric tests were utilized to assess the results of the study. An independent two-tailed t-test was conducted comparing German-speakers' average comprehension response time to English-speakers' average comprehension response time. Means were calculated by determining the time that transpired between when a sentence ended and when subjects responded indicating comprehension. English-speaking subjects were significantly faster in their response time (M = 409.51 ms, SD = 341.68 ms) than German-speaking subjects (M = 726.39 ms, SD = 265.13 ms). Statistically, t = 2.36 and p = 0.029. A two-tailed Mann–Whitney U-test comparing German-speaking subjects' and English-speaking subjects' reaction time was also conducted. There was a significant difference between the native English-speaking language group and the native German-speaking language group. The English mean rank was 7.40 and the German mean rank was 14.27, U = 19, p = 0.011.

EEG data readings showed differences between the groups. While overall patterns between groups were similar on all electrodes over time, there were differences in amplitude and frequency between the groups. Averages were broken down into groups according to regions. An overall average was created for the frontal electrodes.

English-speaking subjects had a 40 Hz response upon hearing the verb and no 40 Hz response at the end of the sentence. German-speaking subjects did not have a 40 Hz response upon hearing the verb and did not show one until the end of the sentence.

In a visual inspection of the wavelets, differences were found in the

English   German

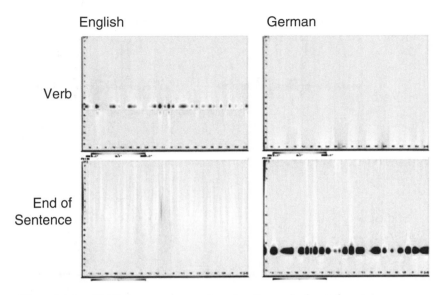

Figure 14.3   40 Hz response upon hearing the verb, frontal region

overall frontal average wavelet (Figure 14.3). Native English-speakers had gamma activity ranging in intensity from −100 μV to 100 μV in a steady band ranging from 36 Hz to 39 Hz in their frontal electrode average surrounding the marker of the verb. German-speakers had very little gamma activity surrounding the marker of the verb in their frontal electrode average. In contrast, native German-speakers had gamma activity ranging in intensity from −100 μV to 100 μV in a steady band ranging from 29 Hz to 33 Hz surrounding the end of the sentence marker in their frontal electrode average. When inspecting the parietal leads, no difference in pattern was found. Rather, both groups had similar gamma activity in all three markers (Figure 14.4).

Discussion

The interconnectors of brain regions and the comparison of activity in various regions of the brain can be understood by recourse to the work of Luria (1970). His work, which recognized that sensory and motor activity are related to specific brain regions, focused on how complex behavioral processes are not related to similar specific regions. For such complex processes an integration of a number of different regions of the brain is required. He postulated that three major regions of the brain existed and that each region was related to different specific functions. Complex

English   German

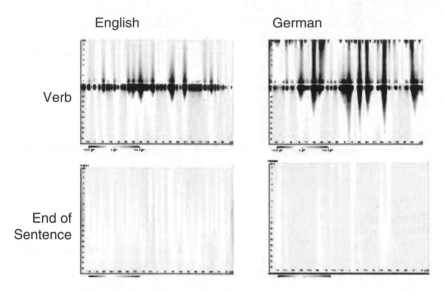

Note: 40 Hz activity for both German and English subjects occurred at the same time in the parietal region.

Figure 14.4   40 Hz response upon hearing the verb, parietal region

human behavior for him required the interaction of all of these regions. The first region, which primarily regulated energy levels and tone of the cortex, was located in the brainstem and reticular formation. The second region in the area of the cortex – which included the parietal area – was responsible for sensory integration. The third and largest region, the frontal lobes, was the seat of complex behavior such as planning, complying with social dictates and decision-making activities. The activity in the parietal region indicates that, while both groups were storing information at the same time, the use as reflected in frontal activity occurred at different times for the two groups. Such findings are consistent with Luria's theory of regions two and three.

As indicated by the results, native English-speaking Americans differed from native German-speaking Germans in both comprehension reaction time and EEG measured response. Consistent with our hypothesis, native German-speakers took significantly more time to indicate when they understood a sentence than did native English-speakers. This result is consistent with the ideas of Vygotsky (1986) and the theory that individuals from different cultures develop unique language processing strategies that affect behavior. A deliberative cognitive style used by Germans could account for this difference in comprehension reaction time.

The hypothesis was further supported by EEG 40 Hz wavelets that showed different patterns of activity in relation to time and brain region. As predicted, both native English-speakers and native German-speakers had 40 Hz activity while they listened and responded to sentences. However, a difference in timing of 40 Hz activity was found between the groups with native English-speakers having on average 40 Hz activity earlier in each comprehension task than the native German-speakers. In the frontal region native English-speakers had 40 Hz activity surrounding the verb whereas native German-speakers had 40 Hz activity later surrounding the end of the sentence. This difference in the timing of 40 Hz is consistent with the idea of a more deliberative cognitive style, which was reflected in manual reaction time. In the parietal region, however, both groups had comparable 40 Hz activity surrounding the verb, a finding consistent with Luria's approach.

STUDY 2: DECISION-MAKING DIFFERENCES BETWEEN NATIVE ENGLISH AND GERMAN-SPEAKERS

Given the results of this first study, it was further hypothesized that a deliberative cognitive style shown by the German group would transfer to decision-making. This hypothesis was investigated in a second study. In order to perform a second study to compare the two groups on the time required to make a decision, a decision-making task was required.

Gonzalez et al. (2005) studied framing effects and risky decisions using the Asian disease model. In this model subjects are presented with scenarios involving problems that are either framed positively or negatively and are asked to make a choice between a certain (sure) or probabilistic (risky) option. Her results showed differences in reaction time between positive and negative frames as well as differences in risky versus safe decisions. These results were also reflected by differences in fMRI.

Gonzalez's work indicated that this model would serve as a useful decision-making task when using neurophysiologic measures. The use of this task was ideal since the goal of the second study was not to replicate Gonzalez's findings but rather to ascertain whether differences in decision-making time and brain activity could be found between the two language groups. It was expected that native German-speakers would take longer to make a choice for both positively and negatively framed problems and would have a later onset of gamma activity than their native English-speaking counterparts.

The Asian Disease Model
Positive
The USA is preparing for an outbreak of a disease that is expected to kill 600 000 people. There are two plans to stop it. Scientific estimates of the outcomes are: → Option A has a 1/3 chance of saving 600 000 people and a 2/3 chance of saving no one (risk-seeking) → Option B will save 200 000 people (risk-averse) Which plan would you choose? A or B?
Negative
The USA is preparing for an outbreak of a disease that is expected to kill 600 000 people. There are two plans to stop it. Scientific estimates of the outcomes are: → If option A is used, there is a 1/3 chance that nobody will die, and a chance that 600 000 people will die (risk-seeking) → If option B is used, 400 000 people will die (risk-averse) Which plan would you choose? A or B?

Figure 14.5   Decision-making task

Method

A similar sample as that of the first study was utilized. That is, a total of 11 native English-speaking people and 10 native German-speaking people participated in the study. As before, the German subjects were local 'au pairs' who had recently arrived from Germany. All subjects were right-handed college-aged women (19–22 years) who were enrolled in classes at a university.

Subjects were presented with instructions in their native language through a PowerPoint presentation. They were given ten problems each framed positively and negatively resulting in a total of 20 problems. The problems were in the format of the Asian disease problem, with the option of one certain outcome and one risky outcome (Figure 14.5). Presentation software was used to present the problems on a computer screen.

Each trial began with a 10-second presentation of the problem on the computer screen. Then after 10 seconds, the two choices were added to the display and the cumulative display remained visible on the screen for 18 seconds. Subjects were instructed to make their decision by clicking one of two options on a computer mouse. Subjects clicked the left side of the mouse for option A and the right side of the mouse for option B. Subjects entered their choice any time after the choices were made visible on the screen. A warning bell sounded indicating that time was about to expire if the subjects did not make a choice within the 18-second interval for each problem. Each problem trial was followed by a rest period of 12 seconds in order to reduce EEG overlap for each trial. Five fixation periods of 25 seconds were distributed evenly throughout the experiment to obtain a baseline measure of brain activation and once again to prevent overlap in EEG data. During these rest periods a '+' was displayed in the center of the computer screen. Subjects were given four practice problems after reading the instructions and were allowed to ask any questions before they began the actual experiment.

EEG data was collected using the 64-channel EEG machine produced by Bio Semi. The cap was placed on the subject's head, conductive gel was inserted into each electrode opening and then corresponding electrodes were connected. Subjects were seated in a comfortable leather recliner in front of the computer monitor, through which they read the instructions.

Results

Again, parametric and non-parametric tests were utilized to assess the results of the study. Overall, the German subjects took significantly longer to make a decision in the framing study (M = 12 683.84 ms, SD = 4206.42 ms) than the English subjects (M = 9001.52 ms, SD = 1452.92 ms). Statistically, $t = -2.61$ with $p = 0.0184$. (Mean values represent the time in milliseconds that elapsed from the time subjects were presented with a choice and when they actually made their choice.) A Mann-Whitney U-test revealed a significant difference with German subjects taking longer to make a decision. The German group mean rank was 13 and the English mean rank was 6, $U = 9$, $p = 0.005$. Both native English and native German-speakers took a longer amount of time to make a decision when a question was framed negatively as compared to when it was framed positively. These results support the findings of Gonzalez et al. (2005).

Native German-speakers took significantly longer to make a decision on a question that was framed positively (M = 10 839.29 ms, SD = 2139.46 ms) than native English-speakers (M = 8338.28 ms, SD = 1812.47 ms). Statistically, t = –2.69, p = 0.0162. A Mann–Whitney U-test supported the findings of the t test. The English mean rank was 6.56 and the German mean rank was 11.75; U = 14 and p = 0.034. Native German-speakers also took significantly longer to make a decision on a question framed negatively (M = 13 562.03 ms, SD = 4261.25 ms) than did native English-speakers (M = 9664.78, SD = 1409.74). Statistically, t = –2.73, p = 0.0149. Again, a Mann–Whitney U-test supported the findings of the t test. The English mean rank was 6.00 and the German mean rank was 12.38; U = 9 and p = 0.009.

In addition, both native English and native German-speakers took longer to respond when choosing a risky option as compared to choosing a safe option. Native German-speakers took significantly longer when choosing a risky option (M = 11 974.8 ms, SD = 1810.39 ms) as compared to native English-speakers (M = 9088.58 ms, SD = 1329.94 ms). Statistically, t = –3.78, p = 0.0018. A Mann–Whitney U-test supported the findings of the t test. The English mean rank was 5.13 and the German mean rank was 11.88; U = 5 and p = 0.005. Native German-speakers also took longer when choosing a safe option (M = 11 266.77 ms, SD = 1898.61 ms) as compared to native English-speakers (M = 8247.59 ms, SD = 762.65 ms). Statistically, t = –4.40, p = 0.0005. A Mann–Whitney U-test supported the findings of the t test. The English mean rank was 4.75 and the German mean rank was 12.25; U = 2 and p = 0.002. As in the first study, neurophysiologic differences were found between the two groups. EEG results indicated that gamma activity occurred at a later onset for native German-speaking subjects than it did for native English-speaking subjects when making a decision (Figure 14.6).

General Discussion

In both the comprehension and decision-making studies native German-speaking subjects took longer than native English-speaking subjects. These findings are consistent with the hypothesis of a more deliberative cognitive style in the native German-speakers that reflects itself in a general language processing strategy across situations. Not only are the behavioral differences in the predicted direction, but the underlying neurological differences also followed this predicted pattern.

We argue that the lexicology and grammar of a language have a role

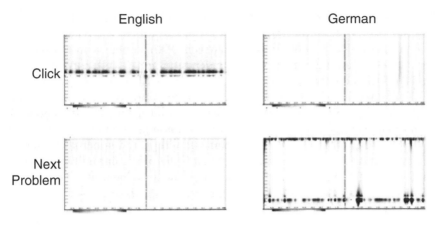

Note: English-speaking subjects had a 40 Hz response at the time of their decision. German-speaking subjects did not exhibit a 40 Hz response at this time, but instead showed the 40 Hz response at the end of the problem.

Figure 14.6   40 Hz response, decision-making task, frontal region

beyond the traditional one of determining how speakers conceptualize the world around them. Language is acted upon by the internal framework of the brain. In order to understand the nature of conflict at the level of observed behavioral differences, we should also understand the micro-language processing strategies that may underlie these differences. These two studies demonstrate that social neuroscience may provide a new way of understanding micro-processes in cross-cultural negotiations and con-flict resolution.

In order to understand the effect of differing cultures on negotiations and conflict management, we need to examine these interactions on a more micro level. The reason that much variance is left unexplained in extant research is that macro-level models are difficult to translate into specific interaction patterns in negotiations. We contend that individuals from differing cultures will differ, not just in their observable norms and behaviors (that have been studied previously), but also in their underlying neuropsychology – their ways of understanding and ascribing meaning to interactions (see Nisbett et al., 2001). In other words, while previous studies have primarily examined external behaviors that are indicative of culture, very little research has examined internal cognitive processes that may also reflect cultural differences.

Thanasoulas (2001) provides an interesting overview of the traditional literature examining the acquisition of secondary languages. He notes that the field of foreign language teaching prides itself in having moved beyond the notion that language is merely a code to be mastered through the assimilation of grammatical rules and some aspects of the relevant social context (Kramsch, 1993). Indeed, there is now an emphasis on 'walking in the shoes' of another culture while understanding this different culture in relation to one's own.

Language is indeed a code, albeit in a far more subtle manner than traditionally portrayed. It is more than a social institution shaping and shaped by society as portrayed by Armour-Thomas and Gopaul-McNicol (1998). Rather, it is also the key to understanding a fundamental, underlying biological process by which individuals of a particular culture process information. Ironically, the diplomat and scholar Wihelm von Humboldt (quoted in Salzmann, 2003, p. 142), captured the essence of this notion when he wrote:

> The spiritual traits and the structure of the language of a people are so intimately blended, that, given either of the two, one should be able to derive the other from it to the fullest extent . . . Language is the outward manifestation of the people: their language is their spirit, and their spirit is their language; it is difficult to imagine any two things more identical.

Von Humboldt was writing in the context of language and culture being intertwined with each other. He was expressing a notion much akin to that of Bruner (1996) who noted that although meanings are in the mind, they have their beginnings and hold their significance in the culture in which they are created.

We assert that the lexicology and grammar of a language have a role beyond the traditional one of determining how speakers conceptualize the world around them. We would modify the observation of Durkheim (1947) who suggested that 'language is not merely the external covering of a thought; it is also its internal framework'. Language is acted upon by the internal framework of the brain. Failure to utilize language to gain insight to this internal processing framework must lead to some degree of breakdown in the transmission of knowledge, even in the presence of language proficiency and cultural immersion.

Limitations

As with all studies, this one has limitations that may constrain its generalizability. The sample size is small, though comparable to other recent neuroscience studies (see Gonzalez et al., 2005; Kaan et al., 2007; Krause et al., 2006). The small sample size reflects the nature of research in neuroscience in that studies take longer and are more complicated in procedures in which brain activity is measured. Our respondents were also all women, a possible limiting factor. Because of the specialized requirements of the study – needing, as we did, to compare native German-speaking with native English-speaking respondents – finding a suitable sample was difficult. Replication with other groups of different ages and gender in their native country of Germany was not possible. Drawing on a relatively homogeneous sample of German-speaking versus English-speaking women allowed us to have comparable sub-samples that differed primarily in their native language and did not differ in terms of other major demographic variables.

PRACTICAL IMPLICATIONS AND OPPORTUNITIES FOR FURTHER RESEARCH

The findings indicate that it is important to realize that not only do people from different cultures speak differently, they also think differently and such differences are rooted in different neurological activity taking place at different times. The effects of culture on brain activity and physiology gives further support to the extent of physical changes due to culture. This chapter is reflective of the current increase in research activity with regard to the impact of culture on neurological processes. For example, Tan et al. (2008), using fMRI, provided experimental support for the Worf hypothesis relating language to perception. Willems et al. (2008), in their work on semantic integration and linguistic information, made use of ERP by means of time-frequency analysis. Also Park (2007) conducted the first functional imaging studies of culture and cognition. Park's group found different neural activation when East Asians were compared with Westerners. In her work she also found an increase in brain regions associated with spatial perception in a study of London taxi drivers.

To increase understanding of the impact of culture upon negotiating styles, further research should examine the effect of deliberative cognitive styles on a range of other behaviors. For example, it would be worthwhile to understand culture's impact upon the phenomenon of tolerance for ambiguity. Do cultures exhibiting a more deliberative cognitive style have higher or lower tolerance for ambiguity? Further aspects of decision-making practices and processes should also be examined. Besides studies aimed at investigating the range of influence, more work is needed to understand the relationship between syntax and neurophysiologic functioning. What has been done in this area has only begun to scratch the surface. A second area for further research will involve methodological advances allowing examination of real-time neurophysiologic effects doing ongoing negotiations. Recent negotiation research has used a methodology which allows measurement of responses by negotiators engaged in actual negotiations with a 'counterpart' who is actually simulated by the computer (for example, Van Kleef et al., 2006). By measuring brain wave activity during a simulated negotiation, future research can provide more refined understanding of how negotiators with differing cognitive styles would respond to identical negotiation prompts and parameters.

Clearly, utilization of this 'new' language code is essential in such business activities as cross-cultural negotiations and marketing and sales. More fundamentally, it is critical in the transference of business knowledge. Kedia and Bhagat (1988) note that there are three types of knowledge transfer: product-embodied, process-embodied and person-embodied. It is in the latter two cases where an understanding of the code becomes invaluable. Perhaps, just as researchers such as Hofstede (1980) have constructed ordinal scales to position behavioral tendencies of different cultures relative to one another, future research might attempt a similar ranking of brain language processing across cultures.

The marriage between the work of Hofstede and others with the knowledge gained from brain physiology provides an opportunity to address and better understand differences in negotiating style. Hoftstede's (1980) work is based on attitudinal measures of cultural tendencies. Extending this study, we are beginning to supply the biological underpinnings for these attitudinal observations. Such knowledge should facilitate better communication and thus more opportunity for integrative solutions in cross-cultural negotiations. For example, a better understanding by negotiators of language syntax may provide a more nuanced understanding of a counterpart's cognitive processes, and thus promote more tolerance and less anxiety. An American negotiator confronting a German negotiator's more deliberative style may better understand that this slower style is indicative of the German negotiator's cognitive processing tendencies rather than an attempt by the negotiator to intentionally slow down the process. A German negotiator, confronting the American's more direct, fast-paced style, may better understand the need to explicitly ask for more time to make a better decision. Both negotiators will be better able to understand the cultural base for different styles, rather than imputing a negative motivation to their counterpart. This more nuanced cultural knowledge may lead to an increased possibility of integrative negotiation outcomes.

An awareness of the impact of culture on perception and cognition must be taken into consideration by business negotiators. A 'crash course' in cultural differences, as some corporations provide, is not enough for global negotiators. What is needed is a respect for cultural differences and a deep-seated appreciation for language differences in order to avoid cultural miscues.

REFERENCES

Adair, W.L. and J.M. Brett (2005), 'The negotiation dance: time, culture, and behavioral sequences in negotiation', *Organization Science*, **16**, 33–51.
Adler, N.J. and J.L. Graham (1987), 'Business negotiations: Canadians are not just like Americans', *Canadian Journal of Administrative Science*, **4**, 211–38.
Adler, N.J., J.L. Graham and T.S. Gehrke (1987), 'Business negotiations in Canada, Mexico, and the US', *Journal of Business Research*, **15** (4), 411–29.
Adler, N.J., R. Brahm and J.L. Graham (1992), 'Strategy implementation: a comparison of face-to-face negotiations in the People's Republic of China and the United States', *Strategic Management Journal*, **13**, 449–66.
Adolphs, R. (2003), 'Cognitive neuroscience of human social behavior', *Neuroscience Reviews*, **4**, 165–78.
Allerheiligen, R., J.L. Graham and C.-Y. Lin (1985), 'Honesty in interorganizational negotiations in the United States, Japan, Brazil, and the Republic of China', *Journal of Macromarketing*, **5**, 4–16.
Armour-Thomas, E. and S. Gopaul-McNicol (1998), *Assessing Intelligence: Applying a Bio-Cultural Model*, Thousand Oaks, CA: Sage Publications.
Bazerman, M.H. and J.S. Carroll (1987), 'Negotiator cognition', *Research in Organizational Behavior*, **9**, 247–88.
Bazerman, M.H. and M.A. Neale (1983), 'Heuristics in negotiation: limitations to effective dispute resolution', in M.H. Bazerman and R.J. Lewicki (eds), *Negotiating in Organizations*, Beverly Hills, CA: Sage.
Brett, J.M. (2001), *Negotiating Globally: How to Negotiate Deals, Resolve Disputes, and Make Decisions Across Cultural Boundaries*, San Francisco, CA: Jossey-Bass.
Bruner, J. (1996), *The Culture of Education*, Cambridge, MA: Harvard University Press.
Cacioppo, J.T. and G.G. Bernston (1992), 'Social psychological contributions to the decade of the brain: doctrine of multilevel analysis', *American Psychologist*, **47**, 1019–28.
Cacioppo, J.T., G.G. Berntson, T.S. Lorig, C.J. Norris, E. Rickett and H. Nusbaum (2003), 'Just because you're imaging the brain doesn't mean you can stop using your head: a primer and set of first principles', *Journal of Personality and Social Psychology*, **85**, 650–61.
Cacioppo, J.T., D.G. Amaral, J.J. Blanchard et al. (2007), 'Social neuroscience: progress and implications for mental health', *Perspectives on Psychological Science*, **2** (2), 99–123.
Chua, E.G. and W.B. Gudykunst (1987), 'Conflict resolution styles in low- and high-context cultures', *Communication Research Reports*, **4**, 32–7.
Crick, F. and C. Koch (1997), 'Towards a neurobiological theory of consciousnesses', in N. Block, O. Flanagan and G. Guzeldere (eds), *The Nature of Consciousness*, Cambridge, MA: MIT Press, pp. 277–92.
Damasio, A. (1999), *The Feeling of What Happens: Body and Emotion in the Making of Consciousness*, San Diego, CA: Harcourt.
Durkheim, E. (1947), *The Elementary Forms of Religious Life*, New York: The Free Press.
Friederici, A.D. and S. Frisch (2000), 'Verb argument structure processing: the role of verb-specific and argument-specific information', *Journal of Memory and Language*, **43**, 476–507.

Gelfand, M.J. and J.M. Brett (eds) (2004), *The Handbook of Negotiation and Culture*, Palo Alto, CA: Stanford Business Books.
Gelfand, M.J. and M.J. Christakopoulou (1999), 'Culture and negotiator cognition: judgment accuracy and negotiation processes in individualistic and collectivistic cultures', *Organizational Behavior and Human Decision Processes*, **79**, 248–69.
Gelfand, M.J. and N. Dyer (2000), 'A cultural perspective on negotiation: progress, pitfalls, and prospects', *Applied Psychology: An International Review*, **49**, 62–99.
Gelfand, M.J., L.H. Nishii, K.M. Holcombe, N. Dyer, K. Ohbuchi and M. Fukuno (2001), 'Cultural influences on cognitive representations of conflict: interpretations of conflict episodes in the United States and Japan', *Journal of Applied Psychology*, **86**, 1059–74.
Gelfand, M.J., M. Erez and Z. Aycan (2007), 'Cross-cultural organizational behavior', *Annual Review of Psychology*, **58**, 479–514.
Gonzalez, C., J. Dana, H. Koshino and M. Just (2005), 'The framing effect and risky decisions: examining cognitive functions with fMRI', *Journal of Economic Psychology*, **26**, 1–20.
Graham, J.L. (1985), 'The influence of culture on the process of business negotiations: an exploratory study', *Journal of International Business Studies*, **16**, 81–96.
Graham, J.L., L.I. Evenko and M.N. Rajan (1993), 'An empirical comparison of Soviet and American business negotiations', *International Journal of Business Studies*, **23**, 387–418.
Hagoort, P., C. Brown and J. Groothusen (1993), 'The syntactic positive shift (SPS) as an ERP measure of syntactic processing', *Language and Cognitive Processes*, **8**, 439–83.
Haig, A., E. Gordon, J. Wright, R. Meares and H. Bahramali (2000), 'Gamma-band EEGs predict autonomic responses during mental arithmetic', *Neuroreport*, **11** (4), 669–75.
Hald, L.A., M.C.M. Bastiaansen and P. Hagoort (2006), 'EEG theta and gamma responses to semantic violations in online sentence processing', *Brain and Language*, **96**, 90–105.
Hall, E. and M. Hall (1990), *Understanding Cultural Differences: Germans, French and Americans*, Yarmouth, ME: Intercultural Press.
Hampden-Turner, C. and F. Trompenaars (1993), *The Seven Cultures of Capitalism*, Garden City, NY: Doubleday.
Hofstede, G. (1980), *Culture's Consequences: International Differences in Work-related Values*, Thousand Oaks, CA: Sage.
Hofstede, G. (1991), *Cultures and Organizations: Software of the Mind*, Berkshire, UK: McGraw-Hill.
Hofstede, G. and D. Bond (1988), 'The Confucius connection: from cultural roots to economic growth', *Organizational Dynamics*, **16**, 4–21.
Kaan, E., R. Wayland, M. Bao and C. Barkley (2007), 'Effects of native language and training on lexical tone perception: an event-related potential study', *Brain Research*, **1148**, 113–22.
Kedia, B. and R. Bhagat (1988), 'Cultural constraints on transfer of technology across nations: implications for research in international and comparative management', *Academy of Management Review*, **13**, 559–71.
Knight, R.T., D.L. Woods and D. Scabini (1993), 'Anatomical substrates of

auditory selective attention: behavioral and electrophysiological effects of posterior association cortex lesions', *Cognitive Brain Research*, **1**, 227–40.

Kotik-Friedgut, B. (2006), 'Development of the lurian approach: a cultural neurolinguistic perspective', *Neuropsychology Review*, **16** (1), 43–51.

Kramsch, C. (1993), *Context and Culture in Language Teaching*, Oxford: Oxford University Press.

Krause, C., P. Grönholm, A. Leinonen, M. Laine, A. Säkkinen and C. Söderholm (2006), 'Modality matters: the effects of stimulus modality on the 4- to 30-Hz brain electric oscillations during a lexical decision task', *Brain Research*, **1110**, 182–92.

Kutas, M. and C.K. Van Petten (1994), 'Psycholinguistics electrified: event-related brain potential investigations', in M.A. Gernsbaccher (ed.), *Handbook of Psycholinguistics*, San Diego, CA: Academic Press, pp. 83–143.

Luria, A.R. (1970), 'The functional organization of the brain', *Scientific American*, **222** (3), 66–78.

Llinas, R. and D. Pare (1996), 'The brain as a closed system modulated by the senses', *The Mind–Brain Continuum: Sensory Processes*, Cambridge, MA: MIT Press, pp. 1–18.

Markus, H.R. and S. Kitayama (1991), 'Culture and the self: implications for cognition, emotion, and motivation', *Psychological Review*, **98**, 224–53.

McCarthy, J.F., K. Horne and M. O'Connor (2002), '40-hz event-related potential as a measure of linguistic comprehension', International Academy of Linguistics Behavioral and Social Sciences, Las Vegas, Nevada.

Morris, M.W. and M.J. Gelfand (2004), 'Cultural differences and cognitive dynamics: expanding the cognitive perspective on negotiation', in M.J. Gelfand and J.M. Brett (eds), *The Handbook of Negotiation and Culture*, Palo Alto, CA: Stanford Business Books, pp. 45–70.

Nisbett, R.E., K. Peng, I. Choi and A. Norenzayan (2001), 'Culture and systems of thought: holistic versus analytic cognition', *Psychological Review*, **108** (2), 291–310.

Nobre, A.C. and G. McCarthy (1995), 'Language-related field potentials in the anterior–medial temporal lobe: II. Effects of word type and semantic priming', *Journal of Neuroscience*, **15**, 1090–99.

Park, D.C. (2007), 'Eastern brain/western brain: neuroimaging cultural differences in cognition', Association for Psychological Science, Washington, DC.

Pearson, V.M.S. and W.G. Stephan (1998) 'Preferences for styles of negotiation: a comparison of Brazil and the US', *International Journal of Intercultural Relations*, **22**, 67–83.

Pinkley, R.L. (1990), 'Dimensions of conflict frame: disputant interpretations of conflict', *Journal of Applied Psychology*, **75**, 117–26.

Pruitt, D.G. and P.J. Carnevale (1993), *Negotiation in Social Conflict*, Buckingham: Open University Press.

Reinvang, I. (1999), 'Cognitive event-related potentials in neuropsychological assessment', *Neuropsychology Review*, **9**, 231–48.

Rogoff, B. (1990), *Apprenticeship in Thinking: Cognitive Development in Social Context*, New York: Oxford University Press.

Salzmann, Z. (2003), *Language, Culture and Society: An Introduction to Linguistic Anthropology*, Boulder, CO: Westview Press.

Sanfey, A.G. (2007), 'Decision neuroscience: new directions in studies of judgment and decision making', *Current Directions in Psychological Science*, **16**, 151–5.

Schwartz, S.H. (1992), 'Universal in the content and structure of values: theoretical advances and empirical tests in 20 countries', in M. Zanna (ed.), *Advances in Experimental Psychology*, Vol. 25, Orlando, FL: Academic Press, pp. 1–65.

Schwartz, S.H. (1994), 'Beyond individualism/collectivism: new cultural dimensions of values', in U. Kim, H.C. Triandis, C. Kagitcibasi, S.-C. Choi, and G. Yoon (eds), *Individualism and Collectivism: Theory, Method, and Applications*, Thousand Oaks, CA: Sage, pp. 85–122.

Tan, L., A. Chan, P. Kay, P. Khong, L. Yip and K. Luke (2008), 'Language affects patterns of brain activation associated with perceptual decision', *PNAS Proceedings of the National Academy of Sciences of the United States of America*, **105** (10), 4004–9.

Thanasoulas, D. (2001), 'The importance of teaching culture in the foreign language classroom', *Radical Pedagogy*, **3**, available at http://radicalpedagogy. icaap.org.

Thompson, L. (1990), 'Negotiation behavior and outcomes: empirical evidence and theoretical issues', *Psychological Bulletin*, **108**, 515–32.

Ting-Toomey, S. (1986), 'Conflict styles in black and white subjective cultures', in Y.Y. Kim (ed.), *Current Research in Interethnic Communication*, Beverly Hills, CA: Sage, pp. 75–89.

Ting-Toomey, S., G. Gao, P. Trubisky et al. (1991), 'Culture, face maintenance, and styles of handling interpersonal conflict: a study of five cultures', *International Journal of Conflict Management*, **2**, 275–92.

Tinsley, C.H. (1998), 'Models of conflict resolution in Japanese, German, and American cultures', *Journal of Applied Psychology*, **83**, 316–23.

Tinsley, C.H. (2001), 'How negotiators get to yes: predicting the constellation of strategies used across cultures to negotiate conflict', *Journal of Applied Psychology*, **86**, 583–93.

Torrence, C. and G.P. Compo (1998), 'A practical guide to wavelet analysis', *Bulletin of the American Meteorological Society*, **79** (1), 61–78.

Van Kleef, G.A., C.K.W. De Dreu and S.R. Manstead (2006), 'Supplication and appeasement in conflict and negotiation: the interpersonal effects of disappointment, worry, guilt, and regret', *Journal of Personality and Social Psychology*, **91**, 124–42.

Vygotsky, L. (1986), *Thought and Language*, newly revised and edited by A. Kozulin, Cambridge, MA: MIT Press.

Vygotsky, L. (1987), 'Thinking and speech', in R.W. Rieber and A.S. Carton (eds), *The Collected Works of L.S. Vygotsky* (trans. by N. Minick), New York: Plenum Press.

Weiss, T. (1992), 'A conceptual framework for intercultural/international communication', Paper presented at the Annual Eastern Michigan University Conference on Languages and Communication for World Business and the Professions, 11th, Ypsilanti, Michigan, 25–28 March, p. 6.

Willems, R., R. Oostenveld and P. Hagoort (2008), 'Early decreases in alpha and gamma band power distinguish linguistic from visual information during spoken sentence comprehension', *Brain Research*, **1219**, 78–90.

15. Brain and human behavior in organizations: a field of neuro-organizational behavior

Constant D. Beugré

INTRODUCTION

This chapter introduces a new field, neuro-organizational behavior (neuro-OB), defined as the study of the impact of brain structures on human behavior in organizations. The reason for incorporating the effects of the brain in the study of human behavior in organizations is perhaps best symbolized by White's (1992) assertion that a science of human life that ignores the brain is akin to a study of the solar system that leaves out the sun. There is also an increased attention toward understanding the neurobiology of decision making although the organizational science literature has been slow in responding to such research interest. Although organizational scholars have given pre-eminence to mental processes, they have limited their effort to cognitive processes (information processing, memory, perception) or emotional arousal (anger, frustration, resentment) in explaining behavior in organizations. As a consequence, there has been a missing cognitive neuroscience perspective in organization study (Butler and Senior, 2007).

Recently, however, Lee and Chamberlain (2007) introduced the concept of organizational cognitive neuroscience to refer to the study of the processes within the brain that underlie or influence human decisions, behaviors and interactions within organizations or in response to organizational manifestations or institutions. Studying the brain is essential to understanding how people make decisions as managers, employees, customers and economic agents. If understanding the brain is important in explaining human behavior, then three main questions arise: (1) What are the neural bases of behaviors displayed in the workplace? (2) Can a neuroscientific approach add new insights to our understanding of human behaviors in organizations? (3) Can knowledge using a neuroscientific perspective help to improve management practice?

The purpose of this chapter is to address these questions. In so doing, the chapter proposes a new field, neuro-OB, which is at the intersection of cognitive psychology, organizational behavior, neuroscience, social cognitive neuroscience and the emerging field of neuroeconomics (Camerer, 2007; Camerer et al., 2004; Glimcher, 2003; Glimcher et al., 2009; Lowenstein et al., 2008). Although the study of the role of the brain in management decision is not entirely new, incorporating the disparate bodies of knowledge into a coherent conceptual framework constitutes somewhat of a novelty and sets the premise for neuro-OB. I am in no way claiming to have 'invented' a new field; rather, in this chapter I am attempting to develop an integrative paradigm that paves the way for conceptual, empirical and experimental research on the role of the brain in organizational behavior. This is particularly important because the building block of human behavior is really the human brain. In fact, organizational behavior scholars study issues and topics that describe the actions of people in organizations populated by other people. Similarly, research in neuroeconomics and social cognitive neuroscience focuses on the neural basis of phenomena, such as fairness, trust, cooperation and decision making that are of interest to organizational scholars.

Developing a field of neuro-OB may have implications for both theory and practice. From a theoretical standpoint, a field of neuro-OB may help to improve our understanding of how people make decisions in the workplace. Specifically, such a field may help to explain how the brain influences the types of behaviors people display in work settings. Not only will organizational scholars explore which brain structures are responsible for particular behaviors, but they may also develop strategies to predict them. From the practical standpoint, a field of neuro-OB may help managers to better understand employee behavior in the workplace. For instance, knowing that pressures to meet looming deadlines activate brain regions that are responsible for emotional reactions may help managers to delay their decisions or seek inputs from others to avoid making rash decisions. The chapter is organized as follows. First, I delineate the field of neuro-OB. Next, I explore the potential domains of interest for organizational researchers intended to use a neuroscientific perspective in their research. I then discuss the research and management implications of neuro-OB.

DELINEATING THE FIELD OF NEURO-OB

Although the field of neuro-OB does not exist yet, I provide a working definition that may help to delineate it from other fields, such as organizational behavior, neuroscience, cognitive psychology, social cognitive neuroscience and neuroeconomics. Neuro-OB refers to the study of the

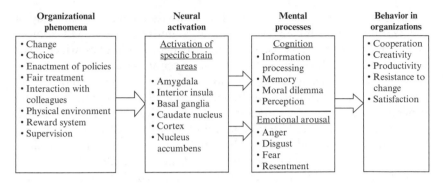

Organizational phenomena	Neural activation	Mental processes	Behavior in organizations
• Change • Choice • Enactment of policies • Fair treatment • Interaction with colleagues • Physical environment • Reward system • Supervision	<u>Activation of specific brain areas</u> • Amygdala • Interior insula • Basal ganglia • Caudate nucleus • Cortex • Nucleus accumbens	<u>Cognition</u> • Information processing • Memory • Moral dilemma • Perception <u>Emotional arousal</u> • Anger • Disgust • Fear • Resentment	• Cooperation • Creativity • Productivity • Resistance to change • Satisfaction

Figure 15.1   Neural basis of organizational behavior

impact of the brain on behavior that occurs in organizations, profit or non-profit. Defined as such, neuro-OB is different from organizational behavior in so far that it uses a neuroscientific perspective in the study of human behavior in organizations. Organizational behavior is generally defined as the study of human behavior in organizations. Thus, it is an aggregation of anthropological, economic, political science, psychological and sociological knowledge. Neuro-OB includes three levels of analysis, neural, cognitive and behavioral. The neural level focuses on identifying the brain regions that are activated when organizational members display particular types of behavior. The cognitive level concerns internal mental processes that rely on these neural substrates, such as memory and information processing (Lee and Chamberlain, 2007), and the behavioral level concerns behaviors displayed by organizational members.

Figure 15.1 indicates that organizational phenomena activate the neural circuitry. Specific brain regions may be activated by particular organizational events. Such neural activation leads to mental processes including cognitions and emotional arousal. Some brain regions are involved in cognitive processes, whereas others are implicated in emotional arousal. For instance, the ventromedial prefrontal cortex, the nucleus accumbens and the amygdala have been linked to affective processing (Damasio, 1994), whereas the prefrontal cortex is concerned with planning for the long term and representing anticipation of future events. Thus, neuro-OB considers the neural circuitry as the point of departure for explaining human behavior in organizations.

Neuro-OB is different from cognitive psychology and social cognitive neuroscience. The goal of cognitive psychology is to understand the underlying mental architecture that supports cognitive functions (Poldrack, 2006). Social cognitive neuroscience combines the tools of cognitive neuroscience with questions and theories from various social sciences (Lieberman, 2007, p. 260). It encompasses the empirical study of the neural mechanisms underlying social cognitive processes (Blakemore et al., 2004). Neuro-OB is also different from neuroeconomics, which deals with the study of the impact of the brain on economic decisions (Camerer et al., 2004; Glimcher, 2003). Neuroeconomics merges methods from neuroscience and economics to better understand how the human brain generates decisions in economic and social contexts (Fehr et al., 2005). Thus, neuro-OB is a multidisciplinary discipline that draws its knowledge and methods from cognitive psychology, neuroeconomics, neuroscience, organizational behavior and social cognitive neuroscience.

Although neuro-OB is different from the allied disciplines described above, it shares some commonalities with them. All these disciplines rely on neuroscientific methods to explain human behavior. Neuro-OB may be considered as the application of neuroeconomics and social cognitive neuroscience theories to the workplace. For instance, the topics of fairness, reciprocity and trust are studied in neuroeconomics and social cognitive neuroscience. The difference, however, is that neuro-OB focuses on these topics within organizations. Applying such concepts in organizational settings is particularly important because people spend most of their adult lives as members of organizations. In fact, work is a central element of an individual's personal identity. Neuro-OB is embedded in organizational behavior, neuroeconomics and social cognitive neuroscience. Having delineated the field of neuro-OB, I now turn to its domain of interest.

RESEARCH QUESTIONS IN NEURO-OB

Almost all topics studied in organizational behavior, neuroeconomics and social cognitive neuroscience can be explored by neuro-OB because the ability of researchers to directly observe brain activity has recently increased. Discussing all of them is beyond the scope of this chapter, particularly due to space constraints. I will therefore focus on those that have received research attention in neuroeconomics and social cognitive neuroscience, two fields close to neuro-OB. Specifically, I will discuss the neural foundations of fairness, ethics and moral cognition, motivation and incentives, trust and cooperation, change and uncertainty to the extent that these phenomena are ubiquitous within modern organizations. Moreover, they have received increased attention in the literature in neuroeconomics and social cognitive neuroscience that are contributive disciplines to neuro-OB.

It is well established that the search for reward and the avoidance of punishment is a common behavior observed in humans. Such behaviors also occur in the workplace. There is evidence that the search for pleasurable outcomes and the avoidance of painful ones may have neural bases. Two questions are relevant when exploring the neural basis of organizational behavior. First, could a neuroscientific approach advance our understanding of human behavior in organizations? Second, could knowledge gleaned from the use of neuroscientific methods improve management practice? Before answering these two questions, I review the extant literature on the neural basis of behaviors that are of interest to organizational behavior scholars. Because neuroscientific investigation of organizational behavior is still lacking, I will rely on the extant literature on neuroeconomics and social cognitive neuroscience with the intent of applying it to organizational settings.

THE NEURAL BASIS OF FAIRNESS

Research in neuroeconomics demonstrates that the anterior insula is activated when facing situations leading to decisions of fairness or unfairness and to emotional responses, such as pain and disgust (Sanfey et al., 2003). Knoch et al. (2006) showed that disruption of the right but not the left, dorsolateral prefrontal cortex (DLPFC), by low-frequency repetitive transcranial magnetic stimulation, substantially reduces participants' willingness to reject their partners' intentionally unfair offers in the Ultimatum Game. However, the participants in the experiment still judge such offers as unfair. The authors interpret these results by concluding that the right DLPFC plays a key role in the implementation of fairness-related behaviors. Fairness also activates the ventromedial prefrontal cortex (VMPFC) (McCabe et al., 2001), whereas unfairness activates the dorsomedial prefrontal cortex (Decety et al., 2004). Tabibnia et al. (2008) found that the orbitofrontal cortex was associated with fairness preferences. 'A basic sense of fairness and unfairness is essential to many aspects of societal and personal decision-making and underlies notions as diverse as ethics, social policy, legal practice, and personal morality' (Sanfey et al., 2003, p. 1757). However, fairness is not the only behavior that has been proven to have a neural basis. Research evidence also shows a neural basis for ethics and moral cognitions, behaviors that are fundamental in organizational settings.

THE NEURAL BASIS OF ETHICS AND MORAL COGNITIONS IN ORGANIZATIONS

Reynolds (2006) proposed a neurocognitive model of ethics in which he emphasizes the role of neurons in assessing ethical decisions. He specifically notes that 'cognitive models with their insistence on linear progression or movements from stage to stage, are incapable of explaining why managers "know," without being able to explain why, that a particular course of action is ethical and another is not' (ibid., p. 742). Cohen (2005) notes that personal moral dilemmas activate the medial prefrontal cortex (MPFC) associated with emotional arousal, whereas impersonal moral dilemmas elicit activity in the prefrontal cortex, which is associated with cognitive processes. Prehn et al. (2008) contend that both cognitive and emotional components play an important role in formulating moral judgments. Moll et al. (2002) demonstrate that viewing moral and non-moral pleasant visual stimuli activates a common network of brain areas that includes the amygdala, the orbitofrontal cortex (OFC), the medial frontal gyrus (MedFG) and the cortex surrounding the right posterior temporal sulcus (pSTS). Thus, people may develop 'moral prototypes' against which incoming stimuli are compared. Moll et al. (2008) found that the DLPFC, the anterior prefrontal cortex, the mPFC, the VMPFC and the superior temporal sulcus region (STS) are implicated in moral cognition and behavior.

THE NEURAL BASIS OF REWARDS

Brain regions involved in reward include the ventral striatum, the DLPFC, the orbital prefrontal cortex, the nucleus accumbens and the amygdala. Neuroeconomic evidence indicates that people develop a propensity to experience direct pain when they spend money (Camerer et al., 2004; McClure et al., 2004). When participants earned money by responding correctly to a stimulus rather than just receiving equivalent rewards with no effort, there was a greater activity in the striatum – a reward region of the brain. Earned money is more rewarding in the brain than unearned money (Camerer et al., 2004). These findings may have direct implications for managers. Tying compensation to performance may be more rewarding for employees than compensation that is not performance based. The expectation of a reward is likely to stimulate the nucleus accumbens. In organizational settings the prospect of a pay increase or a promotion may motivate employees. Dickhaut et al. (2003) found more activity in the OFC when thinking about gains compared to losses, and more activity in the inferior parietal and cerebellar areas when thinking about losses. When people experience pleasure or anticipate pleasure, the nucleus accumbens is activated. The insula is activated when people experience pain, taste something bad, anticipate pain or see a disgusting picture.

People respond to monetary incentives because the limbic system quickly gets used to new stimuli and reacts only to the unexpected, such as a financial windfall (Camerer et al., 2004; McClure et al., 2004). Unexpected rewards or rewards higher than expected produce a phasic increase in the firing rate of the dopamine neurons at the time of their delivery (Caldú and Dreher, 2007). Applied to work settings, employees may respond to bonuses and rewards that are unexpected because they activate the brain's reward circuitry. The 'juice reward' experiment may apply to organizational settings. Promising a pay increase, a bonus or a promotion in exchange for good performance may motivate employees to work harder to the extent that the expectation of reward is likely to stimulate the nucleus accumbens – the seat of dopamine receptors. The expectation of reward is so powerful that people tend to downplay the potential risks when they see opportunities for large rewards. We must acknowledge, however, that there are non-monetary incentives that activate the brain's reward circuitry. Research shows that cooperation engages several areas from the brain reward circuitry including the nucleus accumbens, the caudate nucleus and the VMPFC. Tabibnia and Lieberman (2007) note that fairness and cooperation are rewarding in themselves to the extent that they activate the brain's reward circuitry.

THE NEURAL BASIS OF TRUST AND COOPERATION IN ORGANIZATIONS

Many relations in the workplace depend on trust and cooperation. Indeed, humans are biologically endowed to engage in exchanges, which require trust and cooperation. These two forms of social interactions are believed to have neural underpinnings as demonstrated by research in neuro-economics. McCabe et al. (2001) found that players who cooperated more often with others showed increased activation in Broadman area 10 and in the thalamus. The trust game in neuroeconomics may account for the role of the brain in trust. The game involves a trustee and an investor. Berg et al. (1995) developed the trust game. In this game two players are randomly and anonymously matched, one as investor and the other as trustee. The amount sent by the investor is considered as a measure of trust and the amount returned by the trustee is a measure of trustworthiness. Trust is required in the workplace for collaborative work, such as teamwork or commitment to an organization. For example, equity theory (Adams, 1965) suggests that employees believe that their outcomes should be proportional to their inputs compared to relevant others. The occurrence of such events would lead to trust. The reciprocation of trust would be for employees to work hard and show commitment and loyalty to their organization. Whereas fairness and trust elicit reciprocation, unfairness and distrust engender non-reciprocation.

NEURAL BASIS OF CHANGE AND UNCERTAINTY IN ORGANIZATIONS

Why do people resist change? Are there neural underpinnings of resistance to change? Do people resist change because the human brain is wired to do so? Change involves situations of uncertainty where the likelihood of different outcomes is unknown. Such uncertainty may activate particular brain regions. Camerer et al. (2004) describe the amygdala as an internal 'hypochondriac' which provides quick and dirty emotional signals in response to potential fears (p. 561). The amygdala is a brain structure implicated in many different kinds of phenomena, such as attitudes, stereotyping, person perception and emotion (Ochsner and Lieberman, 2001). Another brain region that is implicated in reactions to uncertainty is the insula. The insula is a region that processes information from the nervous system about bodily states, such as physical pain, hunger, the pain of social exclusion, disgusting odors and choking (Camerer et al., 2004, p. 568). This suggests a neural basis of 'fear of the unknown' influencing choices (Camerer et al., 2004). Applied to organizational settings, one may speculate that the anterior insula may be involved when people face change. Specifically, it may help to explain employee resistance to change. To the extent that change increases uncertainty and 'fear of the unknown', it may activate the anterior insula. The prefrontal cortex is also involved in uncertainty and change. It is considered as the seat of willpower – the ability to take the long-term perspective in evaluating risks and rewards (Morse, 2006). Thus, its activation may provide a means for employees to anticipate change and thereby respond to it in a more positive way.

When faced with uncertainty, these brain regions may be activated, thereby eliciting defensive responses. Novel stimuli require more cognitive effort, whereas familiar situations require less cognitive effort. The construct of automaticity – one of the key functions of the brain – may help to better understand why people resist change. Automaticity implies that behaviors may become automatic and effortless. For example, experience and practice may cause a rather complex behavior to become automatic. As Camerer et al. (2004) note, 'When good performance becomes automatic (in the form of procedural knowledge), it is typically hard to articulate, which means human capital of this sort is difficult to reproduce by teaching others' (p. 560). Automaticity may also help to explain the extent to which it is difficult to share tacit knowledge in organizations. It may also account for the role of experience in learning and performance to the extent that the existence of prototypes may play an important role in this process. People compare new events to prototypes already stored in memory. In explaining how entrepreneurs recognize opportunities for new ventures, Baron (2006) notes that experienced, repeat entrepreneurs generally search for opportunities in areas or industries where they are already knowledgeable. Such a comparison helps individuals make decisions fast and effortless for familiar situations, whereas novel ones require more cognitive effort.

Neuroscientific evidence shows that the basal ganglia is activated when people perform routine tasks, whereas change activates the amygdala and the orbital frontal cortex, which leads to emotional expressions. Thus, people may resist change because adopting new processes would require the involvement of the prefrontal cortex, which requires more cognitive effort. The adoption of new processes may also involve possible gains as well as losses. To the extent that people are more sensitive to losses than gains (Kahneman and Tversky, 1979) they may tend to resist new situations where the potential for loss may well exist. These findings demonstrate that research in organizational change could benefit from a neuroscientific perspective. By exploiting the type of knowledge about brain organization and function, and determining which brain systems are associated with a particular behavior, researchers may be able to better understand the behavior (Cohen, 2005).

NEURAL BASIS OF COGNITION AND EMOTION IN ORGANIZATIONS

Classical economics emphasizes the rational choice model. However, research in behavioral economics and particularly neuroeconomics has presented evidence to the contrary. Such research has demonstrated that emotions play a key role in decision making. Pillutla and Murnighan (1996) and Van Winden (2007) suggest that punishment in a game like the Ultimatum Game is more driven by anger about the appropriation of resources than a concern for fairness, indicating that emotions guide such behavior. As Phelps (2006) put it, the neural circuitry of emotion and cognition interact from early perception to decision making and reasoning. Damasio (1994), Bechara and Damasio (2005) and Glimcher et al. (2007) show that emotions play an important role in decisions. The somatic marker hypothesis (Bechara et al., 1999; Damasio, 1994), suggests that decision making is a process that deeply depends on emotions. In a study using the gambling task, Bechara et al. (1999) found that patients with amygdala damage as well as those with VMPFC damage were impaired on the gambling task and unable to develop anticipatory skin conductance responses (SCRs) while they ponder risky choices. However, patients with VMPFC were able to generate SCRs when they received a reward or a punishment unlike patients with amygdala damage.

Implications for Research and Practice

Neuro-OB intends to focus on the neural basis of human behavior in organizations. In so doing, it contends that the analysis of work behavior should start at the neural level, a layer of analysis that has been missing in the extant literature in organizational behavior. This approach may offer opportunities for new research insights as well as guidelines for management practice.

Implications for Research

Neuro-OB may offer several research opportunities by borrowing theories and techniques from neuroscience, neuroeconomics and social cognitive neuroscience. The chapter has outlined some of the behaviors whose neural underpinnings may illuminate research in neuro-OB. By using a neuro-scientific approach, organizational scholars could look inside the 'black box' to better explore management decisions and employee behavior. Research in neuro-OB could also help to explain the reasons why some managers may prefer short-term versus long-term planning. An understanding of the human brain and its impact on decision-making may help organizational scholars to better explain such decisions. Second, neuro-OB could help organizational scholars to better analyze employee reactions to work events. Why do some incentives motivate employees, while others do not? Similarly, how do employees react to situations of fairness and unfairness? Do experiences of fairness stimulate the same brain structures than experiences of unfairness? Neuro-OB could also contribute to knowledge about creativity in organizations to the extent that 'we know too little about what circumstances or organizational conditions are necessary to unleash and promote creativity, and how one optimizes creativity from an organizational point of view' (Coates, 2003, p. 8). Looking inside the brain could contribute to the advancement of knowledge related to human behavior at work.

However, knowledge about the role of the human brain in organizational behavior cannot be accumulated without sound experimental and/ or empirical studies. Thus, organizational scholars should familiarize themselves with neuroscientific tools, such as electro-encephalogram (EEG), functional magnetic resonance imaging (fMRI) and position emission tomography (PET). One of the older techniques, EEG, measures electrical activity on the outside of the brain using scale electrodes. However, it does not directly measure internal brain activity. fMRI uses magnetic resonance imaging to measure oxygenated blood flow in the brain, which is correlated with neural input, whereas PET injects a radioactive solution in which glucose is a more direct correlate of neural activity (Camerer, 2007). 'fMRI and PET are good for roughly identifying areas that are active in a task. Once candidate circuits are established, it is useful to ask whether behavior is changed when parts of the circuit are broken or disrupted' (ibid., p. C30). These methods can be divided between those measuring electromagnetic activity of the brain and those sensitive to changes in cerebral blood flow or metabolism. EEG is part of the former, whereas PET and fMRI are part of the latter.

Despite their sophistication and their ability to provide valuable information about the role of brain structures in management decisions, these techniques present two major limitations. The first limitation is that they rely on reverse inference in which the engagement of a particular cognitive process is inferred from the activation of a particular brain region. Reverse inference reasons backward from the presence of brain activation to the engagement of a particular cognitive function (Poldrack, 2006). Although such inferences are not deductively valid, they can still provide some useful information (ibid.). According to Poldrack (2006), there are two ways in which to improve confidence in reverse inferences: (1) increase the selectivity of response on the brain region of interest and (2) increase the prior probability of the cognitive process in question. Confidence in reverse inference can also be increased by focusing on the convergence of evidence from multiple techniques and the activation in two or more regions thought to underlie the same mental processes, particularly if those regions are known to work together in a network (Tabibnia and Lieberman, 2007). The second limitation of these technologies is that they produce largely correlative measures of brain activity, making it difficult to examine the causal role of specific brain activations for choice behavior (Glimcher et al., 2009). To the extent that these technologies point out only correlations between brain activity and behavior, organizational scholars using them must be careful when drawing conclusions and/or making predictions. Research addressing the neural basis of organizational behavior could lead to the accumulation of knowledge that may prove useful for management practice.

Implications for Practice

Two recent articles in *Harvard Business Review* (Morse, 2006) and *HR Magazine* (Fox, 2008) indicate an emerging interest in the application of neuroscience and neuroeconomics knowledge to management practice. Morse (2006) notes that neuroscience can enhance managers' understanding of their own decisions to the extent that the brain is involved in several business decisions; whether negotiating an acquisition, hiring an employee, jockeying for a promotion, granting a loan or trusting a partner. Such understanding can result in better management of the decision-making process. Fox (2008) observes that neuroplasticity, the brain's ability to adapt, may account for employees' ability to change and learn new skills and technologies. However, the author advises that training should be repackaged with technology and conducted in small groups to improve retention. These two professional articles focusing on the role of the brain in advancing management practice suggest that neuro-OB could have practical implications in at least two areas: (1) management decision making and (2) understanding employee behavior. Neuro-OB could help managers to better assess their own decisions. When making strategic decisions, managers could realize that brain regions responsible for cognitions and emotional arousal may be implicated. They could use such awareness to better assess the extent to which their own decisions are a mix of rationality and emotionality. Thus, when they are emotionally aroused because of specific circumstances, managers could delay critical decisions or seek valuable inputs from others. Knowledge from neuro-OB could also help managers to better understand employee behavior and its causes. Research indicates that human beings may have a natural aversion for inequity (Cohen, 2005; Sanfey et al., 2003; Tabibnia et al., 2008). This inequity aversion is so strong that people are willing to sacrifice personal gains to prevent another person from receiving an inequitably better outcome (Fehr and Schmidt, 1999). Inequity aversion may lead to a desire to punish others who have acted unfairly. Such desire can skew decision-making (Morse, 2006).

Using such knowledge, managers could strive to create fair working environments, to the extent that such environments could foster trust, cooperation and creativity. Managers could also be sensitive to the role that emotions play in human behavior. Such knowledge could help managers to develop a theory of mind (Premack and Woodruff, 1978). Theory of mind refers to a person's ability to understand other people's motor intentions and actions, goals, beliefs and thoughts (Singer, 2009). It involves a network of brain areas including the STS, the mPFC and the temporal poles (ibid.). Theory of mind may help managers to better assess their employees' mental states and consequently deal with them in a more positive manner. Specifically, it may help managers to predict employee actions and reactions more accurately.

CONCLUSION

The main goal of neuro-OB is to build knowledge of human behavior in organizations that is grounded in management and organizational theory while using neuroscientific methods and techniques. It is construed as a sub-field of organizational behavior. Although the discipline of neuro-OB does not exist yet, it is my hope that the present chapter will spark interest in the role of brain structures in management decisions, making neuro-OB a field worthy of scientific inquiry. If successful, neuro-OB could help unify the biological sciences and the social sciences in explaining human behavior at work.

REFERENCES

Adams, S.J. (1965), 'Inequity in social exchange', in L. Berkowitz (ed.), *Advances in Experimental Social Psychology*, Vol. 2, New York: Academic Press, pp. 267–99.

Baron, R.A. (2006), 'Opportunity recognition as pattern recognition: how entrepreneurs "connect the dots" to identify new business opportunities', *Academy of Management Perspectives*, **20** (1), 104–19.

Bechara, A. and H. Damasio (2005), The somatic marker hypothesis. A neural theory of economic decisions', *Games and Economic Behavior*, **52** (2), 336–72.

Bechara, A., H. Damasio, A.R. Damasio and G.P. Lee (1999), 'Different contributions of the human amygdala and ventromedial prefrontal cortex to decision making', *Journal of Neuroscience*, **19**, 5473–81.

Berg, J., J. Dickhaut and K. McCabe (1995), 'Trust, reciprocity, and social history', *Games and Economic Behavior*, **10**, 122–42.

Blakemore, S.J., J. Winston and U. Frith (2004), 'Social cognitive neuroscience: where are we heading?', *Trends in Cognitive Sciences*, **8** (5), 216–22.

Butler, M.J.R. and C. Senior (2007), 'Toward an organizational cognitive neuroscience', in C. Senior and M.J.R. Butler (eds), *The Social Cognitive Neuroscience of Organizations, Annals of the New York Academy of Sciences*, Vol. 118, Boston, MA: Blackwell Publishing, pp. 1–17.

Caldú, X. and J.C. Dreher (2007), 'Hormonal and genetic influences on processing reward and social information', in C. Senior and M.J.R. Butler (eds), *The Social Cognitive Neuroscience of Organizations, Annals of the New York Academy of Sciences*, Vol. 118, Boston, MA: Blackwell Publishing, pp. 43–73.

Camerer, C.L. (2007), 'Neuroeconomics: using neuroscience to make economic predictions', *Economic Journal*, **117** (519), C26–C42.

Camerer, C.L., G. Loewenstein and D. Prelec (2004), 'Neuroeconomics: why economics needs brains', *Scandinavian Journal of Economics*, **106** (3), 555–79.

Coates, J.F. (2003), 'Brain science will change human resources', *Employee Relations Today*, Winter, 1–9.

Cohen, J.D. (2005), 'The vulcanization of the human brain: a neural perspective on interactions between cognition and emotion', *Journal of Economic Perspectives*, **19** (4), 3–24.

302   *Neuroeconomics and the firm*

Damasio, A.R. (1994), *Descartes' Error: Emotion, Reason, and the Human Brain*, London: Macmillan.
Decety, J., P.L. Jacksonm, J.A. Sommerville, T. Chaminade and A.N. Meltzoff (2004), 'The neural bases of cooperation and competition: an fMRI investigation', *Neuroimage*, **23**, 744–51.
Dickhaut, J., K. McCabe, J.C. Ngode, A. Rustichini and J.V. Pardo (2003), 'The impact of the certainty context on the process of choice', *Proceedings of the National Academy of Sciences of the United States of America*, **100**, 3536–41.
Fehr, E. and K.M. Schmidt (1999), A theory of fairness, competition, and cooperation', *Quarterly Journal of Economics*, **114**, 817–68.
Fehr, E., U. Fischbacher and M. Kosfeld (2005), 'Neuroeconomic foundations of trust and social preferences', *AEA Papers and Proceedings*, **95** (2), 346–51.
Fox, A. (2008), 'The brain at work', *HR Magazine*, March, 37–42.
Glimcher, P.W. (2003), *Decisions, Uncertainty, and the Brain, The Science of Neuroeconomics*, Cambridge, MA: MIT Press.
Glimcher, P.W., J. Kable and K. Louie (2007), 'Neuroeconomic studies of impulsivity: now or just as soon as possible?', *American Economic Review*, **97**, 142–7.
Glimcher, P.W., C.F. Camerer, E. Fehr and R.A. Poldrack (2009), 'Introduction: a brief history of neuroeconomics', in P.W. Glimcher, C.F. Camerer, E. Fehr and R.A. Poldrack (eds), *Neuroeconomics: Decision Making and the Brain*, New York: Academic Press, pp. 1–12.
Kahneman, D. and A. Tversky (1979), 'Prospect theory: an analysis of decision under uncertainty', *Econometrica*, **47**, 263–91.
Knoch, D., A. Pascual-Leone, K. Myer, V. Yreyer and E. Fehr (2006), 'Diminishing reciprocal fairness by disrupting the right prefrontal cortex', *Science*, **314** (5800), 829–32.
Lee, N. and L. Chamberlain (2007), 'Neuroimaging and psychophysiological measurement in organizational research', in C. Senior and M.J.R. Butler (eds), *The Social Cognitive Neuroscience of Organizations, Annals of the New York Academy of Sciences*, Vol. 118, Boston, MA: Blackwell Publishing, pp. 18–42.
Lieberman, M. (2007), 'Social cognitive neuroscience: a review of core processes', *Annual Review of Psychology*, **58** (1), 259–89.
Lowenstein, G., S. Rick and J.D. Cohen (2008), 'Neuroeconomics', *Annual Review of Psychology*, **59** (1), 647–72.
McCabe, K., D. Houser, L. Ryan, V. Smith and T. Trouard (2001), 'A functional imaging study of cooperation in two-person reciprocal exchange', *Proceedings of the National Academy of Sciences of the United States of America*, **98**, 11832–5.
McClure, S.M., D.I. Laibson, G. Loewenstein and J.D. Cohen (2004), 'Separate neural systems value immediate and delayed monetary rewards', *Science*, **306**, 503–7.
Moll, J., R. de Oliveira-Souza, P.J. Eslinger, I.E. Gramati and J. Mourao–Miranda (2002), 'The neural correlates of moral sensitivity: a functional magnetic resonance imaging investigation of basic and moral emotions', *Journal of Neuroscience*, **22** (7), 2730–36.
Moll, J., R. de Oliveira-Souza and R. Zahn (2008), 'The neural basis of moral cognition: sentiments, concepts, and values', *Annals of the New York Academy of Sciences*, **1124**, 161–80.
Morse, G. (2006), 'Decisions and desire', *Harvard Business Review*, January, 42–51.

Ochsner, K.N. and M.D. Lieberman (2001), 'The emergence of social cognitive neuroscience', *American Psychologist*, **56** (9), 717–34.

Phelps, E.A. (2006), 'Emotion and cognition: insights from studies of the human amygdala', *Annual Review of Psychology*, **57**, 27–53.

Pillutla, M.M. and J.K. Murnighan (1996), 'Unfairness, anger, and spite: emotional rejections of ultimatum offers', *Organizational Behavior and Human Decision Processes*, **68**, 208–24.

Poldrack, R.A. (2006), 'Can cognitive processes be inferred from neuroimaging?', *Trends in Cognitive Sciences*, **10** (2), 59–63.

Prehn, K., I. Wartenburger, K. Meriau et al. (2008), 'Individual differences in moral judgment competence influence neural correlates of socio-normative judgments', *Social Cognitive and Affective Neuroscience*, **3** (1), 33–46.

Premack, D. and G. Woodruff (1978), 'Does the chimpanzee have a theory of mind?', *Behavioral Brain Science*, **1**, 515–26.

Reynolds, J.S. (2006), 'A neurocognitive model of the ethical decision making process: implications for study and practice', *Journal of Applied Psychology*, **91**, 737–48.

Sanfey, A.G., J.K. Rilling, J.A. Aronson, L.E. Nystrom and J.D. Cohen (2003), 'The neural basis of economic decision-making in the Ultimate Game', *Science*, **300**, 1755–8.

Singer, T. (2009), 'Understanding others: brain mechanisms of theory of mind and empathy', in P.W. Glimcher, C.F. Camerer, E. Fehr and R.A. Poldrack (eds), *Neuroeconomics: Decision Making and the Brain*, New York: Academic Press, pp. 251–68.

Tabibnia, G. and M.D. Lieberman (2007), Fairness and cooperation are rewarding: evidence from social cognitive neuroscience', in C. Senior and M.J.R. Butler (eds), *The Social Cognitive Neuroscience of Organizations*, Annals of the New York Academy of Sciences, Vol. 118, Boston, MA: Blackwell Publishing, pp. 90–101.

Tabibnia, G., A.B. Satpute and M.D. Lieberman (2008), 'The sunny side of fairness: preference for fairness activates reward circuitry (and disregarding unfairness activates self-control circuitry)', *Psychological Science*, **19** (4), 339–47.

Van Winden, F. (2007), 'Affect and fairness in economics', *Social Justice Research*, **20** (1), 35–52.

White, E. (1992), *The End of the Empty Organism: Neurobiology and the Sciences of Human Action*, Westport, CT: Praeger.

Index